1963

VERSIONS OF CENSORSHIP

AN ALDINE LIBRARY EDITION

This book may be kept

VERSIONS
OF
CENSORSHIP

An Anthology edited by
John McCormick and Mairi MacInnes

ALDINE PUBLISHING COMPANY / CHICAGO

First published 1962 as a Doubleday Anchor Original
Aldine Library Edition first published 1962
ALDINE PUBLISHING COMPANY
64 East Van Buren Street
Chicago 5, Illinois

Printed in the United States of America

ACKNOWLEDGMENTS are hereby made for permission to reprint the following: "The *Index Librorum Prohibitorum*" from *The Vatican Story* by Bernard Wall, © 1956 by Bernard Wall, reprinted by permission of Harper & Brothers. "A Few Tips About Science" from *The Life of Galileo* by Bertolt Brecht, translated by Desmond I. Vesey, 1960, reprinted by permission of Helene Brecht-Weigel & Methuen & Co. Ltd., London. "Soviet Genetics: The Real Issue" by Sir Julian Huxley, by permission of the author. "Khrushchev and the Trade-Unionists" by permission of The New York *Times*. "The Factual Heresy" from *A Discord of Trumpets*, © 1956 by Claud Cockburn, reprinted by permission of Simon and Schuster, Inc. "Liberty of the Press in the United States" and "Unlimited Power of the Majority" from *Democracy in America* by Alexis de Tocqueville, edited by Phillips Bradley, published by Alfred A. Knopf, Inc. and Vintage Books, Inc.; by permission of Alfred A. Knopf, Inc. "Freedom of Speech and the First Amendment" by Zechariah Chafee, Jr., reprinted by permission of the publishers from Howard Mumford Jones, editor, *Primer of Intellectual Freedom*, Cambridge, Mass.: Harvard University Press, © 1949, by the President and Fellows of Harvard College. "Defence of the Freedom to Read" by Henry Miller, © by the author; reprinted by permission of New Directions. "Ketman" by Czeslaw Milosz, reprinted from *The Captive Mind* by Czeslaw Milosz, by permission of Alfred A. Knopf, Inc., © 1951, 1953 by the author. "The Prevention of Literature" from *Shooting an Elephant And Other Essays* by George Orwell, © 1945, 1946, 1949, 1950, by Sonia Brownell Orwell; reprinted by permission of Harcourt, Brace & World, Inc. and Martin Secker & Warburg Ltd. "The Necessity of Immoral Plays" from the Preface to *The Shewing-Up of Blanco Posnet* by George Bernard Shaw, by permission of the Public Trustee and The Society of Authors. "Dream-Censorship" reprinted from *New Introductory Lectures on Psychoanalysis* by Sigmund Freud, translated by W. J. H. Sprott; by permission of W. W. Norton

& Co., Inc., © 1933 by Sigmund Freud. "The Letter to M. d'Alembert on the Theatre" by J.-J. Rousseau, translated by Alan Bloom as *Politics and the Arts*, 1960; by permission of The Free Press of Glencoe, Illinois. "The Expediency of Toleration," being chapter XX of *Tractatus Theologico-Politicus* by Benedict de Spinoza, translated by A. G. Wernham; by permission of the Clarendon Press, Oxford.

Excerpts from *Paideia* by Werner Jaeger, reprinted by permission of Oxford University Press, Inc. Excerpts from *The Myth of the State* by Ernst Cassirer, reprinted by permission of the Yale University Press. Excerpts from *Plato Today* by R. H. S. Crossman, reprinted by permission of George Allen & Unwin, Ltd. Excerpts from *The Catholic Viewpoint on Censorship* by Harold C. Gardiner, S.J., reprinted by permission of Doubleday & Company, Inc.

CONTENTS

CENSORSHIP and IMAGINATION

I.   CENSORSHIP AND LITERATURE

II.   CENSORSHIP AND THE THEATRE

INTRODUCTION

One part of the fascination that censorship exercises is that like "love" or "freedom" or "democracy," it does not readily lend itself to definition. Censorship and all it implies in terms both of our historical understanding and of issues of enormous moment in contemporary life defies brief definition because it is an idea that always engages our prejudices, penetrates to the dim regions where our manners and mores take form, and shapes our attitude to the rule law, while at the same time the responses it evokes, whether pernicious or benevolent, depend upon the actualities of the historical moment. Censorship fascinates us because its theory demands some decision on its practice whenever there is an intellectual or political crisis; it is one of the gauges of civilization; it is a measure of individual rationality and liberalism. As our world grows smaller and areas of choice diminish, the issue that censorship poses becomes more pressing even as our responses become weary and indecisive. History, which has accelerated so powerfully in recent decades, has diffused our attention, and we tend to overlook the most urgent of the threats to ourselves from ourselves.

Although censorship is by nature protean, we have attempted in the matter that follows to construct a definition out of cases, both historical and contemporary, that seemed to us to penetrate to the core of the subject. Although our exhibits are arranged in roughly chronological order, we have frequently violated chronology in the belief that the historicist's approach is unsatisfying here and in fidelity to a conviction that our juxtapositions make possible certain insights that conventional chronology obscures.

The word "censor" is derived from Latin *censere*, "to assess or estimate," which in turn derives from the Greek verb "to estimate." In ancient Rome, dating from about 443 B.C., the censors were two officials appointed to preside over the *census,* or the registration of citizens for the purpose of determining the duties they owed to the community. A. H. G. Greenidge writes, "In the etymology of the word lurks the idea of the arbitrary assignment of burdens or duties. Varro defines *census* as *arbitrium,* and derives the name *censores* from the position of these magistrates as *arbitri populi.* This original idea of 'discretionary power' was never entirely lost; although ultimately it came to be more intimately associated with the appreciation of morals than with the assignment of burdens. From the point of view of its moral significance the censorship was the Roman manifestation of that state control of conduct which was a not unusual feature of ancient societies." The ancient etymology of the word "censor," together with the lurking suggestion of the arbitrary assignment of burdens, reminds us that the phenomenon of censorship originates in tribal society and is at least as old as authority itself.

This derivation also is our justification for beginning with Milton's *Areopagitica* rather than with a more ancient source. Historically, there was no true debate about censorship before the technological fact of the invention and diffusion of printing and the intellectual turmoil of the Reformation. The lack of challenge to the institution of censorship before the Renaissance reflects the state of human liberty in the ancient tribal organization of the city-state. To quote Fustel de Coulanges from later in our text: the citizens of the ancient city-state "knew neither liberty in private life, liberty in education, nor religious liberty. The human person counted for very little against that holy and almost divine authority which was called country or the state. . . . The ancients, especially the Greeks, always exaggerated the importance, and above all the rights of society; this was largely due, doubtless, to the sacred and religious character with which society was clothed in the beginning."

Involuntary subjection to censorship by the Greek or early Roman was, then, a function of his belief, not only in the theological sense, but also empirically, since it did not occur to him that society could survive other than through the supremacy of a single social cause. However, freedom of discussion existed simultaneously with this belief, as we know from

Herodotus' praise of Athens as well as from Plato's record of
Socrates' saying that without liberty of utterance he would
prefer to die, but there had always been authoritative voices
demanding a restriction of the popular licence and allowing,
at the most, free discussion in an élite, for an élite, kept within
bounds by that form of self-censorship based upon devotion to
a single common good. This ancient twofold pattern survived
the appearance of Christianity with only the slightest of
modifications.

The Christian idea of conscience, until the Reformation, was
linked with belief in Right Reason (*ratio recta*): the conviction that while man is free to choose evil over good, he is divinely inspired to know which course is evil and which good.
The doctrine of right reason conspired to fortify the practice
of self-censorship as medieval social and clerical organization
continued and extended the ancient assumption of the élite.
Thus, the Church did not institute the Index until the Council
of Trent, 1545–63. The early Church Fathers read and debated
works of heresy without hindrance from authority. Bitter theological debates, too, taking place as many did within the
stronghold of the medieval Church itself, seldom roused suppression. On the other hand, even before the Reformation, the
end of the fifteenth century found the Church élite (to use
our former terms) resisting all questioning of its authority from
the outside and resorting, when needed, to inquisitorial methods and censorship to defend its unique position. To quote the
authoritative historians of the period:

> Beneath the official orthodoxy of states, although belief
> remained lively and, in general, constant, ran an uninter-
> rupted current of heretical thought. The Cathars were for-
> gotten, together with the Zealot Franciscans and the
> Fraticelli; but the Vaudois went on professing that the
> Church betrayed the Gospel, and the heirs of Joachim of
> Flora did not give up hope that the world might be re-
> newed through the intervention of the Spirit. Wycliffe and
> John Huss in turn declared the necessity of giving the
> little-known Bible to the faithful. Certain affirmations of
> principle, certain rules of method, on which the ancient

daring of the heresies agreed with the young philological and historical science of the humanists, were resolutely produced, and the men of the sixteenth century accepted them without flinching. Already their formidable efficacy was able to show itself; an entire people could rise up at the name of the Gospel, in which they read the denial of the theologians' teaching.*

Not only, in effect, were the great heretical movements puritanical, but they were also against the prerogative of the "élite" when it gave evidence, through misuse of Church power, through the signs of wealth, and through the degradation of the Papacy by such a Pope as Alexander VI, of its unworthiness. The efforts of the Church to suppress these movements had two results. First, in defending the authority of the Papacy and the clergy, they militated against popular movements among the laity. Secondly, by defending the prerogative of the priesthood passed down from St. Peter by the laying on of hands, they were naturally against the setting up of another standard, common to clergy and laity alike—and therefore in effect anti-sacerdotal—that is, the Gospel. Often the Church's attempt to keep the Gospel out of the hands of their congregations was based on a belief that untutored minds might be led into heresy by reading the Gospel, through misunderstanding. In these actions by the Church we see the origins of the censoring problems of our own day, with the repetition of the old pattern of an élite, which, however free among members of its own kind, practiced a self-censorship in regard to the outsiders, and which, according to the nature of its power, sometimes imposed a censorship on them, rigorous or loose, against the natural revolutions caused by changing circumstances which tend to set the élite aside or replace it with another.

With John Milton's *Areopagitica*, the issues of censorship, which have been to this juncture implicit, explode into the modern world. The Renaissance and Reformation have shown a change in man's concept of himself and his place in the universe. The slow spread of printing, literacy, and education have

---

* Henri Pirenne, et al.: *La Fin du Moyen Age* (Paris: Presses Universitaires de France, 1931), p. 245 [editors' translation].

already raised, in all its threat and promise, the prospect of an informed laity. Censorship as a benevolent and voluntary device for protecting belief is in process of change to censorship as a device for obstructing every manner of thought. The modern lines of battle are drawn up. While *Areopagitica* is at once a history of censorship, a splendid display of the Renaissance mind at work, and a prophecy of our difficulties today, Milton's argument rests upon the issue of belief; it derives from his humanist, Protestant interpretation of right reason, and contains an expression of his intolerance of Roman Catholicism. Thus we include *Areopagitica* under our first heading, *Censorship and Belief*. The material in this section extends back to Plato for an illustration of belief in the non-theological sense, while *Areopagitica* itself and the Roman Catholic Index pose the issue of censorship involving theological belief. The case of Galileo is melodramatically appropriate to our heading, in its confrontation of the ideal of free speculation at odds with religious dogma. The selection from Bertolt Brecht's play, *The Life of Galileo*, is a wry, oblique commentary on how a gifted unorthodox Communist writer interpreted the central issue of obstructive censorship. Finally, in the selection from Spinoza, we see the liberated, unorthodox, but still believing Renaissance mind at the task of convincing secular government of the inevitability of toleration. Belief and fact find accommodation, and we are on the threshold of the new science.

With the second section, *Censorship and Fact*, the issue shifts from abstract belief to the mundane and the material. By "fact" we intend not only "data," but also the impact upon the human spirit of the scientific method. The inductive method soon spread from the laboratory to political philosophy, which is to say into society itself. Now concepts of liberty and freedom become totally secular, while the issue between scientists themselves and the censors moves from canon to civil law in some cases; in others, to the murky ground on which rationalist assertions of the natural scientist's freedom clash with governmental convenience. Three centuries of allegiance to the new science have not clarified the problem. Thus we move from Hobbes's materialist determinism to the Lysenko case and to conflicts in the U.S. between atomic science and national security without a sense of violation.* It may well be that we are involuntarily returning to those habits of mind of the ancient city-state, in which a kind of freedom was exercised without reference to the paramount rights of freedom of *private* conscience.

Part II of this section, *Censorship and the News,* takes us to more familiar, or at least less controversial, matter. Out of a flood of possible exhibits we have centered on the vastly important question of definition. The selections from Jefferson, Tocqueville, and Horace Walpole give a necessary historical dimension to the definition, while the account of Premier Khrushchev's interview with the American Trade-Unionists and the selection by Claud Cockburn challenge certain accepted opinions about the very nature of news. The obscure but significant case of Abner Kneeland, together with the authoritative statements by Chafee and the selections by Malin, represent the complex legal aspects of press censorship in this country. We discover that the modern newspaper is a logical extension of the scientific method of the seventeenth century, and that its challenge to censorship is similar to the challenge of science itself: it is made in the name of free inquiry, popular education, and a barely rational, post-medieval assumption that facts are *good,* that fact, in fact, transcends fact.

By entitling the third section *Censorship and Imagination,* we have tried to place the issue of censorship and art where we feel it belongs: not first on pornography, although that is of course involved, but upon the question of what art is and how it functions in society. We include Judge Bryan's important opinion concerning *Lady Chatterley's Lover* in recognition of the fact that the argument has so often been conducted over the issue of pornography. But we also include Henry Miller's defense of *Sexus* because Miller places the argument where it belongs, in terms of what a work of art is in its essence. While *De l'Allemagne* is not strictly a work of art, it is included here for its spirited account of how the machinery of government can be directed against a work of the imagina-

* The link was suggested by G. de Santillana, *The Crime of Galileo* (Chicago: Phoenix Books, 1955).

tion and because Mme. de Staël writes in the accents of the artist outraged.

The classic selections from Milosz and Orwell take us into the modern landscape of hallucination, where imagination is often trapped and blinded. The second part of *Censorship and Imagination* deals with the theatre. It testifies to the fact that the theatre has always been peculiarly liable to persecution, since its challenge to authority is fully open and public. Lord Chesterfield and Bernard Shaw present eloquent arguments against censorship, whereas Rousseau's "Letter to M. d'Alembert" not only gives the case for censorship of the theatre, but also takes the argument back to the ancient city-state and its emphasis on public morale. In a limited sense Rousseau answers some of Milton's arguments in *Areopagitica*, to some extent performing for us the task of linking censorship and the imagination with the entire history of censorship in its many manifestations.

The concluding section is called *Self-Censorship*, not to confuse the reader with a term already used to define a pre-Renaissance habit of mind, but to indicate that the modern world is not finally a rational one. If we are children of the Renaissance, we are also children of Freud. Freud's dream censor is as powerful as the Roman officials of the third century B.C. Freud and Dostoyevsky between them open up that modern vista where neurosis and politics meet; in their shadow we debate whether the withholding of a report written by scientists under government contract is an instance of censorship or not. In their shadow we debate whether atomic scientists should have exercised the pre-Renaissance form of self-censorship because of their awareness of the post-Freudian world, and withheld their discoveries in nuclear physics.

In its complexities, the manifold guises of censorship trick us into apathy. People are fond of answers, and when no clear rapid answer is forthcoming, they are likely to feel that no question has been asked. We have not seen it as our task to provide answers. If this collection indicates anything, it is that no single answer is appropriate to all historical and social situations. We have tried to provide notes toward a chapter in the history of ideas, both to fill out the past and to indicate the complexity, ubiquity, and urgency of censorship in the modern time. Unlike other chapters in the history of ideas, this one can have no ending. If our data suggests as much to the reader, we shall have succeeded a little in our purpose.

JOHN MC CORMICK

MAIRI MAC INNES

New York 1961

CENSORSHIP and BELIEF

COMMENT: On the Background of *Areopagitica*

In 1639 John Milton, then a man of 31 and a dedicated poet with his promised work still unwritten, broke off his travels abroad to return to an England on the brink of civil war. "It was a time," he wrote later,

> when Charles, having broken the peace, was renewing what is called the episcopal war with the Scots, in which the Royalists being routed in the first encounter, and the English being universally and justly disaffected, the necessity of his affairs at last obliged him to convene a parliament. As soon as I was able I hired a spacious house in the city, for myself and my books; where I again, with rapture, resumed my literary pursuits, and where I calmly awaited the issue of the contest, which I trusted to the wise conduct of Providence, and to the courage of the people. The vigour of the Parliament had begun to humble the pride of the bishops. As long as the liberty of speech was no longer subject to control, all mouths began to be opened against the bishops. They said that it was unjust that they alone should differ from the model of other Reformed Churches; that the government of the Church should be according to the pattern of other churches, and particularly the word of God. This awakened all my attention and my zeal. I saw that a way was opening for the establishment of real liberty; that the foundation was laying for the deliverance of man from the yoke of slavery and superstition; that the principles of religion, which were the first objects of our care, would exert a salutary influence on the manners and constitution

of the republic. And as I had from my youth studied the distinctions between religious and civil rights, I perceived that, if ever I wished to be of use, I ought at least not to be wanting to my country, to the Church, and to so many of my fellow-Christians, in a crisis of so much danger. I therefore determined to relinquish the other pursuits in which I was engaged, and to transfer the whole force of my talents and my industry to this one important object.

The way in which Milton served the cause of freedom was by engaging in the writing of pamphlets. He became a propagandist on a high but influential level. Later his services were to be recognized by appointment to a minor official post; in the days to which we refer he was able to appeal to Parliament from an independent position as a private citizen, in the instance of *Areopagitica* likening himself, in the seventeenth century manner, to a figure in classical times, the Athenian orator Isocrates, who, on the eve of the despotism of Philip of Macedon, publicly appealed for a return to the old Athenian democracy and the Council of the Areopagos who guarded it. What Parliament had done to provoke a comparison with those days of similarly declining liberties was, in 1643, to pass an "Order for the Regulating of Printing, and for suppressing the great late abuses and frequent disorders in Printing many false Scandalous, Seditious, Libellous, and unlicensed Pamphlets, to the great defamation of Religion and Government." Such was the Long Parliament's first serious effort to control the press. When Charles I had been so pressed for funds as to convene it in 1637, the Long Parliament had forthwith abolished the former organ of censorship, the infamous Star Chamber. In the interim, some printers had tired of waiting for the government to protect their copyrights and printed whatever would bring them money, infringing copyrights and having theirs infringed in return. Now, in 1643, it was the trade situation as much as the ideological one that had brought forth the new order for the regulation of printing.

In brief, it declared that no order of Parliament was to be printed except by commission of the House. All books were to be licensed and also entered in the Stationers' Register. No book in the privilege of the Company was to be printed without the license or consent of the Company. If books were to be entered under a particular name or imported from abroad, the license of the owner was required. Certain officers of the Company and of Parliament were empowered to make searches, apprehend delinquent authors, or printers, and to seize unlawful printing presses together with nut, spindle, and materials, and, in the event of opposition, to break open doors and locks.

The order had the effect of re-establishing the booksellers and printers (the stationers) as their own arbiters, in place of the bishops, who derived their power directly from the King, as head of the Church of England. The new licensing personnel were not bishops and their chaplains working through the Star Chamber, but lawyers, doctors, Members of Parliament, and a schoolmaster, and in the case of books of divinity, Presbyterian ministers. "Small pamphlets, portraitures, pictures and the like" were to be reviewed by the Clerk of the Stationers' Company. As Parliament gave the Company its powers, the Company obliged Parliament by responding with its political loyalty. When Charles moved his Court from London to Oxford, he was wise enough to take his own printer, but the other printers were Presbyterians and happy to be rid of Archbishop Laud's chaplains and *imprimaturs*. We can see, then, that Parliament had not much to fear from the flood of schismatic and sectarian pamphlets or even the scurrilous and fearfully libelous ones that were abroad.

We must look deeper for the motives that impelled an order for censorship even in such heroic days, when the passion for liberty was as hot as it has ever been, among all kinds and classes of men.

Injurious trade practices as well as sedition and heresy were certainly, in the minds of the Members of the House, responsible for the order. What is perhaps surprising to us is that an alternative was not worth more official consideration. Clearly, freedom of the press was not up till then a birthright, nor was it claimed to be. It seems hardly to have been realized that printing had radically altered the significance of language. But control of the press by bishops, who had come, since Elizabethan days, to be hated for their political influence, was re-

vealing at last the increasing *power* of the press. At this point
Milton could readily call into question a further and necessary
freedom of discussion. He wrote at a time when the anti-
Episcopalians, the Parliamentarians, were experiencing their
greatest triumphs with the sword. They might, Milton held,
enjoy triumphs of the spirit too, which would, by the nature of
truth, worst their enemies as effectively.

By 1644, when he wrote *Areopagitica*, the Civil War had
been in progress for two years, and the outcome was beginning
to be clear. In this year the fiercely anti-prelatical Scots had
driven into northern England, the Earl of Essex had, though
briefly, advanced into royalist Cornwall on behalf of Parliament, and the Parliamentary forces had triumphed over Prince
Rupert and the King's men at Marston Moor. Plans were well
underway for the formation of the New Model Army, that
godly, russet-coated body of men who were, by their own
words, "called forth and conjured, by the severall Declarations
of Parliament, to the defence of our owne and the people's
just rights and liberties." *Areopagitica* appeared in November.
It shared the glorious spirit of the Republican side. The Long
Parliament, that was to peter out so ignominiously, was still
vigorous and young, and Milton was not blind, or pitiful, or
ignored as he was to be, though even now he was petitioning
Parliament for the correction of a measure that as he saw it
ran counter to the spirit of the age, a threat to the religious
faith and civil purpose which up to then had so successfully
opposed the arbitrarily wielded powers of Charles I. Truth, as
Brecht says, is the daughter of time, not of authority, and the
time that gave us *Aeropagitica* shows us in the attitude of the
text itself that the new establishment felt uncertain of the
temper for liberty which had brought it into power. Its uncertainty was to become more apparent as that temper failed,
and shows up in its measures of intolerance and self-right-
eousness.

The style of *Areopagitica* shows very clearly that Milton
was facing up to a certain amount of havering on Parliament's
part; he is exhorting, rather than persuading; his enemy is
fear, not a counter-argument. What he is doing is stating the
full case for liberty of printing so that the opposition may be

overwhelmed, and his tools are his resources of Hebrew and classical scholarship, his imagination, and the great seventeenth century English prose style. Unfortunately this magnificent language is now beyond most people; those long, harmonious, periodic sentences don't seem quite honest; how can you be both full-blown and exact? Our notion of honest prose favors the drab, curtailed, and pseudo-scientific. This stuff of Milton's is nothing that fits in neatly with our notion of puritanism. Though we tend to think of puritanism as a plain style, *Areopagitica* shows a much more fundamental puritanism: a belief that Reason, in itself, is a power for good. What seems to a modern reader to be ornamental flourish turns out on closer inspection to be substantiation of the argument; in Milton's writing there are no asides. While he is exhorting, he is at the same time given over to the power of reason in language, both comprehensively and precisely. To render the argument of *Areopagitica* in Basic English would be simply impossible.

The pieces of this anthology which follow reflect one part or another of his argument. Therefore we print the *Areopagitica* nearly entire, omitting only such short passages as back his argument with the classical instances approved in his century but now lost to the common reader. Where the sense is made difficult by vocabulary or reference, we clarify it in notes which appear at the end, explaining only what is necessary for the understanding of the whole.

The edition is that published in 1931 by the Columbia University Press.

Areopagitica is written in the form of an address to the Parliament which has recently passed the licensing decree. It begins with a long eulogy comparing Parliament to other great assemblies of the past. Milton suggests that Parliament would show its superiority to these other assemblies by its ability to listen to reason and a willingness to repeal one of its own acts.

TEXT: *Areopagitica* by John Milton

. . . If ye be thus resolv'd, as it were injury to thinke ye were not, I know not what should withhold me from presenting ye with a fit instance wherein to shew both that love of truth which ye eminently professe and that uprightnesse of your judgement which is not wont to be partiall to your selves; by judging over again that Order which ye have ordain'd *to regulate Printing. That no Book, pamphlet, or paper shall be henceforth Printed, unlesse the same be first approv'd and licenc't by such,* or at least one of such as shall be thereto appointed. For that part which preserves justly every mans Copy to himselfe, or provides for the poor, I touch not, only wish they be not made pretenses to abuse and persecute honest and painfull Men, who offend not in either of these particulars. But that other clause of Licencing Books, which we thought had dy'd with his brother *quadragesimal* and *matrimonial*[1] when the Prelats expir'd,[2] I shall now attend with such a Homily, as shall lay before ye, first the inventors of it to bee those whom ye will be loath to own; next what is to be thought in generall of reading, what ever sort the Books be; and that this Order avails nothing to the suppressing of scandalous, seditious, and libellous Books, which were mainly intended to be supprest. Last, that it will be primely to the discouragement of all learning, and the stop of Truth, not only by disexercising and blunting our abilities in what we know already, but by hindring and cropping the discovery that might bee yet further made both in religious and civill Wisdome.

I deny not, but that it is of greatest concernment in the Church and Commonwealth, to have a vigilant eye how Bookes demeane themselves as well as men; and thereafter to confine, imprison, and do sharpest justice on them as malefactors: For Books are not absolutely dead things, but doe contain a potencie of life in them to be as active as that soule was whose progeny they are; nay they do preserve as in a violl the purest efficacie and extraction of that living intellect that bred them. I know they are as lively, and as vigorously productive, as those fabulous Dragons teeth;[3] and being sown up and down, may chance to spring up armed men. And yet on the other hand unlesse warinesse be us'd, as good almost kill a Man as kill a good Book; who kills a Man kills a reasonable creature, Gods Image; but hee who destroyes a good Booke, kills reason it selfe, kills the Image of God, as it were in the eye. Many a man lives a burden to the Earth; but a good Booke is the pretious life-blood of a master spirit, imbalm'd and treasur'd up on purpose to a life beyond life. 'Tis true, no age can restore a life, whereof perhaps there is no great losse; and revolutions of ages doe not oft recover the losse of a rejected truth, for the want of which whole Nations fare the worse. We should be wary therefore what persecution we raise against the living labours of publick men, how we spill that season'd life of man preserv'd and stor'd up in Books; since we see a kinde of homicide may be thus committed, sometimes a martyrdome, and if it extend to the whole impression, a kinde of massacre, whereof the execution ends not in the slaying of an elementall life, but strikes at that ethereall and fift essence, the breath of reason it selfe, slaies an immortality rather then a life. . . .

[Milton shows that there has been very little censorship in the great commonwealths of the past. The early Church declared only which books were not approved, until after the year 800.]

After which time the Popes of *Rome,* engrossing what they pleas'd of Politicall rule into their owne hands, extended their dominion over mens eyes, as they had before over their judgements, burning and prohibiting to be read what they fansied not; yet sparing in their censures, and the Books not many which they so dealt with; till *Martin* the 5 by his Bull[4] not only prohibited, but was the first that excommunicated the reading of hereticall Books; for about that time *Wicklef* and

Husse[5] growing terrible, were they who first drove the Papall
Court to a stricter policy of prohibiting. Which cours *Leo* the
10, and his successors follow'd, untill the Councell of Trent,
and the Spanish Inquisition engendring together brought forth,
or perfeted those Catalogues, and expurging Indexes[6] that
rake through the entralls of many an old good Author, with
a violation wors then any could be offer'd to his tomb. Nor
did they stay in matters Hereticall, but any subject that was
not to their palat, they either condemn'd in a prohibition, or
had it strait into the new Purgatory of an Index. To fill up the
measure of encroachment, their last invention was to ordain
that no Book, pamphlet, or paper should be Printed (as if
S. *Peter* had bequeath'd them the keys of the Presse also out
of Paradise) unlesse it were approv'd and licenc't under the
hands of 2 or 3 glutton Friers . . . Sometimes 5 *Imprimaturs*
are seen together dialogue-wise in the Piatza of one Title page,
complementing and ducking each to other with their shav'n
reverences, whether the Author, who stands by in perplexity
at the foot of his Epistle, shall to the Presse or to the spunge.
These are the prety responsories, these are the deare Antipho-
nies that so bewitcht of late our Prelats, and their Chaplaines
with the goodly Eccho they made; and besotted us to the gay
imitation of a lordly *Imprimatur*, one from Lambeth house,
another from the West end of *Pauls;*[7] so apishly Romanizing,
that the word of command still was set downe in Latine; as if
the learned Grammaticall pen that wrote it, would cast no ink
without Latine: or perhaps, as they thought, because no vulgar
tongue was worthy to expresse the pure conceit of an *Imprimatur;* but rather, as I hope, for that our English, the language
of men ever famous, and formost in the atchievements of liberty, will not easily finde servile letters anow to spell such a
dictatorie presumption English. And thus ye have the Inventors and the originall of Book-licencing ript up, and drawn as
lineally as any pedigree. We have it not, that can be heard of,
from any ancient State, or politie, or Church, nor by any
Statute left us by our Ancestors elder or later; nor from the
moderne custom of any reformed Citty, or Church abroad; but
from the most Antichristian Councel, and the most tyrannous
Inquisition that ever inquir'd. Till then Books were ever as

freely admitted into the World as any other birth; the issue
of the brain was no more stifl'd then the issue of the womb:
no envious *Juno*[8] sate cros-leg'd over the nativity of any mans
intellectuall off-spring; but if it prov'd a Monster, who denies,
but that it was justly burnt, or sunk into the Sea . . .

Dionysius Alexandrinus was about the year 240, a person of
great name in the Church for piety and learning, who had
wont to avail himself much against hereticks by being con-
versant in their Books; untill a certain Presbyter laid it scrupu-
lously to his conscience, how he durst venture himselfe among
those defiling volumes. The worthy man loath to give offence
fell into a new debate with himselfe what was to be thought;
when suddenly a vision sent from God, it is his own Epistle
that so averrs it, confirm'd him in these words: Read any books
what ever come to thy hands, for thou art sufficient both to
judge aright, and to examine each matter. To this revelation
he assented the sooner, as he confesses, because it was answerable to that of the Apostle to the Thessalonians, Prove all
things, hold fast that which is good. And he might have added
another remarkable saying of the same Author; To the pure
all things are pure, not only meats and drinks, but all kinde
of knowledge whether of good or evill; the knowledge cannot
defile, nor consequently the books, if the will and conscience
be not defil'd. For books are as meats and viands are; some
of good, some of evill substance; and yet God in that unapocry-
phall vision, said without exception, Rise *Peter*, kill and eat,
leaving the choice to each mans discretion. Wholesome meats
to a vitiated stomack differ little or nothing from unwholesome;
and best books to a naughty[9] mind are not unappliable to occasions of evill. Bad meats will scarce breed good nourishment
in the healthiest concoction; but herein the difference is of bad
books, that they to a discreet and judicious Reader serve in
many respects to discover, to confute, to forewarn, and to illustrate. . . .

I conceive therefore, that when God did enlarge the universall diet of mans body, saving ever the rules of temperance,
he then also, as before, left arbitrary the dyeting and repast-
ing of our minds; as wherein every mature man might have
to exercise his owne leading capacity. How great a vertue is

temperance, how much of moment through the whole life of
man? yet God committs the managing so great a trust, without particular Law or prescription, wholly to the demeanour
of every grown man. And therefore when he himself tabl'd the
Jews from heaven, that Omer[10] which was every mans daily
portion of Manna, is computed to have bin more then might
have well suffic'd the heartiest feeder thrice as many meals.
For those actions which enter into a man, rather than issue
out of him, and therefore defile not, God uses not to captivat
under a perpetuall childhood of prescription, but trusts him
with the gift of reason to be his own chooser; there were but
little work left for preaching, if law and compulsion should
grow so fast upon those things which hertofore were govern'd
only by exhortation. *Salomon* informs us that much reading
is a wearines to the flesh; but neither he, nor other inspir'd
author tells us that such, or such reading is unlawfull: yet
certainly had God thought good to limit us herein, it had bin
much more expedient to have told us what was unlawfull, then
what was wearisome. As for the burning of those Ephesian
books by St. *Pauls* converts, tis reply'd the books were magick,
the Syriack so renders them. It was a privat act, a voluntary
act, and leaves us to a voluntary imitation: the men in remorse burnt those books which were their own; the Magistrat
by this example is not appointed: these men practiz'd the
books, another might perhaps have read them in some sort
usefully. Good and evill we know in the field of this World
grow up together almost inseparably; and the knowledge of
good is so involv'd and interwoven with the knowledge of evill,
and in so many cunning resemblances hardly to be discern'd,
that those confused seeds[11] which were impos'd on *Psyche*
as an incessant labour to cull out, and sort asunder, were not
more intermixt. It was from out the rinde of one apple tasted,
that the knowledge of good and evill as two twins cleaving
together leapt forth into the World. And perhaps this is that
doom which *Adam* fell into of knowing good and evill, that
is to say of knowing good by evill. As therefore the state of
man now is; what wisdome can there be to choose, what continence to forbeare without the knowledge of evill? He that
can apprehend and consider vice with all her baits and seem-

ing pleasures, and yet abstain, and yet distinguish, and yet prefer that which is truly better, he is the true wayfaring Christian. I cannot praise a fugitive and cloister'd vertue, un-exercis'd & unbreath'd, that never sallies out and sees her adversary, but slinks out of the race, where that immortall garland is to be run for, not without dust and heat. Assuredly we bring not innocence into the world, we bring impurity much rather: that which purifies us is triall, and triall is by what is contrary. That vertue therefore which is but a youngling in the contemplation of evill, and knows not the utmost that vice promises to her followers, and rejects it, is but a blank vertue, not a pure; her whitenesse is but an excrementall[12] whitenesse; Which was the reason why our sage and serious Poet *Spencer*, whom I dare be known to think a better teacher then *Scotus* or *Aquinas*,[13] describing true temperance under the person of *Guion*, brings him in with his palmer through the cave of Mammon, and the bowr of earthly blisse that he might see and know, and yet abstain. Since therefore the knowledge and survay of vice is in this world so necessary to the constituting of human vertue, and the scanning of error to the confirmation of truth, how can we more safely, and with lesse danger scout into the regions of sin and falsity then by reading all manner of tractats, and hearing all manner of reason? And this is the benefit which may be had of books promiscuously read. But of the harm that may result hence three kinds are usually reckn'd. First, is fear'd the infection that may spread; but then all human learning and controversie in religious points must remove out of the world, yea the Bible it selfe; for that oftimes relates blasphemy not nicely, it describes the carnall sense of wicked men not unelegantly, it brings in holiest men passionately murmuring against providence through all the arguments of *Epicurus:* in other great disputes it answers dubiously and darkly to the common reader. . . . Seeing therefore that those books, and those in great abundance which are likeliest to taint both life and doctrine, cannot be supprest without the fall of learning, and of all ability in disputation, and that these books of either sort are most and soonest catching to the learned, from whom to the common people what ever is hereticall or dissolute may quickly

be convey'd, and that evill manners are as perfectly learnt
without books a thousand other ways which cannot be stopt,
and evill doctrine not with books can propagate, except a
teacher guide, which he might also doe without writing, and
so beyond prohibiting, I am not able to unfold, how this
cautelous[14] enterprise of licencing can be exempted from the
number of vain and impossible attempts. And he who were
pleasantly dispos'd, could not well avoid to lik'n it to the exploit of that gallant man who thought to pound up the crows
by shutting his Parkgate. Besides another inconvenience, if
learned men be the first receivers out of books, & dispredders
both of vice and error, how shall the licencers themselves be
confided in, unlesse we can conferr upon them, or they assume to themselves above all others in the Land, the grace of
infallibility, and uncorruptednesse? And again, if it be true,
that a wise man like a good refiner can gather gold out of
the drossiest volume, and that a fool will be a fool with the
best book, yea or without book, there is no reason that we
should deprive a wise man of any advantage to his wisdome,
while we seek to restrain from a fool, that which being restrain'd will be no hindrance to his folly. For if there should
be so much exactnesse always us'd to keep that from him
which is unfit for his reading, we should in the judgement of
Aristotle not only, but of *Salomon,* and of our Saviour, not
voutsafe him good precepts, and by consequence not willingly
admit him to good books; as being certain that a wise man
will make better use of an idle pamphlet, then a fool will do
of sacred Scripture. 'Tis next alleg'd we must not expose our
selves to temptations without necessity, and next to that, not
imploy our time in vain things. To both these objections one
answer will serve, out of the grounds already laid, that to all
men such books are not temptations, nor vanities; but usefull
drugs and materialls wherewith to temper and compose effective and strong med'cins, which mans life cannot want.[15]
The rest, as children and childish men, who have not the art
to qualifie and prepare these working mineralls, well may be
exhorted to forbear, but hinder'd forcibly they cannot be by
all the licencing that Sainted Inquisition could ever yet contrive; which is what I promis'd to deliver next, That this order

of licencing conduces nothing to the end for which it was fram'd; and hath almost prevented me by being clear already while thus much hath bin explaining.[16] See the ingenuity[17] of Truth, who when she gets a free and willing hand, opens her self faster, then the pace of method and discours can overtake her. It was the task which I began with, To shew that no Nation, or well instituted State, if they valu'd books at all, did ever use this way of licencing; and it might be answer'd, that this is a piece of prudence lately discover'd. To which I return, that as it was a thing slight and obvious to think on, so if it had bin difficult to finde out, there wanted not among them long since, who suggested such a cours; which they not following, leave us a pattern of their judgement, that it was not the not knowing, but the not approving, which was the cause of their not using it. *Plato,* a man of high autority indeed, but least of all for his Commonwealth, in the book of his laws, which no City ever yet receiv'd, fed his fancie with making many edicts to his ayrie Burgomasters, which they who otherwise admire him, wish had bin rather buried and excus'd in the *genial* cups of an *Academick* night-sitting. By which laws he seems to tolerat no kind of learning, but by unalterable decree, consisting most of practicall traditions, to the attainment whereof a Library of smaller bulk then his own dialogues would be abundant. And there also enacts that no Poet should so much as read to any privat man, what he had writt'n, untill the Judges and Law-keepers had seen it, and allow'd it: But that *Plato* meant this Law peculiarly to that Commonwealth which he had imagin'd, and to no other, is evident. Why was he not else a Law-giver to himself, but a transgressor, and to be expell'd by his own Magistrats; both for the wanton epigrams and dialogues which he made, and his perpetuall reading of *Sophron Mimus,* and *Aristophanes,* books of grossest infamy, and also for commending the latter of them though he were the malicious libeller of his chief friends, to be read by the Tyrant *Dionysius,* who had little need of such trash to spend his time on? But that he knew this licencing of Poems had reference and dependence to many other proviso's there set down in his fancied republic, which in this world could have no place: and so neither he himself, nor any Magistrat, or City ever imitated that cours, which tak'n apart from those other collaterall injunctions must needs be vain and fruitlesse. For if they fell upon one kind of strictnesse, unlesse their care were equall to regulat all other things of like aptnes to corrupt the mind, that single endeavour they knew would be but a fond[18] labour; to shut and fortifie one gate against corruption, and be necessitated to leave others round about wide open. If we think to regulat Printing, thereby to rectifie manners, we must regulat all recreations and pastimes, all that is delightfull to man. No musick must be heard, no song be set or sung, but what is grave and *Dorick*.[19] There must be licencing dancers, that no gesture, motion, or deportment be taught our youth but what by their allowance shall be thought honest; for such *Plato* was provided of; It will ask more then the work of twenty licencers to examin all the lutes, the violins, and the ghittarrs in every house; they must not be suffer'd to prattle as they doe, but must be licenc'd what they may say. And who shall silence all the airs and madrigalls, that whisper softnes in chambers? The Windows also, and the *Balcone's* must be thought on, there are shrewd books, with dangerous Frontispices set to sale; who shall prohibit them, shall twenty licencers? . . . Who shall regulat all the mixt conversation of our youth, male and female together, as is the fashion of this Country, who shall still appoint what shall be discours'd, what presum'd, and no furder? Lastly, who shall forbid and separat all idle resort, all evill company? These things will be, and must be; but how they shall be lest hurtfull, how lest enticing, herein consists the grave and governing wisdom of a State. To sequester out of the world into *Atlantick* and *Eutopian* polities,[20] which never can be drawn into use, will not mend our condition; but to ordain wisely as in this world of evill, in the midd'st whereof God hath plac't us unavoidably. Nor is it *Plato's* licencing of books will doe this, which necessarily pulls along with it so many other kinds of licencing, as will make us all both ridiculous and weary, and yet frustrat; but those unwritt'n, or at least unconstraining laws of vertuous education, religious and civill nurture, which *Plato* there mentions, as the bonds and ligaments of the Commonwealth, the pillars and the sustainers of every writt'n Statute; these they be which

will bear chief sway in such matters as these, when all licencing will be easily eluded. Impunity and remissenes, for certain
are the bane of a Commonwealth, but here the great art lyes
to discern in what the law is to bid restraint and punishment,
and in what things perswasion only is to work. If every action
which is good, or evill in man at ripe years, were to be under
pittance,[21] and prescription, and compulsion, what were vertue but a name, what praise could be then due to well-doing,
what grammercy to be sober, just or continent? many there be
that complain of divin Providence for suffering *Adam* to trans-
gresse, foolish tongues! when God gave him reason, he gave
him freedom to choose, for reason is but choosing; he had bin
else a meer artificiall *Adam,* such an *Adam* as he is in the
motions.[22] We our selves esteem not of[23] that obedience, or
love, or gift, which is of force: God therefore left him free,
set before him a provoking object, ever almost in his eyes;
herein consisted his merit, herein the right of his reward, the
praise of his abstinence. Wherefore did he creat passions
within us, pleasures round about us, but that these rightly temper'd are the very ingredients of vertu? They are not skilfull
considerers of human things, who imagin to remove sin by removing the matter of sin; for, besides that it is a huge heap
increasing under the very act of diminishing, though some
part of it may for a time be withdrawn from some persons,
it cannot from all, in such a universall thing as books are; and
when this is done, yet the sin remains entire. Though ye take
from a covetous man all his treasure, he has yet one jewell
left, ye cannot bereave him of his covetousnesse. Banish all
objects of lust, shut up all youth into the severest discipline
that can be exercis'd in any hermitage, ye cannot make them
chaste, that came not thither so: such great care and wisdom
is requir'd to the right managing of this point. Suppose we
could expell sin by this means; look how much we thus expell
of sin, so much we expell of vertue: for the matter of them
both is the same; remove that, and ye remove them both alike.
This justifies the high providence of God, who though he command us temperance, justice, continence, yet powrs out before
us ev'n to a profusenes all desirable things, and gives us minds
that can wander beyond all limit and satiety. Why should we

then affect a rigor contrary to the manner of God and of nature, by abridging or scanting those means, which books freely
permitted are, both to the triall of vertue, and the exercise of
truth. It would be better done to learn that the law must needs
be frivolous which goes to restrain things, uncertainly and yet
equally working to good, and to evill. And were I the chooser,
a dram of well-doing should be preferr'd before many times as
much the forcible hindrance of evill-doing. For God sure esteems the growth and compleating of one vertuous person,
more then the restraint of ten vitious. And albeit what ever
thing we hear or see, sitting, walking, travelling, or conversing
may be fitly call'd our book, and is of the same effect that
writings are, yet grant the thing to be prohibited were only
books, it appears that this order hitherto is far insufficient to
the end which it intends. . . . If then the order shall not be
vain and frustrat, behold a new labour, Lords and Commons,
ye must repeal and proscribe all scandalous and unlicenc't
books already printed and divulg'd; after ye have drawn them
up into a list, that all may know which are condemn'd, and
which not; and ordain that no forrein books be deliver'd out
of custody, till they have bin read over. This office will require the whole time of not a few overseers, and those no vulgar men. There be also books which are partly usefull and
excellent, partly culpable and pernicious; this work will ask as
many more officials, to make expurgations, and expunctions,
that the Commonwealth of learning be not damnify'd. In fine,
when the multitude of books encrease upon their hands, ye
must be fain to catalogue all those Printers who are found
frequently offending, and forbidd the importation of their
whole suspected *typography*. In a word, that this your order
may be exact, and not deficient, ye must reform it perfectly
according to the model of *Trent* and *Sevil*,[24] which I know
ye abhorre to doe. Yet though ye should condiscend to this,
which God forbid, the order still would be but fruitlesse and
defective to that end whereto ye meant it. If to prevent sects
and schisms, who is so unread or so uncatechis'd in story, that
hath not heard of many sects refusing books as a hindrance,
and preserving their doctrine unmixt for many ages, only by
unwritt'n traditions. The Christian faith, for that was once a

schism, is not unknown to have spread all over *Asia*, ere any Gospel or Epistle was seen in writing. If the amendment of manners be aym'd at, look into Italy and Spain, whether those places be one scruple the better, the honester, the wiser, the chaster, since all the inquisitionall rigor that hath bin executed upon books.

Another reason, whereby to make it plain that this order will misse the end it seeks, consider by the quality which ought to be in every licencer. It cannot be deny'd but that he who is made judge to sit upon the birth, or death of books whether they may be wafted into this world, or not, had need to be a man above the common measure, both studious, learned, and judicious; there may be else no mean mistakes in the censure of what is passable or not; which is also no mean injury. If he be of such worth as behoovs him, there cannot be a more tedious and unpleasing journey-work, a greater losse of time levied upon his head, then to be made the perpetuall reader of unchosen books and pamphlets, oftimes huge volumes. There is no book that is acceptable unlesse at certain seasons; but to be enjoyn'd the reading of that at all times, and in a hand scars legible, whereof three pages would not down at any time in the fairest Print, is an imposition which I cannot beleeve how he that values time, and his own studies, or is but of a sensible nostrill should be able to endure. In this one thing I crave leave of the present licencers to be pardon'd for so thinking: who doubtlesse took this office up, looking on it through their obedience to the Parlament, whose command perhaps made all things seem easie and unlaborious to them; but that this short triall hath wearied them out already, their own expressions and excuses to them who make so many journeys to sollicit their licence, are testimony anough. Seeing therefore those who now possesse the imployment, by all evident signs wish themselves well ridd of it, and that no man of worth, none that is not a plain unthrift of his own hours is ever likely to succeed them, except he mean to put himself to the salary of a Presse-corrector, we may easily foresee what kind of licencers we are to expect hereafter, either ignorant, imperious, and remisse, or basely pecuniary. This is what I had to shew wherein this order cannot conduce to that end, whereof it bears the intention.

I lastly proceed from the no good it can do, to the manifest hurt it causes, in being first the greatest discouragement and affront, that can be offer'd to learning and to learned men. It was the complaint and lamentation of Prelats, upon every least breath of a motion to remove pluralities, and distribute more equally Church revennu's, that then all learning would be for ever dasht and discourag'd. But as for that opinion, I never found cause to think that the tenth part of learning stood or fell with the Clergy: nor could I ever but hold it for a sordid and unworthy speech of any Churchman who had a competency left him. If therefore ye be loath to dishearten utterly and discontent, not the mercenary crew of false pretenders to learning, but the free and ingenuous sort of such as evidently were born to study, and love lerning for it self, not for lucre, or any other end, but the service of God and of truth, and perhaps that lasting fame and perpetuity of praise which God and good men have consented shall be the reward of those whose publisht labours advance the good of mankind, then know, that so far to distrust the judgement & the honesty of one who hath but a common repute in learning, and never yet offended, as not to count him fit to print his mind without a tutor and examiner, lest he should drop a scism, or something of corruption, is the greatest displeasure and indignity to a free and knowing spirit that can be put upon him. . . . He who is not trusted with his own actions, his drift not being known to be evill, and standing to the hazard of law and penalty, has no great argument to think himself reputed in the Commonwealth wherin he was born, for other then a fool or a foreiner. When a man writes to the world, he summons up all his reason and deliberation to assist him; he searches, meditats, is industrious, and likely consults and conferrs with his judicious friends; after all which done he takes himself to be inform'd in what he writes, as well as any that writ before him; if in this the most consummat act of his fidelity and ripenesse, no years, no industry, no former proof of his abilities can bring him to that state of maturity, as not to be still mistrusted and suspected, unlesse he carry all his considerat diligence, all his midnight watchings, and expence of *Palladian* oyl,[25] to the hasty view of an unleasur'd licencer, perhaps much his younger, perhaps far his inferiour in judgement, perhaps one who never knew the labour of book-writing, and if he be not repulst, or slighted, must appear in Print like a punie[26] with his guardian, and his censors hand on the back of his title to be his bayl and surety, that he is no idiot, or seducer, it cannot be but a dishonor and derogation to the author, to the book, to the priviledge and dignity of Learning. And what if the author shall be one so copious of fancie, as to have many things well worth the adding, come into his mind after licencing, while the book is yet under the Presse, which not seldom happ'ns to the best and diligentest writers; and that perhaps a dozen times in one book. The Printer dares not go beyond his licenc't copy; so often then must the author trudge to his leavgiver, that those his new insertions may be viewd; and many a jaunt will be made, ere that licencer, for it must be the same man, can either be found, or found at leisure; mean while either the Presse must stand still, which is no small damage, or the author loose his accuratest thoughts, & send the book forth wors then he had made it, which to a diligent writer is the greatest melancholy and vexation that can befall. And how can a man teach with autority, which is the life of teaching, how can he be a Doctor in his book as he ought to be, or else had better be silent, whenas all he teaches, all he delivers, is but under the tuition, under the correction of his patriarchal licencer to blot or alter what precisely accords not with the hidebound humor which he calls his judgement. When every acute reader upon the first sight of a pedantick licence, will be ready with these like words to ding the book a coits distance from him, I hate a pupil teacher, I endure not an instructer that comes to me under the wardship of an overseeing fist. I know nothing of the licencer, but that I have his own hand here for his arrogance; who shall warrant me his judgement? The State Sir, replies the Stationer, but has a quick return, The State shall be my governours, but not my criticks; they may be mistak'n in the choice of a licencer, as easily as this licencer may be mistak'n in an author: This is some common stuffe; and he might adde from Sir *Francis Bacon*, That *such authoriz'd books are but the language of the times.* For though a licencer should happ'n to be judicious more then ordnary, which will be a great jeopardy of the next succession, yet his very office, and his commission enjoyns him to let passe nothing but what is vulgarly receiv'd already. Nay, which is more lamentable, if the work of any deceased author, though never so famous in his life time, and even to this day, come to their hands for licence to be Printed, or Reprinted, if there be found in his book one sentence of a ventrous edge, utter'd in the height of zeal, and who knows whether it might not be the dictat of a divine Spirit, yet not suiting with every low decrepit humor of their own, though it were *Knox* himself, the Reformer of a Kingdom that spake it, they will not pardon him their dash: the sense of that great man shall to all posterity be lost, for the fearfulnesse, or the presumptuous rashnesse of a perfunctory licencer. And to what an author this violence hath bin lately done, and in what book of greatest consequence to be faithfully publisht, I could now instance, but shall forbear till a more convenient season. Yet if these things be not resented seriously and timely by them who have the remedy in their power, but that such iron moulds as these shall have autority to knaw out the choisest periods of exquisitest books, and to commit such a treacherous fraud against the orphan remainders of worthiest men after death, the more sorrow will belong to that haples race of men, whose misfortune it is to have understanding. Henceforth let no man care to learn, or care to be more then worldly wise; for certainly in higher matters to be ignorant and slothfull, to be a common stedfast dunce will be the only pleasant life, and only in request.

And as it is a particular disesteem of every knowing person alive, and most injurious to the writt'n labours and monuments of the dead, so to me it seems an undervaluing and vilifying of the whole Nation. I cannot set so light by all the invention, the art, the wit, the grave and solid judgement which is in England, as that it can be comprehended in any twenty capacities how good soever, much lesse that it should not passe except their superintendence be over it, except it be sifted and strain'd with their strainers, that it should be uncurrant without their manuall stamp. Truth and understanding are not such wares as to be monopoliz'd and traded in by tickets and statutes, and standards. We must not think to make a staple commodity of all the knowledge in the Land, to mark and licence it like our broad cloath, and our wooll packs. What is it but a servitude like that impos'd by the Philistims, not to be allow'd the sharpning of our own axes and coulters, but we must repair from all quarters to twenty licencing forges. Had any one writt'n and divulg'd erroneous things & scandalous to honest life, misusing and forfeiting the esteem had of his reason among men, if after conviction this only censure were adjudg'd him, that he should never henceforth write, but what were first examin'd by an appointed officer, whose hand should be annext to passe his credit for him, that now he might be safely read, it could not be apprehended lesse then a disgracefull punishment. Whence to include the whole Nation, and those that never yet thus offended, under such a diffident and suspectfull prohibition, may plainly be understood what a disparagement it is. So much the more, when as dettors and delinquents may walk abroad without a keeper, but unoffensive books must not stirre forth without a visible jaylor in thir title. Nor is it to the common people lesse then a reproach; for if we be so jealous over them, as that we dare not trust them with an English pamphlet, what doe we but censure them for a giddy, vitious, and ungrounded people; in such a sick and weak estate of faith and discretion, as to be able to take nothing down but through the pipe of a licencer. That this is care or love of them, we cannot pretend, whenas in those Popish places where the Laity are most hated and dispis'd the same strictnes is us'd over them. Wisdom we cannot call it, because it stops but one breach of licence, nor that neither; whenas those corruptions which it seeks to prevent, break in faster at other dores which cannot be shut.

And lest som should perswade ye, Lords and Commons, that these arguments of lerned mens discouragement at this your order, are meer flourishes, and not reall, I could recount what I have seen and heard in other Countries, where this kind of inquisition tyrannizes; when I have sat among their lerned men, for that honor I had, and bin counted happy to be born in such a place of *Philosophic* freedom, as they suppos'd England was, while themselvs did nothing but bemoan the servil

condition into which lerning amongst them was brought; that
this was it which had dampt the glory of Italian wits; that
nothing had bin there writt'n now these many years but flattery and fustian. There it was that I found and visited the
famous *Galileo* grown old, a prisner to the Inquisition, for
thinking in Astronomy otherwise then the Franciscan and
Dominican licencers thought. And though I knew that England
then was groaning loudest under the Prelaticall yoak, never-
thelesse I took it as a pledge of future happines, that other
Nations were so perswaded of her liberty. Yet was it beyond
my hope that those Worthies were then breathing in her air,
who should be her leaders to such a deliverance, as shall never
be forgott'n by any revolution of time that this world hath to
finish. When that was once begun, it was as little in my fear,
that what words of complaint I heard among lerned men of
other parts utter'd against the Inquisition, the same I should
hear by as lerned men at home utterd in time of Parlament
against an order of licencing . . . While things are yet not constituted in Religion, that freedom of writing should be restrain'd by a discipline imitated from the Prelats, and learnt
by them from the Inquisition to shut us up all again into the
brest of a licencer, must needs give cause of doubt and discouragement to all learned and religious men. Who cannot but
discern the finenes of this politic drift, and who are the con-
trivers; that while Bishops were to be baited down, then all
Presses might be open; it was the peoples birthright and priviledge in time of Parlament, it was the breaking forth of light.
But now the Bishops abrogated and voided out of the Church,
as if our Reformation sought no more, but to make room for
others into their seats under another name, the Episcopall arts
begin to bud again, the cruse of truth must run no more oyle,
liberty of Printing must be enthrall'd again under a Prelaticall
commission of twenty, the privilege of the people nullify'd, and
which is wors, the freedom of learning must groan again, and
to her old fetters; all this the Parlament yet sitting. Although
their own late arguments and defences against the Prelats
might remember them that this obstructing violence meets for
the most part with an event utterly opposite to the end which
it drives at: instead of suppressing sects and schisms, it raises

them and invests them with a reputation: *The punishing of wits enhaunces their autority,* saith the Vicount St. *Albans, and a forbidd'n writing is thought to be a certain spark of truth that flies up in the faces of them who seeke to tread it out.* This order therefore may prove a nursing mother to sects, but I shall easily shew how it will be a step-dame to Truth: and first by disinabling us to the maintenance of what is known already.

Well knows he who uses to consider, that our faith and knowledge thrives by exercise, as well as our limbs and complexion. Truth is compar'd in Scripture to a streaming fountain; if her waters flow not in a perpetuall progression, they sick'n into a muddy pool of conformity and tradition. A man may be a heretick in the truth; and if he beleeve things only because his Pastor sayes so, or the Assembly so determins, without knowing other reason, though his belief be true, yet the very truth he holds, becomes his heresie. There is not any burden that som would gladlier post off to another, then the charge and care of their Religion. There be, who knows not that there be of Protestants and professors who live and dye in as arrant an implicit faith, as any lay Papist of Loretto.[27] A wealthy man addicted to his pleasure and to his profits, finds Religion to be a traffick so entangl'd, and of so many piddling accounts, that of all mysteries he cannot skill[28] to keep a stock going upon that trade. What should he doe? fain he would have the name to be religious, fain he would bear up with his neighbours in that. What does he therefore, but resolvs to give over toyling, and to find himself out som factor, to whose care and credit he may commit the whole managing of his religious affairs; som Divine of note and estimation that must be. To him he adheres, resigns the whole warehouse of his religion, with all the locks and keyes into his custody; and indeed makes the very person of that man his religion; esteems his associating with him a sufficient evidence and commendatory of his own piety. So that a man may say his religion is now no more within himself, but is becom a dividuall movable, and goes and comes neer him, according as that good man frequents the house. He entertains him, gives him gifts, feasts him, lodges him; his religion comes home at night, praies, is liberally supt, and sumptuously laid to sleep, rises, is saluted. and after the malmsey, or some well spic't bruage, and better breakfasted then he whose morning appetite would have gladly fed on green figs between *Bethany* and *Ierusalem,* his Religion walks abroad at eight, and leavs his kind entertainer in the shop trading all day without his religion.

Another sort there be who when they hear that all things shall be order'd, all things regulated and setl'd; nothing writt'n but what passes through the custom-house of certain Publicans that have the tunaging and the poundaging[29] of all free spok'n truth, will strait give themselvs up into your hands, mak'em & cut'em out what religion ye please; there be delights, there be recreations and jolly pastimes that will fetch the day about from sun to sun, and rock the tedious year as in a delightfull dream. What need they torture their heads with that which others have tak'n so strictly, and so unalterably into their own pourveying. These are the fruits which a dull ease and cessation of our knowledge will bring forth among the people. How goodly, and how to be wisht were such an obedient unanimity as this, what a fine conformity would it starch us all into? Doubtles a stanch and solid peece of framework as any January could freeze together . . .

There is yet behind of what I purpos'd to lay open, the incredible losse, and detriment that this plot of licencing puts us to, more then if som enemy at sea should stop up all our hav'ns and ports, and creeks, it hinders and retards the importation of our richest Marchandize, Truth: nay it was first establisht and put in practice by Antichristian malice and mystery on set purpose to extinguish, if it were possible, the light of Reformation, and to settle falshood; little differing from that policie wherewith the Turk upholds his *Alcoran,* by the prohibition of Printing. 'Tis not deny'd, but gladly confest, we are to send our thanks and vows to heav'n, louder then most of Nations, for that great measure of truth which we enjoy, especially in those main points between us and the Pope, with his appertinences the Prelats: but he who thinks we are to pitch our tent here, and have attain'd the utmost prospect of reformation, that the mortall glasse wherein we contemplate, can shew us, till we come to *beatific* vision, that man by this very opinion declares, that he is yet farre short of Truth.

Truth indeed came once into the world with her divine Master, and was a perfect shape most glorious to look on: but when he ascended, and his Apostles after him were laid asleep, then strait arose a wicked race of deceivers, who as that story goes of the *Ægyptian Typhon* with his conspirators, how they dealt with the good *Osiris,* took the virgin Truth, hewd her lovely form into a thousand peeces, and scatter'd them to the four winds. From that time ever since, the sad friends of Truth, such as durst appear, imitating the carefull search that *Isis* made for the mangl'd body of *Osiris,* went up and down gathering up limb by limb still as they could find them. We have not yet found them all, Lords and Commons, nor ever shall doe, till her Masters second comming; he shall bring together every joynt and member, and shall mould them into an immortall feature of lovelines and perfection. Suffer not these licencing prohibitions to stand at every place of opportunity forbidding and disturbing them that continue seeking, that continue to do our obsequies to the torn body of our martyr'd Saint. . . .

Lords and Commons of England, consider what Nation it is wherof ye are, and wherof ye are the governours: a Nation not slow and dull, but of a quick, ingenious, and piercing spirit, acute to invent, suttle and sinewy to discours, not beneath the reach of any point the highest that human capacity can soar to. Therefore the studies of learning in her deepest Sciences have bin so ancient, and so eminent among us, that Writers of good antiquity, and ablest judgement have bin perswaded that ev'n the school of *Pythagoras,* and the *Persian* wisdom took beginning from the old Philosophy of this Iland. And that wise and civill Roman, *Julius Agricola,* who govern'd once here for *Cæsar,* preferr'd the naturall wits of Britain, before the labour'd studies of the French. Nor is it for nothing that the grave and frugal *Transilvanian* sends out yearly from as farre as the mountanous borders of *Russia,* and beyond the *Hercynian* wildernes, not their youth, but their stay'd men, to learn our language, and our *theologic* arts. Yet that which is above all this, the favour and the love of heav'n we have great argument to think in a peculiar manner propitious and propending towards us. Why else was this Nation chos'n before any other, that out of her as out of *Sion* should be proclam'd and sounded forth the first tidings and trumpet of Reformation to all *Europ*. And had it not bin the obstinat perversnes of our Prelats against the divine and admirable spirit of *Wicklef*, to suppresse him as a schismatic and *innovator*, perhaps neither the *Bohemian Husse* and *Jerom*, no nor the name of *Luther*, or of *Calvin* had bin ever known: the glory of reforming all our neighbours had bin compleatly ours. But now, as our obdurat Clergy have with violence demean'd the matter, we are become hitherto the latest and the backwardest Schollers, of whom God offer'd to have made us the teachers. Now once again by all concurrence of signs, and by the generall instinct of holy and devout men, as they daily and solemnly expresse their thoughts, God is decreeing to begin some new and great period in his Church, ev'n to the reforming of Reformation it self: what does he then but reveal Himself to his servants, and as his manner is, first to his English-men; I say as his manner is, first to us, though we mark not the method of his counsels, and are unworthy. Behold now this vast City; a City of refuge, the mansion house of liberty, encompast and surrounded with his protection; the shop of warre hath not there more anvils and hammers waking, to fashion out the plates and instruments of armed Justice in defence of beleaguer'd Truth, then there be pens and heads there, sitting by their studious lamps, musing, searching, revolving new notions and idea's wherewith to present, as with their homage and their fealty the approaching Reformation: others as fast reading, trying all things, assenting to the force of reason and convincement. What could a man require more from a Nation so pliant and so prone to seek after knowledge. What wants there to such a towardly and pregnant soile, but wise and faithfull labourers, to make a knowing people, a Nation of Prophets, of Sages, and of Worthies. We reck'n more then five months yet to harvest; there need not be five weeks, had we but eyes to lift up, the fields are white already. Where there is much desire to learn, there of necessity will be much arguing, much writing, many opinions; for opinion in good men is but knowledge in the making. Under these fantastic terrors of sect and

schism, we wrong the earnest and zealous thirst after knowledge and understanding which God hath stirr'd up in this City.
What some lament of, we rather should rejoyce at, should
rather praise this pious forwardnes among men, to reassume
the ill deputed care of their Religion into their own hands
again. . . . And that we are to hope better of all these supposed sects and schisms, and that we shall not need that solicitude honest perhaps though over timorous of them that vex
in this behalf, but shall laugh in the end, at those malicious
applauders of our differences, I have these reasons to perswade
me.

First, when a City shall be as it were besieg'd and blockt
about, her navigable river infested, inrodes and incursions
round, defiance and battell oft rumor'd to be marching up ev'n
to her walls, and suburb trenches, that then the people, or
the greater part, more then at other times, wholly tak'n up
with the study of highest and most important matters to be
reform'd, should be disputing, reasoning, reading, inventing,
discoursing, ev'n to a rarity, and admiration, things not before
discourst or writt'n of, argues first a singular good will, con-
tentednesse and confidence in your prudent foresight, and safe
government, Lords and Commons; and from thence derives it
self to a gallant bravery and well grounded contempt of their
enemies, as if there were no small number of as great spirits
among us, as his was, who when Rome was nigh besieg'd by
Hanibal, being in the City, bought that peece of ground at
no cheap rate, whereon *Hanibal* himself encampt his own
reg'ment. Next it is a lively and cherfull presage of our happy
successe and victory. For as in a body, when the blood is fresh,
the spirits pure and vigorous, not only to vital, but to rationall
faculties, and those in the acutest, and the pertest operations
of wit and suttlety, it argues in what good plight and constitution the body is, so when the cherfulnesse of the people is so
sprightly up, as that it has, not only wherewith to guard well
its own freedom and safety, but to spare, and to bestow upon
the solidest and sublimest points of controversie, and new invention, it betok'ns us not degenerated, nor drooping to a fatall
decay, but casting off the old and wrincl'd skin of corruption to
outlive these pangs and wax young again, entring the glorious

waies of Truth and prosperous vertue destin'd to become great
and honourable in these latter ages. Methinks I see in my mind
a noble and puissant Nation rousing herself like a strong man
after sleep, and shaking her invincible locks: Methinks I see
her as an Eagle muing[30] her mighty youth, and kindling her
undazl'd eyes at the full midday beam; purging and unscaling
her long abused sight at the fountain it self of heav'nly radiance; while the whole noise of timorous and flocking birds,
with those also that love the twilight, flutter about, amaz'd at
what she means, and in their envious gabble would prognosti-
cat a year of sects and schisms.

What should ye doe then, should ye suppresse all this
flowry crop of knowledge and new light sprung up and yet
springing daily in this City, should ye set an *Oligarchy* of
twenty ingrossers over it, to bring a famin upon our minds
again, when we shall know nothing but what is measur'd to
us by their bushel? Beleeve it, Lords and Commons, they who
counsell ye to such a suppressing, doe as good as bid ye suppresse your selves; and I will soon shew how. If it be desir'd
to know the immediat cause of all this free writing and free
speaking, there cannot be assign'd a truer then your own mild,
and free, and human government; it is the liberty, Lords and
Commons, which your own valorous and happy counsels have
purchast us, liberty which is the nurse of all great wits; this is
that which hath rarify'd and enlightn'd our spirits like the influence of heav'n; this is that which hath enfranchis'd, en-
larg'd and lifted up our apprehensions degrees above themselves. Ye cannot make us now lesse capable, lesse knowing,
lesse eagerly pursuing of the truth, unlesse ye first make your
selves, that made us so, lesse the lovers, lesse the founders of
our true liberty. We can grow ignorant again, brutish, formall,
and slavish, as ye found us; but you then must first become
that which ye cannot be, oppressive, arbitrary, and tyrannous,
as they were from whom ye have free'd us. That our hearts
are now more capacious, our thoughts more erected to the
search and expectation of greatest and exactest things, is the
issue of your owne vertu propagated in us; ye cannot suppresse that unlesse ye reinforce an abrogated and mercilesse
law, that fathers may dispatch at will their own children. And

who shall then sticke closest to ye, and excite others? Not he who takes up armes for cote and conduct and his four nobles of Danegelt.[31] Although I dispraise not the defence of just immunities, yet love my peace better, if that were all. Give me the liberty to know, to utter, and to argue freely according to conscience, above all liberties . . .

And now the time in speciall is, by priviledge to write and speak what may help to the furder discussing of matters in agitation. The Temple of *Janus*[32] with his two *controversal* faces might now not unsignificantly be set open. And though all the windes of doctrin were let loose to play upon the earth, so Truth be in the field, we do injuriously by licencing and prohibiting to misdoubt her strength. Let her and Falshood grapple; who ever knew Truth put to the wors, in a free and open encounter. Her confuting is the best and surest suppressing. He who hears what praying there is for light and clearer knowledge to be sent down among us, would think of other matters to be constituted beyond the discipline of *Geneva*, fram'd and fabric't already to our hands. Yet when the new light which we beg for shines in upon us, there be who envy, and oppose, if it come not first in at their casements. What a collusion is this, whenas we are exhorted by the wise man to use diligence, *to seek for wisdom as for hidd'n treasures* early and late, that another order shall enjoyn us to know nothing but by statute. When a man hath bin labouring the hardest labour in the deep mines of knowledge, hath furnisht out his findings in all their equipage, drawn forth his reasons as it were a battell raung'd, scatter'd and defeated all objections in his way, calls out his adversary into the plain, offers him the advantage of wind and sun, if he please; only that he may try the matter by dint of argument, for his opponents then to sculk, to lay ambushments, to keep a narrow bridge of licencing where the challenger should passe, though it be valour anough in shouldiership, is but weaknes and cowardise in the wars of Truth. For who knows not that Truth is strong next to the Almighty; she needs no policies, nor stratagems, nor licencings to make her victorious, those are the shifts and the defences that error uses against her power: give her but room, & do not bind her when she sleeps, for then she speaks not true, as the old *Proteus* did, who spake oracles only when he was caught & bound, but then rather she turns herself into all shapes, except her own, and perhaps tunes her voice according to the time, as *Micaiah* did before *Ahab,* untill she be adjur'd into her own likenes. Yet is it not impossible that she may have more shapes then one. What else is all that rank of things indifferent, wherein Truth may be on this side, or on the other, without being unlike her self. What but a vain shadow else is the abolition of *those ordinances, that hand writing nayl'd to the crosse,* what great purchase is this Christian liberty which *Paul* so often boasts of. His doctrine is, that he who eats or eats not, regards a day, or regards it not, may doe either to the Lord. How many other things might be tolerated in peace, and left to conscience, had we but charity, and were it not the chief strong hold of our hypocrisie to be ever judging one another. I fear yet this iron yoke of outward conformity hath left a slavish print upon our necks; the ghost of a linnen decency[33] yet haunts us. We stumble and are impatient at the least dividing of one visible congregation from another, though it be not in fundamentalls; and through our forwardnes to suppresse, and our backwardnes to recover any enthrall'd peece of truth out of the gripe of custom, we care not to keep truth separated from truth, which is the fiercest rent and disunion of all. We doe not see that while we still affect by all means a rigid externall formality, we may as soon fall again into a grosse conforming stupidity, a stark and dead congealment of *wood and hay and stubble* forc't and frozen together, which is more to the sudden degenerating of a Church then many *subdichotomies* of petty schisms. Not that I can think well of every light separation, or that all in a Church is to be expected *gold and silver and pretious stones:* it is not possible for man to sever the wheat from the tares, the good fish from the other frie; that must be the Angels Ministery at the end of mortall things. Yet if all cannot be of one mind, as who looks they should be? this doubtles is more wholsome, more prudent, and more Christian that many be tolerated, rather then all compell'd. I mean not tolerated Popery, and open superstition, which as it extirpats all religions and civill supremacies, so it self should be extirpat, provided first that all charitable and compassionat means be us'd to win and regain the weak and the misled: that also which is impious or evil absolutely either against faith or maners no law can possibly permit, that intends not to unlaw it self: but those neighboring differences, or rather indifferences, are what I speak of, whether in some point of doctrine or of discipline, which though they may be many, yet need not interrupt *the unity of Spirit,* if we could but find among us *the bond of peace.* . . .

NOTES ON MILTON'S *AREOPAGITICA*

1. *quadragesimal and matrimonial*—Lenten and marriage licenses, the former referring to permission to eat meat in Lent. Both licenses used to be obtained from bishops. Milton thought of marriage as a civil contract rather than a sacrament.
2. *when the Prelats expir'd*—*prelates* refers to the civil status of the bishops in the House of Lords, from which they were expelled in 1641.
3. *fabulous Dragons teeth*—Jason sowed the teeth of the Colchian dragon, as Medea bade him, and the teeth sprang up as armed men.
4. *Martin the 5*—Pope, 1417–1431. The Bull is the boss-like seal on Papal legal instruments, used of the document itself.
5. *Wicklef and Husse*—fourteenth-century Church reformers. Huss was burnt at the stake in 1415.
6. *expurging Indexes*—the *Index Expurgatorius* bowdlerized, the *Index Librorum Prohibitorum* wholly prohibited books. The former started with the Italian Inquisition; the Council of Trent approved it in 1559. Both indexes are still in operation.
7. *Lambeth house . . . Pauls*—the Archbishop of Canterbury's residence is still at Lambeth; the Bishop of London had a palace bordering on old St. Paul's, which was burnt down in the Great Fire of 1666.
8. *no envious Juno*—when Alcmena labored to give birth to Hercules, Juno, goddess of childbirth, jealous of the child's father, her own husband Jupiter, refused her any help, and the midwife sat cross-legged, in the ancient belief that this would prevent a woman giving birth. But a false report was sent out that a child had been born, the midwife got up, and Hercules was delivered.
9. *naughty*—worthless, empty, of naught.
10. *Omer*—a unit of measure for the manna, mentioned in Exodus.

11. *those confused seeds*—a story from *The Golden Ass* of Apuleius. Venus hated Psyche because her son Cupid had fallen in love with her. To torment the girl, Venus set her to sort out a mountain of various seeds before evening. The ants took pity on Psyche and performed the task for her.

12. *excrementall*—*excrement* used to have the same meaning as *excrescence*—an outgrowth. *Excrementall whitenesse* means superficial whiteness.

13. *Spencer . . . Aquinas*—Edmund Spenser, who wrote the episode of Guyon as part of *The Faerie Queene;* John Duns Scotus, the famous schoolman of the thirteenth century; St. Thomas Aquinas, 1225–1274.

14. *cautelous*—deceitful.

15. *want*—do without.

16. *while . . . explaining*—while I have been involved in explanation.

17. *ingenuity*—ingenuousness.

18. *fond*—foolish.

19. *Dorick*—the style of ancient military music.

20. *Atlantick and Eutopian polities*—political systems of ideal states such as Bacon's *New Atlantis* or More's *Utopia*.

21. *under pittance*—proportioned.

22. *a meer artificiall Adam . . . motions*—just a mechanical Adam, as he is in the puppet shows.

23. *esteem not of*—do not esteem.

24. *model of Trent and Sevil*—i.e., the Inquisition.

25. *Palladian oyl*—scholars studied by oil light. The goddess concerned with their labors was Pallas Athena, goddess of wisdom, and the olive tree that gave the oil was sacred to her.

26. *punie*—little boy.

27. *Loretto*—a shrine in Italy.

28. *skill*—manage.

29. *tunaging and poundaging*—customs-levying.

30. *muing*—renewing by moulting.

31. *cote and conduct . . . Danegelt*—coat and conduct money was raised for clothing and moving troops. Danegelt was money raised to save England from the Danish invasions; here it refers to ship money levied by Charles I for the Navy without consent of Parliament.
    A noble = 6s.8d.

32. *Temple of Janus*—Janus was the two-headed god whose temple was open in war, shut in peace (when there was no controversy).

33. *linnen decency*—as of surplices, the outer covering of the clergy.

COMMENT: On Whether Plato
Would Have Expelled Milton from the
Republic

The *Areopagitica* presented Milton with one difficulty and it presents us with yet another, which will be discussed in the next section. Milton's difficulty was to reconcile his admiration of Plato with Plato's advocacy of censorship in the *Republic*. With this exception, the best minds, according to Milton, had always been against censorship. He does not succeed in bringing the exception into line by declaring that Plato wrote of an ideal, rather than of an actual, state, since the *Republic* is clearly concerned with the righting of current abuses in Plato's day, and so bases itself on human nature as Plato sees it, rather than on the nature of ideal creatures.

In general the *Republic* is directed at solving the problem of the state through the realization and perpetuation of strong and stable human character. It does not set out to provide a rule-of-thumb guide to state management, nor is it a political work except insofar as it deals with the production of good citizens through right education. Elsewhere, for example in dealing with the death of Socrates, where he obviously had political concerns but certainly not educational ones, Plato puts a strong plea for free speech into the mouth of his beloved master Socrates, who says that he would rather die than not voice his opinions. Only up to a point, then, is Milton right in declaring that Plato is dealing with a utopian world.

Plato has a good deal to say about the selection of literature for children in the *Republic*. It is revealing to see what he thinks of Homer, whom his contemporaries considered supremely educational. Homer's poetry suffered, Plato said, be-

cause it did not tell the truth. For poetry not to be useful in
this way was unthinkable for the Greeks. Not until the coming
of Christianity could poetry be judged by a purely aesthetic
standard. Plato pointed out that his governing élite could not
behave in a godlike way or be god-fearing or heroic if they
read in Homer that the gods lied or were frivolous or that
great heroes like Achilles gave way to unmanly passion; nor
could they be brave in war if Homer's description of the world
of the dead made them afraid to die.

Modern people go on believing that children have to be
shown what is expected of them in the way of nobility and
goodness. But since the Freudian revolution they have come
to see that the individual "is engaged in the perpetual human
task of keeping inner and outer reality separate yet inter-
related," as a psychiatrist has put it; in other words, a certain
amount of fright or excitement of one kind or another, presented through books or other media, helps with the task of
self-control and self-knowledge through the enjoyment of that
fright or other excitement. Of course, therapy is not always
uppermost in mind; but we would say that Plato would defeat his own purpose if he prevented his élite from enjoying
the sort of knowledge of life obtained through story. We would
say that delinquency, or failure of the strength of mind Plato
looked for, came not from bad examples or the stimulation of
fear, but from psychotic features of previous origin, and is only
triggered by the immediate stimulus. We would not deeply
disagree over the use of censorship to limit and direct children's
actual studies, however, if Plato did not carry these arguments
a step further when applying them to the adult world.

When you meet with admirers of Homer [Socrates says
to Glaucon], who tell you that he has been the educator
of Hellas and that on questions of human conduct and
culture he deserves to be constantly studied as a guide by
whom to regulate your whole life, it is well to give a
friendly hearing to such people, as entirely well-meaning
according to their lights, and you may acknowledge Homer to be the first and greatest of the tragic poets; but
you must be quite sure that we can admit into our com-

monwealth only the poetry which celebrates the praises of the gods and of good men. If you go further and admit the honeyed muse in epic or in lyric verse, then pleasure and pain will usurp the sovereignty of law and of the principles always recognized by common consent as the best. . . . So now, since we have recurred to the subject of poetry, let this be our defence: it stands to reason that we could not but banish such an influence from our commonwealth.[1]

The exclusion of ignoble or unworthy material begs of course the question of who was to do the excluding. This is the strongest argument in favor of Milton's view that Plato's was a "fancied republic, which in this world could have no place." However, we have stronger objections to the argument for censorship advanced by the *Republic*.

We commonly hear Plato quoted on the subject of censorship as if he advanced his theoretical remedy for the misfortunes of *our* time, rather than of his own. Milton was less qualified to object to this practice than we are, because his knowledge of Plato's day was far more restricted than ours is, and at the same time, in spite of our superior information about ancient society, we are more prone to make false comparisons between the society of the *Republic* and our own, urged on by the similarity between the totalitarian political systems we are all too familiar with and the strongly centralized and directed system of Plato. A new point that we are able to add to the counter-argument of *Areopagitica* is that the Athens of Plato was possessed of a very lively totalitarian spirit already. For ancient religious and patriarchal reasons, the citizens of the ancient city-state, as Fustel de Coulanges writes,

knew neither liberty in private life, liberty in education, nor religious liberty. The human person counted for very little against that holy and almost divine authority which was called country or the state. The state had not only, as we have in our modern societies, a right to administer justice to the citizens; it could strike when one was not guilty, and simply for its own interest. Aristides assuredly had committed no crime, and was not even suspected; but the city had the right to drive him from its territory, for the simple reason that he had acquired by his virtues too much influence, and might become dangerous, if he desired to be. This was called *ostracism*. . . . Now, *ostracism* was not a chastisement; it was a precaution which the city took against a citizen whom it suspected of having the power to injure it at any time. . . . The dangerous maxim that the safety of the state is the supreme law, was the work of antiquity. It was then thought that law, justice, morals, everything should give way before the interests of the country.

It is a singular error, therefore, among all human errors, to believe that in the ancient cities men enjoyed liberty. They had not even the idea of it. They did not believe that there could exist any right as against the city and its gods. We shall see, farther on, that the government changed form several times, while the nature of the state remained nearly the same, and its omnipotence was little diminished. The government was called by turns monarchy, aristocracy, democracy; but none of these revolutions gave man true liberty, individual liberty. To have political rights, to vote, to name magistrates, to have the privilege of being archon,—this was called liberty; but man was not the less enslaved to the state. The ancients, especially the Greeks, always exaggerated the importance, and above all the rights of society; this was largely due, doubtless, to the sacred and religious character with which society was clothed in the beginning.[2]

A Christian moralist of Milton's time would not realize how impossible it would be for an Athenian to write *Areopagitica;* its very conception would have been self-censored. The question whether a man in himself was free or not, which so occupied Milton, would not occur to Plato; for him, individual decision between right and wrong rested entirely on the individual's sense of the public good. It did not depend on a final judgment beyond this world, or a reward in heaven; it did not look hopefully to a martyr's crown or the solace of a good (and private) conscience. Censorship could therefore be projected on a utopian society like Plato's without a thought occurring to him of the transgression of inalienable *private* will, for such liberty as Athens enjoyed was that of a body of men almost perpetually and precariously at war with other cities and in danger of being enslaved by them. Honor, as the due recognition of a man's worth, was the ancient conception that still lingered behind the wisdom of the guardian élite who were to rule the Republic. For most of us in the modern Western world, as for Milton, wisdom is closely connected with the liberty of choice and an ancient conception of the overwhelming importance of a man's relations with his God, which take precedence over his relations with his fellow men.

What is extraordinary about Plato's Republic and what marks the difference between it and the totalitarian systems of our day is the place it gives to wisdom. Wisdom could be gained, according to Plato, only by highly gifted natures after long discipline and experience, and happiness would come to cities only when possessors of wisdom were in command, since they would despise power and riches and all honors except the honor of doing right. Such was Plato's effort to rationalize the religious and patriarchal authority of the state: to have the superior intelligences govern the rest. The inferior intelligences would lack insight, and could therefore be made happy on political and religious myths—"noble lies," as Plato called them, which appeal to their emotions and stimulate them to obey the law. R. H. S. Crossman explains what "noble lies" Plato had in mind:

> By the 'noble lie' Plato meant propaganda, the technique of controlling the behaviour of the stupid majority: and he believed that this was the only sort of general education which the civilian should receive. He must, in fact, be content with the education which Plato had prepared for the children of the ruling class, since politically and morally he would always remain a child. Just as children are told improving stories to prevent them from biting their nails or stealing or telling lies, so the civilian must be fed on propaganda to prevent him from asserting his right to self-government. One such story Plato himself

suggested: 'Yes,' I said, 'you are no doubt right; but still listen to the rest of the tale. "You in this city are all brothers," so we shall tell our tale to them, "but God as he was fashioning you, put gold in those of you who are capable of ruling; hence they are deserving of most reverence. He put silver in the auxiliaries, and iron and copper in the farmers and the other craftsmen. For the most part your children are of the same nature as yourselves, but because you are all akin, sometimes from gold will come a silver offspring, or from silver a gold, and so on all round. Therefore the first and weightiest command of God to the rulers is this—that more than aught else they be good guardians of and watch zealously over the offspring, seeing which of those metals is mixed in their souls; if their own offspring have an admixture of copper or iron, they must show no pity, but giving it the honour proper to its nature, set it among the artisans or the farmers; and if on the other hand in these classes children are born with an admixture of gold and silver, they shall do them honour and appoint the first to be guardians, the second to be auxiliaries. For there is an oracle that the city shall perish when it is guarded by iron or copper." '3

Philosophy for the ruler, and propaganda for the rest —this, says Plato, is the best way of avoiding bloodshed in the establishment and maintenance of the 'dictatorship of the best'. The mistake of Socrates had been his belief that the Law of Reason was suitable for everyone. He had condemned rhetoric and sophistical education altogether and tried to convert the city of Athens to philosophy. But philosophy and reason are poison to the masses. Misunderstood and perverted by them, they merely intensify social unrest. The masses need not the truth, but a convenient falsehood. They, like Adam and Eve, must be forbidden to eat of the Tree of the Knowledge of Good and Evil—for their own sakes. The philosopher-king therefore will not condemn propaganda altogether, but will demand the absolute control of it by the Government. Literature, music, religion, science—everything which can disturb their minds must be censored by the rulers and regulated so as to promote the loyalty of the masses to the new regime. The perfect State will be for the civilian quite literally 'a fool's paradise', controlled by a few wise men, who out of their compassion for the masses provide them with superstitions and ceremonies and popular philosophies fit for their feeble capacities.

Plato's philosophy is the most savage and the most profound attack upon liberal ideas which history can show. It denies every axiom of 'progressive' thought and challenges all its fondest ideals. Equality, freedom, self-government—all are condemned as illusions which can be held only by idealists whose sympathies are stronger than their sense. The true idealist, on Plato's view, will see men as they are, observe their radical inequalities, and give to the many not self-government but security, not freedom but prosperity, not knowledge but the 'noble lie'. The perfect State is not a democracy of rational equals, but an aristocracy in which a hereditary caste of cultured gentlemen care with paternal solicitude for the toiling masses.[4]

Milton's knowledge of Plato was based mostly on the *Timaeus*. It is doubtful whether he would have been so concerned to explain Plato's arguments for censorship if he had understood the philosopher's attitude to the civilian-non-élite in the *Republic*. For Milton was above all a believer in the reason of the common people, and this would be cause enough for Plato to banish the poet from his imaginary state. Milton was also a believer in unorthodoxies such as divorce, and he had a generally acknowledged sympathy with opposition, particularly with the person of Lucifer in *Paradise Lost*. But there is also reason to believe that any poet of our era would be banished. As we have seen, most of Plato's concern over the weakening effects of literature was directed toward poetry likely to be read by school children; he was also concerned, however, over the effects of poetic drama, which were particularly potent because of its origins in religious celebration. So strong were these effects that a play by Phrynichus on the Persian capture of Miletus, which on its first performance had moved the audience to tears of shame, was banned by the archon of Athens, presumably on the grounds that it weakened public morale. As Jaeger says:

> The undisputed supremacy of Attic tragedy, which lasted for a hundred years, coincided chronologically and spiritually with the rise, greatness, and decline of the secular power of Athens. Within that period tragedy attained that domination over the Athenian people which we see reflected in the allusions of the comic poets. . . . Tragedy furthered the intellectual and moral degeneration which Thucydides correctly asserted to have been the ruin of Athens, just as it had given the state strength and cohesion during its rise and glorified it at the zenith of its power. . . . The men of that age never felt that the nature and influence of tragedy were purely and simply aesthetic. Its power over them was so vast that they held it responsible for the spirit of the whole state; and although as historians we may believe that even the greatest poets were representatives, not the creators, of the national spirit, our belief cannot alter the fact that the Athenians held them to be their spiritual leaders, with a responsibility far greater and graver than the constitutional authority of successive political leaders. Only by keeping that in mind can we understand the attacks made on the freedom of poetry in Plato's *Republic*—attacks which seem so inexplicable and repulsive to a liberal mind.
>
> Yet the idea that the tragic poet was responsible for the spirit of the state cannot have been the original conception of his function; for the age of Pisistratus thought of poetry as a thing to be enjoyed. It was created by the tragedies of Aeschylus: it was Aeschylus whom Aristophanes conjured up from the lower world as the only man (in the absence of a Platonic censorship) who could recall poetry to its true function.[5]

"Its power over them was so vast that they held it responsible for the spirit of the whole state. . . ." Even though the author of these words is referring to poetic tragedy, we cannot, even by extending his words to refer to *any* kind of literature, draw parallels with the power of literature in our day.

For various reasons, even the optimistic among us would not say that the most respectable writers have much to do with the spirit of the state. And many think romantically of the artist as a man by nature in opposition to the state. Milton was a republican in the early unspoilt days of a republic; he saw himself as a poet among the great poets of the past; yet he went largely without honor, even in the days of the republic.

The *Republic*, then, would banish poets because they awoke people to pain and pleasure, which Plato found a weakness. Our tradition of compassion urges us to cherish the weak and to regard pleasure and pain as the human condition which we disregard at our peril. We are alarmed by the intellectual purity and strength of the *Republic*. But on his side Plato would surely view our apathy toward poets with even more alarm. He would say that if we neglect them, we choose to live on a very low level, where wanton stupidity and pride may take precedence over principle.

COMMENT: On Milton's Intolerance of the Roman Catholic Church

The chief stumbling block with which *Areopagitica* presents the modern reader is not, however, the fact that Plato advocated censorship in the *Republic*, but that .Milton preached freedom of printing *except for the writings of the Roman Catholic Church*. We have seen that the *Republic* offers a possible prototype of a totalitarian state, although of a most enlightened kind, and we accordingly make mental reservations as we read it before accepting it as the perfect solution to our worldly ills. But Milton's one exception to freedom of expression has been in no way made more tolerable by experience; his exception merely destroys his argument. Harold C. Gardiner, S.J., in his *Catholic Viewpoint on Censorship,* which bears the *imprimatur* of Cardinal Spellman and a *nihil obstat* to signify the approval of his Church, affirms that it would be wrong to read *Areopagitica* without noting the special conditions of Milton's time. While attempting to do so—and to do so is neither to invalidate Milton's relevance for our time nor to indemnify his intolerance of the writings of the Roman Catholic Church—we have to consider it illogical that Milton thought the influence of the "Papists" so fearfully destructive that the very freedom of the people and the sovereignty of reason he was defending could not withstand it. It is just as illogical as the intention of those who would penalize Americans for reading Communist tracts or carefully considering Soviet arguments as arguments, on the grounds that they may thereby become contaminated and so willingly give up the spirit of free inquiry which brought them there in the first place. "Papistry" was the bogey of Milton's day just as Communism is of ours, and we hope that it provides some comment on the practical disadvantage of censorship to note that the bogey is no longer the same. With this in mind, we hope we may fairly inquire into the censorship that the Roman Catholic Church exercises today.

Before we do so, however, we should like to make clear that we are not concerned with making a full history or exemplar of censorship in any of the sections that follow. Censorship has played such a universally ugly part in the history of faith that we do not attempt to give it full coverage; the Protestant churches were as prompt to enforce it as the powers of the Counter-Reformation, and they are as active today as the Roman Catholic Church is. However, they are far more haphazard and subject to fashion. Comstock laws, Blue Laws, and so on, belong to the history of prudery and to the history of anti-Catholicism rather than to doctrinal Protestantism. The Roman Catholic Church alone makes censorship part of its doctrine. What exactly is this doctrine?

First we must note that the Church's attitude is not unlike that of Plato toward the mass of the non-élite in the *Republic:* the Church too considers itself the guardian of the people. The law of reason is not for most people. At the close of the Middle Ages, at the time of the invention of printing, the suppression of vernacular scriptural texts was due as much to fear of heresy caused through misunderstanding by simple souls, as to fear that a flock might cut itself off from its pastor by turning to new sources of information and teaching.

On the general Catholic attitude toward censorship within the secular state, Father Gardiner says:

> The Catholic viewpoint is that law is to be loved because it is rational and because of its origin and purpose. Its origin is from God; its ultimate purpose is rationally to assure greater freedom.
>
> One of the necessary postulates of law (or of the exercise of law through authority) is the community's coercive power, the restriction and punishment of evil-doing, of infringements of the law. This onerous element is not less to be loved than the expansive aspects, for it is des-

tined for the same purpose, to facilitate the exercise of freedom.

It follows, therefore, that society, which has the right and duty to establish laws for the common good, has, by the same title, the right *and the duty* to exercise coercion. It would seem superfluous to emphasize this truth were it not for the fact that most of the controversy about censorship seems to rest fundamentally at exactly this crux. A great number of those who oppose censorship in any shape or form deny implicitly (though they may never advert to the fact) that society has the *right* to censor —especially the state in a pluralistic society like the one in which we live. We aver in these pages that the state not only has the *right* but is solemnly bound by the *duty* to censor, under certain circumstances.

It seems odd that this can apparently be the stand of opponents of censorship, since they are quite ready to admit other coercive powers of the state. No one of them would question the right of the state to arrest traffic-law violators, for instance, or to throw dope peddlers into jail, but when it comes to any restrictions or controls in the matter of freedom of expression, they will not only deny the state's duty to protect the common good, but will even call into question its right.[6]

When it appears to a man that the state is doing wrong, he has surely a duty to "call into question its right" to do so. It might well be considered wrong, for example, to throw dope peddlers into jail when the question of dope addiction has been far more successfully solved in countries that do not treat addicts as criminals. It might well be considered wrong of the state, too, to enforce censorship if censorship could be shown to defeat its own purpose and also to produce worse evils than those it tries to cure. Traffic-law violators belong to a different species of problem, as there is little argument about what is morally right or wrong, but only about whether or not regulations for the common convenience have been obeyed. These analogies apart, however, there is a practical argument to advance against Father Gardiner's equally practical one, and it is the argument that Lord Erskine used in defence of Tom Paine: "Other liberties are held *under* governments, but the liberty of opinion keeps governments themselves in due subjection to their duties." In this argument there is no question of the rightness or wrongness of the opinions raised; they are regarded only as an instrument of keeping the power of the state in check.

The attitude of the Church to the state differs according to the state. In Spain and Ireland the censorship is far more stringent than in South American countries; the degree of censorship depends on the degree of anti-clericalism, or on how far the teaching of the Church is applied by those in power. In general the *Index Librorum Prohibitorum* is the source of such censorship. The description of it that follows is by an English Catholic layman; he does not represent the official Catholic viewpoint.

TEXT: "The *Index Librorum Prohibitorum*" from *The Vatican Story* by Bernard Wall

What is the Index?

It is a small book of about five hundred pages with an introduction in Italian—a language which, after all, most priests can understand up to a point. It consists of a list of the books condemned by the Holy Office. It contains some decrees in Latin in the full text—notably the one condemning Charles Maurras and the French Royalist newspaper, *L'Action Française:*

DECRETUM

'Damnantur quaedam opera Caroli Maurras et ephem-
erides 'L'action Française . . .'
        die 29 ianuarii 1914
        et die 29 decembris 1926*

But texts are rare. Usually the Index prints only the title of the book, the author, publisher and date, with the date of the decree by which the book was condemned. The title of the book is printed in the language in which it was first known in Rome.

Two things strike one's eye immediately. One is that most of the books condemned are of an abstruse or eccentric theological nature—sea-shells abandoned on the shores of long-dead controversies. Thus we find:

* DECREE. Are condemned whatsoever works of Charles Maurras and the daily newspaper 'L'Action Française . . .'

'The Abominations of the Papacy or the Irrefutable Demonstration that the Roman Pope is Antichrist: an excerpt from the book The Final Ruin of Rome in the year of Our Lord 1666 . . .'

Or:

'Discourse (A Seasonable) showing how that the Oaths of Allegiance and Supremacy contain nothing which any good Christian ought to Boggle at.' By W. B.

Or:

'Letter (A) from Rome showing an exact Conformity between Popery and Paganism, or the Religion of the present Romans derived from that of their heathen Ancestors. Middleton. Conyers, 1755.'

Some of the books are in Greek, many in Latin and many in French. The French excelled in 'Open Letters', so we get 'Lettre d'un évêque à un collègue', 'Lettre d'un abbé . . .' and so on. Sometimes the titles are anodyne: what, one wonders, can be the objection to the 'Lettre d'un avocat à un de ses amis sur l'onguent pour la bruslure, 1664'? On the list I also discover the Basilikon Doron of King James I of England, The Book of Common Prayer, Addison's Notes on Italy and Milton's Latin Letters. And here are a few names of better-known writers whose books, individually (or sometimes en bloc), are on the Index: Balzac, Honoré de, Omnes Fabulae Amatoriae—'all amatory fables' seems to mean 'all novels'; Bentham, Jérémie (sic); Abbé Brémond; Thomas Browne; Ernesto Bonaiuti; Ernest Dimnet; Fogazzaro for The Saint; D'Annunzio—omnes fabulae amatoriae; Oliver Goldsmith's History of England; Gregorovius; Henry Hallam; La Fontaine; Andrew Marvell; John Stuart Mill; St. George Mivart (for an article proving there was 'happiness in Hell' in the old Nineteenth Century); Montaigne's Essaies; Lady Sydney Morgan; Victor Hugo's Les Misérables; Pascal's Pensées (with Voltaire's notes); Ranke's History of the Popes; Ernest Renan; Samuel Richardson; Jean-Jacques Rousseau; Georges Sand; Spinoza; Stendhal—omnes fabulae amatoriae; Sterne—A Sentimental Journey; Voltaire;

Zola. . . . Of the works condemned I have selected a number of English names, but they are far fewer than the French, Italian and even the German. There are not many modern writers on the Index. The best-known ones are Gide, Sartre and Alberto Moravia.

I have written enough to show that the list is entirely unsystematic. It condemns Alberto Moravia for indecency. It does not condemn D. H. Lawrence or James Joyce. Balzac, who considered himself to be a supporter of the monarchy and of Catholicism, is condemned, but many of the French writers of the nineteenth century who are known for their bitter attacks on Catholic institutions are not mentioned.

What is the function of the Index? During the struggles of the Reformation, when it began, banned books were seized by Catholic governments, including the papal one, and burnt. But recently, when the 'amatory fables' of Alberto Moravia were put on the Index, their sales probably increased even in Italy; and the officials of the Holy Office, when they walk through Rome, see huge posters advertising films based on them and starring the irresistible Signora Lollobrigida. Is the Index another survival that serves no useful purpose? A prohibition made by an organization that has totalitarian habits though it lacks the means to enforce its will? And how do Roman Catholics throughout the world react to it?

Here some distinctions must be made. In Italy the literary intelligentsia is anti-clerical almost to a man, and priests, peasants and members of the clerical bourgeoisie either do not read at all or do not read 'profane' books. Hence the majority of people likely to take the Index seriously are not affected by it. In countries such as England I have been told that the Index 'has never been promulgated'. English Catholics have no idea what books are on the Index and what are not: and I have never heard of an English Catholic who asked himself before reading a book whether or not it was on the Index. Indeed this is scarcely surprising if it be borne in mind that in Catholic schools students read such writers as Voltaire in the normal course of their education. There is an entirely different situation in Ireland where many writers are banned whose works are not on the Roman Index—including the best-known Catholic novelists. The Irish censors concentrate on sex regardless of literary merit or context and do not seem interested in other kinds of immorality in books.

When books are put on the Index, says Canon D., it is a means of showing that the organization of the Catholic Church does not approve of them as purporting to expound Catholic doctrine. More books by Catholics than by Protestants or agnostics are on the Index precisely because in their case ambiguity might arise. It is reasonable, he adds, that any organization should have the right to say who does and who doesn't expound what it thinks and who is and who isn't suitable to belong to it. Even so it is hard to see what such an incomplete and unsystematic list of prohibited books can achieve from the point of view of those who publish it. It exists perhaps more out of habit and inertia than for any other reason.

COMMENT: On Reason, Truth, and Church Policy

The policy now followed by the Church, according to the historian of Catholic censorship, is "to characterize pernicious books and to place upon believers the responsibility of condemning them for themselves,"[7] but according to Mr. Wall, practice is much more arbitrary than this suggests. The Reformation did not, as is often thought, mean a clean break with the practices of the past. On the contrary, the various sects of Protestantism held it to be their right and duty to supervise and control the productions of the printing press and the reading of the people. Only a lack of machinery and the limitations of territorial power prevented thorough censorship after the break with Rome. If a printer was penalized in one city, he could easily move his press to a city offering more favorable conditions, and perhaps a more favorable set of tenets. However, the work of publishing material for popular circulation begins for practical purposes with the Reformation. If the invention of printing was new, so was the great popular demand for information, which of course meant information in the vernacular and not in the learned tongues—hitherto the vehicle of the Church—which in turn meant greater scope for printers.

It is worth noting that the *Decameron*, which was recently taken out of a local public library in England for indecency, was originally expurgated of *heretical* passages. Fear of heresy had even prevented the study of Hebrew, and for a time only Protestant scholars were able to take an interest in it; Greek too was discouraged, at least in Catholic France, which banished Robert Estienne with his printing presses. In Leipzig, Leyden, and Oxford Greek was studied all the more ardently.

Gradually the rights of censorship passed from the ecclesiastical to the secular authority. It is important to notice that they did not pass into abeyance: though in France censorship was dispensed by the theological department of the Sorbonne, this department did not represent the Church itself. In England the Crown (nominally head of the English Church as well) also assumed the habit of passing out letters patent for the right to make the publishing of a certain book a monopoly. When the grant of letters patent was made to an author, it became the equivalent of a copyright. So much was restriction of the right of discussion *assumed* to be part of government that Sir Thomas More in his *Utopia* makes it punishable by death for an individual to criticize the conduct of the ruling power. His own defence against Henry VIII's prosecution of him for his failure to recognize Henry as head of the newly-formed English church was based on the plea that More did not actually deny recognition—not that More had a right to say what he wished, *or* that the King was simply wrong. This had, of course, always been the general attitude throughout the Middle Ages, partly due to the recognition of the King's divine right to govern, partly due to the fact that for the medieval thinker, freedom of spirit was not possible in the narrow circle of human history. Only in obedience to the Will of God lay perfect freedom. Politics as an art was prevented from attaining any importance until the Renaissance. Therefore, although Dante criticized the Church fiercely for political reasons, the *Divine Comedy* was not censored. It was unusual to apply censorship for other than reasons of heresy.

The medieval thinker longed for repose in God; when the discovery of Greek texts revived the arguments about a legal, well-regulated state here on earth, the objects of thought began to change and some doubt arose over the nature of civil liberty. The fixed order of things was also called into question by Copernican theories that the earth was not the center of the universe, and by the discovery of the New World; but whether these theories could be confirmed by observation and report or not—and the Professor of Philosophy at Padua refused to look into Galileo's telescope—the difficulty was not fear of the truth, for that was already well in hand, but reconciliation with the scriptures and the system of logic which already had, it was thought, laid bare the structure of the universe. And always behind the Church's seeming attacks on freedom of expression (as they appear to us) lay the desire to save souls tempted into heresy from eternal hell-fire.

Freedom, we have to admit, is a very obscure term both philosophically and politically. Ethical freedom is a much simpler thing, as Ernst Cassirer points out in a discussion of modern political myths:

> . . . Men act as free agents not because they possess a *liberum arbitrium indifferentiae*. It is not the absence of a motive but the character of the motives that mark a free action. In the ethical sense a man is a free agent if these motives depend upon his own judgment and own conviction of what moral duty is. According to Kant freedom is equivalent to autonomy. It does not mean "indeterminism," it rather means a special kind of determination. It means that the law which we obey in our actions is not imposed from without but that the moral subject gives this law to itself.
>
> In the exposition of his own theory Kant always warns us against a fundamental misunderstanding. Ethical freedom, he declares, is not a fact but a postulate. It is not *gegeben* but *aufgegeben;* it is not a gift with which human nature is endowed; it is rather a task, and the most arduous task that man can set himself. It is not datum, but a demand; an ethical imperative. To fulfil this demand becomes especially hard in times of a severe and dangerous social crisis when the breakdown of the whole public life seems to be imminent. At these times the individual begins to feel a deep mistrust in his own powers. Freedom is not a natural inheritance of man. In order to possess it we have to create it. If man were simply to follow his natural instincts he would not strive for freedom; he would rather choose dependence. Obviously it is much easier to depend upon others than to think, to judge, and to decide for himself. That accounts for the fact that both in individual and in political life freedom is so often regarded much more as a burden than a privilege. Under

extremely difficult conditions man tries to cast off this burden. Here the totalitarian state and the political myths
step in. The new political parties promise, at least, an escape from the dilemma. They suppress and destroy the
very sense of freedom; but, at the same time, they relieve
men from all personal responsibility.[8]

It is doubtful whether Milton viewed the Roman Catholic
Church in the way that Cassirer views the totalitarian state;
Milton saw the Church rather as the purveyor of falsehoods.
However, we can see now the danger from which Milton suffered—he feared to be deprived of choice, and he feared to
have his reason smothered by a world in which reason has far
less value than the value he himself assigned to it. Therefore
he urged himself into a totally false step and argued that all
words from that source should be cut off, in order that freedom
might be saved. The confusion arose partly from the peril of
the Commonwealth in which he wrote, partly from an over-
lapping of those ideas of things we loosely call "truth." In the
case of the representation of the Universe in *Paradise Lost*
there was apparently no difficulty: in spite of Milton's acquaintance with Galileo and admiration for him, his description of the crystalline spheres in the poem has nothing to do
with Galileo's findings concerning the nature and situation and
motion of the earth. In any case, Milton behaved as a rationalist theologian of his time, little concerned with a synthesis,
very much concerned with the new empiricism; and any
effort to understand his intolerance of the Church of Rome
must take into consideration his view that the Church's denial
of the supremacy of Reason as the chief instrument of choice
between good and evil logically excluded it from the ground
of religious "truth."

TEXT: The Condemnation and Recantation of Galileo

[The text that follows is a translation by Gebler with changes by Professor Giorgio de Santillana.]

Noi, Gasparo del titolo di S. Croce in Gerusalemme *Borgia;*
Fra Felice Centino del titolo di S. Anastasia, detto *d'Ascoli;*
Guido del titolo di S. Maria del Popolo *Bentivoglio;*
Fra Desiderio *Scaglia* del titolo di S. Carlo detto di Cremona;
Fra Antonio *Barberino* detto di S. Onofrio;
Laudivio *Zacchia* del titolo di S. Pietro in Vincula detto di S. Sisto;
Berlingero del titolo di S. Agostino *Gessi;*
Fabricio del titolo di S. Lorenzo in pane e perna *Verospi,* chiamati Preti;
Francesco del titolo di S. Lorenzo in Damaso *Barberini;* e Martio di S. Maria Nuova *Ginetti,* Diaconi,

by the grace of God, cardinals of the Holy Roman Church, Inquisitors-General by the Holy Apostolic See specially deputed against heretical pravity throughout the whole Christian Commonwealth.

Whereas you, Galileo, son of the late Vincenzo Galilei, Florentine, aged seventy years, were in the year 1615 denounced to this Holy Office for holding as true the false doctrine taught by some that the Sun is the center of the world and immovable and that the Earth moves, and also with a diurnal motion; for having disciples to whom you taught the same doctrine; for holding correspondence with certain mathematicians of Germany concerning the same; for having printed certain letters, entitled "On the Sunspots," wherein you developed the same doctrine as true; and for replying to the objections from the Holy Scriptures, which from time to time were urged against it, by glossing the said Scriptures according to your own meaning: and whereas there was thereupon produced the copy of a document in the form of a letter, purporting to be written by you to one formerly your disciple, and in this divers propositions are set forth, following the position of Copernicus, which are contrary to the true sense and authority of Holy Scripture:

This Holy Tribunal being therefore of intention to proceed against the disorder and mischief thence resulting, which went on increasing to the prejudice of the Holy Faith, by command of His Holiness and of the Most Eminent Lords Cardinals of this supreme and universal Inquisition, the two propositions of the stability of the Sun and the motion of the Earth were by the theological Qualifiers qualified as follows:

The proposition that the Sun is the center of the world and does not move from its place is absurd and false philosophically and formally heretical, because it is expressly contrary to the Holy Scripture.

The proposition that the Earth is not the center of the world and immovable but that it moves, and also with a diurnal motion, is equally absurd and false philosophically and theologically considered at least erroneous in faith.

But whereas it was desired at that time to deal leniently with you, it was decreed at the Holy Congregation held before His Holiness on the twenty-fifth of February, 1616, that his Eminence the Lord Cardinal Bellarmine should order you to abandon altogether the said false doctrine and, in the event of your refusal, that an injunction should be imposed upon you by the Commissary of the Holy Office to give up the said doctrine and not to teach it to others, not to defend it, nor even discuss it; and failing your acquiescence in this injunction, that you should be imprisoned. And in execution of this decree, on the following day, at the Palace, and in the presence of his Eminence, the said Lord Cardinal Bellarmine, after being gently admonished by the said Lord Cardinal, the command was enjoined upon you by the Father Commissary of the Holy Office of that time, before a notary and witnesses, that you were altogether to abandon the said false opinion and not in future to hold or defend or teach it in any way whatsoever, neither verbally nor in writing; and, upon your promising to obey, you were dismissed.

And, in order that a doctrine so pernicious might be wholly rooted out and not insinuate itself further to the grave prejudice of Catholic truth, a decree was issued by the Holy Congregation of the Index prohibiting the books which treat of this doctrine and declaring the doctrine itself to be false and wholly contrary to the sacred and divine Scripture.

And whereas a book appeared here recently, printed last year at Florence, the title of which shows that you were the author, this title being: "Dialogue of Galileo Galilei on the Great World Systems"; and whereas the Holy Congregation was afterward informed that through the publication of the said book the false opinion of the motion of the Earth and the stability of the Sun was daily gaining ground, the said book was taken into careful consideration, and in it there was discovered a patent violation of the aforesaid injunction that had been imposed upon you, for in this book you have defended the said opinion previously condemned and to your face declared to be so, although in the said book you strive by various devices to produce the impression that you leave it undecided, and in express terms as probable: which, however, is a most grievous error, as an opinion can in no wise be probable which has been declared and defined to be contrary to divine Scripture.

Therefore by our order you were cited before this Holy Office, where, being examined upon your oath, you acknowledged the book to be written and published by you. You confessed that you began to write the said book about ten or twelve years ago, after the command had been imposed upon you as above; that you requested license to print it without, however, intimating to those who granted you this license that you had been commanded not to hold, defend, or teach the doctrine in question in any way whatever.

You likewise confessed that the writing of the said book is in many places drawn up in such a form that the reader might fancy that the arguments brought forward on the false side are calculated by their cogency to compel conviction rather than to be easy of refutation, excusing yourself for having fallen into an error, as you alleged, so foreign to your intention, by the fact that you had written in dialogue and by the natural complacency that every man feels in regard to his own subtleties and in showing himself more clever than the generality of men in devising, even on behalf of false propositions, ingenious and plausible arguments.

And, a suitable term having been assigned to you to prepare your defense, you produced a certificate in the handwriting of his Eminence the Lord Cardinal Bellarmine, procured by you, as you asserted, in order to defend yourself against the calumnies of your enemies, who charged that you had abjured and had been punished by the Holy Office, in which certificate it is declared that you had not abjured and had not been punished but only that the declaration made by His Holiness and published by the Holy Congregation of the Index had been announced to you, wherein it is declared that the doctrine of the motion of the Earth and the stability of the Sun is contrary to the Holy Scriptures and therefore cannot be defended or held. And, as in this certificate there is no mention of the two articles of the injunction, namely, the order not "to teach" and "in any way," you represented that we ought to believe that in the course of fourteen or sixteen years you had lost all memory of them and that this was why you said nothing of the injunction when you requested permission to print your book. And all this you urged not by way of excuse for your error but that it might be set down to a vainglorious ambition rather than to malice. But this certificate produced by you in your defense has only aggravated your delinquency, since, although it is there stated that said opinion is contrary to Holy Scripture, you have nevertheless dared to discuss and defend it and to argue its probability; nor does the license artfully and cunningly extorted by you avail you anything, since you did not notify the command imposed upon you.

And whereas it appeared to us that you had not stated the full truth with regard to your intention, we thought it necessary to subject you to a rigorous examination at which (without prejudice, however, to the matters confessed by you and set forth as above with regard to your said intention) you answered like a good Catholic. Therefore, having seen and maturely considered the merits of this your cause, together with your confessions and excuses above-mentioned, and all that ought justly to be seen and considered, we have arrived at the underwritten final sentence against you:

Invoking, therefore, the most holy name of our Lord Jesus Christ and of His most glorious Mother, ever Virgin Mary, by this our final sentence, which sitting in judgment, with the counsel and advice of the Reverend Masters of sacred theology and Doctors of both Laws, our assessors, we deliver in these writings, in the cause and causes at present before us between the Magnificent Carlo Sinceri, Doctor of both Laws, Proctor Fiscal of this Holy Office, of the one part, and you Galileo Galilei, the defendant, here present, examined, tried, and confessed as shown above, of the other part—

We say, pronounce, sentence, and declare that you, the said Galileo, by reason of the matters adduced in trial, and by you confessed as above, have rendered yourself in the judgment of this Holy Office vehemently suspected of heresy, namely, of having believed and held the doctrine—which is false and contrary to the sacred and divine Scriptures—that the Sun is the center of the world and does not move from east to west and that the Earth moves and is not the center of the world; and that an opinion may be held and defended as probable after it has been declared and defined to be contrary to the Holy Scripture; and that consequently you have incurred all the censures and penalties imposed and promulgated in the sacred canons and other constitutions, general and particular, against such delinquents. From which we are content that you be absolved, provided that, first, with a sincere heart and unfeigned faith, you abjure, curse, and detest before us the aforesaid errors and heresies and every other error and heresy contrary to the Catholic and Apostolic Roman Church in the form to be prescribed by us for you.

And, in order that this your grave and pernicious error and transgression may not remain altogether unpunished and that you may be more cautious in the future and an example to others that they may abstain from similar delinquencies, we ordain that the book of the "Dialogue of Galileo Galilei" be prohibited by public edict.

We condemn you to the formal prison of this Holy Office during our pleasure, and by way of salutary penance we enjoin that for three years to come you repeat once a week the seven penitential Psalms. Reserving to ourselves liberty to moderate, commute, or take off, in whole or in part, the aforesaid penalties and penance.

And so we say, pronounce, sentence, declare, ordain, and reserve in this and in any other better way and form which we can and may rightfully employ.

And then, Galileo:

I, Galileo, son of the late Vincenzo Galilei, Florentine, aged seventy years, arraigned personally before this tribunal and kneeling before you, Most Eminent and Reverend Lord Cardinals Inquisitors-General against heretical pravity throughout the entire Christian commonwealth, having before my eyes and touching with my hands the Holy Gospels, swear that I have always believed, do believe, and by God's help will in the future believe all that is held, preached, and taught by the Holy Catholic and Apostolic Church. But, whereas—after an injunction had been judicially intimated to me by this Holy Office to the effect that I must altogether abandon the false opinion that the Sun is the center of the world and immovable and that the Earth is not the center of the world and moves and that I must not hold, defend, or teach in any way whatsoever, verbally or in writing, the said false doctrine, and after it had been notified to me that the said doctrine was contrary to Holy Scripture—I wrote and printed a book in which I discuss this new doctrine already condemned and adduce arguments of great cogency in its favor without presenting any solution of these, I have been pronounced by the Holy Office to be vehemently suspected of heresy, that is to say, of having held and believed that the Sun is the center of the world and immovable and that the Earth is not the center and moves:

Therefore, desiring to remove from the minds of your Eminences, and of all faithful Christians, this vehement suspicion justly conceived against me, with sincere heart and unfeigned faith I abjure, curse, and detest the aforesaid errors and heresies and generally every other error, heresy, and sect whatsoever contrary to the Holy Church, and I swear that in future I will never again say or assert, verbally or in writing, anything that might furnish occasion for a similar suspicion regarding me; but, should I know any heretic or person suspected of heresy, I will denounce him to this Holy Office or to the Inquisitor or Ordinary of the place where I may be. Further, I swear and promise to fulfil and observe in their integrity all penances that have been, or that shall be, imposed upon me by this Holy Office. And, in the event of my contravening (which God forbid!) any of these my promises and oaths, I submit myself to all the pains and penalties imposed and promulgated in the sacred canons and other constitutions, general and particular, against such delinquents. So help me God and these His Holy Gospels, which I touch with my hands.

Having recited, he signed the attestation:

I, the said Galileo Galilei, have abjured, sworn, promised, and bound myself as above; and in witness of the truth thereof I have with my own hand subscribed the present document of my abjuration and recited it word for word at Rome, in the convent of the Minerva, this twenty-second day of June, 1633.[9]

COMMENT: On the Historical Galileo and the Figure of Parable

The accusation of Galileo by a board of cardinals and his subsequent recantation culminated a well-known sorry affair, which, if we are to believe a recent author,[10] owed its existence as much to Galileo's habit of writing in Italian instead of Latin and to the Jesuits' wish to get even with the Dominicans over cosmological matters, as to any clearly formulated wish of the Catholic hierarchy to stop the rot in the old order of the universe. "Any superior court would have had to reverse the sentence and order the defendant freed and proceedings started against the Master of the Holy Palace." But there was, of course, no superior court, and Galileo, to his surprise, was haled off to a lifetime of house-arrest. Although Galileo's book, the *Dialogue on the Great World Systems,* was not released from the Index until 1822, we cannot blame the Curia for being no quicker than any other authority in reversing its decisions; it is more surprising that the inevitability of the Copernican opinion of the revolution of the earth about the sun was not seen to be confirmed by Galileo's observations, even if it was necessary to make him say that he did not believe in them. Through the unwillingness of the Inquisition to desire anything more of Galileo than blind obedience, the liberty of the Church itself was put in jeopardy and the intellectual life of Rome snuffed out. This was a good deal more than the censorship of a book or two: it was even more than the extinction of a man—though between the two, as Milton points out, there is little to choose. Though we must not allow it to pardon anything, we must remember that Galileo was unlucky; documents were juggled, the Papacy changed hands. In fact, if he had not been unlucky, Galileo would have been allowed to have his opinions and his proofs of his opinions, since he had at all times submitted to spiritual authority. But for the misfortune to spring from the secular power of that authority was a consequence of a situation in which church and state were not divided. In America the pressures of spiritual authority in such a situation are apt to be exaggerated or minimized and seldom understood.

The masterpiece of the great Communist poet and dramatist Bertolt Brecht, from which we quote part of the last scene, deals with Galileo as a spiritual coward in the time-honored way. The churchmen are depicted as brilliant intellectual men who are afraid that Galileo's discoveries will destroy the authority of the church. In one of the most brilliant scenes of the play, the new Pope, Urban VIII, a mathematician from whom Galileo had expected a new tolerance, is persuaded by the Grand Inquisitor that Galileo should be shown the instruments of torture. But we know from Professor de Santillana's study that it was doubtful what heresy Galileo was charged under, and that the Pope refrained from saying that Galileo's opinions were actually heretical; so that the situation came about, historically speaking, in a much more chancy fashion than Brecht shows us. It would be foolish to imagine that Brecht's view is due to his Communist persuasions, although they perhaps made it easier for him to see the Church as a much more homogeneous body than it would seem from within the fold.

The Galileo that Brecht gives us is a man of active, lively mind, of a certain sensuality—"when I eat," he says, "I get good ideas." In the scene that follows, he is under house-arrest in the country. He spends his time ostensibly listening to tracts read him by his daughter, Virginia. Andrea Sarti, his former pupil, comes to visit him. Andrea is here represented as a man who once idolized Galileo and who now despises him for having betrayed the cause of science. Because he is an idealist he believes, when Galileo hands him a new work, the *Discourses on Two New Sciences,* written in secret, that Galileo has recanted in order to gain time to write this book. But Galileo sees himself as a coward who has retarded the appearance of scientific fact for centuries. And though it is not for us to judge

Galileo, his view of himself is the one that strikes us as more honorable than Sarti's: more honorable because in the end more honest about motives and more ashamed of his old failure to stand by his opinion. We must remember that Brecht does not show the historical Galileo's outward and apparently sincere submission to the Church in spiritual matters, which must be a factor in *our* estimate of his case. The breaking of Galileo, as it appears both historically and in Brecht's play was, as Professor de Santillana points out, a social degradation. Censorship works on society in social ways, though it may employ morals as its instruments.

TEXT: "A Few Tips About Science"
from *The Life of Galileo* by Bertolt Brecht

[(*From Scene 14*) *translated by Desmond I. Vesey*]

ANDREA: Fabricius in Amsterdam has charged me to enquire after your health.

GALILEO: My health is all right. They pay a great deal of attention to me.

ANDREA: I am glad I shall be able to report that you are in good health.

GALILEO: Fabricius will be pleased to hear it. And you can inform him that I live in suitable comfort. By the depth of my repentance I have been able to retain the favour of my superiors so far as to be permitted to engage in scientific work—within certain limits and under the supervision of the Church.

ANDREA: Yes. We, too, have heard that the Church is satisfied with you. Your complete submission has had its effect. It has ensured, as the authorities will have noted with satisfaction, that in Italy no further work containing new ideas has been published since you submitted.

GALILEO *listening:* Unfortunately there are countries which refuse the protection of the Church. I fear that the condemned teachings may be disseminated there.

ANDREA: There, too, as a result of your recantation, there has been a set-back most gratifying to the Church.

GALILEO: Really? *Pause.* Nothing of Descartes? Nothing from Paris?

ANDREA: Yes. At the news of your recantation he stuffed his treatise on the Nature of Light into a drawer.

A long pause.

GALILEO: I am anxious about certain scientific friends whose feet I have set upon the path of error. Have they been enlightened by my recantation?

ANDREA: In order to be able to do scientific work, I intend to go to Holland. The bull is not permitted to do what Jupiter does not permit himself.

GALILEO: I understand.

ANDREA: Federzoni is once again grinding lenses in some shop in Milan.

GALILEO *laughs:* He knows no Latin.

Pause.

ANDREA: Fulganzio, our little monk, has given up research and has returned to the bosom of the Church.

GALILEO: Yes.

Pause.

GALILEO: My superiors are looking forward to my spiritual recuperation. I am making better progress than might have been expected.

ANDREA: Ah!

VIRGINIA: The Lord be praised.

GALILEO *harshly:* Go and see to the geese, Virginia.

Virginia goes out angrily. As she passes, the monk speaks to her.

THE MONK: I don't trust that man.

VIRGINIA: He's harmless. You can hear what they say. *As she goes:* We've got some fresh goat's cheese.

The monk follows her out.

ANDREA: I shall travel through the night in order to be able to cross the frontier tomorrow morning. May I leave?

GALILEO: I don't know why you came, Sarti. In order to upset me? I live cautiously and I think cautiously, ever since I've been here. But in spite of that I have my relapses.

ANDREA: I'd rather not excite you, Signor Galilei.

GALILEO: Barberini called it the itch. He himself was never quite free of it. I've been writing again.

ANDREA: Oh?

GALILEO: I have finished writing the 'Discorsi'.

ANDREA: What? 'The Conversations between two Branches of Science: Mechanics and the Laws of Falling Bodies'? Here?

GALILEO: Oh, they give me paper and quills. My superiors are no fools. They know that ingrained vices cannot be cured overnight. They protect me from unfortunate results by locking it away page by page.

ANDREA: Oh God!

GALILEO: Did you say anything?

ANDREA: They're making you plough water! They give you paper and quills just to soothe you! How could you ever write anything with that prospect before your eyes?

GALILEO: Oh, I am the slave of my habits.

ANDREA: The 'Discorsi' in the hands of the monks! And Amsterdam and London and Prague hungry for them!

GALILEO: I can hear Fabricius wailing, insisting on his pound of flesh, while he sits safely in Amsterdam.

ANDREA: Two new branches of science as good as lost!

GALILEO: It will doubtless cheer him and some others to hear that I risked the last miserable remains of my peace of mind by making a copy, behind my own back so to speak, using up the last ounce of light of the bright nights for the last six months.

ANDREA: You have a copy?

GALILEO: My vanity has hitherto restrained me from destroying it.

ANDREA: Where is it?

GALILEO: 'If thine eye offend thee, pluck it out.' Whoever wrote that knew more about comfort than I. I call it the height of stupidity to hand it over. But since I have never managed to keep myself away from scientific work you might as well have it. The copy is in the globe. If you were to risk taking it to Holland, you would of course have to shoulder full responsibility. In that case you would have bought it from someone who had access to the original in the Holy Office.

Andrea walks across to the globe and takes out the manuscript.

ANDREA: The 'Discorsi'!

He thumbs through the pages.

ANDREA *reads:* 'My project is to establish an entirely new science dealing with a very old subject—Motion. Through experiments I have discovered some of its properties which are worth knowing.'

GALILEO: I had to do something with my time.

ANDREA: This will found a new science of physics.

GALILEO: Stuff it under your coat.

ANDREA: And we thought you had become a renegade! My voice was raised loudest against you!

GALILEO: And quite right, too. I taught you science and I denied the truth.

ANDREA. This changes everything, everything.

GALILEO: Yes?

ANDREA: You concealed the truth. From the enemy. Even in the field of ethics you were a thousand years ahead of us.

GALILEO: Explain that, Andrea.

ANDREA: In common with the man in the street, we said: he will die, but he will never recant.—You came back: I have recanted, but I shall live.—Your hands are tainted, we said. —You say: better tainted than empty.

GALILEO: Better tainted than empty. Sounds realistic. Sounds like me. New science, new ethics.

ANDREA: I of all people ought to have known. I was eleven years old when you sold another man's telescope to the Venetian Senate. And I saw you make immortal use of that instrument. Your friends shook their heads when you bowed before a child in Florence, but science caught the public fancy. You always laughed at our heroes. 'People that suffer bore me', you said. 'Misfortune comes from insufficient foresight.' And: 'Taking obstacles into account, the shortest line between two points may be a crooked one.'

GALILEO: I recollect.

ANDREA: Then, in 1633, when it suited you to retract a popular point in your teachings, I should have known that you were only withdrawing from a hopeless political squabble in order to be able to carry on with your real business of science.

GALILEO: Which consists in . . .

ANDREA: . . . The study of the properties of motion, mother of machines, which will make the earth so inhabitable that heaven can be demolished.

GALILEO: Aha.

ANDREA: You thereby gained the leisure to write a scientific work which only you could write. Had you ended in a halo of flames at the stake, the others would have been the victors.

GALILEO: They are the victors. And there is no scientific work which only one man can write.

ANDREA: Then why did you recant?

GALILEO: I recanted because I was afraid of physical pain.

ANDREA: No!

GALILEO: I was shown the instruments.

ANDREA: So there was no plan?

GALILEO: There was none.

Pause.

ANDREA *loudly:* Science knows only one commandment: contribute to science.

GALILEO: And that I have done. Welcome to the gutter, brother in science and cousin in treachery! Do you eat fish? I've got fish. What stinks is not fish but me. I sell cheap; you are a buyer. Oh irresistible sight of a book, the sacred goods! Mouths water, and curses drown. The Great Babylonian, the murderous cow, the scarlet woman, opens her thighs and everything is different! Hallowed be our haggling, whitewashing, death-fearing society!

ANDREA: Fear of death is human! Human weaknesses are no concern of science.

GALILEO: No! My dear Sarti, even in my present situation I still feel capable of giving you a few tips about science in general, in which you have involved yourself.

A short pause.

GALILEO *academically, his hands folded over his stomach:* During my free hours, of which I have many, I have gone over my case and have considered how the world of science, in which I no longer count myself, will judge it. Even a wool-merchant, apart from buying cheaply and selling dear, must also be concerned that trade in wool can be carried on unhindered. In this respect the pursuit of science seems to me to require particular courage. It is concerned with knowledge, achieved through doubt. Making knowledge about everything available for everybody, science strives to make sceptics of them all. Now the greater part of the population is kept permanently by their princes, landlords and priests in a nacreous haze of superstition and outmoded words which obscure the machinations of these characters.

The misery of the multitude is as old as the hills, and from pulpit and desk is proclaimed as immutable as the hills. Our new device of doubt delighted the great public, which snatched the telescope from our hands and turned it on its tormentors. These selfish and violent men, who greedily exploited the fruits of science to their own use, simultaneously felt the cold eye of science turned on a thousand-year-old, but artificial misery which clearly could be eliminated by eliminating them. They drenched us with their threats and bribes, irresistible to weak souls. But could we deny ourselves to the crowd and still remain scientists? The movements of the stars have become clearer; but to the mass of the people the movements of their masters are still incalculable. The fight over the measurability of the heavens has been won through doubt; but the fight of the Roman housewife for milk is ever and again lost through faith. Science, Sarti, is concerned with both battle-fronts. A humanity which stumbles in this age-old nacreous haze of superstition and outmoded words, too ignorant to develop fully its own powers, will not be capable of developing the powers of nature which you reveal. What are you working for? I maintain that the only purpose of science is to ease the hardship of human existence. If scientists, intimidated by self-seeking people in power, are content to amass knowledge for the sake of knowledge, then science can become crippled, and your new machines will represent nothing but new means of oppression. With time you may discover all that is to be discovered, and your progress will only be a progression away from mankind. The gulf between you and them can one day become so great that your cry of jubilation over some new achievement may be answered by a universal cry of horror.—I, as a scientist, had a unique opportunity. In my days astronomy reached the market-places. In these quite exceptional circumstances, the steadfastness of one man could have shaken the world. If only I had resisted, if only the natural scientists had been able to evolve something like the Hippocratic oath of the doctors, the vow to devote their knowledge wholly to the benefit of mankind! As things now stand, the best one can hope for is for a race of inventive dwarfs who can be hired for anything. Moreover, I am now convinced, Sarti, that I never was in real danger. For a few years I was as strong as the authorities. And I surrendered my knowledge to those in power, to use, or not to use, or to misuse, just as suited their purposes. *Virginia has entered with a dish and stops still.* I have betrayed my profession. A man who does what I have done cannot be tolerated in the ranks of science.

VIRGINIA: You have been received into the ranks of the faithful. *She walks forward and places the dish upon the table.*

GALILEO: Right.—I must eat now.

Andrea holds out his hand. Galileo looks at his hand without taking it.

GALILEO: You yourself are a teacher, now. Can you bring yourself to take a hand such as mine? *He walks over to the table.* Someone passing through sent me geese. I still enjoy my food.

ANDREA: So you are no longer of the opinion that a new age has dawned?

GALILEO: I am. Take care when you go through Germany.— Hide the truth under your coat.

ANDREA *incapable of leaving:* With regard to your estimation of the author we were talking about, I don't know how to answer you. But I cannot believe that your murderous analysis will be the last word.

GALILEO: Many thanks, signor. *He begins to eat.*

VIRGINIA *showing Andrea out:* We do not care for visitors from the past. They excite him.

Andrea leaves. Virginia returns.

GALILEO: Have you any idea who could have sent the geese?

VIRGINIA: Not Andrea.

GALILEO: Perhaps not. What is the night like?

VIRGINIA *at the window:* Clear.

COMMENT: On Political Freedom
and Other People's Beliefs

The advocacy of religious toleration in the text that follows is a good deal less high-minded than Milton's. Whereas Milton assumes that a noble mind can work only in freedom, and that freedom itself produces a nobility of mind, and that these two arguments make censorship undesirable, Benedict de Spinoza, a Jew whose forebears had found refuge in the Dutch Republic from the Inquisition in Spain, was brought to the opinion, by the experience of the Jewish nation and by historical study, that religious toleration was politically expedient. Spinoza calls self-interest a natural law. Like Hobbes, his master, Spinoza was constructing a mechanics of thought as a counterpart to the new scientific method which Galileo had applied to physics, and self-interest belongs in his theory of human development.

When the Dutch Republic came into being in 1579 with the Union of Utrecht, its charter declared that "every citizen should remain free in his religion, and no man be molested or questioned on the subject of divine worship." Philip II's efforts to enforce Catholicism in all parts of the Netherlands had led to his defeat there: but the growing strength of the Calvinist Church began to militate for uniformity of religion once more when the Princes of Orange and the Calvinists found common cause against republicanism and official toleration of all religious beliefs. Spinoza's *Tractatus Theologico-Politicus* was published at Hamburg in 1670. The last chapter is called "That in a free state everyone may think what he pleases, and say what he thinks." Behind its plea for religious toleration lies the author's recognition of the need to limit the civil demands of the religious powers on political grounds. He is concerned with the necessity for a legal way of dissenting from the laws, and with the nature of sovereign power itself.

In brief, Spinoza declares not so much that God is omnipotent and that all power comes from Him, as that God is power itself; that as human thought, feeling, and volition are in accordance with laws of nature, they exist in accordance with the laws by which God Himself manifests His power. Men cannot relinquish their right to decide for themselves, and a wise ruler will not enforce uniformity of religion, which would not only have economic disadvantages, but also require coercion of those who might refuse it—a policy which might be disastrous.

TEXT: "The Expediency of Toleration" from *Tractatus Theologico-Politicus* by Benedict de Spinoza [*translated by A. G. Wernham*]

Could thought be controlled as easily as speech, all governments would rule in safety, and none would be oppressive; for
everyone would live as his rulers wanted, and his judgements
of true and false, good and bad, fair and unfair, would be
determined entirely by their will. However, as I have already
noted at the start of Chapter XVII, it is impossible for thought
to be completely subject to another's control, because no one
can give up to another his natural right to reason freely and
form his own judgement about everything, nor can he be compelled to do so. This is why a government is regarded as oppressive if it tries to control men's minds, and why a sovereign
is thought to wrong its subjects, and to usurp their right, if
it seeks to tell them what they should embrace as true and reject as false, and to prescribe the beliefs which should inspire
their minds with devotion to God; for in such matters an individual cannot alienate his right even if he wishes. Admittedly a man's judgement can be influenced in many ways,
some of them hardly credible; so much so, in fact, that though
not directly under another's command it may depend entirely
on his words, and thus in that respect can properly be called
subject to his right. Yet in spite of all that political skill has
been able to achieve in this field, it has never been completely
successful; men have always found that individuals were full
of their own ideas, and that opinions varied as much as tastes.
Even Moses, who by extraordinary ability, and not by decep-

tion, had so captivated the mind of his people that it regarded him as a superman, divinely inspired in everything he said and did, was not immune from its criticisms and misrepresentations; and this is still more true of the other kings. Yet were such immunity conceivable at all it would be in a monarchy; not in a democracy where all or most men are colleagues in the government. The reason for this, I think, is plain to everyone.

Thus no matter how completely a ruler has convinced his subjects that he has the right to do everything, and is the interpreter of law and piety, he will never be able to prevent them from passing their own individual judgements on everything, and from feeling different emotions accordingly. It is true that he has the right to treat as enemies all who are not in complete agreement with him on every point; but what I am discussing now is not his right, but the good of the state. Admittedly he has the right to rule with the utmost violence, and to hale citizens off to execution on the most trivial pretexts; but everyone will deny that he can do so with the approval of sound reason. Indeed, just because he cannot do such things without great danger to the whole state, we may even deny that he has full power to do them, and hence deny that he has full right to do them either; since, as I have shown, a sovereign's right is determined by its power.

If no man, then, can surrender his freedom to judge and think as he pleases, and everyone is master of his own thoughts by perfect natural right, the attempt to make men speak only as the sovereign prescribes, no matter how different and opposed their ideas may be, must always meet with very little success in a state; for even men of great experience cannot hold their tongues, far less the mass of the people. It is a common human failing to confide one's plans to others even when secrecy is needed: hence government will be most oppressive where the individual is denied the freedom to express and communicate his opinions, and moderate where this freedom is allowed him. Yet it must also be admitted that words can be treasonable as well as deeds; and so, though it is impossible to deprive subjects of such freedom entirely, it will be quite disastrous to grant it to them in full. Hence we must now inquire how far it can and must be granted to everyone if the peace of the state and the right of the sovereign are to be preserved. This inquiry, as I said at the start of Chapter XVI, was the main object of the concluding Chapters.

It is abundantly clear from my previous account of the basis of the state that its ultimate purpose is not to subject men to tyranny, or to restrain and enslave them through fear, but rather to free everyone from fear so that he may live in all possible security, i.e. may preserve his natural right to exist and act in the best possible way, without harm to himself or his neighbour. It is not, I say, the purpose of the state to change men from rational beings into brutes or puppets; but rather to enable them to exercise their mental and physical powers in safety and use their reason freely, and to prevent them from fighting and quarrelling through hatred, anger, bad faith, and mutual malice. Thus the purpose of the state is really freedom. We also saw that to create a state the one thing needful was that all power to make decisions should be vested either in all collectively, or in a few, or in one man; for the great diversity of men's free judgements, the claim of each to have a monopoly of wisdom, and their inability to think alike and speak with one voice made it impossible for men to live at peace unless everyone surrendered his right to act entirely as he pleased. Thus it was only his right to act as he pleased that everyone surrendered, and not his right to think and judge. This means that while a subject necessarily violates his sovereign's right by acting contrary to its decree, there is no violation whatever in his thinking and judging, and therefore also saying, that the decree is ill-advised; as long as he does no more than express or communicate his opinion, and only defends it out of honest rational conviction, and not out of anger, hatred, or a desire to introduce any change in the state on his own authority. For example, suppose a man shows that some law is contrary to sound reason, and thus maintains that it should be repealed; if he at the same time submits his opinion to the judgement of the sovereign (which alone is competent to pass and repeal laws), and meanwhile does nothing contrary to what that law commands, then, of course, he ranks with all good citizens as a benefactor of the state. But if he breaks the law in order to accuse the magistrate of injustice and to stir up mob hatred against him, or makes a seditious attempt to repeal the law against the magistrate's will, he is simply an agitator and a rebel. This shows how everyone can express and communicate his opinions without infringing the right and authority of the sovereign, i.e. without disturbing the peace of the state; he must leave the determination of all actions to the sovereign, and do nothing contrary to its decree, even though the actions required are frequently in conflict with what he thinks, and declares, to be good. He can do this without violating justice and piety; indeed, he must do this if he wants to be just and pious. For justice, as I have already shown, depends entirely on the sovereign's will; so no one can be just unless he lives by its published decrees. Piety . . . attains its highest expression in the service of public peace and tranquillity; but peace could not be preserved if everyone were to follow his own will; so it is impious, as well as unjust, for a subject to follow his own will and contravene his sovereign's decree, for if this were universally permitted it would inevitably lead to the destruction of the state. He cannot even contravene the judgement and dictate of his own reason in carrying out the sovereign's decrees, for it was with the full approval of his own reason that he decided to transfer his right to determine his actions to the sovereign. But my main point can be confirmed from actual practice; for at meetings of public authorities, both sovereign and subordinate, it is rare for anything to be done by the unanimous vote of all the members, yet everything *is* done by the common decision of all, of those, that is, who voted against the measure as well as of those who voted for it. However I must return to my subject.

A consideration of the basis of the state has shown us how everyone can exercise freedom of judgement without infringing the sovereign's right. It enables us to determine just as easily which beliefs are seditious; they are those which, when accepted, immediately destroy the covenant whereby everyone surrendered the right to act as he pleased. For instance, if anyone believes that the sovereign does not have absolute right, or that nobody is bound to keep promises, or that everyone should live as he pleases, or holds other similar views which directly contradict the said covenant, he is seditious; not so much, to be sure, because of his judgement and opinion as because of the action which it involves; i.e. because merely by thinking in this way he breaks the promise he has given either tacitly or expressly to the sovereign. Hence other beliefs which do not involve action like the breaking of the covenant, the taking of vengeance, and the venting of anger, are not seditious; except perhaps in a state which is in some way corrupt, i.e. a state where superstitious and ambitious men, who cannot tolerate liberal minds, have gained such a reputation that their authority has more weight with the masses than that of the sovereign. Admittedly there are also some beliefs which, although apparently purely theoretical, are advanced and disseminated from hostility to the sovereign; but I have already dealt with these in Chapter XV, and still left reason free. Finally, if we reflect that a man's devotion to the state, like his devotion to God, can only be known from his actions, i.e. from his charity towards his neighbour, we can have no doubt that a good state allows everyone the same freedom to philosophize as I have shown to be permitted by faith. I grant that such freedom sometimes leads to trouble; but the same is true of any institution, no matter how wisely planned. He who seeks to determine everything by law will aggravate vices rather than correct them. We must necessarily permit what we cannot prevent, even though it often leads to harm. Things like extravagance, envy, greed, and drunkenness are a source of much evil; yet we put up with them because they cannot be prevented by legal enactment, vices though in fact they are. Much more then must we allow independence of judgement; for it is certainly a virtue, and it cannot be suppressed. Besides, it leads to no trouble which cannot be forestalled by the influence of the magistrates (as I shall presently show); to say nothing of the fact that it is quite indispensable for the advancement of the arts and sciences, for these are cultivated with success only by men whose judgement is free and unbiased.

But let us assume that such freedom can be suppressed, and that men can be so thoroughly coerced that they dare not whisper a word which is not prescribed by the sovereign. Will it ever come to pass that they also think nothing but what it wills? Assuredly not. Then the inevitable result will be this. Every day men will be saying one thing and thinking another; belief in another's word, a prime necessity in a state, will thus be undermined, nauseating sycophancy and deceitfulness encouraged; and hence will come frauds and the destruction of all honest dealing. In fact, however, the assumption that everyone can be made to speak to order is quite impossible. The more the sovereign tries to deprive men of freedom of speech, the more stubbornly is it opposed; not indeed by money-grubbers, sycophants, and the rest of the shallow crew, whose supreme happiness is to gloat over the coins in their coffers and to have their bellies well stuffed, but by those who, because of their culture, integrity, and ability, have some independence of mind. Ordinary human nature is such that men find nothing more irritating than to have the views which they hold to be true branded as criminal, and the beliefs which inspire them to piety towards God and man held up against them as wickedness; this encourages them to denounce the laws, and to go to all lengths against the magistrate, in the belief that it is not disgraceful but highly laudable to stir up sedition and attempt the most outrageous crimes in such a cause. Given, then, that human nature is such, it follows that laws which proscribe beliefs do not affect the wicked but the liberal-minded, that they are passed to annoy the good rather than to restrain the malicious, and that they cannot be upheld without great danger to the state. In any case, such laws are utterly useless; for those who regard the proscribed beliefs as sound will be unable to obey the laws which proscribe them, while those who reject such beliefs as false welcome these laws as privileges, and are so proud of them that the magistrate can never repeal them even if he wishes. Then there are the dangers which I showed to follow from them in discussing my second lesson from Jewish history in Chapter XVIII above. Finally, the readiness of magistrates to settle the disputes of scholars by legislation has been the main source of innumerable divisions in the church; for were men not captivated by the hope of getting the laws and the magistrate on their side, of triumphing over their opponents amid the general applause of the mob, and of attaining high office, they would never quarrel with such spite or be driven by such frenzy. And these are the findings of experience as well as of reason; for each new day brings instances to show that laws which prescribe what everyone must believe, and forbid men to say or write anything against this or that opinion, are often passed to gratify, or rather, to appease the anger of those who cannot abide independent minds, but by their savage influence can easily change the fervour of an unruly people into frenzy, and direct it against anyone they please. Yet how much better would it be to curb the furious anger of the mob, instead of passing useless laws which can only be broken by those who love the virtues and the arts, and reducing the state to such straits that it cannot support men of liberal views? What greater calamity to a state can be imagined than that good men should be sent into exile as malefactors because they hold unorthodox beliefs and cannot pretend otherwise? What, I say, is more disastrous than that men should be branded as public enemies and haled off to execution for no crime or misdeed, but simply because they have independent minds; and that the scaffold, the terror of the wicked, should become a glorious stage for presenting —to the signal disgrace of the sovereign—supreme examples of courage and endurance? For men whose consciences are clear do not fear death or beg for mercy like criminals, since their minds are not tormented by remorse for deeds of shame; they think it a merit, not a punishment, to die for a good cause, and an honour to die for freedom. And since they give their lives for a cause that is beyond the ken of fainéants and fools, hateful to the unruly, and dear to the good, what are men taught by their death? Only to emulate them, or at least to hold them in reverence.

If honesty, then, is to be valued above servility, and sovereigns are to retain full control, without being forced to yield to agitators, it is necessary to allow freedom of judgement, and so to govern men that they can express different and conflicting opinions without ceasing to live in harmony. This method of government is undoubtedly best, and least subject to inconveniences; for it is best suited to human nature. I have shown that in a democracy (which comes nearest to the natural condition) all make a covenant to act, but not to judge and think, in accordance with the common decision; that is, because all men cannot think alike, they agree that the proposal which gets the most votes shall have the force of a decree, but meanwhile retain the authority to revoke such decrees when they discover better. Thus the less freedom of judgement men are allowed, the greater is the departure from the most natural condition, and, in consequence, the more oppressive is the government. To show in addition that the sovereign's authority is sufficient to prevent all inconveniences arising from such freedom, and can easily restrain men from harming one another, no matter how openly their opinions are in conflict, we need not go far afield; for examples are ready to hand. Take the city of Amsterdam, whose enjoyment of this freedom has made it great and admired by the whole world. In this flourishing state, this city without a peer, men of every race and sect live in the greatest harmony, and before they entrust their goods to anyone there are only two things they want to know: whether he is rich or poor, and whether he is honest or dishonest. His religion or sect does not matter, for it has no influence on the decision of lawsuits; and no sect whatsoever is so detested that its members (provided that they harm no one, give every man his own, and live decent lives) are refused the protection of the civil authorities. In the past, when statesmen and the Provincial Estates began to take sides in the religious controversy between the Remonstrants and the Counter-Remonstrants, this was not the case. The result of their intervention was a division in the church; and that period provided abundant evidence that laws passed about religion, i.e. to settle religious disputes, are more apt to provoke men than to reform them, that they enable some to assume unbounded licence, and, finally, that the cause of schisms is not great zeal for the truth (which is, of course, the source of comradeship and sociability), but great ambition to rule. From which it is clearer than noonday that the real disrupters are those who condemn the writings of others, and seditiously incite the insolent mob against their authors, rather than the authors themselves, who generally write for the learned only, appealing to reason alone; and furthermore, that the real disturbers of peace are those who seek to abolish freedom of judgement in a free state, although it cannot be suppressed.

I have thus shown:—

I. That it is impossible to deprive men of the freedom to say what they think.

II. That this freedom can be granted to everyone without infringing the right and authority of the sovereign; and that everyone can keep it without infringing that right as long as he does not use it as a licence to introduce anything into the state as a law, or to do anything contrary to the accepted laws.

III. That it is no danger to the peace of the state; and that all troubles arising from it can easily be checked.

IV. That it is no danger to piety either.

V. That laws passed about speculative matters are utterly useless; and finally,

VI. That this freedom not only can be granted without danger to public peace, piety, and the right of the sovereign, but actually must be granted if they are all to be preserved. For where the opposite course is taken, and attempts are made to deprive men of it, and where the opinions of the dissenters—not their wills, which alone are capable of moral error—are called to account, the punishment inflicted on good men seems more like martyrdom than punishment, provokes instead of intimidating the rest, and moves them to pity, if not to vengeance. Good faith and honest dealing are undermined, lickspittles and rascals encouraged, and opponents exult because concessions have been made to their anger, and they have converted the sovereign to a creed of which they are the recognized interpreters. They thus make bold to usurp its authority and right, and have the effrontery to boast that since they have been chosen by God directly their commands are divine; and to require that the sovereign's, which are merely human, should give way to the divine commands, i.e. to their own. No one can fail to see that all this is quite incompatible with the well-being of a state. I therefore conclude here, as I did above in Chapter XVIII, that it is safest for a state to make piety and religion consist wholly in the practice of charity and equity; to confine the sovereign's right in the religious as well as in the secular sphere to the control of actions alone; and otherwise to allow everyone both to think what he pleases and to say what he thinks.

My treatise being now complete, it only remains to say expressly that it contains nothing which I would not willingly submit to the examination and judgement of my country's rulers. If anything I have written is in their judgement contrary to my country's laws or detrimental to the general welfare, I am ready to retract it. I know that, being human, I may have made errors; but I have taken great pains to avoid error, and, above all, to see that everything I wrote should be in complete accord with my country's laws, with piety, and with sound morals.

NOTES ON CENSORSHIP AND BELIEF (pp. 35–84)

1. *The Republic of Plato,* translated by F. M. Cornford (New York and London: Oxford University Press, 1945), p. 339.
2. Numa Denis Fustel de Coulanges, *The Ancient City,* translated by Willard Small (New York: Doubleday Anchor Books, 1956), pp. 222–23.
3. Quoted by R. H. S. Crossman, *Plato Today* (London: Allen & Unwin, 1959), p. 90.
4. *Ibid.,* pp. 90–91.
5. Werner Jaeger, *Paideia,* Vol. I, translated by Gilbert Highet (New York: Oxford University Press, 1945), p. 246.
6. Harold C. Gardiner, S.J., *The Catholic Viewpoint on Censorship* (New York: Doubleday, 1958), p. 29.
7. S. J. Putnam, *The Censorship of the Church of Rome,* Vol. I (New York, 1906), p. 60.
8. Ernst Cassirer, *The Myth of the State* (New Haven: Yale University Press, 1946), pp. 287–88.
9. Quoted from Giorgio de Santillana, *The Crime of Galileo,* translated by Gebler with Professor Santillana's revision (Chicago: Phoenix Books, 1955), pp. 306–10 and 312–13.
10. *Ibid., passim.*

CENSORSHIP and FACT

1. CENSORSHIP and SCIENCE

COMMENT

The previous section was concerned with religious faith and efforts to hold it within bounds by means of censorship. Even in the situation which Milton advocated in *Areopagitica,* he tried to maintain the state of freedom by keeping out Roman Catholicism. In the case of Galileo, the Church was attempting, even against its best interests, to keep men's image of the world from changing and men from being upset over the traditional teaching of the Church, by the suppression of certain new opinions about the world. The existence of one belief is a threat to another belief, and the prosecution of the one leads to the prosecution of the other; with the cessation of prosecution, both beliefs tend to lose their threatening force and to take on some of the other's characteristics; such, it would seem, is the mirroring force of hatred. But we are concerned here with the earlier stages. Counter-Reformation followed Reformation, the excesses of Calvin followed the excesses of the Inquisition. Toleration as a principle in itself became an article of belief among the forebears of the Unitarians, and a political principle with Spinoza. With the widening of the middle ground, the reorientation of wealth and interest with the discovery of the New World, and the vision of the heavenly systems advanced by Galileo, the practice of censorship reflected the new secular spirit and the change in the character of authority.

In nothing is the change in the character of authority so

clearly reflected as in the changed significance of the word *freedom*. Whereas for the medieval thinker liberty lay in acknowledgment of God's will, for the Renaissance thinker, however much he felt that the former idea held good, liberty had to be redefined by virtue of new necessities, chief among them the extended responsibilities of citizens toward their own nations.

The sub-title of *Leviathan* (1651) is "the Matter, Form, and Power of a Commonwealth Ecclesiastical and Civil." How far does the power of government extend? As far, Hobbes says, as necessity. The materialism of his answer was shocking to many; in spite of attributing final causality to God, he described a largely determined world; and, unlike Spinoza, he ignored what we may perhaps call the assumed supremacy of the conscience.

TEXT: "Of the Liberty of Subjects" from *Leviathan* by Thomas Hobbes

Liberty, or Freedom, signifieth, properly, the absence of opposition; by opposition, I mean external impediments of motion; and may be applied no less to irrational, and inanimate
creatures, than to rational. For whatsoever is so tied, or en-
vironed, as it cannot move but within a certain space, which
space is determined by the opposition of some external body,
we say it hath not liberty to go further. And so of all living
creatures, whilst they are imprisoned, or restrained, with walls,
or chains; and of the water whilst it is kept in by banks, or
vessels, that otherwise would spread itself into a larger space,
we use to say, they are not at liberty, to move in such manner, as without those external impediments they would. But
when the impediment of motion, is in the constitution of the
thing itself, we use not to say; it wants the liberty; but the
power to move; as when a stone lieth still, or a man is fastened
to his bed by sickness.

And according to this proper, and generally received meaning of the word, a FREEMAN, *is he, that in those things,
which by his strength and wit he is able to do, is not hindered
to do what he has a will to.* But when the words *free,* and
liberty, are applied to any thing but bodies, they are abused;
for that which is not subject to motion is not subject to impediment: and therefore, when it is said, for example, the way is
free, no liberty of the way is signified, but of those that walk
in it without stop. And when we say a gift is free, there is
not meant any liberty of the gift, but of the giver, that was
not bound by any law or covenant to give it. So when we
speak freely, it is not the liberty of voice, or pronunciation,
but of the man, whom no law hath obliged to speak other-

wise than he did. Lastly, from the use of the word *free-will*, no liberty can be inferred of the will, desire, or inclination, but the liberty of the man; which consisteth in this, that he finds no stop, in doing what he has the will, desire, or inclination to do.

Fear and liberty are consistent; as when a man throweth his goods into the sea for *fear* the ship should sink, he doth it nevertheless very willingly, and may refuse to do it if he will; it is therefore the action of one that was *free:* so a man sometimes pays his debt, only for *fear* of imprisonment, which because nobody hindered him from detaining, was the action of a man at *liberty*. And generally all actions which men do in commonwealths, for *fear* of the law, are actions, which the doers had *liberty* to omit.

Liberty, and *necessity* are consistent: as in the water, that hath not only *liberty* but a *necessity* of descending by the channel; so likewise in the actions which men voluntarily do: which, because they proceed from their will, proceed from *liberty;* and yet, because every act of man's will, and every desire, and inclination proceedeth from some cause, and that from another cause, in a continual chain, whose first link is in the hand of God the first of all causes, proceed from necessity. So that to him that could see the connexion of those causes, the *necessity* of all men's voluntary actions, would appear manifest. And therefore God, that seeth, and disposeth all things, seeth also that the liberty of man in doing what he will, is accompanied with the *necessity* of doing that which God will, and no more, nor less. For though men may do many things, which God does not command, nor is therefore author of them; yet they can have no passion, nor appetite to anything, of which appetite God's will is not the cause. And did not his will assure the *necessity* of man's will, and consequently of all that on man's will dependeth, the *liberty* of men would be a contradiction, and impediment to the omnipotence and *liberty* of God. And this shall suffice, as to the matter in hand, of that natural *liberty,* which only is properly called *liberty*.

But as men, for the attaining of peace, and conservation of themselves thereby, have made an artificial man, which we call a commonwealth; so also have they made artificial chains,

called *civil laws*, which they themselves, by mutual cove-
nants, have fastened at one end, to the lips of that man, or
assembly, to whom they have given the sovereign power; and
at the other end to their own ears. These bonds, in their own
nature but weak, may nevertheless be made to hold, by the
danger, though not by the difficulty of breaking them. . . .[1]

COMMENT: On the Exercise of Government and the Exercise of Science

The lengths to which the coercive powers of authority might go (with licence, according to Hobbes's theory) had been common experience before the Civil War in England. Indeed, the Civil War had been a result of that experience. In a way, then, only the possible justification of such measures, through the formulation of the necessities governing authority and the axiomatic method of Hobbes's philosophy, was new. Machiavelli had written that "a free government must be perpetually making new regulations to secure its liberty," but this was mere pragmatism. Hobbes was comprehensive: since all originated with God, necessity began with Him. "Whatever effects are hereafter to be produced, shall have a necessary cause, so that all the effects that have been or shall be produced have their necessity in things antecedent." And the state was a body, like other bodies; men could understand it by isolating its elements and seeing the intellectual integration of the whole.

Such language hints at three new events of interest to anyone looking at the uses of censorship: first, the evidence of the "New Science" at work; second, the application of scientific methods outside the field of science proper; and third, the foreshadowing of political systems, most nearly realized in our own day, in which freedom is based on obedience to the will of the ideological authority.

"The New Science" is, of course, science as we understand it today. Francis Bacon best describes what was new about it to him in his *Novum Organum*.

"Our course and method, however (as we have often said, and again repeat), are such as not to deduce effects from effects, nor experiments from experiments (as the empirics do) but in our capacity of legitimate interpreters of nature, to deduce causes and axioms from effects and experiments; and new effects and experiments from those causes and axioms."

And again: "For we are of opinion, that if men had at their command a proper history of nature and experience, and would apply themselves steadily to it, and could bind themselves to two things: 1. to lay aside received opinions and notions; 2. to restrain themselves, till the proper season, from generalization, they might, by the proper and genuine exertion of their minds, fall into our way of interpretation without the aid of any art. For interpretation is the true and natural act of the mind, when all obstacles are removed."

Although Francis Bacon had too metaphysical a mind to inaugurate a new system of scientific inquiry, he helped break the hold of Aristotle and the rooted belief that nature could be explained from self-evident principles. His *New Atlantis* certainly led to the formation of the Royal Society in 1660—a body of experimenters and inventors who, as a learned society, made a notable contribution to the dissemination of new techniques and information. The inductive basis of modern science owes far more to Isaac Newton than to Bacon. Bacon seemed aware of no kind of deduction except the Aristotelian syllogism and was ignorant of the importance of mathematics in deduction. However, his *Novum Organum*, intended to be part of a greater work which he left unfinished, was widely read a century after his death in 1626, long after Newton had revealed a fundamentally new way of working, founded "not on self-evident notions but on notions which would turn out, in their consequences, to match the facts of experience." We still find valid Bacon's description of the instilled impediments to the observation, interpretation, and the checking of the interpretation by observation, that make up the scientific method of inquiry. These impediments Bacon calls "Idols."

> The idols and false notions which have already preoccupied the human understanding, and are deeply rooted in it, not only so beset men's minds that they become difficult of access, but even when access is obtained will again meet and trouble us in the instauration of the sci-

ences, unless mankind when forewarned guard themselves with all possible care against them.

Four species of idols beset the human mind, to which (for distinction's sake) we have assigned names, calling the first Idols of the Tribe, the second Idols of the Den, the third Idols of the Market, the fourth Idols of the Theatre.

The formation of notions and axioms on the foundation of true induction is the only fitting remedy by which we can ward off and expel these idols. It is, however, of great service to point them out; for the doctrine of idols bears the same relation to the interpretation of nature as that of the confutation of sophisms does to common logic.

The idols of the tribe are inherent in human nature and the very tribe or race of man; for man's sense is falsely asserted to be the standard of things; on the contrary, all the perceptions both of the senses and the mind bear reference to man and not to the universe, and the human mind resembles those uneven mirrors which impart their own properties to different objects, from which rays are emitted and distort and disfigure them.

The idols of the den are those of each individual; for everybody (in addition to the errors common to the race of man) has his own individual den or cavern, which intercepts and corrupts the light of nature, either from his own peculiar and singular disposition, or from his education and intercourse with others, or from his reading, and the authority acquired by those whom he reverences and admires, or from the different impressions produced on the mind, as it happens to be preoccupied and predisposed, or equable and tranquil, and the like; so that the spirit of man (according to its several dispositions), is variable, confused, and, as it were, actuated by chance; and Heraclitus said well that men search for knowledge in lesser worlds, and not in the greater or common world.

There are also idols formed by the reciprocal intercourse and society of man with man, which we call idols of the market, from the commerce and association of men with each other; for men converse by means of language, but words are formed at the will of the generality, and there arises from a bad and unapt formation of words a wonderful obstruction to the mind. Nor can the definitions and explanations with which learned men are wont to guard and protect themselves in some instances afford a complete remedy—words still manifestly force the understanding, throw everything into confusion, and lead mankind into vain and innumerable controversies and fallacies.

Lastly, There are idols which have crept into men's minds from the various dogmas of peculiar systems of philosophy, and also from the perverted rules of demonstration, and these we denominate idols of the theatre: for we regard all the systems of philosophy hitherto received or imagined, as so many plays brought out and performed, creating fictitious and theatrical worlds. Nor do we speak only of the present systems, or of the philosophy and sects of the ancients, since numerous other plays of a similar nature can be still composed and made to agree with each other, the causes of the most opposite errors being generally the same. Nor, again, do we allude merely to general systems, but also to many elements and axioms of sciences which have become inveterate by tradition, implicit credence, and neglect.[1]

Apart from these internal impediments there exist also external ones, though in science, as in any of the other great objective disciplines, there can strictly be no doctrine involved but only the practice and exercise of certain actions. No notion of usefulness need be involved, nor even the answering of certain questions. Work is done because conceived. Answers and uses appear because that is the nature of things. On occasions when the purity of the inquiry is disturbed, the discipline itself ceases and becomes something else—a practice, sometimes, of someone else's bit of proof. Something of this sort happened in the last stage of the Stalinist era in Soviet Russia, when false scientists (who remind us of Milton's "false priests") forsook their discipline. Sir Julian Huxley's articles appeared in *Nature* in June 1949, during the controversy which followed the publication of Lysenko's theory of genetics. The articles have been slightly abbreviated.

TEXT: "Soviet Genetics: The Real Issue" by Sir Julian Huxley

Now that the long-drawn-out dispute over genetics in the U.S.S.R. has come to a close, with the complete defeat of the neo-Mendelians at the hands of Lysenko, it is time for men of science outside the U.S.S.R. to take stock of the situation and to see what implications and consequences it has for them. I believe that the situation is very grave. There is now a party line in genetics, which means that the basic scientific principle of the appeal to fact has been overridden by ideological considerations. A great scientific nation has repudiated certain basic elements of scientific method, and in so doing has repudiated the universal and supranational character of science.

·That is the major issue. Its discussion has been unfortunately clouded by insistence on subsidiary, minor, and sometimes irrelevant issues. In relation to this main issue, it is subsidiary whether or not Lysenko's claims to have made certain new discoveries are substantiated, and whether his theories are wholly or partly sound. It leaves the main issue untouched if the attempt is made to justify the action taken, on the narrowly practical ground that the agricultural production of the U.S.S.R. must be rapidly increased, or on the more general ground that Marxism must believe in the improvement of the environment and must or would like to believe that such improvements have a permanent effect on heredity. It is of no relevance to the main issue that Mendelism has sometimes been used to justify undesirable theories and actions, such as Nazi racialist theories or the exaggerated theories of inherent class superiority put forward by certain eugenists. It is equally irrelevant that Mendel was a Roman Catholic priest, or that this or that noted geneticist was a political reactionary. It is a subsidiary issue that some geneticists in the U.S.S.R. may have been directly or indirectly 'liquidated'. It is confusing the real issue to recall that in a wholly or partly planned economy the State must decide how money should be spent on scientific research and its application, or that men of science outside the U.S.S.R. cannot always obtain official grants for the researches they want to undertake, or always get their papers accepted for publication; or that capitalist as well as communist countries insist on secrecy for certain kinds of research and deny free publication to their results. All these issues are, I repeat, either irrelevant or merely subsidiary to the major issue, which is the official condemnation of scientific results on other than scientific grounds, and therefore the repudiation by the U.S.S.R. of the concept of scientific method and scientific activity held by the great majority of men of science elsewhere.

To make the issue clear, I will begin by quoting from the report of the proceedings of a meeting of the Praesidium of the U.S.S.R. Academy of Sciences of August 26, 1948, the highest and most powerful scientific authority in the land. . . . When passages are from verbatim translations, I have given them in double quotes (". . ."); when from summarized reports, in single quotes ('. . .').

The Praesidium of the Academy of Sciences passed twelve resolutions. Of these the most important for our purpose are the following (the translation has been slightly condensed):

'(3) The Cytogenetical Laboratory of Cytology, Histology and Embryology headed by N. P. Dubinin, shall be abolished *as unscientific and useless*. The Laboratory of Botanical Cytology at the same institute shall be closed down *on the grounds that it has followed the same incorrect and unscientific line.* . . .

'(4) The Bureau of the Division of Biological Sciences shall be charged with the preparation of plans for scientific research work for the years 1948–50. *In this the Bureau shall be guided by Michurin's teaching,* and shall adjust the scientific research work of biological institutes to the needs of national economy.

'(6) The composition of Scientists' Councils at biological institutes and editorial boards of biological publications shall be checked with the object of removing from them *the parti-*

sans of Morgano-Weismannite genetics and of replacing them by *supporters of progressive Michurnite biology.*

'(7) The Division of History and Philosophy shall be charged with inclusion in its programme of popularization of the achievements of Michurinism and of *critical exposure of the pseudo-scientific Morgano-Weismannite tendency.*

'(11) The Bureau of the Division of Biological Sciences shall revise the syllabuses at biological institutes, *bearing in mind the interests of Michurinism.*'

An explanatory statement follows, including the following remarks: 'At a number of Academy institutes *formal genetics has not been combated with sufficient vigour.* For this the Praesidium of the Academy takes the blame. The Bureau of the Division of Biological Sciences and its head L. A. Orbeli (who was released from his duties as Academician-Secretary under Resolution 1) have failed to give a correct orientation to the biologists of the Academy.

'The report by Lysenko, which has been approved by the Central Committee of the Communist Party, *has exposed the scientific inconsistency of the reactionary idealist theories of the followers of Weismannism*—Schmalhausen, Dubinin, Zhebrak, Navashin and others.'

A letter to Comrade Stalin is summarized as follows: 'A pledge is here given by the Praesidium of the U.S.S.R. Academy of Sciences to further Michurin's biology *and to root out unpatriotic, idealist, Weismannite-Morganist ideology*'.

A further statement by the Praesidium ("To the prosperity of our progressive science") is finally summarized: 'Michurin's materialist direction in biology *is the only acceptable form of science, because it is based on dialectical materialism and on the revolutionary principle of changing Nature for the benefit of the people. Weismannite-Morganist idealist teaching is pseudo-scientific, because it is founded on the notion of the divine origin of the world and assumes eternal and unalterable scientific laws. The struggle between the two ideas has taken the form of the ideological class-struggle between socialism and capitalism on the international scale, and between the majority of Soviet scientists and a few remaining Russian scientists who have retained traces of bourgeois ideology, on a smaller scale. There is no place for compromise. Michurinism and Morgano-Weismannism cannot be reconciled.'* (Note here, among much else of interest, the apparent distinction between *Soviet* and *Russian* scientists.)

There are also now available Lysenko's "Report on Soviet Biology" to the session of the Lenin Academy of Agricultural Sciences, July 31–August 7, 1948, together with his concluding speech, two summaries of the subsequent discussion, and verbatim reports of a few of the speeches. Since this article was first written, a verbatim English translation of the entire discussion, totalling 631 pages, has been published in Moscow. Neither space nor time has been available for the general use of verbatim extracts from this, but I have satisfied myself as to the general accuracy of the summarized citations given below.

These reports, together with the documents already cited, constitute a melancholy landmark in the history of science. They demonstrate that science is no longer regarded in the U.S.S.R. as an international activity of free workers whose prime interest it is to discover new truth and new facts, but as an activity subordinated to a particular ideology and designed only to secure practical results in the interests of a particular national and political system. Consequently the unity of science is denied, and various brands of "good" science— Marxist, Soviet, or materialist—are distinguished from various brands of "bad" science—bourgeois, reactionary, idealist and the like. Further, the primary sanction for scientific theory is no longer consonance with the facts of Nature, but consonance with a political and social philosophy. With this, orthodoxy is once more enthroned; and though this is no longer the theological orthodoxy from the bonds of which the Western world emancipated itself in the seventeenth, eighteenth and nineteenth centuries, the new social-political orthodoxy is equally powerful, employs abuse and force in a similar way, and is equally inimical to the free spirit of science. There is now a scientific party line in the U.S.S.R., and those who stray from it do so at their peril.

It is true that up to the present this complete subordination of science to political authority applies only in genetics. However, tendencies in the same direction have also manifested themselves in the U.S.S.R. with more or less force in other fields of creative and intellectual activity—philosophy, literature, the visual arts and even music—and in other scientific subjects, such as psychology and the theory of probability. Further, once the principle of a dominant orthodoxy has been admitted and acted upon on one field, it can readily be generalized, and the presumption is that it will be. In any event, there can now be no security that other branches of science in the U.S.S.R. will not suffer the same fate as genetics, and be *gleichgeschaltet* in relation to an overriding system.

Let me illustrate these points by quotations, at the same time trying to imagine what would have happened if the controversy had developed in Britain or other centre of "bourgeois science".

In the first place, the two sides have been elaborately labelled, and many of the labels have philosophical or political connotations, often implying approval or condemnation. Thus, neo-Mendelism is usually referred to as *Morgano-Mendelism*, often with one or more of the adjectives *formalist, idealist* or *reactionary* prefixed; or simply as *idealist genetics*. Sometimes it is styled 'Weismannism' (again usually with a pejorative prefix), although in the West, Weismann's particular views are now mainly of historical interest only. We are told that the views of the neo-Mendelians are *mystic, metaphysical, bourgeois, pseudo-scientific,* or even *anti-scientific*.

The followers of Lysenko, on the other hand, are called *Michurinites,* presumably because the Soviet tendency is to justify the present in terms of past authority, and Michurin is being deliberately glorified as a great Russian pioneer in agricultural and biological science (whereas in point of fact he was essentially an empiricist who scored some important practical successes, but whose theoretical speculations have become scientifically negligible in the light of later research). Timiriazev is also often cited as an authority under whose banner Lysenko and his followers are advancing (although his genetical theories are now quite outdated by scientific advance). Further, Michurinism is usually qualified with the adjective *scientific, materialist,* or *progressive*. The term So-

viet genetics is not infrequently used, and Lysenko employs the phrase *Soviet creative Darwinism.*

Subtlety of description is pushed to extremes by B. M. Zavadovsky, who distinguishes between *Mendelism* as a system of established facts, and *Mendelianism* as Mendelism distorted by reactionary idealist and metaphysical elements. (But Zavadovsky was in a very awkward position, as an ardent and important member of the Communist Party who had for several decades done a great deal to popularize neo-Mendelism.)

In Britain, I suppose we should have heard simply of certain new claims of Lysenko which required confirmation, and of certain new theories of his which were in conflict with accepted views; or perhaps the matter would have developed into a general dispute between neo-Mendelians and Michurinites, in the same way that the quarrel between Karl Pearson and Bateson developed into a general dispute between biometricians and Mendelians some forty-odd years ago. Individual participants in the controversy might have been stigmatized as old-fashioned or uncritical; but there would certainly have been no wholesale attaching of philosophical, political or moral labels.

In the second place, the chief two touchstones in the controversy in the U.S.S.R. have been, not scientific fact and verification of theory by experiment, but immediate practical utility on one hand and correctness of doctrine on the other. The criterion of practical utility is probably of less general significance. In any event, it is not universally applied. I can testify from personal experience at the time of the celebrations of the Academy of Sciences in 1945, that there was in many fields, including ecology, genetics, systematics and general biology as a whole, an admirable balance between 'pure' and 'applied' work in the U.S.S.R., and that some branches of science with negligible practical applications, such as vertebrate palæontology, were extremely flourishing. However, in the case of genetics, the utilitarian criterion has been drastically employed —largely, I imagine, because the controversy has been so largely guided by Lysenko, and Lysenko is an agriculturist whose primary aim has been to achieve success through spectacular practical results.

Thus, in his "Report" Lysenko (1948) says: "Socialist Agriculture, the collective and State farming system, has given rise to a Soviet biological science, founded by Michurin—a science *new in principle* [italics mine throughout, unless otherwise stated], developing in close union with agronomical practice. . . . It is no exaggeration to say that *Morgan's feeble metaphysical 'science'* . . . can stand no comparison with our *effective Michurinist agrobiological science.*"

Lysenko later refers to Michurin as "the great transformer of Nature", and says "in our country the Morganist cytogeneticists find themselves confronted by the *practical effectiveness of the Michurin trend* in agrobiological science". With reference to the special laboratory under Zhebrak, set up in the Timiriazev Academy by the Ministry of Agriculture, to study polyploidy (which, I may mention, has obtained some extremely interesting results), Lysenko merely says that, in his view, "it has produced literally nothing of practical value. Here is one example, . . . to show how useless is the practical and theoretical programme of our domestic Morganist cytogeneticists". Finally, in the conclusion of his "Report", he writes that *"a scientific handling of practical problems is the surest way to a deeper knowledge of the laws of development of living nature"* (italics his)—a sweeping assertion in obvious contradiction with many events in the history of science.

In the discussion, the same thesis is reiterated. Thus Nemchinov states that the task of agricultural science is to change Nature for the benefit of socialist economy (*nota bene,* not of humanity in general), and Lobanov says that Soviet agricultural science must 'aim at the successful solution of practical problems' (a statement with which no one would quarrel if it were not constantly extended to mean that all genetics must be directed *only* to the solution of practical problems). Some of the speakers even went further. Olshansky states that Morgano-Mendelism '*obstructs* the work of practical breeding and seed-growing'; and Dubinin's interesting study of the selective effect of environment on the genetic composition of a population of *Drosophila,* because it is of no immediate practical value, is described by Yakushkin as '*a monstrous deviation from the tasks of a Soviet scientist*'. Babajanyan, when asked by Rapoport why he shut his eyes to the existence of useful as opposed to deleterious mutations in *Drosophila,* answered *"because they are useful mutations for a useless object".* Previously he had said "Who wants what by their very nature are useless *Drosophilas?"* There could not be a clearer repudiation of the idea that one of the basic functions of science is to obtain knowledge and understanding. Dimitriev condemns all scientific work (in genetics) which does not assist practical agriculture, and criticizes Schmalhausen and others *'for expressing views incompatible with progressive improvement in agriculture'.* (Apparently, he regards it as irrelevant whether the views happen to be true or not.)

On the other hand, some speakers give the practical criterion a twist and assert that 'Morgano-Mendelism is a bourgeois philosophy *seeking nothing but the exploitation of Nature'* (Dvorjankin); and that 'self-pollination and selection of selfed lines of maize use Morganist techniques, which made seed-production difficult *and play into the hands of capitalist seed-firms'* (Feiginson).

One of the reasons given by the Academy for closing down the Cytogenetical Laboratory under Dubinin (see above) is that it is "useless". (The Academy must have forgotten Faraday's answer to a questioner who asked him what was the use of his work: "What is the use of a baby?")

In Britain, the practical utility of this or that discovery or the immediate applicability of this or that theory would doubtless have been discussed; but no one would have questioned the desirability of leaving a considerable free sector to pure research, whether on the two-fold ground, usually accepted here, that one of the aims of science is to increase knowledge irrespective of practical results, and that practical results do, as a matter of fact, often spring from what appear to be the most impractical investigations, or, in the case of a minority, for the latter reason only. More Government money might have gone into Michurinite work if the Government and its advisers had been impressed by Lysenko's claims; but it is safe to say that no laboratory turning out a considerable volume of research results would have been closed down as useless.

Most central to the issue is the appeal to doctrine and authority instead of to observational and experimental verification. As a result, a basic effect of the controversy has been to establish, in the fields of genetics and evolution, a scientific orthodoxy, which in its turn is related to and dependent upon a philosophical orthodoxy. And the philosophical orthodoxy is, of course, linked with the social and political orthodoxy of Communism and the authority of the Communist Party in the U.S.S.R. The upshot is that science in the U.S.S.R. must now do its work in a totally different atmosphere and on totally different intellectual foundations from those in other countries. . . .

I have tried to present in some detail the situation concerning genetic science in the U.S.S.R. This must be related to a more general picture—the situation of thought and creative expression under Communism—though I can here only touch on its broad lines. In what follows, I shall use 'thought' as a convenient brief general term, to cover not only philosophy, but also creative expression in letters, art and music.

In the U.S.S.R., as is now common knowledge, thought in this extended sense has been to a greater or lesser extent compulsorily socialized—subordinated to an over-riding social philosophy and subjected to State (political) control, so that its freedom or autonomy is consciously and expressly restricted. It is, of course, obvious that thought is nowhere completely autonomous, being always limited by its material, social, and spiritual or intellectual environment; but this limitation is, in the Western world of to-day, for the most part an automatic conditioning, not a conscious restriction, and is moderate in extent.

The restriction of thought and expression in the U.S.S.R. operates rather differently in different fields. In politics it of course operates through the one-party system, which allows freedom of political thought or expression only within the limits of communist party doctrine.

In history and the social sciences, restriction is as severe, and perhaps even more productive of distortion (as an example of the distortion of history, I may cite the fact that in the Museum of the Revolution there is not—or was not in 1945 when I was in Moscow—any mention of the part played by Trotsky in the Revolution).

In philosophy, it appears to operate by reference to a tradition of authority and orthodoxy. To read the recent discussions on philosophy in the U.S.S.R. (summarized in *Europe* two years ago) is rather like being transported back to one of the Councils of early Christianity, except that the authorities with whom one must conform are not the Fathers of the Church, but Marx, Engels, Lenin and Stalin. The function of philosophy in the U.S.S.R. is not to explore the bases of human thought and action in general, but to clarify and develop a particular philosophy, that of neo-Marxism (as we may call Marxism as brought up to date since 1917), which provides the theoretical basis for political activity. In the arts, on the other hand, the positive criterion to which they must conform is "socialist realism", as opposed to the negative criterion of "formalism". These criteria are interpreted rather differently in different arts —in music, for example, a good deal of subtlety has to be employed to give a sense to the term *realism;* but rather crudely it may be said that "socialist realism" is intended as the justification of the belief that the arts should be easily intelligible to every citizen, and should have as their only, or at least their prime, function the social one of providing emotional outlet, focus and drive for the activities of society in war and peace, as against that of new exploration or of expression for the individual artist, or of private enjoyment by the individual citizen.

In natural science, it is too much to suggest that everything shall be readily intelligible to everybody. On the other hand, there is apparently in many fields, and perhaps notably in agriculture, a tendency to stress the practical aspects of science in providing control over Nature, as against the 'pure' aspect, as providing knowledge and understanding of Nature. It is therefore sought to associate the practical workers in applied science as closely as possible with research; and to achieve this it is desirable that scientific theories should be of as simple a nature as possible. Elaborate and unfamiliar theoretical constructions (such as that of neo-Mendelism) cannot be expected to appeal to the practical man who is anxious for results and likes to feel he understands the great adventure in which he is participating. They can therefore be conveniently discouraged by being branded as formalist (as well as being stig-matized as politically undesirable if that too is required).

The attack on the theory of probability is another example of the appeal to naïve practicability. Soviet science does not want mere probability in its theories, because it wants cer-tainty of results: this is in no sense an unfair travesty of the position taken by Lysenko himself—it would presumably be overcomplicated and difficult to explain that only by means of the theory of probability is it possible to evaluate whatever degree of certainty a scientific result may have.

In the particular case of genetics, it would seem that Ly-senko's theories have a greater appeal to the practical man, because of their *simpliste* nature, in equating the highly com-plex processes of heredity to the apparently simpler and, at any rate, more familiar ones of digestion and assimilation, and in their naïve view that environment acts directly upon heredity to produce adaptation, instead of indirectly *via* the mechanism of selection; and further, in using Michurin's homely ideas, such as the 'shaking' or 'shattering' of the 'heredity', instead of trying to analyse what really happens in the complex biological entities and processes that are actually involved.

It should in all fairness be noted that many branches of Rus-sian science have not been treated in the same fashion as ge-netics. There appears to be no specifically Marxian ideology, still less any party line, prescribed for chemistry or biochem-istry, for mathematics (apart from probability theory), for geology, palæontology, ecology, taxonomy, plant physiology, etc. This is presumably because their pursuit has not yet raised any issues of ideological importance.

Whatever the reasons, the "socialization" of biological sci-ence in the U.S.S.R. has proceeded along the lines I have in-dicated—appeal to immediate utility, to the partial or total ex-clusion of the appeal to the discovery of new facts and new truth; appeal to national patriotism and class sentiment, so that science is regarded primarily as an instrument of the class struggle and its national extensions; the subordination of scien-tific to philosophical theory, and of scientific activity to an over-riding socio-political point of view; and finally, the appeal to authority, in the shape of a party line, in regard to scientific research and education. In passing, it must be noted that a great deal of what may be called the philosophical labelling of tendencies in science has been exceedingly arbitrary, and often, in my opinion, actually erroneous. Thus, as already mentioned, it is a perversion of terms to call neo-Mendelism *idealist* and *anti-materialist* when its chief merit has been the discovery of the material basis of inheritance. As regards the name-calling of individual geneticists, I knew Morgan intimately, and know that it is absurd to impute any philosophical or political motives to him; and Muller, who is stigmatized a 'bourgeois' or 'reactionary', was actually in difficulties in the United States for some years of his most fruitful period because of his left-wing and pro-Russian attitude. In any case, a fact is a fact whether discovered by a communist or a fascist, whether in the United States or in the U.S.S.R.

In any event, science in the U.S.S.R., together with other fields of intellectual thought and creative expression, has now become in principle an activity to be exercised in subordination to an over-riding doctrine. This doctrine is doubtless in part a deliberate rationalization of the political practice and aims of the rulers of the U.S.S.R., but none the less for that, constitutes an extremely powerful driving force for the Soviet State and Soviet society. According to this doctrine, the developing socialist society of the U.S.S.R. in particular, and of communist countries in general, finds itself involved in a desperate and inevitable struggle with capitalist society in the other major countries of the world. Not only is that struggle inevitable, but it admits of no compromise: according to the official philosophy of Soviet communism, it must continue until the victory of communism is assured.

Science accordingly comes to be regarded as an organ of the developing socialist society and therefore as one of its weapons in its struggle against the rest of the world. Furthermore, the socio-political struggle is transferred into science, which is then seen as divided into two camps, as inevitably and as irreconcilably opposed as, in the view of orthodox Soviet political philosophy, are communism and capitalism, the communist and the bourgeois or capitalist type of society.

It has puzzled many observers to note that in the genetics

controversy the official Soviet scientists have abandoned one element in orthodox Marxism, namely, the principle that advance is effected through the reconciliation of opposites, by the reconciliation of thesis and antithesis in a higher synthesis. However, the explanation is, I think, the simple one I have just advanced, namely, that the scientific controversy has been subordinated to and indeed made a part of the class struggle, and so has come to partake of the irreconcilability which the Marxists have always pronounced to be a feature of the more general socio-political conflict.

One further consequence of this state of affairs is the injection of patriotism and xenophobia into science, as we have already cited. For some little time past, rebukes have been administered to Soviet scientific workers for servility to foreign or bourgeois scientific theories, and the principle of secrecy in science has been extended further in the U.S.S.R. than elsewhere, since Soviet scientists in general, and not only those engaged on war research, have been warned not to speak freely to foreign scientists about scientific discoveries in the U.S.S.R.

Once this over-riding system of ideological criteria is set up for science, it becomes all too easy for men of science who enjoy political power, or are in a position of authority, to use it for the discomfiture of their scientific opponents; and, in fact, in reading the summary of the discussion on Soviet biology, one cannot escape the conclusion that Lysenko and his followers have thus taken advantage of the situation. Because a system of authority and orthodoxy exists in the U.S.S.R., and because within such a system certain philosophic labels connote blame and condemnation, those labels, it would seem, have often been attached with the deliberate purpose of administering a thorough beating to one party to a scientific dispute.

The idea of subordinating scientific activity to ideological and political considerations is at least understandable in a society such as the U.S.S.R. What is difficult to understand is how, in the case of genetics, this subordination has been pushed so far as to deny the validity of well-established facts and concepts, and to proscribe an entire branch of science, while giving official approval to an alternative system which is demonstrably inadequate from the point of view of scientific method, and the facts and concepts of which have not been properly established.

Russian science in general stands at a high level. How can the Academy have given its blessing to Michurinism, whose facts are notoriously and obviously dubious and whose crude interpretative principles bear no resemblance to a scientific theory in the accepted sense? And how can it have pronounced the scientific condemnation of Mendelian genetics, seeing that in its fifty years of existence it has steadily developed until in all other countries it is accepted as one of the most vigorous and successful branches of science?

Equally puzzling, how can the political authorities have given official sanction and exclusive encouragement to Michurinism, when impartial scientific advice, if given without any political pressure, would have told them that its methods and ideas, when not definitely false, are inadequate and unscientific, in that they do not meet normal scientific criteria? Do they not know that bad science cannot produce good practical results?

Clearly, no one outside Russia can answer such questions. But one may hazard a guess. My guess is that many factors have been involved. As regards practice, Lysenko and his school are continuing to obtain results, partly through improvements in agronomy which have nothing to do with genetics; partly through genetic methods which, although claimed as Michurinist, are in reality based on Mendelism; and partly through the enthusiasm which Lysenko has been able to inspire among agriculturists. So the practical bankruptcy of Michurinism is for a time disguised. The political authorities appear unable to distinguish between scientific theories in the proper sense of the word, and vague interpretative hypotheses which are so flexible that they can be adjusted *post hoc* to account for a great deal that is really better explained on quite other principles. So the theoretically expected crash may be long postponed.

Then Marxism, since the Revolution, has always had pro-Lamarckian and anti-Mendelian leanings. This is partly because Lamarckism promises short-cuts both to agricultural and social improvements, while Mendelism cannot do so, and in its earlier stages was not of much service in many practical fields; partly because Mendelism has an anti-egalitarian element, the implications of which have been much exaggerated in the U.S.S.R. as a stick with which to beat eugenists and racialists; partly because the direct effect of environment and heredity postulated by Lamarckism seems at first sight much more "natural" as well as simpler than the indirect effect, *via* the natural selection of mutations, which Western genetics has demonstrated, but which Lysenko dismisses as "unthinkable".

A further factor would seem to have been the rise of a patriotic nationalism in the U.S.S.R., which has affected science as well as all other fields. Michurin was one of the few Russians who could be selected as having made distinctive contributions to agricultural improvement. He had been favoured by Lenin; his views not only fitted in with Lysenko's, but with the Lamarckian bias I have just mentioned. He could be, and was, made one of the chief symbols of a distinctively Soviet genetics, and once this was done, neo-Mendelism, being irreconcilable with Michurinism, could be branded as bourgeois, foreign and unpatriotic.

Finally, there was the fact of Lysenko, an admirable figurehead for the anti-Mendelian faction in the Communist party, and quick to turn all these other factors to account in his own interest.

As for the Academy of Sciences, I do not see how its action can be explained, except as a result of the subordination of science to politics and ideology. Once a party line in biology had been laid down, the Academy had to toe it like everybody else. . . .

It is, of course, true that the freedom and autonomy of science have been infringed upon in countries other than the U.S.S.R. The total nature of modern war is such that secrecy is imposed on all men of science carrying on research for war purposes, even in peace-time. This, however, affects only a fraction of scientific work. What is in dispute is merely the limit of the 'secret sector'; and men of science are still free to devote themselves to work of a non-military nature. Freedom of publication is also limited in certain branches of industrial research; but here again science as a whole is not involved.

Again, in some countries, such as the Argentine, many university scientists have been dismissed for political reasons. But even in such cases politics does not presume to dictate the *scientific* admissibility of theories or branches of science.

The nearest approach in the Western world to ideological control of science was the legislation prohibiting the teaching of evolution in Tennessee and some other States of the U.S.A. But even this was partial in the sense that it affected only a few States, and only the public institutions in those States.

So far as I am aware, in modern times it is only in the U.S.S.R. (and, though to a somewhat lesser extent, in Germany under Hitler) that science has lost its inherent intellectual autonomy, in the sense that the admissibility of its theories, laws and facts is judged not on their scientific merits but in relation to political and philosophical doctrines, and research and scientific thought are subordinated to the directives of a political party.

As a direct consequence of this, science as a whole has lost its unity. It is no longer in essentials a world activity, that is, one transcending the partial frameworks of nationalism and religion, but has become split into two. The Nazis tried to split it into German, Aryan or Nordic science as opposed to non-Aryan, Jewish or Bolshevik science; the Russians have now succeeded in splitting it into Soviet, Marxist, Communist or materialist science as against foreign, bourgeois, capitalist or idealist science.

Nazi Germany paid for its attacks on scientific autonomy and unity by a deterioration in the quality of its scientific work. The U.S.S.R. will doubtless in due time pay an equally heavy price. But this can provide no satisfaction, except perhaps to the minority whose hostility to the U.S.S.R. over-rides all other considerations. All men of science worthy of the name, all who really believe in the possibility of progress for the human species as a whole, and in science as an indispensable agency for securing that progress, all who believe that the search for new truth is one of the highest activities of man, must feel acute regret at the action of the U.S.S.R. through its Academy of Sciences.

But regret is barren. We ask immediately whether there is

nothing to be done. In the first place, we must realize that the action of the U.S.S.R. is only an extreme and exaggerated manifestation of a general situation. The general situation is constituted by the familiar trend towards a greater centralization and a greater organisation of society. This again is regretted by some; but it would appear to be inevitable in the present stage of the world's history, and many consider it to be a necessary prerequisite not only for the greater efficiency of the social organism but also in the long run for the greater happiness and fuller development of individuals. There are, however, good and bad ways, or at least more desirable and less desirable ways, in which this trend can be realized. This applies both to broad social and economic organisation, and also to the way in which science is to be integrated with the rest of the life of society—for clearly science cannot escape the operation of the general trend.

Our question—whether there is nothing to be done—now resolves itself into three more particular questions. What can men of science do to see that the general trend towards the integration of society develops in the best possible way? What can men of science do to see that the integration of science with other social activities does not infringe on its autonomy and its unity? And what can men of science do to modify the policy of the U.S.S.R. in subordinating science to philosophical and political orthodoxy?

Although the first question is perhaps the most important, it is difficult to find an answer to it, and especially a generally agreed answer, and I do not propose to do more than touch upon the matter. I personally would suggest something of this sort. It is of great importance for a society to possess some kind of ideological driving force. National patriotism may suffice in times of war, but not in peace. When religious belief is strong, it may provide the ideological drive; but this is assuredly not the case in the Western world to-day, where religion is not only fragmented into many churches and sects, but also no longer provides a dominant appeal to the majority of people. In the U.S.S.R. and other communist countries, on the other hand, communism does provide such an appeal, and an appeal both theoretical and practical in nature. To provide an equally powerful and equally general appeal, I believe that only some kind of dynamic or evolutionary humanism will suffice, a belief that man has the duty of carrying the general process of evolution to new heights, and that in discharging that duty rightly he will be providing and ever expanding new possibilities of fuller living for future generations. If so, then this evolutionary humanism must be based on science, and it will be the task of the men of science not only to provide the material basis for the heightened standards of living, but also the theoretical and philosophic background for the new ideology—what for a religion would be its theological framework. . . .

The second question is more specific and more immediate. I may perhaps re-phrase it thus: How should men of science act in the face of the increasing concern of the State with science, and the consequent increasing pressure of the State on science?

Can they accept the existence of an official scientific policy? Can they accept the possibility that the majority of men of science shall be paid by the State and that the major cost of scientific work shall be borne on Government funds? Can they accept official direction as to what subjects shall be investigated?

I think that they can (indeed, that they must)—but with certain clearly formulated provisos. A Government is at perfect liberty to embark on a large-scale and comprehensive official scientific policy. It can legitimately decide that that policy shall be predominantly practical—designed to raise the standard of life, to improve health, to increase production, or to promote military efficiency. It can legitimately demand that the scientific curriculum throughout all stages of education should be adequate and should be framed so as to give the best possible understanding of Nature and man's place in Nature, of the social functions of science and of its intellectual and practical importance. It can legitimately insist on large-scale educational campaigns outside the school and university system to help the general population to understand the value and importance of science as a whole or of this or that branch of scientific work, or to make them feel that they are actively and intelligently participating in the nation's scientific effort. It can legitimately do everything in its power to check superstition, to combat unscientific or anti-scientific attitudes of mind, and to promote an understanding of scientific method, and of its value and importance.

Probably all men of science would agree that it is legitimate, and most of them that it is desirable, for a Government to embark on such a policy. But they would assuredly only agree on certain conditions. In the first place, they would say a Government has no right to pronounce in any way on the truth or falsity of any scientific facts, laws or theories, nor to exert pressure in favour of their acceptance or rejection by scientists. It must not subordinate the intellectual autonomy of science to any other criteria, whether religious, philosophical, or political, nor seek to impose upon scientific truth standards other than its own, nor relate scientific activity to any orthodoxy or authoritarian principle, nor, most of all, impose a scientific orthodoxy.

As implication of this, it must consult scientific opinion in forming its scientific policy, and leave all essentially scientific decisions in the hands of men of science. On the educational side of its scientific policy, it must, of course, consult educationists as well as scientists, and recognize their autonomy in their own sphere.

It must recognize the special characteristics of science and the scientific method—the fact that it is essentially a universal activity; that for its advance it depends very largely on freedom of publication, which in its turn implies freedom for other scientific workers to test and re-test published conclusions; that major advances in scientific knowledge cannot be planned to order, and that new possibilities of practical advance often derive from the most unexpected quarters, including investigations undertaken with no practical aim.

As a consequence of these characteristics of science, the State should permit the utmost freedom of publication consonant with military security; it should encourage the international exchange of publications and research workers to the fullest extent; and it should not insist on all research, even all research paid for out of Government funds, being directed to immediate practical objectives, but should leave a considerable "unplanned sector" of fundamental research to the free choice of the pure scientist.

In education, while not in any way minimizing the importance of science as an organised body of tested knowledge, it should also recognize the value of the scientific method—of free inquiry and free discussion, with reference back to fact where possible, as against dogmatic assertion and unreflective assimilation. . . .

COMMENT: On Governmental Direction of Science

Interference of the sort exercised by the Soviet hierarchy, which surely involves the use of simple censorship—the withholding of the written word—led in Lysenko's case to odd conclusions; but even more, it led to the extinction of pure science in his case—that is, what was ostensibly a scientific conclusion was reached by a botched travesty of the recognized discipline. Science pursued for its own sake is universally significant and is by its nature available to all. When a national fence is put round it, it ceases to be universal; it becomes something relative to national aims, diplomatics, national images, and the rest. If a scientist is prevented from practicing his discipline, he is undergoing, in no matter what more lenient degree, the treatment of Galileo. This may be inevitable if a scientist goes to work for an organization rather than for his discipline, but it is equally inevitable that the discipline suffers if it is interfered with. Science, in fact, which not long ago had the respect and privilege once accorded Latin medieval scholarship, seems now in process of becoming as national as that scholarship became with the development of vernaculars.

In the passage that follows we can see something of the muddle that attends a scientific operation that has to be kept immune from the rest of the world for reasons of national security. It is taken from the publication of the United States Atomic Energy Commission on the hearing before the Personnel Security Board, spring 1954, which was engaged *In the Matter of J. Robert Oppenheimer*. The extract is from the end of John J. McCloy's testimony. At the time of the hearing Mr. McCloy was no longer a public servant; during the war he had been Assistant Secretary of War under Henry L. Stimson, and when the war was over, he became U.S. High Commissioner in Germany. Though not a scientist, he was perfectly able to see the necessary conditions for the practice of science. His testimony, with its odd, startling wish to explain and be understood, together with the decent and restrained inter-jections of the interlocutors, revealing their desire to hear him out, are a better commentary on the pathetic irrele-vancies of the inquiry for the pursuits and desires of science—even in a war—than anything we can say.

TEXT: "Natural Science and National Security" from *In the Matter of J. Robert Oppenheimer*, quoting John J. McCloy, et al.

MR. MC CLOY. There is another aspect to this question of security, if I may just go on, that troubles me and I have been thinking about it a good bit since I have read the charges and the reply of Dr. Oppenheimer, and have talked to a number of people who are somewhat familiar with this whole subject. It seems to me that there are two security aspects. One is the negative aspect. How do you gauge an individual in terms of his likelihood of being careless with respect to the use of documents or expressions, if he is not animated by something more sinister? There is also for want of a better expression the positive security. I remember very vividly the early days when the warnings that Neils Bohr—I was not in Washington when Neils Bohr first came over, but I saw him from time to time after that—when he announced to us and to the President that the uranium atom had been split, and we might look forward with some concern to the possibility that the Germans would have an atomic weapon, and our eagerness at that time to take on, practically speaking, anyone who had this quality of mind that could reach in back of and beyond, from the layman's point of view, at least, and deal with this concept and reduce it to reality.

As I try to look back to that period, I think we would have taken pretty much anybody who had certainly the combination of those qualities, the theoretical ability, plus the practical sense, to advance our defense position in that field. In those days we were on guard against the Nazis and the Germans. I think we would have grabbed one of them if we thought he had that quality, and surrounded him with as much security precautions as we could. Indeed, I think we would have probably taken a convicted murderer if he had that capacity. There again is this question of the relative character of security. It depends somewhat on the day and age that you are in.

I want to emphasize particularly this affirmative side of it. The names we bandied about at that time included a number of refugees and a number of people that came from Europe. I have the impression—I may be wrong about it—but I have the impression that a very large element of this theoretical thinking did emanate from the minds of those who immigrated from this country, and had not been generated here as far as it had been in Europe. There were names like Fermi and Wigner and Teller, Rabi, another queer name, Szilard, or something like that—but I have the impression they came over here, and probably embued with a certain anti-Nazi fervor which tended to stimulate thinking, and it is that type of mind that we certainly needed then.

We could find, so to speak, practical atomic physicists, and today there are great quantities of them being trained, and whether we are getting this finely balanced imagination which can stretch beyond the practicalities of this thing is to my mind the important aspect of this problem. The art is still in its infancy and we still are in need of great imagination in this field.

In a very real sense, therefore, I think there is a security risk in reverse. If anything is done which would in any way repress or dampen that fervor, that verve, that enthusiasm, or the feeling generally that the place where you can get the greatest opportunity for the expansion of your mind and your experiments in this field is the United States, to that extent the security of the United States is impaired.

In other words, you can't be too conventional about it or you run into a security problem the other way. We are only secure if we have the best brains and the best reach of mind in this field. If the impression is prevalent that scientists as a whole have to work under such great restrictions and perhaps great suspicion, in the United States, we may lose the next step in this field, which I think would be very dangerous for us.

From my own experience in Germany, although they were very backward in this field, and in that respect there is a very interesting instance which I have seen referred to in print——

MR. GRAY. Mr. McCloy, may I interrupt you for a minute? As a lawyer, you must observe we allow very considerable latitude in these hearings, and we have tried in no way to circumscribe anything that any witness wishes to say, and in fact, almost anything the lawyers wanted to say has gone into the record. You were asked a question, I believe, by Mr. Garrison, about Dr. Oppenheimer's—it has been a long time and I have forgotten.

MR. GARRISON. Loyalty, and him as a security risk.

MR. GRAY. Yes. Whereas I think your views are entitled to great weight on these matters generally, I would respectfully and in the most friendly spirit, suggest that we not wander too far afield from this question.

THE WITNESS. I didn't mean to wander too far.

MR. GRAY. Yes, sir.

THE WITNESS. I did want to make one point. I have been asked this recently in New York frequently: Do you think that Dr. Oppenheimer is a security risk, and how would I answer that. This is long before I had any idea I was going to be called here. What do you mean by security, positive, negative, there is a security risk both ways in this thing. It is the affirmative security that I believe we must protect here. I would say that even if Dr. Oppenheimer had some connections that were somewhat suspicious or make one fairly uneasy, you have to balance his affirmative aspect against that, before you can finally conclude in your own mind that he is a reasonable security risk, because there is a balance of interest there; that he not only is himself, but that he represents in terms of scientific inquiry—I am very sorry if I rambled on about that and I didn't mean to.

MR. GRAY. I don't want to cut you off at all, but you were getting back about something of the Nazis during the war.

THE WITNESS. Yes. Let me tell you why I did that, if I may.

MR. ROBB. Mr. Chairman, may I interpose one thought. I think the rules do provide that no witness will be allowed to argue from the witness stand. I think the witness should bear that in mind, if I might suggest it.

THE WITNESS. Yes. I don't mean to argue. I am trying honestly to answer the question whether this man is a security risk in my judgment from what I know of him.

MR. ROBB. I understand. . . .

[There follows a cross-examination in which Mr. McCloy is asked whether—since at the time of the inquiry he is Chairman of the Board of the Chase National Bank—he would employ as a bank teller a man whom he did not wholly trust. Mr. Mc-Cloy replies that he does not get the analogy and is allowed to go on.]

THE WITNESS. One of my tasks in Germany was to pick up Nazi scientists and send them over to the United States. These Nazi scientists a few years before were doing their utmost to overthrow the United States Government by violence. They had a very suspicious background. They are being used now, I assume—whether they are still, I don't know, because I am not in contact with it—on very sensitive projects in spite of their background. The Defense Department has been certainly to some extent dependent upon German scientists in connection with guided missiles. I suppose other things being equal, you would like to have a perfectly pure, uncontaminated chap, with no background, to deal with these things, but it is not possible in this world. I think you do have to take risks in regard to the security of the country. As I said at the beginning, even if they put you—I won't be personal about it—but let us say put Mr. Stimson or anybody in charge of the innermost secrets of our defense system, there is a risk there. You can't avoid the necessity of balancing to some degree.

So I reemphasize from looking at it, I would think I would come to the conclusion if I were Secretary of War, let us balance all the considerations here and take the calculated risk. It is too bad you have to calculate sometimes. But in the last analysis, you have to calculate what is best for the United States, because there is no Maginot Line in terms—it is just as weak as the Maginot Line in terms of security.

MR. GRAY. Do you understand that it is beyond the duty of this board to make the ultimate decision as to who shall be employed by the Government on the basis of his indispensability or otherwise?

THE WITNESS. Surely.

MR. GRAY. We are more narrowly concerned with the field of security as we understand the term.

THE WITNESS. I understand that.

MR. GRAY. I think I have no more questions. Dr. Evans.

DR. EVANS. Mr. McCloy, you say you talked to Bohr?

THE WITNESS. Yes; Neils Bohr.

DR. EVANS. Where did you talk to Neils?

THE WITNESS. I talked to him abroad and here. He visited Washington, you know.

DR. EVANS. I know. Did he tell you who split the uranium atom over there?

THE WITNESS. Wasn't it Hahn and Straussman?

DR. EVANS. Yes. I am just giving you a little quiz to find out how much you associated.

THE WITNESS. You terrify me.

DR. EVANS. Did you read Smyth's book?

THE WITNESS. Yes; I did. I was also tutored by Rabi; I may say that when Dr. Oppenheimer gave me up as a poor prospect.

DR. EVANS. And you think we should take some chances for fear we might disqualify someone who might do us a lot of good?

THE WITNESS. Yes; I do.

DR. EVANS. You do?

THE WITNESS. Yes.

II. CENSORSHIP and the NEWS

TEXT: "Mr. Krushchev and the Trade-Unionists of America" from The New York *Times,* September 22, 1959

[*The following is part of a verbatim report of the meeting of the Russian leader and some American trade-union officials.*]

KNIGHT. Mr. Chairman, since it took me so long to get the floor, I want to exercise my democratic rights and ask two questions. Mr. Chairman, you have made repeated statements regarding self-determination and the freedom of people from outside interference.

We agree with you on both of these principles. However, we cannot understand, since you say you favor the right of the German people both East and West to decide for themselves on unification, how do you visualize the German people making this decision since you continue to oppose a free and democratic vote by the German people on this issue.

My second question is, in view of your statements favoring self-determination and non-interference in the internal affairs of other nations and your statements supporting peaceful co-existence, how do you reconcile these statements with the harsh military suppression of the Hungarian Freedom Fighters by the Soviet military powers.

KHRUSHCHEV. The capitalists have certainly trained

some very good cadres. May I just give my thoughts aloud? Do you know anything about Germany? Have you ever been there? The German Democratic Republic is based on the most democratic foundations. There is no private ownership of the means of production.

KNIGHT. If it is on the most democratic foundations, then they should not be afraid of a democratic election.

REUTHER. In Eastern Germany there is only a one-party system.

(Interchange of ten voices.)

KNIGHT. Why do you oppose a democratic vote for reunification of Germany?

KHRUSHCHEV. It depends not on me but on the two Germanies.

KNIGHT. But you take a position against democratic re-unification in your propaganda throughout the world.

KHRUSHCHEV. Tell me where I said that. Hungary has its own constitution and laws, and is freely developing.

KNIGHT. Why did the Russians interfere in Hungary?

KHRUSHCHEV. There was no interference. There was a counter-revolution, thugs and hooligans who received arms from outside and took power in Budapest. And the Government asked us for aid and we gave it, and we're proud of it. We are proud of it as a feat. There would be fascism there if we had not.

REUTHER. Was Nagy a Fascist, I thought he was a Communist?

KHRUSHCHEV. Don't mix good things with dirt. [Exchanges around the table.] Have we exhausted the Hungarian question?

CAREY. We have touched on it; we have certainly not exhausted it.

(Phillips brought up the question of radio jamming of Radio Free Europe and Voice of America.)

KHRUSHCHEV. What do you prefer to have for dinner? [Looking at Phillips] What is your favorite dish?

PHILLIPS. Probably roast beef.

KHRUSHCHEV. I, borscht . . . You continue to enjoy roast beef, and I, borscht.

REUTHER. But you prescribe and insist on borscht for all.

KHRUSHCHEV (rising to his feet at 10:22 P. M.). If you don't read what I have stated, what can I expect . . .

REUTHER. You advocate more trade. How come you oppose a free flow of ideas.

KHRUSHCHEV. As head of the working class I will protect workers from capitalist propaganda.

(At this point, unexpectedly, Khrushchev, still on his feet, gave a burlesque demonstration of his idea of the can-can he witnessed during the Hollywood rehearsal of the forthcoming film "Can-Can." He turned his back to the table, bent downward, flipped his coat up and gave an imitation of the can-can.)

KHRUSHCHEV. This is a dance in which girls pull up their skirts. You're going to see that, we are not. This is what you call freedom—freedom for the girls to show their backsides. To us it's pornography. The culture of people who want pornography. It's capitalism that makes the girls that way.

(Khrushchev still on his feet while saying this.)

PHILLIPS. Does the Chairman think that the girls should be prohibited by law from showing their backsides.

KHRUSHCHEV. There should be a law prohibiting the girls from showing their backsides, a moral law.

CAREY. I may not see it, I may not want to see it——

KHRUSHCHEV. Your children will go to see it.

REUTHER. Perhaps it was a stupid movie—it was stupid of them to show it to you. But that has nothing to do with our question of why not a free flow of ideas between our countries?

KHRUSHCHEV. Why don't you want to trade with us? The sausage tastes the same in all countries.

(Khrushchev referred to the press conference statement by Georgi A. Zhukov on cultural exchange.)

CAREY. I will read this press statement and I'm sure that all of our colleagues will follow it up.

SATYUKOV (editor of Pravda). We printed in Pravda in full Reuther's statement at the unemployment conference in Washington. We didn't change a word, but at the same time the New York papers said that it was a Red scheme. We wrote back in Pravda there was no collusion between us and Reuther. The Voice of America didn't broadcast it. If it did, we wouldn't jam it.

REUTHER. No, you wouldn't because that report on unemployment would reflect upon us. But why didn't you and why don't you publish my May Day speech of this year in West Berlin? I invite you to publish and broadcast that speech.

KHRUSHCHEV. We only publish speeches that contribute to friendly relations between countries.

COMMENT: On What News Is

What took place in the above interview was not merely a discussion on self-determination among nations. The ostensible subject was merely the occasion for a great deal of propaganda and maneuvering for propaganda on both sides. However, when Mr. Reuther asked why Mr. Khrushchev opposed a free flow of ideas, the answer enlightens us on the completely different notion of "news" in Soviet Russia. Mr. Khrushchev would "protect" the workers . . . and he accused American trade unionists of calling freedom that absence of moral restraint which permits girls to perform a licentious dance. Finally, in Soviet Russia, they "only publish speeches that contribute to friendly relations between countries."

Mr. Khrushchev may have been exaggerating when he represented Russian newspapers as bodies eager to preserve the right spirit in the Russian public at the expense of the news; to a small extent, even the best newspapers of the West wish to do this—The New York *Times*'s motto is "All the news that's fit to print." But we gather from Russian newspapers themselves that the newspaper public is altogether ignorant of the Western idea of news and our idea of the proper function of a newspaper as simply a source of information. Only recently have news stories as such appeared in *Izvestia;* in *Pravda* there are none. Yet even in the West the value of the free flow of information is constantly being belittled. Recently President Kennedy asked newspaper proprietors to use self-censorship to safeguard matters of national security—a request likely to prove more dangerous than helpful to the American nation if carried out. The value of public opinion depends on the quality and quantity of the information given out by the newspapers. Of course the worst of the sensational press in the West is a long way from a devoted interest in the news and the background to the news, and it was probably to this sort of newspaper that Mr. Khrushchev was referring. It is surprising to find his views shared by an eminent person of the past.

TEXT: "A Nineteenth-Century Opinion of Newspapers" from a letter of Thomas Jefferson to John Norvell, June 11, 1807

Washington

To your request of my opinion of the manner in which a newspaper should be conducted so as to be most useful, I should answer, "by restraining it to true facts and sound principles only." Yet I fear such a paper would find few subscribers. It is a melancholy truth that a suppression of the press could not more completely deprive the nation of its benefits than is done by its abandoned prostitution to falsehood. Nothing can now be believed which is seen in a newspaper. Truth itself becomes suspicious by being put into that polluted vehicle. The real extent of this state of misinformation is known only to those who are in situations to confront facts within their knowledge with the lies of the day. I really look with commiseration over the great body of my fellow citizens who, reading newspapers, live and die in the belief that they have known something of what has been passing in the world in their time; whereas the accounts they have read in newspapers are just as true a history of any other period of the world as of the present except that the real names of the day are affixed to their fables. General facts may indeed be collected from them—such as that Europe is now at war, that Bonaparte has been a successful warrior, that he has subjected a great portion of Europe to his will, etc., etc., but no details can be relied on. I will add that the man who never looks into a newspaper is better informed than he who reads them, inasmuch as he who knows nothing is nearer to truth than he whose mind is filled with false-hoods and errors. He who reads nothing will still learn the great facts, and the details are all false.

Perhaps an editor might begin a reformation in some such way as this: divide his paper into four chapters, heading the first, Truths, 2nd, Probabilities, 3rd, Possibilities, 4th, Lies. The first chapter would be very short, as it would contain little more than authentic papers and information from such sources as the editor would be willing to risk his own reputation for their truth. The second would contain what, from a mature consideration of all circumstances, his judgment should con-clude to be probably true. This, however, should rather con-tain too little than too much. The third and fourth should be professedly for those readers who would rather have lies for their money than the blank paper they would occupy.

COMMENT: On the Function of the Modern Newspaper

A modern answer to Jefferson would of course state that the best newspapers of today are deeply responsible publications. So far as possible, great newspapers like The New York *Times,* *The Christian Science Monitor, The Times* of London, *The Guardian,* and *Le Monde,* present factual accounts, with selection and comment by editors playing small part in the presentation of the news. So far as possible they present actual verbatim reports. The New York *Times* goes further than any in its endeavor to separate comment from the fullest possible coverage. Reporters of this newspaper regard askance the British and Continental European habit of allowing explanation to appear under a journalist's name as part of the actual story, and of allowing the personality of the journalist to appear through such explanations. The "objectivity" of the *Times*'s journalism comes from following the same methods that Thomas Hobbes followed in his examination of phenomena outside the field of natural science, and though language itself and the importance of the journalist prevent a story from being in itself a phenomenon, we tend to regard it as such. How far astray this belief may lead us appears in the discrepancy between the common assumption of how the news is gathered and the knowledgeable account which follows.

Mr. Claud Cockburn was at one time a correspondent of *The Times* of London. He declined a professional plum, the Washington desk of that newspaper, when the Wall Street crash of 1929 had somewhat undermined his faith in capitalism. Believing "news" was created by piecing bits of information together, he started a weekly sheet in which to print the stories which were circulating in influential quarters but which ordinary newspapers dared not touch for fear of prosecution or of scandal. Not responsible to advertisers or to press lords or to what has since come to be called "the Establishment," Cockburn was able to print stories that never appeared elsewhere. The consequences must have occasionally appeared alarming.

TEXT: "The Factual Heresy" from *A Discord of Trumpets* by Claud Cockburn

"If you go on like this," said Mr. John Wheeler-Bennett, then head of the Royal Institute of International Affairs at Chatham House, "you will soon, I should think, be either quite famous or in jail."

"Lots of people," I said, "have been both."

"That," he said, turning upon me his luminous smile and beaming as though an awkward question had now been satisfactorily resolved, "is so."

A lot of people who—by constantly talking of *The Week*, complaining of it, denouncing it as a horrible liar and even praising it—were helping to make this tiny sheet "quite famous" were also of opinion that something terrible must be going to happen to *The Week* pretty soon. Mr. Kingsley Martin, editor of the *New Statesman*, who had been very kind to me personally and wished us well, was one of these. Once he wrote in his column in the *New Statesman* that he had been waiting for a fortnight for the "heavens to fall" as a result of a particular disclosure in *The Week*—it was fairly clear from the context that what the heavens were going to fall upon was me. Another time he came briefly to my office to tell me that he had just read the current issue and wanted to warn me that to his mind the only doubt as to the result was whether I should get out with a heavy fine or suffer a sharp jail sentence into the bargain.

The Criminal Libel Law and the Official Secrets Act—one or other of which we apparently infringed about twice a month —were the instruments which people imagined were going to send me to jail. Since, as I have said, I had no lawyer to bother me about such things and since nobody but myself could pos-

sibly be involved in whatever unpleasantness might arise, I was
saved all the advance worry which nags at people on other
types of paper when they are handling dynamite, and by being simply ignorant on whether I was infringing some law or
not, saved myself from the temptation which otherwise, I make
no doubt, would have often been irresistible—to omit or tone
down reports of facts and reports of rumors merely on the
ground that to publish them might land one in the courts. We
were, of course, repeatedly threatened with libel actions, but
none of them was ever brought and none was ever settled out
of court.

When deciding whether or not to write a story which was
obviously, in the legal sense, libelous but which I believed to
be true and of some public interest, I used instead of a lawyer
a simple criterion of my own: In case he brings an action, I
asked myself, which of us in the end will look more ridiculous?
On the whole, this criterion worked fairly well. When the
emissaries of the libeled came to see me with threats and men-
aces, they were immediately discouraged by the evident pov-
erty of our organization. Their usual technique was then to
demand an unqualified apology. This I invariably refused on
principle although always expressing readiness to write another
story on the same subject giving any facts they might choose
to supply tending to show that the earlier story had been base-
less. It was at this point that one could usually detect from
their expression that the thought passing through their minds
was that which had passed through mine earlier—namely, that
if their client took the case to court he would probably make
more of a monkey out of himself that he was likely to make
out of me.

How often we really infringed the Official Secrets Act or
were suspected by the authorities of espionage or improper relations with public servants for the purpose of extracting state
secrets, I have no idea. For the first eighteen months or so,
at any rate, we were highly suspect—naturally, and for the
same reason that I had been suspect in Berlin, namely, that
we had no easily recognizable fancy dress and the authorities
were somewhat in the position of the drunken Dutchman in the
musical comedy who gets by accident into the middle of a

fancy-dress ball and runs frantically from person to person imploring them, "Do please tell me once and for each what are you *as?*"

Obviously, the authorities would much rather deal with people who are visibly members of some recognized political organization, and I had a lot of evidence that they were considerably worried by not knowing what I was "as."

The real situation was quite otherwise.

Long ago, Wilmott Lewis had drawn my attention to what he called the "factual heresy" or the "illusion of spot news."

It would be tedious to examine the historical phenomena which had produced in the public mind a belief that the desirable thing to read in a newspaper is the "inside news" and still more the illusion in the public mind that the newspaper, or rather the reporter, really has "inside news."

Wilmott Lewis, who was usually right about such matters, took the view that about ninety per cent of what the public conceived to be "inside news" or "spot news" is either something so trivial or obvious that it is not worth writing about or else is not "inside news" at all, in the sense of being something secret and confidential, but is the kind of information which any highly informed and reasonably intelligent person could piece together from, say, a week's reading of all available newspapers and a week's conversation with all available sources. And even this, he used to insist, is not enough. News, he used to say, is in itself nothing. Presentation is almost everything. The entire question, he would insist, is a question of style.

I have seen people who, as he made these observations, came rapidly to the idiotic conclusion that the creative journalistic process is much simpler than it really is—you could see them beginning to imagine that all the man had to do was to sit about reading and talking, and presently, having developed his "style," present the matter in coruscating prose. This, of course, is untrue too, and the reason why Lewis, for example, leaned over backward talking about style, and the reason why it is necessary to do so repeatedly, is that although in the early days of journalism style was emphasized to the point where the role of the "facts" was merely forgotten, nowadays the "factual heresy" is a dangerous one.

To hear people talking about the facts you would think that they lay about like pieces of gold ore in the Yukon days, waiting to be picked up—arduously, it is true, but still definitely and visible—by strenuous prospectors whose subsequent problem was only how to get them to market.

Such a view is evidently and dangerously naïve. There are no such facts. Or if there are, they are meaningless and entirely ineffective; might in fact just as well not be lying about at all until the prospector—the journalist—puts them into relation with other facts; presents them, in fact, and then they become as much a part of a pattern created by him as if he were writing a novel. In that sense, all stories are written backward —they are supposed to begin with the facts and develop from there, but in reality they begin with a journalist's point of view, a conception, and it is the point of view from which the facts are subsequently organized. Journalistically speaking, "in the beginning is the word." All this is difficult and even rather unwholesome to explain to the layman, because he gets the impression that what you are saying is that truth does not matter and that you are publicly admitting what he long ago suspected—that journalism is a way of "cooking" the facts. Really cunning journalists, realizing this and anxious to raise the status of journalism in the esteem of the general public, positively encourage the layman in his mistaken views—they like him to have the picture of these maggotty facts lying about on maybe frozen ground and a lot of noble and utterly unprejudiced journalists with no idea whatever of what they are looking for scrabbling in the ironbound earth and presently bringing home the pure gold of Truth.

When I had to start explaining what *The Week* was trying to do, I did myself a good deal of harm by being rather too frank about this matter. To make matters worse, I went about saying that rumors were just as important, just as significant, just as—in the last analysis—"valid" as "facts."

This shocked people horribly, although if you pressed them and asked whether it was not true that ninety per cent of "information received" by such serious persons as ambassadors and chiefs of police really consists in significant rumors and rumors which can be interpreted by the person who knows enough rumors, they were usually bound to admit that this is indeed the case. Contemporaries on the existing weekly newspapers used to complain that *The Week* published rumors which they themselves refused to publish until they were confirmed. One was reminded of the atheistic young man who has told the believer that he would never believe anything that he did not understand, to which the believer replied, "Young man, your beliefs are likely to be small."

In the same way, people who refused to print anything that was not a confirmed fact were likely to print very little of general interest. And I found that attitude arrogant, for unless one imagines one is God, how on earth can one tell truth from rumor in less than perhaps fifty years? And fifty years is too long to wait if one is in the business of issuing a weekly newspaper.

So far as *The Week*'s news-gathering operations were concerned, they were conducted for the most part on a barter basis with a group of what were then the best informed and most lively-minded correspondents in London.

They included Mr. Farson, correspondent of the Chicago *Daily News;* Mr. Stefan Litauer, correspondent of the Polish News Agency; Mr. Paul Scheffer, correspondent of the *Berliner Tageblatt;* and a varying group of French correspondents.

Two or three times a week we met around noon in Mr. Farson's office at Bush House and pooled our information. And on the days we did not meet, we pooled information over the telephone. To describe this pool as a "group" would be to use too formal a word, but—owing, I think, to Mr. Farson's guidance—we all of us came to realize that there was something to be said for regular exchanges even when there seemed to be no news at all. The mere fact of each in turn going through a kind of "total recall" of what had been said by informants—diplomats, financiers and others—during the course of the past forty-eight hours was clarificatory and often produced a piece of the great jigsaw which otherwise could have been overlooked or forgotten. Usually, of course, there was plenty of news. There was news which, for example, Mr. Farson could not handle for his paper but which was exactly suited to *The Week*. Everyone had something to contribute, everyone picked out of the bag what suited his own requirements. Apart from what *The Week* could directly contribute to the pool, it had a special role to play, a special utility. Of course there were innumerable stories which, for example, Mr. Farson or Mr. Litauer could not venture to send directly to their papers or news agencies but which they could send if they just appeared in *The Week* and could thus be quoted instead of being sent on the responsibility of the correspondents.

The French were particularly good at playing this game. And as time went on, this group—every member of which had his own special contacts with news sources in London, his own confidential sources of news in his own country and a lively awareness between the apparently significant news and the news that really was significant in the light of knowledge of the basic trends—made up a pretty formidable information center.

And then naturally the whole business "snowballed." When it was seen what kind of stories *The Week* uniquely would handle, all sorts of people—for motives sometimes noble and quite often vile—would approach *The Week* to draw its attention to the most extraordinary pieces of more or less confidential information. Sometimes it came from frustrated newspapermen who could not get what they considered vital news into their own papers. More often such confidences were the outcome of obscure financial or diplomatic duels. They would come, for instance, from the councillor of an Embassy who was convinced of the wrongheaded policy of the Foreign Office and the Ambassador and wished, without exposing himself, to put a spoke in their wheel. . . .

COMMENT: On Opinion and the Public

The emergence of responsible Western newspapers out of the scurrilous mass to which Jefferson referred coincided with general enfranchisement and general education. As both these factors were denied in Russia until long after they were established and effective elsewhere, the connection between them and a popular press has been missing in that country. In cases where the connection existed, the independent minority's dissatisfaction with the popular press and the need for comment invited certain newspapers to set themselves up as arbiters and circulators of informed opinion. Today's papers create public opinion as well as reflect it. The way they answer to public opinion on such questions as capital punishment suggests that they act as organs of the public judgment, just as, according to Rousseau, censorship acts as "the declaration of the public judgment." Though it may be curious to think of newspapers acting as censors, Rousseau's words on the function of public censors are strikingly apt as a description of the function of a responsible newspaper as a platform of public dissent. "Public opinion is the form of law which the censor administers, and, like the prince, only applies to particular cases.

"The censorial tribunal, so far from being the arbiter of the people's opinion, only declares it, and, as soon as the two part company, its decisions are null and void . . . The opinions of a people are derived from its constitution; although the law does not regulate morality, it is legislation that gives it birth. When legislation grows weak, morality degenerates; but in such cases the judgment of the censors will not do what the force of the laws has failed to effect."[2]

In America, public opinion tends to be more tacit than in

other countries of the West, and more local, because most newspapers lack national readership and because other platforms of national dissent are lacking. Remarkably few American newspapers can afford a foreign correspondent. Though the character of the nation as a whole and the character of newspapers have changed since he wrote, Tocqueville's indication in 1834 of the kinds of censorship that the American system produces still holds good. Too often, in a flattering appraisal of a situation in which official censorship is lacking, people easily discount the equally strong and dangerous censorship exercised by a narrow, ill-informed public opinion. This after all is exercised by the performance of the general will, in Rousseau's terms; it is therefore incident to rule by the people. The other kind of censorship exercised in the United States, by Post Office and Customs, is carried on outside the terms of the social contract altogether.

TEXT: "Liberty of the Press in the United States" from *Democracy in America* by Alexis de Tocqueville

[The Henry Reeve text; revised by Francis Bowen and Phillips Bradley]

The influence of the liberty of the press does not affect political opinions alone, but extends to all the opinions of men and modifies customs as well as laws. In another part of this work I shall attempt to determine the degree of influence that the liberty of the press has exercised upon civil society in the United States and to point out the direction which it has given to the ideas as well as the tone which it has imparted to the character and the feelings of the Anglo-Americans. At present I propose only to examine the effects produced by the liberty of the press in the political world. I confess that I do not entertain that firm and complete attachment to the liberty of the press which is wont to be excited by things that are supremely good in their very nature. I approve of it from a consideration more of the evils it prevents than of the advantages it ensures.

If anyone could point out an intermediate and yet a tenable position between the complete independence and the entire servitude of opinion, I should perhaps be inclined to adopt it, but the difficulty is to discover this intermediate position. Intending to correct the licentiousness of the press and to restore the use of orderly language, you first try the offender by a jury; but if the jury acquits him, the opinion which was that of a single individual becomes the opinion of the whole country. Too much and too little has therefore been done; go farther, then. You bring the delinquent before permanent magistrates; but even here the cause must be heard before it can be decided; and the very principles which no book would have ventured to avow are blazoned forth in the pleadings, and what was obscurely hinted at in a single composition is thus repeated in a multitude of other publications. The language is only the expression and, if I may so speak, the body of the thought, but it is not the thought itself. Tribunals may condemn the body, but the sense, the spirit of the work is too subtle for their authority. Too much has still been done to recede, too little to attain your end; you must go still farther. Establish a censorship of the press. But the tongue of the public speaker will still make itself heard, and your purpose is not yet accomplished; you have only increased the mischief. Thought is not, like physical strength, dependent upon the number of its agents; nor can authors be counted like the troops that compose an army. On the contrary, the authority of a principle is often increased by the small number of men by whom it is expressed. The words of one strong-minded man addressed to the passions of a listening assembly have more power than the vociferations of a thousand orators; and if it be allowed to speak freely in any one public place, the consequence is the same as if free speaking was allowed in every village. The liberty of speech must therefore be destroyed as well as the liberty of the press. And now you have succeeded, everybody is reduced to silence. But your object was to repress the abuses of liberty, and you are brought to the feet of a despot. You have been led from the extreme of independence to the extreme of servitude without finding a single tenable position on the way at which you could stop.

There are certain nations which have peculiar reasons for cherishing the liberty of the press, independently of the general motives that I have just pointed out. For in certain countries which profess to be free, every individual agent of the government may violate the laws with impunity, since the constitution does not give to those who are injured a right of complaint before the courts of justice. In this case the liberty of the press is not merely one of the guarantees, but it is the only guarantee of their liberty and security that the citizens possess. If the rulers of these nations proposed to abolish the independence of the press, the whole people might answer: Give us the right of prosecuting your offenses before the ordinary tribunals, and perhaps we may then waive our right of appeal to the tribunal of public opinion.

In countries where the doctrine of the sovereignty of the people ostensibly prevails, the censorship of the press is not only dangerous, but absurd. When the right of every citizen to a share in the government of society is acknowledged, everyone must be presumed to be able to choose between the various opinions of his contemporaries and to appreciate the different facts from which inferences may be drawn. The sovereignty of the people and the liberty of the press may therefore be regarded as correlative, just as the censorship of the press and universal suffrage are two things which are irreconcilably opposed and which cannot long be retained among the institutions of the same people. Not a single individual of the millions who inhabit the United States has as yet dared to propose any restrictions on the liberty of the press. The first newspaper over which I cast my eyes, upon my arrival in America, contained the following article:

> In all this affair, the language of Jackson [the President] has been that of a heartless despot, solely occupied with the preservation of his own authority. Ambition is his crime, and it will be his punishment, too: intrigue is his native element, and intrigue will confound his tricks, and deprive him of his power. He governs by means of corruption, and his immoral practices will redound to his shame and confusion. His conduct in the political arena has been that of a shameless and lawless gamester. He succeeded at the time; but the hour of retribution approaches, and he will be obliged to disgorge his winnings, to throw aside his false dice, and to end his days in some retirement, where he may curse his madness at his leisure; for repentance is a virtue with which his heart is likely to remain forever unacquainted. (VINCENNE's *Gazette.*)

Many persons in France think that the violence of the press originates in the instability of the social state, in our political passions and the general feeling of uneasiness that consequently prevails; and it is therefore supposed that as soon as society has resumed a certain degree of composure, the press will abandon its present vehemence. For my own part, I would willingly attribute to these causes the extraordinary ascendancy which the press has acquired over the nation; but I do not think that they exercise much influence on its language. The periodical press appears to me to have passions and instincts of its own, independent of the circumstances in which it is placed; and the present condition of America corroborates this opinion.

America is perhaps, at this moment, the country of the whole world that contains the fewest germs of revolution; but the press is not less destructive in its principles there than in France, and it displays the same violence without the same reasons for indignation. In America as in France it constitutes a singular power, so strangely composed of mingled good and evil that liberty could not live without it, and public order can hardly be maintained against it. Its power is certainly much greater in France than in the United States, though nothing is more rare in the latter country than to hear of a prosecution being instituted against it. The reason for this is perfectly simple: the Americans, having once admitted the doctrine of the sovereignty of the people, apply it with perfect sincerity. It was never their intention out of elements which are changing every day to create institutions that should last forever; and there is consequently nothing criminal in an attack upon the existing laws, provided a violent infraction of them is not intended. They are also of the opinion that courts of justice are powerless to check the abuses of the press, and that, as the subtlety of human language perpetually eludes judicial analysis, offenses of this nature somehow escape the hand which attempts to seize them. They hold that to act with efficacy upon the press it would be necessary to find a tribunal not only devoted to the existing order of things, but capable of surmounting the influence of public opinion; a tribunal which should conduct its proceedings without publicity, which should pronounce its decrees without assigning its motives, and punish the intentions even more than the language of a writer. Whoever should be able to create and maintain a tribunal of this kind would waste his time in prosecuting the liberty of the press; for he would be the absolute master of the whole community and would be as free to rid himself of the authors as of their writings. In this question, therefore, there is no medium between servitude and license; in order to enjoy the inestimable benefits that the liberty of the press ensures, it is necessary to submit to the inevitable evils that it creates. To expect to acquire the former and to escape the latter is to cherish one of those illusions which commonly mislead nations in their times of sickness when, tired with faction and exhausted by effort, they attempt to make hostile opinions and contrary principles coexist upon the same soil. . . .

TEXT: "The Unlimited Power of the Majority" from *Democracy in America* by Alexis de Tocqueville

[The Henry Reeve text; revised by Francis Bowen and Phillips Bradley]

It is in the examination of the exercise of thought in the United States that we clearly perceive how far the power of the majority surpasses all the powers with which we are acquainted in Europe. Thought is an invisible and subtle power that mocks all the efforts of tyranny. At the present time the most absolute monarchs in Europe cannot prevent certain opinions hostile to their authority from circulating in secret through their dominions and even in their courts. It is not so in America; as long as the majority is still undecided, discussion is carried on; but as soon as its decision is irrevocably pronounced, everyone is silent, and the friends as well as the opponents of the measure unite in assenting to its propriety. The reason for this is perfectly clear: no monarch is so absolute as to combine all the powers of society in his own hands and to conquer all opposition, as a majority is able to do, which has the right both of making and of executing the laws.

The authority of a king is physical and controls the actions of men without subduing their will. But the majority possesses a power that is physical and moral at the same time, which acts upon the will as much as upon the actions and represses not only all contest, but all controversy.

I know of no country in which there is so little independence of mind and real freedom of discussion as in America. In any constitutional state in Europe every sort of religious and political theory may be freely preached and disseminated; for there is no country in Europe so subdued by any single authority as not to protect the man who raises his voice in the cause of truth from the consequences of his hardihood. If he is unfortunate enough to live under an absolute government, the people are often on his side; if he inhabits a free country, he can, if necessary, find a shelter behind the throne. The aristocratic part of society supports him in some countries, and the democracy in others. But in a nation where democratic institutions exist, organized like those of the United States, there is but one authority, one element of strength and success, with nothing beyond it.

In America the majority raises formidable barriers around the liberty of opinion; within these barriers an author may write what he pleases, but woe to him if he goes beyond them. Not that he is in danger of an auto-da-fé, but he is exposed to continued obloquy and persecution. His political career is closed forever, since he has offended the only authority that is able to open it. Every sort of compensation, even that of celebrity, is refused to him. Before making public his opinions he thought he had sympathizers; now it seems to him that he has none any more since he has revealed himself to everyone; then those who blame him criticize loudly and those who think as he does keep quiet and move away without courage. He yields at length, overcome by the daily effort which he has to make, and subsides into silence, as if he felt remorse for having spoken the truth.

Fetters and headsmen were the coarse instruments that tyranny formerly employed; but the civilization of our age has perfected despotism itself, though it seemed to have nothing to learn. Monarchs had, so to speak, materialized oppression; the democratic republics of the present day have rendered it as entirely an affair of the mind as the will which it is intended to coerce. Under the absolute sway of one man the body was attacked in order to subdue the soul; but the soul escaped the blows which were directed against it and rose proudly superior. Such is not the course adopted by tyranny in democratic republics; there the body is left free, and the soul is enslaved. The master no longer says: "You shall think as I do or you shall die"; but he says: "You are free to think differently from me and to retain your life, your property, and all that you possess; but you are henceforth a stranger among your people. You may retain your civil rights, but they will be useless to you, for you will never be chosen by your fellow citizens if you solicit their votes; and they will affect to scorn you if you ask for their esteem. You will remain among men, but you will be deprived of the rights of mankind. Your fellow creatures will shun you like an impure being; and even those who believe in your innocence will abandon you, lest they should be shunned in their turn. Go in peace! I have given you your life, but it is an existence worse than death."

Absolute monarchies had dishonored despotism; let us beware lest democratic republics should reinstate it and render it less odious and degrading in the eyes of the many by making it still more onerous to the few.

Works have been published in the proudest nations of the Old World expressly intended to censure the vices and the follies of the times: Labruyère inhabited the palace of Louis XIV when he composed his chapter upon the Great, and Molière criticized the courtiers in the plays that were acted before the court. But the ruling power in the United States is not to be made game of. The smallest reproach irritates its sensibility, and the slightest joke that has any foundation in truth renders it indignant; from the forms of its language up to the solid virtues of its character, everything must be made the subject of encomium. No writer, whatever be his eminence, can escape paying this tribute of adulation to his fellow citizens. The majority lives in the perpetual utterance of self-applause, and there are certain truths which the Americans can learn only from strangers or from experience.

If America has not as yet had any great writers, the reason is given in these facts; there can be no literary genius without freedom of opinion, and freedom of opinion does not exist in America. The Inquisition has never been able to prevent a vast number of anti-religious books from circulating in Spain. The empire of the majority succeeds much better in the United States, since it actually removes any wish to publish them. Unbelievers are to be met with in America, but there is no public

organ of infidelity. Attempts have been made by some governments to protect morality by prohibiting licentious books. In
the United States no one is punished for this sort of books,
but no one is induced to write them; not because all the citizens are immaculate in conduct, but because the majority of
the community is decent and orderly. . . .

COMMENT: On the Emergence of Popular Opinion as a Curb on Power

The emergence of public opinion as a political force, distinct from the mob in having respect for law, and having an effect on the government of the day, appears in the history of John Wilkes, editor of *The North Briton*. From the moment of his accession, George III and his favorite, the Scottish Lord Bute, were bitterly denounced in the press for their efforts to gather power back to the Crown. John Wilkes became the champion of liberty as a consequence of denunciation that went further than most and led to his prosecution for libel against the King. Wilkes was a Member of Parliament (through patronage) and therefore entitled to certain privileges; in his efforts to preserve his parliamentary privilege to utter criticism of the King's policies (which the King conveniently found libelous), Wilkes found himself almost by chance consolidating, if not instituting, once and for all the parallel privilege of the press.

Though the British press had been granted full privileges in 1692, a glance at the supposedly incendiary No. 45 of *The North Briton*, so called in derision of Lord Bute, shows that criticism of authority could not, by our standards, go at all far. The responsibilities of the Crown had been so far taken over by the Prime Minister that if the King had not been set on reclaiming his personal power, Wilkes's censures might easily have been ignored, with the understanding that they were not personally intended. Unfortunately, as the censures were dangerous to the royal policies which the King had adopted to subdue his political enemies, he was pleased to take them as an affront to the Crown itself. Yet in no sense do the censures strike the modern reader as critical of the King personally. The prosecution of Wilkes was clearly a purely party-political attack, and Wilkes appears to us well within his rights as a Member of Parliament to criticize official policy wherever it originated. The precise object of his criticism was the peace concluding the Seven Years' War, by which the King's Party relinquished many of the trophies and prizes of land won in battle by British forces, for the sake of a party-political victory over the Whigs, and especially over Pitt, who had conducted the war; by this wasteful peace treaty, also, the allies of Britain, notably Prussia, were abandoned to pursue the war as best they might.

It is still something of a lesson to read of the ferocity and meanness of the official attack, so neatly paralleled by French police actions today against critics of the Army. It is even more of a lesson to read of the independence and fairness of the judiciary in that corrupt and dissolute age. Wilkes managed to grow in popular esteem both as a victim and as a hero— scandalous, gallant, extremely brave, he forced the issue at all times.

Horace Walpole thought that his recollections of the period were scandalous enough to be sealed for twenty years after his death, and they still keep their sting. We take the text from the first volume, ending the subject long before the author does, as the Wilkes case belongs as much to the history of parliamentary representation as to that of censorship; after the first stage, it is concerned with the long battle for a seat in Parliament to which Wilkes was often elected by the men of Middlesex and as often rejected by his peers.

The extracts begin when Bute ("the Favourite"), having appointed some friends to office, was considering retirement. He was soon to be succeeded by the "Triumvirate," chief of whom was the Lord Grenville, who set out the general warrant by which Wilkes was originally arrested. William Pitt the Elder was at this time in opposition.

TEXT: "The Wilkes Affair" from *Memoirs of the Reign of George III* by Horace Walpole

These successes and the tide of power swelled the weak bladder of the Favourite's mind to the highest pitch. His own style was haughty and distant; that of his creatures insolent. Many persons who had absented themselves from his levée were threatened with the loss of their own, or the places of their relations, and were obliged to bow the knee. But this sunshine drew up very malignant vapours. Scarce was the earl seated but one step below the throne, when a most virulent weekly paper appeared, called the *North Briton*. Unawed by the prosecution of the *Monitor* (another opponent periodic satire, the author of which had been taken up for abusing favourites), and though combated by two Court papers called the *Briton* and the *Auditor* (the former written by Smollet, and the latter by Murphy, and both which the new champion fairly silenced in a few weeks), the *North Briton* proceeded with an acrimony, a spirit, and a licentiousness unheard of before even in this country. The highest names, whether of statesmen or magistrates, were printed at length, and the insinuations went still higher. In general, favouritism was the topic, and the partiality of the Court to the Scots. . . .

On reflection it was not thought advisable to enter on the discussion of such a subject in Westminster Hall; and, as the daring audaciousness of the writer promised little decorum, it was held prudent to wait till he should furnish a less delicate handle to vengeance: a circumspection that deceived and fell heavy on the author, who, being advised to more caution in his compositions, replied, he had tried the temper of the Court by the paper on Mortimer, and found they did not dare to touch him.

This author, who must be so often mentioned in the following pages, was John Wilkes, member of Parliament for Ailesbury. He was of a plebeian family, but inherited a tolerable fortune in Buckinghamshire, and had been bred at Oxford, where he distinguished himself by humorous attacks on whatever was esteemed most holy and respectable. Unrestrained either in his conduct or conversation, he was allowed to have more wit than in truth he possessed; and, living with rakes and second-rate authors, he had acquired fame, such as it was, in the middling sphere of life, before his name was so much as known to the public. His appearance as an orator had by no means conspired to make him more noticed. He spoke coldly and insipidly, though with impertinence; his manner was poor, and his countenance horrid. When his pen, which possessed an easy impudent style, had drawn the attention of mankind towards him, and it was asked, who this saucy writer was? Fame, that had adopted him, could furnish but scurvy anecdotes of his private life. He had married a woman of fortune, used her ill, and at last cruelly, to extort from her the provision he had made for her separate maintenance; he had debauched a maiden of family by an informal promise of marriage, and had been guilty of other frauds and breaches of trust. Yet the man, bitter as he was in his political writings, was commonly not ill-natured or acrimonious. Wantonness, rather than ambition or vengeance, guided his hand; and, though he became the martyr of the best cause, there was nothing in his principles or morals that led him to care under what government he lived. To laugh and riot and scatter firebrands with him was liberty. Despotism will for ever reproach Freedom with the profligacy of such a saint! . . .

As soon as it was known that Lord Bute intended to quit, Wilkes had forborne to publish his *North Britons;* waiting to see the consequences of the change. The tone he had given did not, however, stop. In the City they toasted to Wit, Beauty, Virtue, and Honour, ironic designations of the King, Queen, Princess Dowager, and Lord Bute. The *North Briton,* too, was soon resumed, and on the 23rd of April was published the memorable *forty-fifth* number, which occasioned so much trouble to the author, procured so essential a correction of loose and, till then, undefined power, and produced so many silly conundrums and wretched witticisms on the number itself. This famous paper gave a flat lie to the King himself, for having, by the Favourite's suggestion, assumed the honour of obtaining peace for the King of Prussia.

Nothing could be more just than the satire, nothing more bold than the unmeasured liberty with which it was uttered. The Prussian monarch must have read with scorn, and Europe with laughter, so absurd a boast as our vaunting to have saved an ally whom we had betrayed and abandoned. Ridicule might have handled this vainglorious falsehood with full severity and full security, without passing the bounds which law allows. But when Parliament had connived at the treachery, could it be supposed that it would suffer a private hand to wield the bolt which had slept in the custody of so many corrupt representatives? The lie given in print to the Crown, by an obscure man, was an unparalleled licence. If the King had a particle of power left, or his servants, or his magistrates, of spirit, such an insult could not be passed over. The rashness of his servants contrived to involve the Crown and themselves in inextricable difficulties, and to make the unwarrantable behaviour of Wilkes appear innocent, when compared with the excesses they committed themselves.

I do not mean to lead the reader through the maze of vague and barbarous law-proceedings, which sprang out of this transaction. It did but lay open the undefined or unmeaning magazine of terms which the chicanery or contradictions of ages had heaped together, and it proved that the Crown and the subject might be justified in almost any excesses. The right hand of Nonsense armed the King, and her left defended the subject. The lawyers on either side were employed in discovering springes or loop-holes.

After a week's deliberation Wilkes was seized, April 30th, by three messengers, on a *general warrant,* signed by Lord Halifax. They had been ordered to apprehend him at midnight, but abstained till noon of the 30th. Churchill, his friend, then with him, slipped out of the house, either to secure himself or to give the alarm. Mr. Wood, the Under-Secretary, and Philip Carteret Webbe, a most villanous tool and agent in any iniquity, seized his papers, though he had received intimation time enough to convey away the most material. He was conducted to Lord Halifax's, where he behaved with much firmness and confidence, and grievously wounded the haughty dignity attempted to be assumed by Lord Egremont. They committed him close prisoner to the Tower; a severity rarely, and never fit to be, practised but in cases of most dangerous treason. This treatment served but to increase Wilkes's spirit and wit. He desired to be confined in the same room where Sir William Windham, Lord Egremont's father, had been kept on a charge of Jacobitism; and said he hoped, if there could be found such a chamber in the Tower, that he might not be lodged where any Scotchman had been prisoner.

About the same time, being told of the reasons alleged by the King of Spain for setting aside his eldest son, two of which were, that the Prince squinted, and did not believe the mysteries of our holy religion; then said Wilkes, 'I can never be King of Spain, for I squint, and believe none of those mysteries.'

The rigour of the commitment gave serious alarm; but, the very day on which it happened, Wilkes's friends applied to the Court of Common Pleas for his habeas corpus, expecting it from Lord Chief Justice Pratt, and scorning or despairing of it from Lord Mansfield.

Lord Temple[3] instantly resorted to the Tower, but was denied admittance to the prisoner; a restraint the ministers found the very next day they must take off. Lord Temple then returned to visit Wilkes, as did the Duke of Grafton and some few others of rank; but, in general, the prisoner's character was so bad, and his conduct so rash and unguarded, that few who were either decent or cautious cared to be concerned with him.

The habeas corpus being granted, Wilkes was carried to the Court of Common Pleas, May 3rd. He spoke for an hour, said 'attempts had been made to corrupt him, now to persecute him; he had been worse treated than any rebel Scot.' The crowd in Westminster Hall gave a great shout; the Chief Justice, with great dignity, reproved them. The judges took time to deliberate. The people were profuse of their acclamations to the sufferer.

On the 5th, he wrote a letter to his daughter (a child whom he had placed in a convent in France for her education), and sent it open to Lord Halifax; it congratulated her on living in a *free* country. He was the same day turned out of his commission in the militia.

On the 6th, being again conveyed from the Tower to Westminster Hall, Pratt and the other judges of the Common Pleas unanimously discharged him from his confinement; the Chief Justice delivering their opinions, and dismissing him on his parliamentary privilege, 'because, though privilege of Parliament does not hold against a breach of the peace, it does against what only *tends* to a breach of the peace. . . .'

The Chief Justice had no sooner granted the enlargement of Wilkes, than two of the King's sergeants presented letters to the Court, from the Attorney and Solicitor Generals, demanding to be admitted into the Court, as the case concerned the King's interest. The Attorney, it is said, has a right of interfering in any Court where the King's interest is agitated; it is doubted whether the Solicitor has the same prerogative. To both Pratt answered that they had applied too late. Now did the Court feel the consequence of having forced Pratt to be Chief Justice against his will.

This triumph quite overset the little discretion of which Wilkes had been master. He seemed to put himself into the situation of a King, who, not content with the outworks with which the law has surrounded his person, attempts to employ the law as offensive artillery. Affecting to have been robbed of moveables when his papers were seized, Wilkes entered into a virulent controversy, by letter, with the Secretaries of State; and even endeavoured, though in vain, to obtain warrants for searching their houses. This wild conduct did not help his cause. His next step fell more perniciously on his own head. He erected a printing-press in his own house; and, against the remonstrances of Lord Temple, who never wanted fear where there was room for it, and who had no taste for anything that did not lead directly home to faction, indulged himself in realizing those sallies of his humour and intemperance, which

are scarcely excusable when transient and confined to the jol-
lity of intoxicated moments at table. The Court regarding Lord
Temple as the instigator, not as the Socrates, of this Alcibiades,
removed him from the Lord-Lieutenancy of the county of
Buckingham. The printers, who had been vexed in their business by the orders of the Secretaries of State, and encouraged
by the victory of Wilkes, prosecuted the messengers, and obtained damages to the value of £300. . . .

In one point the Favourite and his rivals agreed; that is, in
the destruction of Wilkes. The rashness and despotic conduct
of the triumvirate had made them parties in the same cause;
they pursuing him with what they called Law, and the Scotch
without attention to any law. . . .

[*The means to persecute Wilkes soon came to hand. On November 15, 1763, in the House of Lords,*]

Lord Sandwich produced a poem, called an *Essay on
Woman*, with notes pretended to be written by Bishop Warburton. It was a performance bawdy and blasphemous to the
last degree, being a parody of Pope's *Essay on Man,* and of
other pieces, adapted to the grossest ideas, or to the most profane. Wilkes and Potter, son of the late Archbishop of Canterbury, had formerly composed this indecent patchwork in
some of their bacchanalian hours; and Wilkes, not content with
provoking the vengeance of the King, of the Princess, of the
Favourite, of twenty subaltern ministers, and of the whole
Scottish nation, had, for the amusement of his idle hours, con-
signed this *innocent* rhapsody to his own printing-press—a folly
unparalleled, though he had intended to restrain the edition
to twelve copies. However, as he could not commit a wanton
imprudence without giving birth to some villany or tyranny in
others, this very poem was now laid before the House of Lords
in consequence of a train of both kinds. One of the copies had
been seized among his papers by Philip Carteret Webbe. Still
was even that ministry ashamed to accuse Wilkes on evidence
which had fallen into their hands by such illegal means—unanswerable proof that they were conscious of their guilt, and
knew they could not justify their proceedings. But the blood-
hounds having thus fallen on the scent, were not to be turned

aside by delicacies. Could they procure another copy the business would be effected—and effected it was. Carteret Webbe set his tools to work, for even hangmen have deputies. There was one Kidgell, a dainty priggish parson, much in vogue among the old ladies for his gossiping and quaint sermons, and chaplain to the Scotch Earl of March. This fellow got at a proof-sheet; and by the treachery of one of Wilkes's printers, who thought himself ill-used, and by the encouragement of his patron, who consulted Lord Bute and Lord Sandwich, and was egged on by them to proceed, Kidgell and Webbe purchased the whole poem: and now did Sandwich, who had hugged this mischief for months in his breast, lay open the precious poem before his brother Lords in strains of more hypocrisy than would have been tolerable even in a professed Methodist. Parts of it were read, most coarsely and disgustingly blasphemous. Lord Lyttelton groaned in spirit, and begged they might hear no more. Bishop Warburton, who had not the luck, like Lord Lyttelton, to have his conversion believed by any one, foamed with the violence of a Saint Dominic; vaunted that he had combated infidelity, and laid it under his feet; and said, the blackest fiends in hell would not keep company with Wilkes, and then begged Satan's pardon for comparing them together.

Lord Temple had got no intelligence of this bomb, and knew little what to say; but concluding, justly, that the piece had been found among Wilkes's papers, condemned the means by which it was obtained. It was instantly voted blasphemous, and a breach of privilege against the person of the Bishop of Gloucester. Lord Sandwich then moved that Wilkes should be voted the author; but even Lord Mansfield condemned so hasty and arbitrary a course, and said it was previously necessary to hear the accused person in his own defence: on which the proceeding was adjourned to the next day but one. I was in a division in the lobby of the House of Commons, when I heard what was passing in the other House, and immediately informed Mr. Pitt. He replied with indignation, 'Why do not they search the Bishop of Gloucester's study for heresy?'

Events now thickened so fast that, to avoid confusion, I will here say a little more on this head. The plot so hopefully laid to blow up Wilkes, and ruin him in the estimation of all the decent and grave, had, at least in the latter respect, scarce any effect at all. The treachery was so gross and scandalous, so revengeful, and so totally unconnected with the political conduct of Wilkes, and the instruments so despicable, odious, or in whom any pretensions to decency, sanctimony, or faith were so preposterous that, losing all sight of the scandal contained in the poem, the whole world almost united in crying out against the informers. Sandwich, in opening the discovery, had canted till his own friends could not keep their countenances. Sir Francis Dashwood was not more notorious for singing profane and lewd catches; and what aggravated the hypocrisy, scarce a fortnight had passed since this holy Secretary of State himself had been present with Wilkes at a weekly club to which both belonged, held at the top of Covent Garden Theatre, and composed of players and the loosest revellers of the age. Warburton's part was only ridiculous, and was heightened by its being known that Potter, his wife's gallant, had had the chief hand in the composition of the verses. However, an intimacy commenced between the Bishop and Sandwich, and some jovial dinners and libations of champagne cemented their friendship. Kidgell, the jackall, published so precise, affected, and hypocritic an account of the transaction, that he, who might have escaped in the gloom of the treachery, completely blasted his own reputation; and falling into debt, was, according to the fate of inferior tools, abandoned by his masters, and forced to fly his country. Though the rank and fortune of Sandwich saved him from disgrace of that kind, he had little reason to exult in his machination. He brought a stigma on himself that counterworked many of his own views and arts; and Churchill the poet has branded his name on this account with lasting colours. The public indignation went so far, that the Beggar's Opera being performed at Covent Garden Theatre soon after this event, the whole audience, when Macheath says, *'That Jemmy Twitcher should peach me, I own surprises me,'* burst out into an applause of application; and the nickname of *Jemmy Twitcher* stuck by the Earl so as almost to occasion the disuse of his title.

While the destruction of the character and fortune of

Wilkes was thus prosecuted in one chamber of Parliament, a plot against his life was hatching in the other; his enemies not being satisfied with all the severities they could wring from the law to ·oppress him. Nor were several servants of the Crown sorry to make his outrages a handle for curtailing liberty itself. The House was no sooner met, than Wilkes rose to make his complaint of the breach of privilege in the seizure of himself and his papers. The Speaker interrupted him. . . . Wilkes then made his complaint. Mr. Pitt approved of Lord North's motion of thanks, but spoke against precipitation. Wilkes's case, he said, was not to be parallelled. He desired to be tried by his peers,—and if he did not, said Pitt, I would force him. *The North Briton*, No. 45, was then read; and two printers being examined, one said he had received it from Wilkes in his own handwriting; the other, that Wilkes and Churchill were the authors of that periodic paper in general. Lord North, who had undertaken the conduct of the parliamentary prosecution against Wilkes, held forth on the sedition of those papers, and of No. 45 in particular. Wilkes, replied his Lordship, however, had not proved that it contained any falsehoods. Mr. Pitt said it was a scandalous, licentious paper, and false; but always distinguishing between the criminal and the illegal proceedings of the ministers. The House, he said, was not a proper place for trying a libel; nor did this tend to excite traitorous insurrections. Was the motion calculated, by inserting the word *traitorous*, to justify what the ministers had done? He himself could never learn exactly what was a libel. Whoever was the patron of these doctrines, *fœnum habet in cornu*. Norton said he did think the paper tended to excite insurrections. Scandalous reflections on private men or magistrates were a libel. Opposing law was treason. Pitt replied, a libel could not be treason. It might, said North, tend to excite treason. Pitt moved to omit the epithet *traitorous*, but the Ministry upholding it, the House divided at eleven at night, and the ministerial phrase was carried by 273 against 111; Sir Alexander Gilmour and Murray, two Scots, and the only two of that nation in opposition, voting with the rest of their countrymen on that occasion. Lord North then moved to have the paper burned by the hangman, which was ordered. Lord North affirmed next, that privilege did not extend to libels, nor to stay justice; which Pitt said was the boldest assertion and attempt ever made without consulting precedents or appointing a committee. He lamented the King was so ill served as to run aground on the liberties of Parliament. He would die, he said, if a day were not appointed for hearing Wilkes. Norton took this up hotly, and said he was called upon by insult and abuse. Pitt replied that he had said the King had been ill served by lawyers and others; and he proposed to take the case of privilege into consideration the next day, and on the following day to hear the complaint of Wilkes, which was agreed to at one in the morning.

The next day, when I went down to the House, I found all the members standing on the floor in great hubbub, questioning, hearing, and eagerly discussing I knew not what. I soon learned that Wilkes about two hours before had been dangerously wounded by Martin in a duel. In the foregoing spring, Wilkes, in one of his *North Britons*, had pointed out Martin by name as a low fellow, and dirty tool of power. Martin had stomached, not digested this; but in the debate on No. 45 the day before, he had risen and called the author of that paper on himself a cowardly, scandalous, and malignant scoundrel, and had repeated the words twice, trembling with rage. Wilkes took no notice; and as he did not, the House did not interfere, as is usual, when personalities happen, and seem to threaten a duel. The next morning Wilkes wrote to Martin, to ask if the words used the day before were meant to be addressed to him as the supposed author of the paper in which Martin had been abused. If Martin had thus intended to point the words, Wilkes owned he had written that paper. Martin replied he had meant him, Wilkes; and as the latter had avowed himself the author, he should not deny, added Martin, what he had said before five hundred people, and gave him a challenge. About noon they went into Hyde Park; Martin alone; Wilkes with Humphrey Cotes in a post-chaise, knowing if he killed Martin that he should have no chance of pardon. Cotes waited at a distance. They changed pistols, both fired, and both missed. Martin fired a second time, and lodged a ball in Wilkes's side, who was going to fire, but dropped his pistol. The wound, though not mortal, proved a bad one.

It was thought an ill symptom of Martin's heroism, that he had smothered the affront for so many months, nor had given vent to his resentment, till the affair with Forbes had left a doubt on Wilkes's courage. If Martin got rid of this imputation, it was but at the expense of a worse charge. It came out, nor could he deny it, that his neighbours in the country had observed him practising to fire at a target for the whole summer. I shall not be thought to have used too hard an expression, when I called this a plot against the life of Wilkes. . . .

On the 23rd of November came on the important question whether the Privilege of Parliament preserved the members from being taken up for writing and publishing libels. At first sight a disinterested person would perhaps think it strange that it should be a question whether a seat in the Legislature should not secure the Legislators from the penalty of breaking the laws, for publishing a libel is undoubtedly illegal; but to those acquainted with our Constitution, it will perhaps appear more extraordinary that a House of Commons should suffer such a question to be proposed to them, and that they should condescend to agitate it. Will our posterity believe that a House of Commons gave it up? but it was *that* House of Commons that had sold itself to approve the late Peace. Still it is to be admired that this cessation of their privileges should be wrung from them after the Court of Common Pleas had declared that Privilege held against everything but treason, felony, and breach of the peace. A libel, at most, but *tended* to a breach of the peace.

The Legislature consists of the three branches of King, Lords, and Commons. Together they form our invaluable Constitution, and each is a check on the other two. But it must be remembered, at the same time, that while any two are checking, the third is naturally aiming at extending and aggrandizing its power. The House of Commons has not seldom made this attempt, like the rest. The Lords, as a permanent and as a proud body, more constantly aim at it: the Crown always. Of liberty a chief and material engine is the liberty

of the Press; a privilege for ever sought to be stifled and an-
nihilated by the Crown. The ministers of the Crown and its
lawyers must misrepresent the liberty of the Press before they
can presume to request the suppression of it. Every grievance
set forth in print is misnamed a libel; and grave laws necessarily disapprove libels. If the Crown can arrive at precluding
Members of Parliament from complaining in print of grievances, no doubt the Crown could debar all other men, who
are of less importance, and whose persons are regarded by no
sacred privilege. Liberty of speech and liberty of writing are
the two instruments by which Englishmen call on one another
to defend their common rights. Liberty of speech is communicated but a little way; the Press gives wings to that voice,
and all men may read what all cannot hear. Freedom of speech
in Parliament is not so valuable as freedom of writing. A man
may hazard many necessary truths in print when he may conceal his name which he might not venture to utter in open
Parliament. If discovered, his privilege used to be his security.
Nor is this a vindication of libels properly so called; but a Court
will call a libel the most just censure of tyranny. Yet could it
not wrest from Members of Parliament the safety of their persons without their own consent—and in what instance did the
Court ask this?—in what instance did the House of Commons
yield it? Mr. Wilkes, one of their own members, had been
taken up by a *General Warrant*, in which his name had not
so much as been mentioned. Contrary to all precedent, he had
been committed *close* prisoner to the Tower—a proceeding so
arbitrary, that a Court of Law had set him free. The House
of Commons sacrificed him and their own privileges, and yet
shame—I mean disgrace, so soon overtook them, that *General
Warrants*, such as that on which Wilkes was arrested, were
given up, condemned, exploded. . . .

The 3rd of December had been appointed for burning *The
North Briton* at the Royal Exchange; but when the magistrates
were assembled for that purpose, and the executioner began
to perform the ceremony, a great riot ensued, the paper was
forced from the hangman, the constables were pelted and
beaten, and Mr. Harley, one of the Sheriffs, had the glass of
his coach broken, and himself was wounded in the face by a

billet snatched from the fire that was lighted to burn the paper, and thrown at him. The cry was, 'Wilkes and Liberty!' A jack-boot and a petticoat—the mob's hieroglyphics for Lord Bute and the Princess, were burned with great triumph and ac-clamations.

On the 6th the Duke of Bedford, who had moved that the Commons might be desired to permit Mr. Harley, member for the City, to attend the House of Lords, called on him, and Blount, the other sheriff, to give an account of the late riot. They said the mob had been encouraged by gentlemen from windows and balconies, particularly from the Union coffee-house. One low man had been taken into custody; another had been rescued by the rioters. One witness said the mob had united two respectable names in a cry of approbation, those of the Duke of Cumberland and Lord Temple, and he had joined in that shout. The Duke of Grafton shrewdly told the marshal's man he must have seen many mobs of party against party; had there appeared two parties on this occa-sion? 'No,' replied the fellow, 'all were of one mind.' The Duke of Bedford, spluttering with zeal and indiscretion, broke forth against Bridgen, the Lord Mayor, and the other magistrates, who, though within hearing, had taken no pains to quell the mob. 'Such behaviour,' he said, 'in any smaller town would have forfeited their franchises. The Common Council had long been setting themselves up against the Parliament, and last year had taken on them to advise the King to refuse his assent to a law that had passed through both Houses. He hoped their Lordships would resent this insult and disrespect to their or-ders.' The Chancellor, alarmed at this injudicious attack on the City, said it would be right to proceed without delay against the actors and abettors of the riot; but, without further proofs, he would not believe the magistrates of London guilty. He moved to vote the rioters perturbators of the peace. This was voted, and thanks to the sheriffs for their behaviour. . . . Wilkes, in the meantime, went on triumphantly with his prose-cutions; and on the 6th of December obtained a verdict of £1000 damages, and costs of suit, against Mr. Wood, the Under-Secretary of State. . . .

[*However, Wilkes saw that the opinion of the House of Commons was against him, and went off privately to France, where his daughter was. During his absence the House declared him an outlaw. But he was to come back, and still an outlaw, to be elected to Parliament again and again, with tremendous popular enthusiasm, against which his enemies could do very little. Meanwhile, Horace Walpole began to consider the turn of events.*]

I . . . had been very seriously alarmed at the strides I had seen made towards arbitrary power; but having beheld the cowardice of Lord Bute, and knowing that of Lord Mansfield, and finding the nation delivered from the influence of Fox, I had flattered myself the danger was over. I had been pleased, too, that Grenville was become the acting minister; having (I confess my blindness) entertained a most favourable opinion of his integrity. He talked nothing but reformation—which, indeed, alone would not have duped me—I had seen too much of patriot hypocrisy! but he went beyond myself in his principles of liberty—I mean, in his discourse. I thought him a grounded Republican; had heard him harangue by the hour against the despotic doctrines of Lord Mansfield. Nor had his venal prostitution of himself to Lord Bute as yet opened my eyes. But I was again roused by the arbitrary treatment of Wilkes, committed close prisoner to the Tower by an indefinite warrant. Lord Bute, I saw, had left his cloak to his successors; yet I could not believe that my friend, Algernon Sydney (for Grenville appeared to me as scarce a less Whig saint), was capable of concurring in such measures. In truth, when I saw Saint Sandwich added to his rubric, I began to be startled. I saw him lean, too, on the Bedfords: them I did not love; and nothing is a more sovereign cure for blindness in friendship than a connection between one's friends and one's enemies. I laboured by those most in Grenville's confidence to detach him from so disreputable an union; but Grenville knew his interest better than I knew him.

COMMENT: On the Dangers of
Preventing the Questioning of Authority

In the Wilkes case, the prosecution of censorship hung on a charge of seditious libel, or libel against the King. In the case that follows, it hangs on a charge of blasphemy, or, as it were, libel against God. The offense of Abner Kneeland, according to the prosecutor, was to circulate a newspaper containing opinions contrary to the Christian religion, although, oddly enough, the defence claimed that the newspaper did not seek to convert others to Kneeland's opinion.

The arguments used by the Attorney of the Commonwealth of Massachusetts, who wished to have the newspaper suppressed, are common even today. In effect he says, "Say what you will so long as you do not offend my belief." People are free to broadcast their opinions, that is, so long as they do not question the validity of accepted opinions. Such is the sense of President Eisenhower's words at Dartmouth College, June 14, 1953:

> Don't join the book burners. Don't think you are going to conceal faults by concealing evidence that they ever existed. Don't be afraid to go into your library and read every book *as long as it does not offend our own ideas of decency.* That should be the only censorship. [Editors' italics].

Such words are purely paternalist; they imply superiority of judgment on the part of authority (but authority is not necessarily superior, as anyone knows). Other bodies have the same attitude—the Roman Catholic Church, the Communist élite in Soviet Russia, Plato in *The Republic,* and prosecuting attorneys in general, as witness the following.

TEXT: "Corruption of the Poor and
Unlearned by Certain Opinions" from
*Report of the Arguments of the Attorney of
the Commonwealth, at Trials of Abner
Kneeland, for Blasphemy, in the Municipal
and Supreme Courts, in Boston, January
and May, 1834*

The law does say, that no man shall in a scurrilous, indecent,
scandalous, obscene manner blaspheme God or the Christian
Religion as contained in the Holy Scriptures. He shall not
treat the faith and opinions of the wisest men without the advantages of learning and patient sober thinking to a total disbelief of all things hitherto held sacred, and to a rejection consequently of all laws and ordinances of the State, which stand
only on an assumption of that truth; that when the Constitution and Laws establish the existence and providence of God
and the Christian Religion and recognize them as part of the
Law of the land, no man shall impiously and contumeliously
reproach them—no man shall in a vulgar, sneering and scoff-
ing manner promulgate doctrines destructive of the peace of
society—and subversive of the happiness of individuals com-
posing it—shall not take away the sanctions of oaths, shall not
sap the foundation of justice and official duty—shall not deprive
men of the reverence they feel for God and religion, shall not
rob them of their present consolations and future hopes, shall
not remove the moral and religious restraints which a belief
in God and Christianity imposes.

This is what the Law prohibits, and this is the offence

charged in this Indictment against this defendant, and this offence of his is aggravated by the vehicle in which he conveys this moral poison—a Newspaper easily circulated, soon read, and finding its way to the poor and unlearned, to those who have not learning nor leisure enough to consider and refute its falsehoods—an offence also aggravated by his pampering that depraved appetite which vulgar and illiterate minds are apt to have for obscenity and scurrilousness, and which all Courts, as *moral Boards of Health,* ought to denounce and restrain.

The religious and moral sense of the people of this happy land is the great anchor, which alone can hold safe the vessel of State in the mighty current of human affairs, which always is flowing and always is strong, and amid the storms which agitate the world—and if the mass of the people were debauched from the principles of religion, which are the true basis of that humanity, charity, moral sense and benevolence, so long our national characteristics, the prostration of our excellent Constitution and laws would soon follow. . . .

There remain some general and important topics involved in this trial of which I would speak briefly, to prevent misunderstanding.

1. The rights of conscience—

I would not impugn them—They are guaranteed by our Institutions—use yours as you please, but leave me mine—abuse not, vilify not, obliterate not my creed—that you have no right to do—offend us not by obscene blasphemy—we have a right to be protected from insult and not have our feelings hurt by offensive and disgusting obscenity. Such is the true construction of religious freedom.

2. The liberty of free discussion.

We indulge it to the utmost latitude—we ask only that it be decent—that it be fair—that it be sincere—that it violate not the laws of the land. . . .

3. The liberty of the Press—

We admit and would support it to the fullest extent—"It has led to many of the blessings both of religion and government, which the world enjoys, and is calculated to advance mankind to still higher degrees of civilization and happiness." But restrain its licentiousness—it may be the engine of mischief as

well as of good. It is the liberty of fire arms—the liberty of the
sword—of the element of fire, to be rightfully and *lawfully*
used on proper occasions, but not for murder or assassination,
for mischief or malice on persons or reputation. . . .

4. Toleration—we tolerate all creeds.

A book that in my opinion contains more truth than any
other book ever published, has said "The fool in his heart saith
there is no God." While the fool says it only in his heart—we
tolerate him—we pity his folly—we pity his blindness. The
Heavens above, the earth beneath declare the glory of God
and all that therein is. "An undevout astronomer is mad."—A
man must be a fool indeed, who in the works around him sees
not proofs of Nature's God. . . .

5. We deprecate religious persecution. We ask only for
maintenance of the laws of the land. We would have nobody
persecuted for religious creeds. We ask only that they should
not withhold the same liberty from others, should not attack
violently or indecently publish libels upon all religions. If they
choose to believe nothing themselves, let them not deprive
others of their heavenly hopes, let them not sap the foundations of morality and law. . . .

Mr. Parker occupied about two hours in this opening address; after which Andrew Dunlap Esq. in behalf of the defendant called several witnesses to prove the general character
of Mr. Kneeland for good morals, and he then entered upon
the defence in a splendid oration, which he was three days
in delivering to the Jury, having commenced at twelve o'clock
on Tuesday, and concluded at four o'clock on Friday after-
noon. . . . [There follows the speech for the prosecution.]

Mr. Parker was [again] more than two hours addressing
the Jury. The next morning Judge Thacher gave them his in-
structions. His charge was reported in the Boston Daily Ad-
vertiser & Patriot of Thursday, 13th February, 1834.

The verdict of the Jury was—GUILTY.—Mr. Kneeland appealed to the Supreme Court and was there put to the bar
again on the 13th of May. His second trial also occupied four
days. . . . [The result of this trial was that] the Jury did not
all agree. Eleven of them agreed on a Verdict of GUILTY in

ten minutes. A personal and political friend of the Defendant's Counsel, was the dissentient Juror. He did not regularly belong on that Jury, and was put there by means of Mr. Dunlap's exertions. . . .

The cause is continued to be put to a new Jury at next November Term.

COMMENT: On Freedom of Speech

If liberty in the United States is to be subject to an official
definition, as the author of the last extract implies, where are
we to infer that true freedom of speech begins? During and
after World War I, federal legislation like the Espionage Act
and state legislation like the notorious "Lusk laws" in New
York again raised this issue. Men were imprisoned, indicted,
tried, convicted, deported, or threatened with deportation for
opposing the war, supporting a minority party, opposing the
sale of Liberty Bonds, "interfering with the draft," or advocating "radicalism." Socialist members of the New York legislature were denied their seats. In the *Harvard Law Review* for
June 1919, Zechariah Chafee, Jr. published a famous essay
entitled "Freedom of Speech in War Time." The substance of
this essay, modernized, forms much of the first chapters of his
book *Free Speech in the United States* (Cambridge, Mass.:
Harvard University Press, 1941). Omitting the citation of cases
and other technical matter and a few minor phrases, the text
is here reprinted from the latest issue of his book.

TEXT: "Freedom of Speech and the First Amendment" from *Free Speech in the United States* by Zechariah Chafee, Jr.

Never in the history of our country since the Alien and Sedition Laws of 1798, has the meaning of free speech been the subject of such sharp controversy as during the years since 1917. Over nineteen hundred prosecutions and other judicial proceedings during the war, involving speeches, newspaper articles, pamphlets, and books, were followed after the armistice by a widespread legislative consideration of bills punishing the advocacy of extreme radicalism. It is becoming increasingly important to determine the true limits of freedom of expression, so that speakers and writers may know how much they can properly say, and governments may be sure how much they can lawfully and wisely suppress.

This book is an inquiry into the proper limitations upon freedom of speech, and is in no way an argument that any one should be allowed to say whatever he wants anywhere and at any time. We can all agree from the very start that there must be some point where the government may step in, and my main purpose is to make clear from many different angles just where I believe that point to lie. We ought also to agree that a man may believe that certain persons have a right to speak or other constitutional rights without at all identifying himself with the position and views of such persons. In a country where John Adams defended the British soldiers involved in the Boston Massacre and Alexander Hamilton represented British Loyalists and General Grant insisted upon amnesty for Robert E. Lee, it is surprising how between 1917 and 1920 it was impossible for any one to uphold the rights of a minority without subjecting himself to the accusation that he shared their opinions. If he urged milder treatment of conscientious objectors, he was a pacifist. If he held that the treaty with Germany should not violate the terms of the armistice, he was a pro-German. This popular argument reached its climax when an opponent of the disqualified Socialist assembly informed the world that he had always suspected Charles Evans Hughes of being disloyal.

I am not an atheist, but I would not roast one at the stake as in the sixteenth century, or even exclude him from the witness stand as in the nineteenth. Neither am I a pacifist or an anarchist or a Socialist or a Bolshevik. I have no sympathy myself with the views of most of the men who have been imprisoned since the war began for speaking out. My only interest is to find whether or not the treatment which they have received accords with freedom of speech. That principle may be invoked just as eagerly in future years by conservatives. Whatever political or economic opinion falls within the scope of the First Amendment ought to be safeguarded from governmental interference by every man who has sworn to uphold the Constitution of the United States, no matter how much he disagrees with those who are entitled to its protection or how lofty the patriotism of those who would whittle away the Bill of Rights into insignificance.

A friend of Lovejoy, the Abolitionist printer killed in the Alton riots, said at the time:

> We are more especially called upon to maintain the principles of free discussion in case of unpopular sentiments or persons, as in no other case will any effort to maintain them be needed.

The free speech clauses of the American constitutions are not merely expressions of political faith without binding legal force. Their history shows that they limit legislative action as much as any other part of the Bills of Rights. The United States Constitution as originally drafted contained no guaranty of religious or intellectual liberty, except that it forbade any religious test oath and gave immunity to members of Congress for anything said in debates. Pinckney, of South Carolina, had sought to insert a free speech clause, grouping liberty of the press with trial by jury and habeas corpus as "essentials in free governments." His suggestion was rejected by a slight majority as unnecessary, in that the power of Congress did not extend to the press, a natural belief before Hamilton and Marshall had developed the doctrine of incidental and implied powers. Hamilton himself defended the omission on the ground that liberty of the press was indefinable and depended only on public opinion and the general spirit of the people and government for its security, little thinking that he himself would frame a definition now embodied in the constitutions of half the states. The citizens of the states were not satisfied, and the absence of the guaranty of freedom of speech was repeatedly condemned in the state conventions and in outside discussion. Virginia, New York, and Rhode Island embodied a declaration of this right in their ratifications of the federal Constitution. Virginia expressly demanded an amendment and Maryland drafted one in its convention, basing it on a very significant reason, to be mentioned shortly. At the first session of Congress a Bill of Rights, including the present First Amendment, was proposed for adoption by the states, and became part of the Constitution December 15, 1791. Massachusetts, Virginia, and Pennsylvania already had similar provisions, and such a clause was eventually inserted in the constitutions of all other states. Thus the guaranty of freedom of speech was almost a condition of the entry of four original states into the Union, and is now declared by every state to be as much a part of its fundamental law as trial by jury or compensation for property taken by eminent domain. Such a widely recognized right must mean something, and have behind it the obligation of the courts to refuse to enforce any legislation which violates freedom of speech.

We shall not, however, confine ourselves to the question whether a given form of federal or state action against pacifist and similar utterances is void under the constitutions. It is often assumed that, so long as a statute is held valid under the Bill of Rights, that document ceases to be of any importance in the matter, and may be henceforth disregarded. On the contrary, a provision like the First Amendment to the federal Constitution,

Congress shall make no law respecting an establishment
of religion, or prohibiting the free exercise thereof; or
abridging the freedom of speech, or of the press; or the
right of the people peaceably to assemble, and to peti-
tion the Government for a redress of grievances

is much more than an order to Congress not to cross the boundary which marks the extreme limits of lawful suppression. It is
also an exhortation and a guide for the action of Congress inside that boundary. It is a declaration of national policy in
favor of the public discussion of all public questions. Such a
declaration should make Congress reluctant and careful in the
enactment of all restrictions upon utterance, even though the
courts will not refuse to enforce them as unconstitutional. It
should influence the judges in their construction of valid speech
statutes, and the prosecuting attorneys who control their enforcement. The Bill of Rights in a European constitution is a
declaration of policies and nothing more, for the courts cannot
disregard the legislative will though it violates the Constitution. Our Bills of Rights perform a double function. They fix a
certain point to halt the government abruptly with a "Thus
far and no farther"; but long before that point is reached they
urge upon every official of the three branches of the state a
constant regard for certain declared fundamental policies of
American life.

Our main task, therefore, is to ascertain the nature and
scope of the policy which finds expression in the First Amendment to the United States Constitution and the similar clauses
of all the state constitutions. We can then determine the place
of that policy in the conduct of war, and particularly the war
with Germany. The free speech controversy during the war
chiefly gathered about the federal Espionage Act . . . This
statute, which imposes a maximum of twenty years' imprisonment and a $10,000 fine on several kinds of spoken or written
opposition to the war, was enacted and vigorously enforced
under a Constitution which provides: "Congress shall make no
law . . . abridging the freedom of speech, or of the press."

Clearly, the problem of the limits of freedom of speech in
war time is no academic question. On the one side, thought-

ful men and journals were asking how scores of citizens could be imprisoned under this Constitution only for their open disapproval of the war as irreligious, unwise, or unjust. On the other, federal and state officials pointed to the great activities of German agents in our midst and to the unprecedented extension of the business of war over the whole nation, so that, in the familiar remark of Ludendorff, wars are no longer won by armies in the field, but by the *morale* of the whole people. The widespread Liberty Bond campaigns, and the shipyards, munition factories, government offices, training camps, in all parts of the country, were felt to make the entire United States a theater of war, in which attacks upon our cause were as dangerous and unjustified as if made among the soldiers in the rear trenches. The government regarded it as inconceivable that the Constitution should cripple its efforts to maintain public safety. Abstaining from countercharges of disloyalty and tyranny, let us recognize the issue as a conflict between two vital principles, and endeavor to find the basis of reconciliation between order and freedom.

At the outset, we can reject two extreme views in the controversy. First, there is the view that the Bill of Rights is a peace-time document and consequently freedom of speech may be ignored in war. This view has been officially repudiated. At the opposite pole is the belief of many agitators that the First Amendment renders unconstitutional any Act of Congress without exception "abridging the freedom of speech, or of the press," that all speech is free, and only action can be restrained and punished. This view is equally untenable. The provisions of the Bill of Rights cannot be applied with absolute literalness, but are subject to exceptions. For instance, the prohibition of involuntary servitude in the Thirteenth Amendment does not prevent military conscription, or the enforcement of a "work or fight" statute. The difficulty, of course, is to define the principle on which the implied exceptions are based, and an effort to that end will be made subsequently.

Since it is plain that the true solution lies between these two extreme views, and that even in war time freedom of speech exists subject to a problematical limit, it is necessary to determine where the line runs between utterances which are protected by the Constitution from governmental control and those which are not. Many attempts at a legal definition of that line have been made, but two mutually inconsistent theories have been especially successful in winning judicial acceptance, and frequently appear in the Espionage Act cases.

One theory construes the First Amendment as enacting Blackstone's statement that "the liberty of the press . . . consists in laying no *previous* restraints upon publications and not in freedom from censure for criminal matter when published." The line where legitimate suppression begins is fixed chronologically at the time of publication. The government cannot interfere by a censorship or injunction *before* the words are spoken or printed, but can punish them as much as it pleases *after* publication, no matter how harmless or essential to the public welfare the discussion may be. This Blackstonian definition is sometimes urged as a reason why civil libels should not be enjoined, so that on this theory liberty of the press means opportunity for blackmailers and no protection for political criticism. Of course, if the First Amendment does not prevent prosecution and punishment of utterances, no serious question could arise about the constitutionality of the Espionage Act.

This Blackstonian theory dies hard, but it ought to be knocked on the head once for all. In the first place, Blackstone was not interpreting a constitution, but trying to state the English law of his time, which had no censorship and did have extensive libel prosecutions. Whether or not he stated that law correctly, an entirely different view of the liberty of the press was soon afterwards enacted in Fox's Libel Act . . . so that Blackstone's view does not even correspond to the English law of the last hundred and twenty-five years. Furthermore, Blackstone is notoriously unfitted to be an authority on the liberties of American colonists, since he upheld the right of Parliament to tax them, and was pronounced by one of his own colleagues to have been "we all know, an anti-republican lawyer."

Not only is the Blackstonian interpretation of our free speech clauses inconsistent with eighteenth-century history, soon to be considered, but it is contrary to modern decisions, thoroughly artificial, and wholly out of accord with a commonsense view of the relations of state and citizen. In some respects this theory goes altogether too far in restricting state action. The total prohibition of previous restraint would not allow the government to prevent a newspaper from publishing the sailing dates of transports or the number of troops in a sector. It would forbid the removal of an indecent poster from a billboard. Censorship of moving pictures before exhibition has been held valid under a free speech clause. And whatever else may be thought of the decision under the Espionage Act with the unfortunate title *United States* v. *The Spirit of '76,* it was clearly previous restraint for a federal court to direct the seizure of a film which depicted the Wyoming Massacre and Paul Revere's Ride, because it was "calculated reasonably so to excite or inflame the passions of our people or some of them as that they will be deterred from giving that full measure of co-operation, sympathy, assistance, and sacrifice which is due to Great Britain, as an ally of ours," and "to make us a little bit slack in our loyalty to Great Britain in this great catastrophe."

On the other hand, it is hardly necessary to argue that the Blackstonian definition gives very inadequate protection to the freedom of expression. A death penalty for writing about socialism would be as effective suppression as a censorship. The government which holds twenty years in prison before a speaker and calls him free to talk resembles the peasant described by Galsworthy:

> The other day in Russia an Englishman came on a street-meeting shortly after the first revolution had begun. An extremist was addressing the gathering and telling them that they were fools to go on fighting, that they ought to refuse and go home, and so forth. The crowd grew angry, and some soldiers were for making a rush at him; but the chairman, a big burly peasant, stopped them with these words: "Brothers, you know that our country is now a country of free speech. We must listen to this man, we must let him say anything he will. But, brothers, when he's finished, we'll bash his head in!"

Cooley's comment on Blackstone is unanswerable:

> . . . *The mere exemption from previous restraints cannot be all that is secured by the constitutional provisions, inasmuch as of words to be uttered orally there can be no previous censorship, and the liberty of the press might be rendered a mockery and a delusion, and the phrase itself a byword, if, while every man was at liberty to publish what he pleased, the public authorities might nevertheless punish him for harmless publications, . . . Their purpose [of the free-speech clauses] has evidently been to protect parties in the free publication of matters of public concern, to secure their right to a free discussion of public events and public measures, and to enable every citizen at any time to bring the government and any person in authority to the bar of public opinion by any just criticism upon their conduct in the exercise of the authority which the people have conferred upon them. . . . The evils to be prevented were not the censorship of the press merely, but any action of the government by means of which it might prevent such free and general discussion of public matters as seems absolutely essential to prepare the people for an intelligent exercise of their rights as citizens.*

If we turn from principles to precedents, we find several decisions which declare the constitutional guaranty of free speech to be violated by statutes and other governmental action which imposed no previous restraint, but penalized publications after they were made. And most of the decisions in which a particular statute punishing for talking or writing is sustained do not rest upon the Blackstonian interpretation of liberty of speech, but upon another theory, now to be considered. Therefore, the severe punishments imposed by the Espionage Act might conceivably violate the First Amendment, although they do not interfere with utterances before publication.

A second interpretation of the freedom of speech clauses limits them to the protection of the use of utterance and not of its "abuse." It draws the line between "liberty" and "license." Chief Justice White rejected:

the contention that the freedom of the press is the free-
dom to do wrong with impunity and implies the right to
frustrate and defeat the discharge of those governmental
duties upon the performance of which the freedom of all,
including that of the press, depends. . . . However com-
plete is the right of the press to state public things and
discuss them, that right, as every other right, enjoyed in
human society, is subject to the restraints which separate
right from wrong-doing.

A statement of the same view in another peace case was
made by Judge Hamersley of Connecticut:

Every citizen has an equal right to use his mental en-
dowments, as well as his property, in any harmless occu-
pation or manner; but he has no right to use them so as to
injure his fellow-citizens or to endanger the vital interests
of society. Immunity in the mischievous use is as incon-
sistent with civil liberty as prohibition of the harmless
use. . . . The liberty protected is not the right to per-
petrate acts of licentiousness, or any act inconsistent with
the peace or safety of the State. Freedom of speech and
press does not include the abuse of the power of tongue
or pen, any more than freedom of other action includes
an injurious use of one's occupation, business, or property.

The decisions in the war were full of similar language, of
which a few specimens will suffice:

In this country it is one of our foundation stones of lib-
erty that we may freely discuss anything we please, pro-
vided that that discussion is in conformity with law, or at
least not in violation of it.

No American worthy of the name believes in anything
else than free speech; but free speech means, not license,
not counseling disobedience of the law. Free speech
means that frank, free, full, and orderly expression which
every man or woman in the land, citizen or alien, may
engage in, in lawful and orderly fashion.

No one is permitted under the constitutional guaranties
to commit a wrong or violate the law.

Just the same sort of distinction was made by Lord Kenyon during the French revolution:

The liberty of the press is dear to England. The licentiousness of the press is odious to England. The liberty of it can never be so well protected as by beating down the licentiousness.

This exasperated Sir James Fitzjames Stephen into the comment, "Hobbes is nearly the only writer who seems to me capable of using the word 'liberty' without talking nonsense."

A slightly more satisfactory view was adopted by Cooley, that the clauses guard against repressive measures by the several departments of government, but not against utterances which are a public offense, or which injure the reputation of individuals.

We understand liberty of speech and of the press to imply not only liberty to publish, but complete immunity from legal censure and punishment for the publication, so long as it is not harmful in its character, when tested by such standards as the law affords.

To a judge obliged to decide whether honest and able opposition to the continuation of a war is punishable, these generalizations furnish as much help as a woman forced, like Isabella in *Measure for Measure,* to choose between her brother's death and loss of honor, might obtain from the pious maxim, "Do right." What is abuse? What is license? What standards does the law afford? To argue that the federal Constitution does not prevent punishment for criminal utterances begs the whole question, for utterances within its protection are not crimes. If it only safeguarded lawful speech, Congress could escape its operation at any time by making any class of speech unlawful. Suppose, for example, that Congress declared any criticism of the particular administration in office to be a felony, punishable by ten years' imprisonment. Clearly, the Constitution must limit the power of Congress to create crimes. But how far does that limitation go?

Shall we say that the constitutional guaranties must be interpreted in the light of the contemporary common law; and that Congress and the state legislatures may punish as they please any speech that was criminal or tortious before 1791? We can all agree that the free speech clauses do not wipe out the common law as to obscenity, profanity, and defamation of individuals. But how about the common law of sedition and libels against the government? Was this left in full force by the First Amendment, although it was the biggest of all the legal limitations on discussion of public matters before the Revolution? No doubt conditions in 1791 must be considered, but they do not arbitrarily fix the division between lawful and unlawful speech for all time.

Clearly, we must look further and find a rational test of what is use and what is abuse. Saying that the line lies between them gets us nowhere. And "license" is too often "liberty" to the speaker, and what happens to be anathema to the judge.

One of the strongest reasons for the waywardness of trial judges during the war was their inability to get guidance from precedents. There were practically no satisfactory judicial discussions before 1917 about the meaning of the free speech clauses. The pre-war courts in construing such clauses did little more than place obvious cases on this or that side of the line. They told us, for instance, that libel and slander were actionable, or even punishable, that indecent books were criminal, that it was contempt to interfere with pending judicial proceedings, and that a permit could be required for street meetings; and on the other hand, that some criticism of the government must be allowed, that a temperate examination of a judge's opinion was not contempt, and that honest discussion of the merits of a painting caused no liability for damages. But when we asked where the line actually ran and how they knew on which side of it a given utterance belonged, we found little answer in their opinions.

Even frequently quoted statements by Justice Holmes in his first Espionage Act decisions are open to the same adverse criticism—they tell us that plainly unlawful utterances are, to be sure, unlawful:

The First Amendment . . . obviously was not intended

to give immunity for every possible use of language . . .
We venture to believe that neither Hamilton nor Madison,
nor any other competent person then or later, ever sup-
posed that to make criminal the counselling of a murder
. . . would be an unconstitutional interference with free
speech.

The most stringent protection of free speech would not
protect a man in falsely shouting fire in a theatre and caus-
ing a panic.

How about the man who gets up in a theater between the
acts and informs the audience honestly, but perhaps mistak-
enly, that the fire exits are too few or locked? He is a much
closer parallel to Frohwerk or Debs. How about James Russell
Lowell when he counseled, not murder, but the cessation of
murder, his name for war? The question whether such per-
plexing cases are within the First Amendment or not cannot
be solved by the multiplication of obvious examples, but only
by the development of a rational principle to mark the limits
of constitutional protection.

"The gradual process of judicial inclusion and exclusion,"
which has served so well to define other clauses in the federal
Constitution by blocking out concrete situations on each side
of the line until the line itself becomes increasingly plain, was
of very little use for the First Amendment before 1917. The
pre-war cases were too few, too varied in their character, and
often too easily solved to develop any definite boundary between lawful and unlawful speech.

Fortunately, we did get during the war years three very
able judicial statements which take us far toward the ultimate
solution of the problem of the limits of free speech, one by
Judge Learned Hand in 1917 and two by Justice Holmes in
1919 . . .

For the moment, however, it may be worth while to forsake
the purely judicial discussion of free speech, and obtain light
upon its meaning from the history of the constitutional clauses
and from the purpose free speech serves in social and political
life.

The framers of the First Amendment make it plain that they

regarded freedom of speech as very important; "absolutely necessary" is Luther Martin's phrase. But they say very little about its exact meaning. That should not surprise us if we recall our own vagueness about freedom of the seas. Men rarely define their inspirations until they are forced into doing so by sharp antagonism. Therefore, it is not until the Sedition Law of 1798 made the limits of liberty of the press a concrete and burning issue that we get much helpful expression of opinion on our problem. Before that time, however, we have a few important pieces of evidence to show that the words were used in the Constitution in a wide and liberal sense.

On October 26, 1774, the Continental Congress issued an address to the inhabitants of Quebec, declaring that the English colonists had five invaluable rights, representative government, trial by jury, liberty of the person, easy tenure of land, and freedom of the press:

> *The last right we shall mention regards the freedom of the press. The importance of this consists, besides the advancement of truth, science, morality and arts in general, in its diffusion of liberal sentiment on the administration of government, its ready communication of thoughts between subjects, and its consequential promotion of union among them, whereby oppressive officials are shamed or intimidated into more honorable and just modes of conducting affairs.*

In 1785 Virginia, which was the first state to insert a clause protecting the liberty of the press in its constitution (1776), enacted a statute drawn by Jefferson for Establishing Religious Freedom. This opened with a very broad principle of toleration: "Whereas, Almighty God hath created the mind free; that all attempts to influence it by temporal punishments or burthens, or by civil incapacitations, tend only to beget habits of hypocrisy and meanness." Though this relates specifically to religion, it shows the trend of men's thoughts, and the meaning which "liberty" had to Jefferson long before the bitter controversy of 1798.

Benjamin Franklin, in discussing the brief "freedom of speech" clause in the Pennsylvania Constitution of 1776, said in 1789 that if by the liberty of the press were to be understood merely the liberty of discussing the propriety of public measures and political opinions, let us have as much of it as you please. On the other hand, if it means liberty to calumniate another, there ought to be some limit.

The reason given by the Maryland convention of 1788 to the people for including a free speech clause in the proposed federal Bill of Rights was: "In prosecutions in the federal courts, for libels, the constitutional preservation of this great and fundamental right may prove invaluable."

The contemporaneous evidence in the passages just quoted shows that in the years before the First Amendment freedom of speech was conceived as giving a wide and genuine protection for all sorts of discussion of public matters. These various statements are, of course, absolutely inconsistent with any Blackstonian theory that liberty of the press forbids nothing except censorship. The men of 1791 went as far as Blackstone, and much farther.

If we apply Coke's test of statutory construction, and consider what mischief in the existing law the framers of the First Amendment wished to remedy by a new safeguard, we can be sure that it was not the censorship. This had expired in England in 1695, and in the colonies by 1725. They knew from books that it destroyed liberty of the press; and if they ever thought of its revival as within the range of practical possibilities, they must have regarded it as clearly prohibited by the First Amendment. But there was no need to go to all the trouble of pushing through a constitutional amendment just to settle an issue that had been dead for decades. What the framers did have plenty of reason to fear was an entirely different danger to political writers and speakers.

For years the government here and in England had substituted for the censorship rigorous and repeated prosecutions for seditious libel, which were directed against political discussion, and for years these prosecutions were opposed by liberal opinion and popular agitation. Primarily the controversy raged around two legal contentions of the great advocates for the defense, such as Erskine and Andrew Hamilton. They argued, first, that the jury and not the judge ought to decide whether the writing was seditious, and secondly, that the truth of the charge ought to prevent conviction. The real issue, however, lay much deeper. Two different views of the relation of rulers and people were in conflict. According to one view, the rulers were the superiors of the people, and therefore must not be subjected to any censure that would tend to diminish their authority. The people could not make adverse criticism in newspapers or pamphlets, but only through their lawful representatives in the legislature, who might be petitioned in an orderly manner. According to the other view, the rulers were agents and servants of the people, who might therefore find fault with their servants and discuss questions of their punishment or dismissal, and of governmental policy.

Under the first view, which was officially accepted until the close of the eighteenth century, developed the law of seditious libel. This was defined as "the intentional publication, without lawful excuse or justification, of written blame of any public man, or of the law, or of any institution established by law." There was no need to prove any intention on the part of the defendant to produce disaffection or excite an insurrection. It was enough if he intended to publish the blame, because it was unlawful in him merely to find fault with his masters and betters. Such, in the opinion of the best authorities, was the common law of sedition.

It is obvious that under this law liberty of the press was nothing more than absence of the censorship, as Blackstone said. All through the eighteenth century, however, there existed beside this definite legal meaning of liberty of the press, a definite popular meaning: the right of unrestricted discussion of public affairs. There can be no doubt that this was in a general way what freedom of speech meant to the framers of the Constitution. Thus Madison, who drafted the First Amendment, bases his explanation of it in 1799 on "the essential difference between the British Government and the American constitutions." In the United States the people and not the government possess the absolute sovereignty, and the legislature as well as the executive is under limitations of power. Hence, Congress is not free to punish anything which was criminal at English common law. A government which is "elective, limited and responsible" in all its branches may well be supposed to require "a greater freedom of animadversion" than might be tolerated by one that is composed of an irresponsible hereditary king and upper house, and an omnipotent legislature.

This contemporary testimony corroborates the conclusion of Professor Schofield:

> One of the objects of the Revolution was to get rid of the English common law on liberty of speech and of the press. . . . Liberty of the press as declared in the First Amendment, and the English common-law crime of sedition, cannot co-exist.

There are a few early judicial decisions to the contrary, but they ought not to weigh against the statements of Madison and the general temper of the time. These judges were surely wrong in holding as they did that sedition was a common-law crime in the federal courts, and in other respects they drew their inspiration from British precedents and the British bench instead of being in close contact with the new ideas of this country. "Indeed," as Senator Beveridge says, "some of them were more British than they were American." "Let a stranger go into our courts," wrote one observer, "and he would almost believe himself in the Court of the King's Bench." Great as was the service of these judges in establishing the common law as to private rights, their testimony as to its place in public affairs is of much less value than the other contemporary evidence of the men who sat in the conventions and argued over the adoption of the Constitution. The judges forgot the truth emphasized by Maitland: "The law of a nation can only be studied in relation to the whole national life." I must therefore strongly dissent, with Justice Holmes, from the position sometimes taken in arguments on the Espionage Act, that the founders of our government left the common law as to seditious libel in force and merely intended by the First Amendment "to limit the new government's statutory powers to penalize utterances as seditious, to those which were seditious under the then accepted common-law rule." The founders had seen seventy English prosecutions for libel since 1760, and fifty convictions under that common-law rule, which made conviction easy. That rule had been detested in this country ever since it was repudiated by jury and populace in the famous trial of Peter Zenger, the New York printer, the account of which went through fourteen editions before 1791. The close relation between the Zenger trial and the prosecutions under George III in England and America is shown by the quotations on reprints of the trial and the dedication of the 1784 London edition to Erskine, as well as by reference to Zenger in the discussions preceding the First Amendment. Nor was this the only colonial sedition prosecution under the common law, and many more were threatened. All the American cases before 1791 prove that our common law of sedition was exactly like that of England, and it would be extraordinary if the First Amendment enacted the English sedition law of that time, which was repudiated by every American and every liberal Englishman, and altered through Fox's Libel Act by Parliament itself in the very next year, 1792. We might well fling at the advocates of this common-law view the challenge of Randolph of Roanoke, "whether the common law of libels which attaches to this Constitution be the doctrine laid down by Lord Mansfield, or that which has immortalized Mr. Fox?" The First Amendment was written by men to whom Wilkes and Junius were household words, who intended to wipe out the common law of sedition, and make further prosecutions for criticism of the government, without any incitement to law-breaking, forever impossible in the United States of America.

It must not be forgotten that the controversy over liberty of the press was a conflict between two views of government, that the law of sedition was a product of the view that the government was master, and that the American Revolution transformed into a working reality the second view that the government was servant, and therefore subjected to blame from its master, the people. Consequently, the words of Sir James Fitzjames Stephen about this second view have a vital application to American law.

To those who hold this view fully and carry it out to all its consequences there can be no such offense as sedition. There may indeed be breaches of the peace which may

destroy or endanger life, limb, or property, and there may
be incitements to such offenses, but no imaginable cen-
sure of the government, short of a censure which has an
immediate tendency to produce such a breach of the
peace, *ought to be regarded as criminal.*

In short, the framers of the First Amendment sought to preserve the fruits of the old victory abolishing the censorship,
and to achieve a new victory abolishing sedition prosecutions.

The repudiation by the constitutions of the English common
law of sedition, which was also the common law of the American colonies, has been obscured by some judicial retention of
the two technical incidents of the old law after the adoption
of the free speech clauses. Many judges, rightly or wrongly,
continued to pass on the criminality of the writing and to reject
its truth as a defense, until statutes or new constitutional provisions embodying the popular view on these two points were
enacted. Doubtless, a jury will protect a popular attack on the
government better than a judge, and the admission of truth
as a defense lessens the evils of suppression. These procedural
changes help to substitute the modern view of rulers for the
old view, but they are not enough by themselves to establish
freedom of speech. Juries can suppress much-needed political
discussion in times of intolerance, so long as the substantive
common law or a statute defines criminal utterances in sweeping and loose terms. Sedition prosecutions went on with shameful severity in England after Fox's Libel Act had given the
jury power to determine criminality. The American Sedition
Act of 1798, which President Wilson declares to have "cut
perilously near the root of freedom of speech and of the press,"
entrusted criminality to the jury and admitted truth as a defense. On the other hand, freedom of speech might exist without these two technical safeguards.

The essential question is not, who is judge of the criminality
of an utterance, but what is the test of its criminality. The
common law and the Sedition Act of 1798 made the test blame
of the government and its officials because to bring them into
disrepute tended to overthrow the state. The real issue in every
free speech controversy is this: whether the state can punish all

words which have some tendency, however remote, to bring
about acts in violation of law, or only words which directly
incite to acts in violation of law.

If words do not become criminal until they have "an immediate tendency to produce a breach of the peace," there is no
need for a law of sedition, since the ordinary standards of
criminal solicitation and attempt apply. Under those standards
the words must bring the speaker's unlawful intention reasonably near to success. Such a limited power to punish utterances rarely satisfies the zealous in times of excitement like a
war. They realize that all condemnation of the war or of conscription may conceivably lead to active resistance or insubor-
dination. Is it not better to kill the serpent in the egg? All
writings that have even a remote tendency to hinder the war
must be suppressed.

Such has always been the argument of the opponents of free
speech. And the most powerful weapon in their hands, since
the abolition of the censorship, is this doctrine of indirect
causation, under which words can be punished for a supposed
bad tendency long before there is any probability that they
will break out into unlawful acts. Closely related to it is the
doctrine of constructive intent, which regards the intent of the
defendant to cause violence as immaterial so long as he intended to write the words, or else presumes the violent intent
from the bad tendency of the words on the ground that a man
is presumed to intend the consequences of his acts. When
rulers are allowed to possess these weapons, they can by the
imposition of severe sentences create an *ex post facto* censorship of the press. The transference of that censorship from the
judge to the jury is indeed important when the attack on the
government which is prosecuted expresses a widespread popular sentiment, but the right to jury trial is of much less value in
times of war or threatened disorder when the herd instinct runs
strong, if the opinion of the defendant is highly objectionable
to the majority of the population, or even to the particular class
of men from whom or by whom the jury are drawn.

Under Charles II trial by jury was a blind and cruel system.
During the last part of the reign of George III it was, to say
the least, quite as severe as the severest judge without a jury

could have been. The revolutionary tribunal during the Reign of Terror tried by a jury. It is worth our frank consideration, whether in a country where the doctrine of indirect causation is recognized by the courts twelve small property-holders, who have been through an uninterrupted series of patriotic campaigns and are sufficiently middle-aged to be in no personal danger of compulsory military service, are fitted to decide whether there is a tendency to obstruct the draft in the writings of a pacifist, who also happens to be a Socialist and in sympathy with the Russian Revolution. This, however, is perhaps a problem for the psychologist rather than the lawyer.

Another significant fact in sedition prosecutions is the well-known probability that juries will acquit, after the excitement is over, for words used during the excitement, which are as bad in their tendency as other writings prosecuted and severely punished during the critical period. This was very noticeable during the reign of George III. It is also interesting to find two juries in different parts of the country differing as to the criminal character of similar publications or even the same publication. Thus Leigh Hunt was acquitted for writing an article, for the printing of which John Drakard was convicted. The acquittal of Scott Nearing and the conviction by the same jury of the American Socialist Society for publishing his book form an interesting parallel.

The manner in which juries in time of excitement may be used to suppress writings in opposition to the government, if bad tendency is recognized as a test of criminality, is illustrated by the numerous British sedition trials during the wars with Revolutionary France and Napoleon, after the passage of Fox's Libel Act. For instance, in the case just mentioned, Drakard was convicted for printing an article on the shameful amount of flogging in the army, under a charge in which Baron Wood emphasized the formidable foe with whom England was fighting, and the general belief that Napoleon was using the British press to carry out his purpose of securing her downfall.

It is to be feared, there are in this country many who are endeavoring to aid and assist him in his projects, by crying down the establishment of the country, and breed-

ing hatred against the government. Whether that is the source from whence the paper in question springs, I cannot say, but I advise you to consider whether it has not that tendency. You will consider whether it contains a fair discussion—whether it has not a manifest tendency to create disaffection in the country and prevent men enlisting into the army—whether it does not tend to induce the soldier to desert from the service of his country. And what considerations can be more awful than these? . . .

The House of Parliament is the proper place for the discussion of subjects of this nature . . . It is said that we have a right to discuss the acts of our legislature. That would be a large permission indeed. Is there, gentlemen, to be a power in the people to counteract the acts of the parliament, and is the libeller to come and make the people dissatisfied with the government under which he lives? This is not to be permitted to any man—it is unconstitutional and seditious.

The same emphasis on bad tendency appears in Lord Ellenborough's charge at Leigh Hunt's trial, although it failed to secure his conviction.

Can you conceive that the exhibition of the words "One Thousand Lashes," with strokes underneath to attract attention, could be for any other purpose than to excite disaffection? Could it have any other tendency than that of preventing men from entering the army?

The same desire to nip revolution in the bud was shown by the Scotch judges who secured the conviction of Muir and Palmer for advocating reform of the rotten boroughs which chose the House of Commons and the extension of the franchise, sentences of transportation for seven and fourteen years being imposed.

The right of universal suffrage, the subjects of this country never enjoyed; and were they to enjoy it, they would not long enjoy either liberty or a free constitution. You will, therefore, consider whether telling the people

that they have a just right to what would unquestionably
be tantamount to a total subversion of this constitution, is
such a writing as any person is entitled to compose, to
print, and to publish.

American sentiment about sedition trials was decisively
shown by an expedition to New South Wales to rescue Muir, a
sort of reverse deportation.

In the light of such prosecutions it is plain that the most vital
indication that the popular definition of liberty of the press,
unpunishable criticism of officials and laws, has become a
reality, is the disappearance of these doctrines of bad tendency
and presumptive intent. In Great Britain they lingered until
liberalism triumphed in 1832, but in this country they disappeared with the adoption of the free speech clauses.

The revival of those doctrines is a sure symptom of an attack
upon the liberty of the press.

Only once in our history prior to 1917 has an attempt been
made to apply these doctrines. In 1798 the impending war
with France, the spread of revolutionary doctrines by foreigners in our midst, and the spectacle of the disastrous operation of those doctrines abroad—facts that have a familiar sound
today—led to the enactment of the Alien and Sedition Laws.
The Alien Law allowed the President to compel the departure
of aliens whom he judged dangerous to the peace and safety of
the United States, or suspected, on reasonable grounds, of
treasonable or secret machinations against our government.
The Sedition Law punished false, scandalous, and malicious
writings against the government, either House of Congress, or
the President, if published with intent to defame any of them,
or to excite against them the hatred of the people, or to stir up
sedition or to excite resistance of law, or to aid any hostile
designs of any foreign nation against the United States. The
maximum penalty was a fine of two thousand dollars and two
years' imprisonment. Truth was a defense, and the jury had
power to determine criminality as under Fox's Libel Act. Despite the inclusion of the two legal rules for which reformers
had contended, and the requirement of an actual intention to
cause overt injury, the Sedition Act was bitterly resented as in-

vading the liberty of the press. Its constitutionality was assailed on that ground by Jefferson, who pardoned all prisoners when he became President; Congress eventually repaid all the fines; and popular indignation at the Act and the prosecutions wrecked the Federalist party. In those prosecutions words were once more made punishable for their judicially supposed bad tendency, and the judges reduced the test of intent to a fiction by inferring the bad intent from this bad tendency.

Whether or not the Sedition Act was unconstitutional, and on that question Jefferson seems right, it surely defeated the fundamental policy of the First Amendment, the open discussion of public affairs. Like the British trials, the American sedition cases showed, as Professor Schofield demonstrates, "the great danger . . . that men will be fined and imprisoned, under the guise of being punished for their bad motives, or bad intent and ends, simply because the powers that be do not agree with their opinions, and spokesmen of minorities may be terrorized and silenced when they are most needed by the community and most useful to it, and when they stand most in need of the protection of the law against a hostile, arrogant majority." When the Democrats got into power, a common-law prosecution for seditious libel was brought in New York against a Federalist who had attacked Jefferson. Hamilton conducted the defense in the name of the liberty of the press. This testimony from Jefferson and Hamilton, the leaders of both parties, leaves the Blackstonian interpretation of free speech in America without a leg to stand on. And the brief attempt of Congress and the Federalist judges to revive the crime of sedition had proved so disastrous that it was not repeated during the next century.

The lesson of the prosecutions for sedition in Great Britain and the United States during this revolutionary period, that the most essential element of free speech is the rejection of bad tendency as the test of a criminal utterance, was never more clearly recognized than in Jefferson's preamble to the Virginia Act for establishing Religious Freedom. His words about religious liberty hold good of political and speculative freedom, and the portrayal of human life in every form of art.

> *To suffer the civil Magistrate to intrude his powers into the field of opinion, and to restrain the profession or propagation of principles on supposition of their ill tendency, is a dangerous fallacy, which at once destroys all religious liberty, because he being of course judge of that tendency, will make his opinions the rule of judgment, and approve or condemn the sentiments of others only as they shall square with or differ from his own.*

Although the free speech clauses were directed primarily against the sedition prosecutions of the immediate past, it must not be thought that they would permit unlimited previous restraint. They must also be interpreted in the light of more remote history. The framers of those clauses did not invent the conception of freedom of speech as a result of their own experience of the last few years. The idea had been gradually molded in men's minds by centuries of conflict. It was the product of a people of whom the framers were merely the mouthpiece. Its significance was not fixed by their personality, but was the endless expression of a civilization. It was formed out of past resentment against the royal control of the press under the Tudors, against the Star Chamber and the pillory, against the Parliamentary censorship which Milton condemned in his *Areopagitica,* by recollections of heavy newspaper taxation, by hatred of the suppression of thought which went on vigorously on the Continent during the eighteenth century. Blackstone's views also had undoubted influence to bar out previous restraint. The censor is the most dangerous of all the enemies of liberty of the press, and ought not to exist in this country unless made necessary by extraordinary perils.

Moreover, the meaning of the First Amendment did not crystallize in 1791. The framers would probably have been horrified at the thought of protecting books by Darwin or Bernard Shaw, but "liberty of speech" is no more confined to the speech they thought permissible than "commerce" in another clause is limited to the sailing vessels and horse-drawn vehicles of 1787. Into the making of the constitutional conception of free speech have gone, not only men's bitter experience of the censorship and sedition prosecutions before

1791, but also the subsequent development of the law of fair comment in civil defamation, and the philosophical speculations of John Stuart Mill. Justice Holmes phrases the thought with even more than his habitual felicity. "The provisions of the Constitution are not mathematical formulas having their essence in their form; they are organic living institutions transplanted from English soil."

It is now clear that the First Amendment fixes limits upon the power of Congress to restrict speech either by a censorship or by a criminal statute, and if the Espionage Act exceeds those limits it is unconstitutional. It is sometimes argued that the Constitution gives Congress the power to declare war, raise armies, and support a navy, that one provision of the Constitution cannot be used to break down another provision, and consequently freedom of speech cannot be invoked to break down the war power. I would reply that the First Amendment is just as much a part of the Constitution as the war clauses, and that it is equally accurate to say that the war clauses cannot be invoked to break down freedom of speech. The truth is that all provisions of the Constitution must be construed together so as to limit each other. In a war as in peace, this process of mutual adjustment must include the Bill of Rights. There are those who believe that the Bill of Rights can be set aside in war time at the uncontrolled will of the government. The first ten amendments were drafted by men who had just been through a war. The Third and Fifth Amendments expressly apply in war. A majority of the Supreme Court declared the war power of Congress to be restricted by the Bill of Rights in Ex parte *Milligan*. If the First Amendment is to mean anything, it must restrict powers which are expressly granted by the Constitution to Congress, since Congress has no other powers. It must apply to those activities of government which are most liable to interfere with free discussion, namely, the postal service and the conduct of war.

The true meaning of freedom of speech seems to be this. One of the most important purposes of society and government is the discovery and spread of truth on subjects of general concern. This is possible only through absolutely unlimited discussion, for, as Bagehot points out, once force is thrown into the argument, it becomes a matter of chance whether it is thrown on the false side or the true, and truth loses all its natural advantage in the contest. Nevertheless, there are other purposes of government, such as order, the training of the young, protection against external aggression. Unlimited discussion sometimes interferes with these purposes, which must then be balanced against freedom of speech, but freedom of speech ought to weigh very heavily in the scale. The First Amendment gives binding force to this principle of political wisdom.

Or to put the matter another way, it is useless to define free speech by talk about rights. The agitator asserts his constitutional right to speak, the government asserts its constitutional right to wage war. The result is a deadlock. Each side takes the position of the man who was arrested for swinging his arms and hitting another in the nose, and asked the judge if he did not have a right to swing his arms in a free country. "Your right to swing your arms ends just where the other man's nose begins." To find the boundary line of any right, we must get behind rules of law to human facts. In our problem, we must regard the desires and needs of the individual human being who wants to speak and those of the great group of human beings among whom he speaks. That is, in technical language, there are individual interests and social interests, which must be balanced against each other, if they conflict, in order to determine which interest shall be sacrificed under the circumstances and which shall be protected and become the foundation of a legal right. It must never be forgotten that the balancing cannot be properly done unless all the interests involved are adequately ascertained, and the great evil of all this talk about rights is that each side is so busy denying the other's claim to rights that it entirely overlooks the human desires and needs behind that claim.

The rights and powers of the Constitution, aside from the portions which create the machinery of the federal system, are largely means of protecting important individual and social interests, and because of this necessity of balancing such interests the clauses cannot be construed with absolute literalness. The Fourteenth Amendment and the obligation of contracts clause, maintaining important individual interests, are modified by the police power of the states, which protects health and other social interests. The Thirteenth Amendment is subject to many implied exceptions, so that temporary involuntary servitude is permitted to secure social interests in the construction of roads, the prevention of vagrancy, the training of the militia or national army. It is common to rest these implied exceptions to the Bill of Rights upon the ground that they existed in 1791 and long before, but a less arbitrary explanation is desirable. Not everything old is good. Thus the antiquity of peonage does not constitute it an exception to the Thirteenth Amendment; it is not now demanded by any strong social interest. It is significant that the social interest in shipping which formerly required the compulsory labor of articled sailors is no longer recognized in the United States as sufficiently important to outweigh the individual interest in free locomotion and choice of occupation. Even treaties providing for the apprehension in our ports of deserting foreign seamen have been abrogated by the La Follette Seamen's Act. The Bill of Rights does not crystallize antiquity. It seems better to say that long usage does not create an exception to the absolute language of the Constitution, but demonstrates the importance of the social interest behind the exception.

The First Amendment protects two kinds of interests in free speech. There is an individual interest, the need of many men to express their opinions on matters vital to them if life is to be worth living, and a social interest in the attainment of truth, so that the country may not only adopt the wisest course of action but carry it out in the wisest way. This social interest is especially important in war time. Even after war has been declared there is bound to be a confused mixture of good and bad arguments in its support, and a wide difference of opinion as to its objects. Truth can be sifted out from falsehood only if the government is vigorously and constantly cross-examined, so that the fundamental issues of the struggle may be clearly defined, and the war may not be diverted to improper ends, or conducted with an undue sacrifice of life and liberty, or prolonged after its just purposes are accomplished. Legal proceedings prove that an opponent makes the best cross-examiner. Consequently it is a disastrous mistake to limit criticism to

those who favor the war. Men bitterly hostile to it may point
out evils in its management like the secret treaties, which its
supporters have been too busy to unearth. If a free canvassing
of the aims of the war by its opponents is crushed by the
menace of long imprisonment, such evils, even though made
public in one or two newspapers, may not come to the attention of those who had power to counteract them until too late.

The history of the years between 1914 and 1919 shows how
the objects of a war may change completely during its progress, and it is well that those objects should be steadily re-
formulated under the influence of open discussion not only by
those who demand a military victory, but by pacifists who take
a different view of the national welfare. Further argument for
the existence of this social interest becomes unnecessary if we
recall the national value of the opposition in former wars.

The great trouble with most judicial construction of the Espionage Act is that this social interest has been ignored and
free speech has been regarded as merely an individual interest,
which must readily give way like other personal desires the
moment it interferes with the social interest in national safety.
The judge [Oliver Wendell Holmes, Jr.] who has done most
to bring social interests into legal thinking said years ago, "I
think that the judges themselves have failed adequately to
recognize their duty of weighing considerations of social advantage. The duty is inevitable, and the result of the often proclaimed judicial aversion to deal with such considerations is
simply to leave the very ground and foundation of judgments
inarticulate and often unconscious." The failure of the courts
in the past to formulate any principle for drawing a boundary
line around the right of free speech not only threw the judges
into the difficult questions of the Espionage Act without any
well-considered standard of criminality, but also allowed some
of them to impose standards of their own and fix the line at a
point which makes all opposition to this or any future war impossible. For example:

> No man should be permitted, by deliberate act, or even
> unthinkingly, to do that which will in any way detract
> from the efforts which the United States is putting forth

or serve to postpone for a single moment the early coming
of the day when the success of our arms shall be a fact.

The true boundary line of the First Amendment can be fixed only when Congress and the courts realize that the principle on which speech is classified as lawful or unlawful involves the balancing against each other of two very important social interests, in public safety and in the search for truth. Every reasonable attempt should be made to maintain both interests unimpaired, and the great interest in free speech should be sacrificed only when the interest in public safety is really imperiled, and not, as most men believe, when it is barely conceivable that it may be slightly affected. In war time, therefore, speech should be unrestricted by the censorship or by punishment, unless it is clearly liable to cause direct and dangerous interference with the conduct of the war.

Thus our problem of locating the boundary line of free speech is solved. It is fixed close to the point where words will give rise to unlawful acts. We cannot define the right of free speech with the precision of the Rule against Perpetuities or the Rule in Shelley's Case, because it involves national policies which are much more flexible than private property, but we can establish a workable principle of classification in this method of balancing and this broad test of certain danger. There is a similar balancing in the determination of what is "due process of law." We can insist upon various procedural safeguards which make it more probable that a tribunal will give the value of open discussion its proper weight in the balance. Fox's Libel Act is such a safeguard . . . And we can with certitude declare that the First Amendment forbids the punishment of words merely for their injurious tendencies. The history of the Amendment and the political function of free speech corroborate each other and make this conclusion plain.

COMMENT: On Restricting the Sale
of Pernicious Material

Chafee's essay goes far to explain the legal position the Constitution assumes with regard to freedom of speech. It is a position that is being constantly assaulted, on the one side by public groups, including the states, which, largely motivated by
self-interest, nevertheless wish to bequeath a purer and better
country to their children, and, on the other, by people who
profit from matter put out to satisfy private appetites for violence, sadism, crime, and so on. Both the traditional pieties
of the country and the diversity of opinion make the law vul-
nerable. The popular press is naturally anti-puritan, as it supports entertainment and itself seeks to entertain. Its earnestness
is devoted mainly to the preservation of popular liberties, including its own. Yet the respect for other people which naturally accompanies a zest for liberty becomes bypassed in the
popular press in favor of exposure; a false candor allows it to
intrude in the region of private lives where the laws concerning
freedom of expression have no significance.

From the earliest times of printing, pamphlets and broad-
sheets have flooded the streets and public places with obscene,
ribald, scandalous comment on the events and figures of the
day. Milton himself in his pamphlets was not above insulting
his opponents in terms no one would dream of using today.
The scandalous anti-Catholic literature that found its way
through the mails during the Kennedy-Nixon presidential cam-
paign of 1960 was the inheritor of this tradition, though what
it has kept in nastiness it has forfeited in gusto: the broad-
sheets of Milton's day were a good deal more Rabelaisian. It
seems as though the tradition of their plain broad humor

passed out of the English-speaking world with the deadening impact of the war of 1914–18.

The following text introduces the difficult question of where the line is to be drawn about the legitimacy of material for sale at the newsstands or to be dispatched through the mails, when its influence may be judged pernicious. It introduces too the legality of impounding material of any sort sent through the mails. What the speaker is doing is not setting up an absolute standard of truth, but referring us back to the law, especially to the legal position set out in the First Amendment to the Constitution, and to the kind of ideas that the men had who wrote the First Amendment. The attitude is a utilitarian one, but it is invested with the same humanism as Milton's. Without this peculiarly American utilitarian humanism, respect for the rule of law has very little value. The speech is taken from the testimony of American Civil Liberties Union before Senate Subcommittees on Juvenile Delinquency and Constitutional Amendments, in January 1960.

"One constitutional amendment (S.J. Res. 116), introduced by Senator James O. Eastland of Mississippi, would allow each state to decide 'on the basis of its own public policy, questions of decency and morality,' and would prevent abridgment of the right of the states to enact legislation in this field. A second constitutional amendment (S.J. Res. 133), offered by Senator Estes Kefauver of Tennessee, would declare that the First Amendment protections of free speech and free press do not apply to obscene material and allow Congress and the states to adopt laws prohibiting such material."

TEXT: "Smut, Corruption, and the Law" by Patrick Murphy Malin

My name is Patrick Murphy Malin. I am the Executive Director of the American Civil Liberties Union, a non-profit membership corporation concerned solely with the protection of the civil liberties of all persons, and I testify on its behalf today. . . .

We in the Union—like other Americans—are deeply aware of the problem of juvenile delinquency, the special area of your concern. It is natural that, in the common desire to meet the challenge posed by the high incidence of juvenile delinquency, there should be sought a simple cause and a quick solution. The emotions of pity and indignation lead to the plausible conclusion that, if we can give some public official broad power to stop the flow of "smut," we shall then have gone a long way to insulate our children from pernicious influences which, unrestrained, lead them into degradation and crime.

Nonetheless, we must bear constantly in mind that, with respect to juvenile delinquency no less than with respect to any other area of anti-social or criminal behavior, minimum standards of constitutionality must not be circumvented in the search for a cure. . . .

In introduction, I wish to state our general policy on the complex and difficult question of obscenity. To begin with, we should recall that the Supreme Court has already told us that we cannot constitutionally reduce all of our literature to a level fit for consumption by children. . . . Beyond that, we hold that the constitutional guarantees of free speech and press apply to all expression, and that there is no special category of "obscenity" or "pornography" to which different constitutional tests apply. To be consistent with our view of civil liberties and constitutional freedoms, an obscenity statute must at least be definite enough to guide the average man, and also require that, before any material can be held to be obscene, it must be found to present beyond a reasonable doubt a clear and present danger of normally inducing behavior which has been made criminal by a valid statute.

We wish to make it clear that we do not profess to be experts on the issue of whether there is a causal relationship between the reading or viewing of books and films and the commission of an illegal act, but we know there is a great difference of expert judgment on the matter. As we said in 1955 in a pamphlet which discussed the relationship between crime comics and juvenile delinquency: "The ACLU believes that comic books, like other mass media, may play an important part in the development of children's minds and behavior. But, in view of the divergent—even contradictory—opinions expressed by responsible and qualified persons, it believes that there is lacking the assurance that crime comics are a significant cause of delinquency."

The need for further research on this basic question was forcefully expressed in the final report of the Senate Subcommittee on Juvenile Delinquency in the first session of the 85th Congress, issued on March 4, 1957. That subcommittee was headed by Senator Kefauver of Tennessee. Under the heading (p. 127) "More Basic Research is Needed in Behavioral Problems," the report states:

"The insistent demands for immediate action programs to prevent and treat juvenile delinquency should not obscure the equally important need for long-range, fundamental research on the nature of man and society. Research provides the necessary basic knowledge concerning human social behavior upon which rational, effective action programs must be based. In the course of its deliberations, the subcommittee was impressed time and time again with the serious gaps in our knowledge of the fundamental mechanisms of human behavior in society. Such knowledge is as essential for a far-reaching solution of juvenile delinquency as it is to other pressing social problems. The subcommittee, therefore, believes that the encouragement of basic research in the social sciences must be an essential feature of any systematic program designed to meet the problems created by delinquent behavior.

"Many expert witnesses before this subcommittee have reported on various phases of research findings to date. In the testimony some solid facts have been combined with interesting speculations and revealing insights. But much remains to be known. The intricate web of interrelationships among home environment, parent-child relationships, community facilities, personality structure, broken homes, intergroup relations, school curricula, religious and spiritual values, and the contents of the mass media of communication has been noted. The exact nature and deeper meaning of these relationships, however, still remains to be unraveled.

"Do disturbed children tend to watch television more than nondisturbed children? What does this mean in terms of the future behavior of the child? What are the basic personality characteristics and family environments of nondelinquent children brought up in disorganized and undesirable neighborhoods? Do comic books reinforce, discourage, or encourage antisocial behavior? Before we can begin to probe thoroughly such questions, we must know a great deal more about the nature of human beings, the course of personality development, and the social and cultural processes that shape and direct human behavior. Basic research can do much in helping us discover and define the general patterns of human social behavior, and thus establish the larger contexts in terms of which the mosaic of questions arising from specific social problems will be seen in proper perspective.

"Research plays a particularly important role in the attack upon social problems. It permits the formulation of hypotheses that can be tested and verified by experiments and systematic observations. It leads to the removal of a body of knowledge from the realm of speculation and subjective opinion, in which each individual deems himself to be an expert, to the realm of assured and demonstrated fact. It substitutes proof for unwarranted assertions. For example, only well-designed research can provide a sound basis for evaluating the controversial allegations about the impact of television and comic books and other mass media upon the study habits and behavior of children and youths."

We are, of course, aware that the United States Supreme Court has upheld the constitutionality of the federal obscenity statute, but we shall continue to press our views for a broader concept of the First Amendment and hope for a change in that ruling. (I might also add that the Union is constantly engaged in re-thinking and re-examining its policy formulations, and that this policy view of ours on obscenity is no exception.)

But you are not here concerned with the constitutionality or civil liberties aspects of the federal criminal obscenity law. Your concern today, and ours, is with the administration by the Post Office of the federal impounding-of-obscene-material law. . . .

Under 39 U.S. Code 259a, the Postmaster General may return to senders any mail addressed to persons who, he believes, are engaged in the dissemination of obscene materials, marking such mail as "unlawful."

S.2562 does not deal expressly with Section 259a; it amends Section 259b, the enforcement arm of 259a. [Section] 259b, as it presently stands, empowers the Postmaster General to impound all mail addressed to the person he believes to be a disseminator of obscene materials, when he finds this necessary to the enforcement of 259a, and within 20 days thereafter to seek and obtain a court order continuing the impounding in accordance with the court's discretion—if the court finds that the continuation of such an order is necessary to the enforcement of 259a. The scope of 259b is no broader, now, than that of 259a—obscenity is the test.

S.2562 would amend Sec. 259b so that the court order extending the interim order of the Postmaster General may be issued on a finding by the court, upon all the evidence before it, that the detention of mail is "necessary to the effective enforcement of Sections 259 and 259a," thereby modifying the present language of Sec. 259b which requires that the court find that the detention of mail is "*reasonable* and necessary to the effective enforcement" of the statute. [Italics supplied.]

The other principal change would extend the length of the Postmaster General's interim order from 20 to 45 days. I shall discuss this first.

It has already been judicially noted that the power of the Post Office Department to impound mail "touches basic freedoms," and that its exercise "may as effectively close down an establishment as the sheriff himself." (*Summerfield* v. *Sunshine Book Company,* 221 F. 2d 42, 45 C.A.D.C. 1954, cert. den. *Stanard* v. *Olesen,* quoting Mr. Justice Douglas). And it has also been held that the 20-day expiration date on an administrative impounding order, absent a sustaining court order, "is the most important of these built-in limitations" upon the exercise of the extraordinary power of the Post Office under Section 259b. (*Toberoff* v. *Summerfield, supra,* 256 F. 2d at 94.) S. 2562 would more than halve this protective limitation.

As noted in the *Toberoff* and other cases, the power to harass by the impounding method is destructive; extended to 45 days, the power to impound becomes the power to destroy—all without the requirement of any hearing, without any due process whatsoever having been afforded, and even without any final determination by the Postmaster General or by any court that the material being disseminated is in fact obscene.

If it is finally determined that the material sent by the disseminator is *not* obscene, then he has been financially punished in the meantime, for 45 days, as severely as the convicted disseminator of obscenity who has had a stiff fine imposed upon him after a criminal trial. If the material be finally found obscene, then the person may still have suffered unjustified interference with his business by non-delivery of all *other* materials not found obscene; for we know of no practical method by which his mail exclusively concerning the non-objectionable parts of the business can be sorted out from the mail dealing with ob-jectionable parts. Though the disseminator may examine his incoming mail "and receive such mail as clearly is not connected with the alleged unlawful activity" (under both the present and the proposed legislation), still this cannot be done—unless the word of the disseminator is taken for which mail is and which is not so connected— without exposing his private correspondence to the scru-tiny of the Post Office official. We submit that this re-quires a person to undergo an unlawful search, and to impound without a warrant, in violation of the Fourth Amendment to the United States Constitution. And we contend that the power to impound without any prior judicial determination, on the mere say-so of a govern-ment official, violates that same prohibition as well as the First Amendment.

As for the other principal amendment of Sec. 259b con-tained in S.2562, that provision apparently seeks to alter the judicial standard for granting or denying an extension of the Postmaster General's interim order by discarding the standard of reasonableness.

We think this is gratuitous, unwarranted and, principally, confusing. Is removing the word "reasonable" intended to sug-gest that a wholly unreasonable showing by the Postmaster General would nonetheless compel the courts to extend his in-terim order? The Postmaster General, under any standard, must produce sufficient evidence to persuade the court to ex-tend the interim order by showing that it is necessary to allow his Department to conclude its investigation under Section 259a. Must he produce a scintilla of evidence, or substantial evidence, or a preponderance of evidence? The statute doesn't say. Consequently, in any case, the court will determine, upon all the circumstances of the case, whether an extension is war-ranted. As amorphous as the term "reasonable" is, it at least has the virtue of being common judicial currency and offers some kind of standard to guide the courts. Reasonable is the reverse of arbitrary. To remove the word "reasonable" from the statute implies that the Congress sanctions the Postmaster

General in proceeding under Sec. 259a arbitrarily, on the flimsiest of grounds or on no grounds at all. We do not believe any government official should be empowered to act arbitrarily, either explicitly or implicitly. Preserving the standard of reasonableness in Sec. 259b will at least serve to remind the Postmaster General that he cannot apply the statute at whim.

On the positive side, we endorse the addition of that language on page 5 (lines 2–8 of the bill) which allows a person against whom an interim order is issued to seek an injunction in the Federal District Court ordering the Postmaster General to lift the order if it is not necessary to the effective enforcement of the statute. In those circumstances where the Postmaster General does not believe an extension of the 45-day period will be necessary, this new provision will assure that the affected party will obtain judicial review of an executive action that would otherwise be free of judicial scrutiny during that period.

Having made these brief observations on what are largely technical aspects of this bill, I want now to state that on the whole we believe that S.2562 only makes a bad law worse. We believe, consistently with our general views on censorship, that Sections 259a and 259b have no place in our statute books.

To us, all censorship is suspect. The powers of a censor are almost inevitably abused. This is shown by the fact that the United States Supreme Court has in recent years reversed as a violation of freedom of speech and press *every* decision of every movie censor board and almost *every* decision of the Postmaster in banning as "obscene" materials from the mails which have come before the Court for review. I shall not bore you with a recital of the list of cases, many of which are listed in an annexed appendix.

The Post Office censorship, moreover, usually operates in secret, unless the publisher goes to court to battle it out or otherwise himself discloses the ban. It has been impossible, so far as we are aware, to obtain from the Post Office a list of titles banned. All that it discloses are the names of authors whose works it has suppressed. But what it has disclosed shows that—like all censors who must necessarily err on the side of suppression—it has acted not only unreasonably, but absurdly. For the Post Office has ruled as obscene works by such authors as Ernest Hemingway, John O'Hara, James Jones, John Steinbeck, Norman Mailer, Charles Jackson, Richard Wright, Somerset Maugham, Alexander Dumas, Voltaire, De Maupassant, Zola and Tolstoi. (De Grazia, *Obscenity and the Mails,* 20 Law and Contemporary Problems 608, 615, 1955.)

Both Sections 259a and 259b in their present and proposed form are entirely unnecessary; the tough penalties prescribed in the federal criminal obscenity law afford ample protection to this country, if protection there need be, against obscene materials. As Judge Bryan noted recently in the "Lady Chatterley's Lover" book case, in New York City, the Postmaster General

". . . has no special competence to determine what constitutes obscenity within the meaning of" [the federal obscenity law] . . .

". . . The determination of such questions is peculiarly for the courts, particularly in the light of the constitutional questions implicit in each case." (*Readers' Subscription, Inc.* v. *Christenberry,* 175 F. Supp. 488—D.S.D.N.Y., 1959.)

If for any reason the criminal obscenity statutes are deemed insufficient to protect the public, we know no reason why the Post Office should not be required to proceed as the Customs Bureau is required to do before it may suppress alleged obscene material, that is, to bring an action in a federal district court to condemn the material. There a jury trial can be had. (See 19 United States Code, Section 1305.) We also note that it has been held, in an opinion written by Mr. Justice Potter Stewart when he was on a Federal Court of Appeals, that a jury trial is the right and appropriate way of determining the question of obscenity. (*United States* v. *Volanski,* 246 F. 2d 842, 1957.)

At this point I would like to insert some comments on H.R. 7379 (passed by the House last session) made by Ernest Angell, the Chairman of our Board of Directors, before the House Subcommittee on Postal Operations on July 31, 1959. . . .

"(a) . . . 259b, as it presently stands, empowers the Postmaster General to impound all mail addressed *to* the person he believes to be a disseminator of obscene materials, when he finds this necessary to the enforcement of 259a, and within 20 days thereafter to seek and obtain a court order continuing the impounding in accordance with the court's discretion—if the court finds that the continuation of such an order is reasonable and necessary to the enforcement of 259a. The scope of 259b is no broader, now, than that of 259a—obscenity as the test.

"H.R. 7379 goes much further. It provides that the impounding order may be issued merely when the Postmaster General determines that such action is in 'the public interest,' and extends its effective period to 45 days. And, when the question is before a court of whether it shall continue the impounding order, the standard will be, not as the present whether such continuance is reasonable and necessary to the enforcement of 259a, but only whether it is 'in the public interest.'

"*The standard.* We believe that the standard for the impounding ban, of merely being 'in the public interest,' is clearly unconstitutional. The Supreme Court has already stricken down as unconstitutional a local law of almost identical language which would have permitted an administrative board to ban the exhibition of motion pictures found by it to be 'prejudicial to the best interests of the city.' *Gelling* v. *Texas,* 343 U.S. 960 (1952). There is no logical distinction between the *Gelling* standard and the proposed Post Office standard of this bill. The language before you is so completely vague that it permits the Postmaster General to invoke whatever personal whim he pleases to clothe with the 'public interest' garment. This is no standard at all. Statutes which prescribe no standards by which to guide the administrative officer have been repeatedly held to be unconstitutional in cases in the free speech area. . . .

"And the danger of such vague statutes, as a practical matter, is shown by the fact that the movie in the *Gelling* case

('Pinky') was banned solely because it showed Negro and white children playing together! This illustrates the potentiality of grave abuse opened up by the proposed legislation.

"We note further that Section 259b in its present form 'indicates the awareness of Congress that the Postmaster General was being therein given great and unusual power, and that strict limitations upon the exercise of such power were required'. . . . No public officer should ever be given such power of unlimited discretion, however exalted his position, however sincere he may be.

"(b) It might be argued that a provision in this bill . . . which would give the vendor of the material the right to obtain an injunction restraining the enforcement of the Postmaster's impounding order, may prevent some of the evil we perceive. While this is a partial protection, it certainly is quite inadequate, for a court order restraining the Postmaster may be granted only if it be shown that the issuance of the order was 'arbitrary and capricious.' Thus, the Postmaster General might be completely wrong, it might not be in the public interest to ban *incoming* mail to the vendor, the *outgoing* material that produced the ban might not be obscene in the final analysis,—but the Postmaster General could be restrained by a court only if he had been 'arbitrary or capricious.' This is a far narrower scope of judicial review of administrative acts than can be found in virtually any other statute in this general area with which we, at least, are familiar.

"(c) *Some confusing ambiguities.* The proposed legislation presents certain ambiguities in the court procedure which may well cause substantial confusion. First, query as to whether there can be an appeal from a court order on a finding that the Postmaster General's order was (or was not) arbitrary or capricious; and if reviewable, what is the scope of the review? Secondly, the proposed legislation provides that an appeal from the order of the court shall be allowed 'as in civil causes,' but it is not clear whether this refers merely to an order of a court procured on a motion of the Postmaster General, or *also* to other types of orders which might be secured during the proceedings governed by 259b. Thirdly, startling uncertainty is created by the wording of (a)(1) that the order of

the Postmaster to hold and detain mail is to be in effect for
20 days, though the order normally will not expire for 'the
45 days'—(a)(3). These two sub-sections flatly contradict
each other as to the status of the order between the 21st and
the 45th days. Fourthly, provision is made for review of the
final order of the Post Office in the United States Court of Appeals, though it is not clear whether this review is in addition
to, or as a substitute for, an injunction proceeding in the District Court.

"(d) The Post Office is aghast at the fact that citizens complain against its attempts to brand as obscene materials which
have been repeatedly ruled by court decisions not to be obscene. It is highly improper for the Post Office as a division
of the executive branch to declaim against the rulings of our
courts; it should accept them. The Post Office has even gone
to the extreme of attacking attorneys who have procured favorable court decisions for their clients. These lawyers are no
more to be condemned than the attorneys for the Post Office
who seek to obtain an 'obscenity' finding as to material which
is later found by the courts to be protected by freedom of
press. We also think it is unseemly and improper for the Post
Office to attack organizations which defend freedom of speech.
We have noted that within the past few years every Post Office censorship case which has reached the United States Supreme Court has resulted in that Court ruling against the Post
Office. Under these circumstances, Postal diatribes of emotional pique against organizations which took positions later
upheld by the courts are understandable—but entirely un-
justifiable.

"We suggest that the Post Office should busy itself with an
attempt more narrowly to construe and correctly to apply the
decision of the Supreme Court in Roth as to what obscenity
means, so that these administrative rulings may be upheld
when they reach the appellate courts. To attempt to evade or
cry down the decisions of the courts is not becoming.

"As the Supreme Court said in Roth v. United States, 354
U.S. 476, on the 'fundamental freedoms of speech and press,'

Ceaseless vigilance is the watchword to prevent their erosion by the Congress or by the States. The door barring federal and state intrusion into this area cannot be left ajar; it must be kept tightly closed and opened only the slightest crack necessary to prevent encroachment upon more important interests. It is therefore vital that the safeguards for judging obscenity safeguard the protection of freedom of speech and press for material which does not treat sex in a manner appealing to prurient interest. 354 U.S. 488.

"No one should be condemned for exercising the 'ceaseless vigilance' which the Supreme Court tells us is necessary. Nor should the door barring federal intrusion into the area of freedom of speech and press be opened by any legislation (such as discussed here) which would vest greater censorship powers in one man, the Postmaster General, than are possessed by a censor board anywhere of which we are aware, save the censors behind the Iron Curtain."

With regard to S.J. Res. 133, we are opposed to this proposed Constitutional Amendment for two reasons.

First, we disagree with the definition of obscenity formulated in the *Roth* case, which is adopted in this proposed amendment. Before stating our disagreements with *Roth*, I should first say that, as far as that decision goes, it seems to us headed in the right direction, since it calls for consideration of the material "as a whole," and presumably requires a trial by jury to determine whether the material offends "contemporary community standards." But we do not believe *Roth*, as a whole, is correct.

As I said in discussing S.2562, our position is that there must be a demonstrable relationship between the material sought to be prohibited and conduct made validly criminal by statute.

Roth, in attempting to define that difficult term "obscene," compounds the problem by requiring us to define "prurient," a term at least as obscure as "obscene," and perhaps more obscure because it calls for a judgment based upon a state of mind. Mr. Justice Douglas says in his book, *The Right of the People* (Doubleday, 1958) at p. 65, "Certainly the common test suggested by courts—whether the publication arouses sexual thoughts—cannot be squared with the First Amendment. A state of mind is not enough; it is the relationship of that state of mind to overt action that would seem to be critical." He continues by stating that "[The First Amendment] should be respected even when we come to offensive material, unless there is such a close nexus between the words and anti-social action that the two can be said to be brigaded. The excesses that must be tolerated will bring less evil than the institution of a regime of censors looking for material that is offensive." We are in agreement with Mr. Justice Douglas.

Our second objection to S.J. Res. 133 relates to the effect the proposed amendment would have upon social diversity and change—considerations that lie at the root of freedom of expression. It seems to us that it would be extremely bad social policy to petrify by Constitutional amendment so amorphous and slippery a concept as "obscenity." To imbed a judicial definition of "obscenity" into the Constitution would attribute to such definition an unwarranted infallibility.

While the ACLU believes the *Roth* definition is unsound because it encompasses too much, there are assuredly those who believe that definition unsound because it encompasses too little. But the day may well come when a case is presented to the Supreme Court which persuasively demonstrates that its definition of "obscenity" is erroneous, in one direction or another, based on new evidence discovered by social scientists. The courts, in this area of uncertainty and doubt, must remain free to fashion new rules based on new evidence. Our system of jurisprudence is far more suitable to deal with the changes which inevitably occur in the area of expression than is the more rigid process of Constitutional amendment.

There is no doubt in my mind that the public and scientific view of obscenity will continue to undergo substantial re-evaluation, as has been the case in the past. For example, D. H. Lawrence, who has been responsible for a good deal of litigation recently, has pointed out that ". . . Hamlet shocked all the Cromwellian Puritans, and shocks nobody today, and some of Aristophanes shocks everybody today and didn't galvanize the later Greeks at all, apparently." (*Sex, Literature and Censorship,* Twayne Publishers, Inc., 1953, p.

69.) However, Lawrence goes on to say: "But even I would censor genuine pornography. It would not be very difficult. In the first place genuine pornography is almost always underworld, it doesn't come into the open. In the second place, you can recognize it by the insult it offers, invariably, to sex, and to the human spirit." (p. 74). And then, as if finally to prove the elusiveness of final standards in this complex problem, he offers a few standards of censorship that by any test would probably run afoul of the First Amendment!

The process of Constitutional amendment—particularly as it affects the area of free expression—should not be invoked to freeze a concept about which there are wide areas of disagreement on the one hand, and for which, on the other hand, there are prospects of ever-increasing knowledge in the future.

It is far more sensible to leave to the legislatures and the courts the task of molding the law in this dynamic area.

With regard to S.J. Res. 116, a proposed amendment to the Constitution which would forbid abridgement of the right of a state "to decide on the basis of its own public policy questions of decency and morality," we offer the following comment.

In addition to the fact that the terms "morality" and "decency" are so vague as to defy precise definition—a virtue towards which all law should aspire, and to which it must aspire to satisfy the Constitution itself—those words might well invite attempted nullification of all the safeguards to individual freedom contained in the Bill of Rights. They would not only allow the states to enact legislation curbing literature believed harmful to juveniles, but also might allow the states to disregard other accumulated freedoms. They might justify the regulation of the right to assembly, dominate the right of privacy protected by the Fourth Amendment, and be reckoned superior to the due process and equal protection clauses of the Fourteenth Amendment.

If this proposed amendment were adopted, it would be counterpoised to the entire Bill of Rights and would compel judicial re-evaluation of all those cases over the last ninety years which have applied the Fourteenth Amendment to determine the extent of the power of the states. It would, I fear, result in serious, if not fatal, setbacks to racial equality. It could in some areas threaten the fair administration of criminal justice.

The states today do not lack the power to deal with activity which their legislatures believe should be subject to criminal sanctions. All they must do is conform to the standards set down in the Constitution. True, they do not have unfettered power to regulate any conduct as they see fit. But this is one of the main reasons for our federal and state constitutions: to require the exercise of police powers in a fair and reasonable and non-arbitrary manner.

Any state which believes that its citizens are threatened by conduct it believes criminal, has the power to adopt legislation to prohibit that conduct. Its own judiciary will have the opportunity to determine if that criminal legislation is consistent with its own Constitution and the Constitution of the United States. The United States Courts will also have the opportunity to weigh that legislation against the United States Constitution. Thus the state and the individual have equal opportunity to present their views in court.

The late Justice Holmes said that the life of the law is experience, not logic. Whatever else he meant, it seems to me that he at least meant that law is not a cold, calculable science, but an art that reflects the society of which it is a part. Part of that judicial art includes enabling the law to fit society's changing views of morality and decency, as reflected in legislation and tested by the courts for adherence to the basic Constitutional safeguards of our citizens in a free society with a democratic government.

NOTES ON CENSORSHIP AND FACT

1. Francis Bacon, *Novum Organum,* translated by W. Wood, Book I, li, xxxviii–xliv.
2. J.-J. Rousseau, *The Social Contract Etc.,* translated by G. D. H. Cole (New York: Everyman's Library, 1913), p. 111.
3. Wilkes's patron.

CENSORSHIP and IMAGINATION

I. CENSORSHIP and LITERATURE

COMMENT

"In matters of art," Mr. John Ciardi has written, "what is official is always inhuman." We might add, "What is official is uninteresting." Officialdom interrupts and destroys art because it has nothing to do with it. When censorship tries to step between serious writer and serious reader, as Mr. Ciardi points out, it cannot be tolerated. Writer and reader must both push it aside, first because art exists for an audience, even if that audience isn't there yet; secondly because people without art lose insight and judgment. Efforts to impose restraint on the naturally shocking aspects of works of the imagination generally result in ignorance and corruption. This is not to say that art is therapeutic—though the kinds of entertainments that take the place of a forbidden art often pretend to be so. To a certain extent, the work of the artist represents the conditions of his world, whether he wills it or not. As R. G. Collingwood wrote:

> The artist must prophesy not in the sense that he foretells things to come, but in the sense that he tells his audience, at the risk of their displeasure, the secrets of their own hearts. But what he has to utter is not, as the individualistic theory of art would have us think, his own secrets. As spokesman of the community, the secrets he must utter are theirs. The reason why they need him is that no community altogether knows its own heart; and

by failing in this knowledge a community deceives itself on the one subject concerning which ignorance means death. For the evils which come from that ignorance the poet as prophet suggests no remedy, because he has already given one. The remedy is the poem itself. Art is the community's medicine for the worst disease of the mind, the corruption of consciousness.

In a sense, then, the work of the censor is always too late. It is absurd to consider a writer writing seriously with his public in the forefront of his mind. And when societies, or representatives of society, declare that this may be said and not that, they are always in danger of absurdity. There is a perfectly natural gap between the sentient being of the single solitary common reader and the sets of permissible utterances that may occur between people of different generations, sex, capabilities, education, culture, and so on. Any attempt to "picket" this gap is going to bring about confusion, and any limitations are a potential threat to the free-ranging mind of the ruminator, which seldom expresses directly a hundredth part of what is communicated to it, but which all the same constitutes an enormous moral force in the world. How far this mind may be publicly acknowledged depends very much on the belief the society has in its own worth.

Henry Miller's *Sexus* (in its Danish edition) had been read widely in Norway for some time before it was incidentally cited as an example of an extant pornographic work during the prosecution of another book for obscenity. When *Sexus* came to be examined for obscenity itself, the Oslo Town Court broad-mindedly drew out testimony from many kinds of experts. But Miller, when he was called on for a statement himself, considered them all absurd. The following is his statement.

TEXT: "Defence of the Freedom to Read," a letter to the Supreme Court of Norway in connection with the *Sexus* case, by Henry Miller

Big Sur, California
27 Feb. 1959.

Dear Mr. Hirsch:

To answer your letter of January 19th requesting a statement of me which might be used in the Supreme Court trial to be conducted in March or April of this year . . . It is difficult to be more explicit than I was in my letter of September 19th, 1957, when the case against my book "Sexus" was being tried in the lower courts of Oslo. However, here are some further reflections which I trust will be found à propos.

When I read the decision of the Oslo Town Court, which you sent me some months ago, I did so with mingled feelings. If occasionally I was obliged to roll with laughter—partly because of the inept translation, partly because of the nature and the number of infractions listed—I trust no one will take offense. Taking the world for what it is, and the men who make and execute the laws for what they are, I thought the decision as fair and honest as any theorem of Euclid's. Nor was I unaware of, or indifferent to, the efforts made by the Court to render an interpretation beyond the strict letter of the law. (An impossible task, I would say, for if laws are made for men and not men for laws, it is also true that certain individuals are made for the law and can only see things through the eyes of the law.)

I failed to be impressed, I must confess, by the weighty,

often pompous or hypocritical, opinions adduced by scholars, literary pundits, psychologists, medicos and such like. How could I be when it is precisely such single-minded individuals, so often wholly devoid of humor, at whom I so frequently aim my shafts?

Rereading this lengthy document to-day, I am more than ever aware of the absurdity of the whole procedure. (How lucky I am not to be indicted as a "pervert" or "degenerate", but simply as one who makes sex pleasurable and innocent!) Why, it is often asked, when he has so much else to give, did he have to introduce these disturbing, controversial scenes dealing with sex? To answer that properly, one would have to go back to the womb—with or without the analyst's guiding hand. Each one—priest, analyst, barrister, judge—has his own answer, usually a ready made one. But none go far enough, none are deep enough, inclusive enough. The divine answer, of course, is—first remove the mote from your own eye!

If I were there, in the dock, my answer would probably be—"Guilty! Guilty on all ninety-seven counts! To the gallows!" For when I take the short, myopic view, I realize that I was guilty even before I wrote the book. Guilty, in other words, because I am the way I am. The marvel is that I am walking about as a free man. I should have been condemned the moment I stepped out of my mother's womb.

In that heartrending account of my return to the bosom of the family which is given in "Reunion in Brooklyn", I concluded with these words, and I meant them, each and every one of them: "I regard the entire world as my home. I inhabit the earth, not a particular portion of it labelled America, France, Germany, Russia . . . I owe allegiance to mankind, not to a particular country, race or people. I answer to God, not to the Chief Executive, whomever he may happen to be. I am here on earth to work out my own private destiny. My destiny is linked with that of every other living creature inhabiting this planet—perhaps with those on other planets too, who knows? I refuse to jeopardize my destiny by regarding life within the narrow rules which are laid down to circumscribe it. I dissent from the current view of things, as regards murder, as regards religion, as regards society, as regards our well-being. I will try to live my life in accordance with the vision I have of things eternal. I say 'Peace to you all!' and if you don't find it, it's because you haven't looked for it".

It is curious, and not irrelevent, I hope, to mention at this point the reaction I had upon reading Homer recently. At the request of the publisher, Gallimard, who is bringing out a new edition of *The Odyssey*, I wrote a short Introduction to this work. I had never read *The Odyssey* before, only *The Iliad*, and that but a few months ago. What I wish to say is that, after waiting sixty-seven years to read these universally esteemed classics, I found much to disparage in them. In *The Iliad*, or "the butchers's manual", as I call it, more than in *The Odyssey*. But it would never occur to me to request that they be banned or burned. Nor did I fear, on finishing them, that I would leap outdoors, axe in hand, and run amok. My boy, who was only nine when he read *The Iliad* (in a child's version), my boy who confesses to "liking murder once in a while", told me he was fed up with Homer, with all the killing and all the nonsense about the gods. But I have never feared that this son of mine, now going on eleven, still an avid reader of our detestable "Comics", a devotee of Walt Disney (who is not to my taste at all), an ardent movie fan, particularly of the "Westerns", I have never feared, I say, that he will grow up to be a killer. (Not even if the Army claims him!) I would rather see his mind absorbed by other interests, and I do my best to provide them, but, like all of us, he is a product of the age. No need, I trust, for me to elaborate on the dangers which confront us all, youth especially, in this age. The point is that with each age the menace varies. Whether it be witchcraft, idolatry, leprosy, cancer, schizophrenia, communism, fascism, or what, we have ever to do battle. Seldom do we really vanquish the enemy, in whatever guise he presents himself. At best we become immunized. But we never know, nor are we able to prevent in advance, the dangers which lurk around the corner. No matter how knowledgable, no matter how wise, no matter how prudent and cautious, we all have an Achilles' heel. Security is not the lot of man. Readiness, alertness, responsiveness—these are the sole defenses against the blows of fate.

I smile to myself in putting the following to the honorable members of the Court, prompted as I am to take the bull by the horns. Would it please the Court to know that by common opinion I pass for a sane, healthy, normal individual? that I am not regarded as a "sex addict", a pervert, or even a neurotic? Nor as a writer who is ready to sell his soul for money? That, as a husband, a father, a neighbor I am looked upon as "an asset" to the community? Sounds a trifle ludicrous, does it not? Is this the same *enfant terrible,* it might be asked, who wrote the unmentionable "Tropics", "The Rosy Crucifixion", "The World of Sex", "Quiet Days in Clichy"? Has he reformed? Or is he simply in his dotage now?

To be precise, the question is—are the author of these questionable works and the man who goes by the name of Henry Miller one and the same person? My answer is yes. And I am also one with the protagonist of these "autobiographical romances". That is perhaps harder to swallow. But why? Because I have been "utterly shameless" in revealing every aspect of my life? I am not the first author to have adopted the confessional approach, to have revealed life nakedly, or to have used language supposedly unfit for the ears of school girls. Were I a saint recounting his life of sin, perhaps these bald statements relating to my sex habits would be found enlightening, particularly by priests and medicos. They might even be found instructive.

But I am not a saint, and probably never will be one. Though it occurs to me, as I make this assertion, that I have been called that more than once, and by individuals whom the Court would never suspect capable of holding such an opinion. No, I am not a saint, thank heavens! nor even a propagandist of a new order. I am simply a man, a man born to write, who has taken as his theme the story of his life. A man who has made it clear, in the telling, that it was a good life, a rich life, a merry life, despite the ups and downs, despite the barriers and obstacles (many of his own making), despite the handicaps imposed by stupid codes and conventions. Indeed, I hope that I have made more than that clear, because what-ever I may say about my own life, which is only *a* life, is merely a means of talking about life itself, and what I have tried, desperately sometimes, to make clear is this, that I look upon life itself as good, good no matter on what terms, that I believe it is *we* who make it unlivable, *we*, not the gods, not fate, not circumstance.

Speaking thus, I am reminded of certain passages in the Court's decision which reflect on my sincerity as well as on my ability to think straight. These passages contain the implication that I am often deliberately obscure as well as pretentious in my "metaphysical and surrealistic" flights. I am only too well aware of the diversity of opinion which these "excursi" elicit in the minds of my readers. But how am I to answer such accusations, touching as they do the very marrow of my literary being? Am I to say "You don't know what you are talking about?" Ought I to muster impressive names —"authorities"—to counterbalance these judgments? Or would it not be simpler to say, as I have before—"Guilty! Guilty on all counts, your Honor!"

Believe me, it is not impish, roguish perversity which leads me to pronounce, even quasi-humorously, this word "guilty". As one who thoroughly and sincerely believes in what he says and does, even when wrong, is it not more becoming on my part to admit "guilt" than attempt to defend myself against those who use this word so glibly? Let us be honest. Do those who judge and condemn me—not in Oslo necessarily, but the world over—do these individuals truly believe me to be a culprit, to be "the enemy of society", as they often blandly assert? What is it that disturbs them so? Is it the existence, the prevalence, of immoral, amoral or unsocial behavior, such as is described in my works, or is it the exposure of such behavior in print? Do people of our day and age really behave in this "vile" manner or are these actions merely the product of a "diseased" mind? (Does one refer to such authors as Petronius, Rabelais, Rousseau, Sade, to mention but a few, as "diseased minds"?) Surely some of you must have friends or neighbors, in good standing too, who have indulged in this questionable behavior, or worse. As a man of the world, I know only too well that the appanage of a priest's frock, a judicial robe, a teacher's uniform provides no guarantee of immunity to the temptations of the flesh. We are all in the same pot,

we are all guilty, or innocent, depending on whether we take
the frog's view or the Olympian view. For the nonce I shall
refrain from pretending to measure or apportion guilt, to say,
for example, that a criminal is more guilty, or less, than a
hypocrite. We do not have crime, we do not have war, revolution, crusades, inquisitions, persecution and intolerance because some among us are wicked, mean spirited, or murderers
at heart; we have this malignant condition of human affairs
because all of us, the righteous as well as the ignorant and
the malicious, lack true forbearance, true compassion, true
knowledge and understanding of human nature.

To put it as succinctly and simply as possible, here is my
basic attitude toward life, my prayer, in other words: "Let
us stop thwarting one another, stop judging and condemning,
stop slaughtering one another". I do not implore you to suspend or withhold judgment of me or my work. Neither I nor
my work is that important. (One cometh, another goeth.)
What concerns me is the harm you are doing to yourselves.
I mean by perpetuating this talk of guilt and punishment, of
banning and proscribing, of whitewashing and blackballing, of
closing your eyes when convenient, of making scapegoats when
there is no other way out. I ask you point blank—does the
pursuance of your limited role enable you to get the most out
of life? When you write me off the books, so to speak, will
you find your food and wine more palatable, will you sleep
better, will you be a better man, a better husband, a better
father than before? These are the things that matter—what
happens to *you*, not what you do to *me*.

I know that the man in the dock is not supposed to ask
questions, he is there to answer. But I am unable to regard
myself as a culprit. I am simply "out of line". Yet I am in the
tradition, so to say. A list of my precursors would make an
impressive roster. This trial has been going on since the days
of Prometheus. Since before that. Since the days of the Arch-
angel Michael. In the not too distant past there was one who
was given the cup of hemlock for being "the corrupter of
youth". To-day he is regarded as one of the sanest, most lucid
minds that ever was. We who are always being arraigned before the bar can do no better than to resort to the celebrated

Socratic method. Our only answer is to return the question.

There are so many questions one could put to the Court, to any Court. But would one get a response? Can the Court of the Land ever be put in question? I am afraid not. The judicial body is a sacrosanct body. This is unfortunate, as I see it, for when issues of grave import arise the last court of reference, in my opinion, should be the public. When justice is at stake responsibility cannot be shifted to an elect few without injustice resulting. No Court could function if it did not follow the steel rails of precedent, taboo and prejudice.

I come back to the lengthy document representing the decision of the Oslo Town Court, to the tabulation of all the infractions of the moral code therein listed. There is something frightening as well as disheartening about such an indictment. It has a medieval aspect. And it has nothing to do with justice. Law itself is made to look ridiculous. Once again let me say that it is not the courts of Oslo or the laws and codes of Norway which I inveigh against; everywhere in the civilized world there is this mummery and flummery manifesting as the Voice of Inertia. The offender who stands before the Court is not being tried by his peers but by his dead ancestors. The moral codes, operative only if they are in conformance with natural or divine laws, are not safeguarded by these flimsy dikes; on the contrary, they are exposed as weak and ineffectual barriers.

Finally, here is the crux of the matter. Will an adverse decision by this court or any other court effectively hinder the further circulation of this book? The history of similar cases does not substantiate such an eventuality. If anything, an unfavorable verdict will only add more fuel to the flames. Proscription only leads to resistance; the fight goes on underground, becomes more insidious therefore, more difficult to cope with. If only one man in Norway reads the book and believes with the author that one has the right to express himself freely, the battle is won. You cannot eliminate an idea by suppressing it, and the idea which is linked with this issue is one of freedom to read what one chooses. Freedom, in other words, to read what is bad for one as well as what is good for one—or, what is simply innocuous. How can one guard against evil, in short, if one does not know what evil is?

But it is not something evil, not something poisonous, which this book *Sexus* offers the Norwegian reader. It is a dose of life which I administered to myself first, and which I not only survived but thrived on. Certainly I would not recommend it to infants, but then neither would I offer a child a bottle of *aqua vite*. I can say one thing for it unblushingly—compared to the atom bomb, it is full of lifegiving qualities.

COMMENT: On the American Legal Attitude to Obscene Literature

At present, the U. S. Post Office seizes any mail it considers obscene. As Mr. David Loth writes in *The Erotic in Literature,* "if the local official is upheld in Washington, the sender is notified that it will be burned unless within fifteen days he can 'show cause' why it should not be. If pressed, the department orders a hearing, and the sender always has the right of appeal to a Federal court. Believers in efficiency would do away with these delays and restraints, which actually are available only to someone of means."

When *Lady Chatterley's Lover* by D. H. Lawrence was re-issued unexpurgated by the Grove Press and copies were seized in the mails, the case was brought to trial and Judge Bryan delivered the following judgment. The reader will see that Judge Bryan has had, like former justices, to take into account Lawrence's motives in writing the book. However, to refer back to the extract from Collingwood, the writer's motives, whether deliberately moral or immoral, are irrelevant to his true effect, which is to show the community its own secret heart. We may justly wonder whether a legal preoccupation with the nature and effect of obscenity, which has busied lawyers and publishers for so long, does not endanger the natural function of all literature—whether good or bad—under the perhaps mistaken pretext of protecting the young or innocent.

TEXT: Opinion by Judge Bryan on *Lady Chatterley's Lover*

UNITED STATES DISTRICT COURT—Southern District
of New York

Grove Press, Inc. and Readers' Subscription, Inc.,
Plaintiffs,

—against—

Civil 147-87

Robert K. Christenberry, individually and as
Postmaster of the City of New York,
Defendant.

OPINION

BRYAN, *District Judge:*

These two actions against the Postmaster of New York, now consolidated, arise out of the denial of the United States mails to the recently published Grove Press unexpurgated edition of "Lady Chatterley's Lover" by D. H. Lawrence.

Plaintiffs seek to restrain the Postmaster from enforcing a decision of the Post Office Department that the unexpurgated "Lady Chatterley's Lover", and circulars announcing its availability, are non-mailable under the statute barring obscene matter from the mails. They also seek a declaratory judgment to the effect (1) that the novel is not "obscene, lewd, lascivious, indecent or filthy" in content or character, and is not non-mailable under the statute or, in the alternative, (2) that if the novel be held to fall within the purview of the statute, the statute is to that extent invalid and violates plaintiffs' rights in contravention of the First and Fifth Amendments.

Grove Press, Inc., one of the plaintiffs, is the publisher of the book. Readers' Subscription, Inc., the other plaintiff, is a book club which has rights to distribute it.

Defendant has moved and plaintiffs have cross-moved for summary judgment, pursuant to Rule 56, F. R. C. P. There are no disputed issues of fact. The cases are before me for final determination on the pleadings, the decision of the Postmaster General, the record before him and supplemental affidavits.

On April 30, 1959 the New York Postmaster withheld from dispatch some 20,000 copies of circulars deposited for mailing by Readers' Subscription, which announced the availability of the new Grove edition of Lady Chatterley. At about the same time he also detained a number of copies of the book which had been deposited for mailing by Grove Press.

On May 8, 1959 letters of complaint issued by the General Counsel of the Post Office Department were served on Grove and Readers' Subscription alleging that there was probable cause to believe that these mailings violated 18 U. S. C. § 1461, and advising them of a departmental hearing. The respondents filed answers denying these allegations and a hearing was held before the Judicial Officer of the Post Office Department on May 14, 1959.

The General Counsel, as complainant, introduced the Grove edition and the circulars which had been detained and rested.

The respondents offered (1) testimony as to their reputation and standing in the book publishing and distribution fields and their purpose in publishing and distributing the novel; (2) reviews of the book in leading newspapers and literary periodicals throughout the country; (3) copies of editorials and comments in leading newspapers concerning publication of the book and its anticipated impact; (4) news articles dealing with the banning of the book by the Post Office; and (5) expert testimony by two leading literary critics, Malcolm Cowley and Alfred Kazin, as to the literary stature of the work and its author, contemporary acceptance of literature dealing with sex and sex relations and their own opinions as to the effect of the book on its readers. The editorials and comments and the news articles were excluded.

The Judicial Officer before whom the hearing was held did not decide the issues. On May 28 he issued an order referring the proceedings to the Postmaster General "for final departmental decision."

On June 11, 1959 the Postmaster General rendered a departmental decision finding that the Grove edition "is obscene and non-mailable pursuant to 18 U. S. Code § 1461," and that the Readers' Subscription circulars "give information where obscene material, namely, the book in issue in this case, may be obtained and are non-mailable * * *."

This litigation, which had been commenced prior to the decision, was then brought on for hearing.

I

The basic question here is whether the unexpurgated "Lady Chatterley's Lover" is obscene within the meaning of 18 U. S. C. § 1461, and is thus excluded from the protections afforded freedom of speech and the press by the First Amendment.

However, the defendant takes the position that this question is not before me for decision. He urges that the determination by the Postmaster General that this novel is obscene and non-mailable is conclusive upon the court unless it is found to be unsupported by substantial evidence and is clearly wrong. He argues, therefore, that I may not determine the issue of obscenity *de novo*.

Thus, an initial question is raised as to the scope of the court's power of review. In the light of the issues presented, the basis of the Postmaster General's decision, and the record before him, this question is not of substance.

(1) Prior to *Roth* v. *United States,* the Supreme Court had "always assumed that obscenity is not protected by the freedoms of speech and press." However, until then the constitutional question had not been directly passed upon by the court. In *Roth* the question was squarely posed.

The court held, in accord with its long-standing assumption, that "obscenity is not within the area of constitutionally protected speech or press."

The court was faced with a dilemma. On the one hand it was required to eschew any impingement upon the cherished freedoms of speech and the press guaranteed by the Constitution and so essential to a free society. On the other hand it was faced with the recognized social evil presented by the purveyance of pornography.

The opinion of Mr. Justice Brennan for the majority makes it plain that the area which can be excluded from constitutional protection without impinging upon the free speech and free press guarantees is narrowly limited. He says (p. 484):

> "All ideas having even the slightest redeeming social importance—unorthodox ideas, controversial ideas, even ideas hateful to the prevailing climate of opinion—have the full protection of the guarantees, unless excludable because they encroach upon the limited area of more important interests."

He gives stern warning that no publication advancing such ideas can be suppressed under the guise of regulation of public morals or censorship of public reading matter. As he says (p. 488):

> "The fundamental freedoms of speech and press have contributed greatly to the development and well-being of our free society and are indispensable to its continued growth. Ceaseless vigilance is the watchword to prevent their erosion by Congress or by the States. The door barring federal and state intrusion into this area cannot be left ajar; it must be kept tightly closed and opened only the slightest crack necessary to prevent encroachment upon more important interests."

It was against these constitutional requirements that the Court laid down general standards for judging obscenity, recognizing that it was "vital that [such] standards * * * safeguard the protection of freedom of speech and press for material which does not treat sex" in an obscene manner. The standards were "whether to the average person, applying contemporary community standards, the dominant theme of the material taken as a whole appeals to prurient interest."

The Court did not attempt to apply these standards to a specific set of facts. It merely circumscribed and limited the excluded area in general terms.

Plainly application of these standards to specific material may involve no little difficulty as the court was well aware. Cases involving "hard core" pornography, or what Judge Woolsey referred to as "dirt for dirt's sake," purveyed furtively by dealers in smut, are relatively simple. But works of literary merit present quite a different problem, and one which the majority in *Roth* did not reach as such.

Chief Justice Warren, concurring in the result, said of this problem:

> "° ° ° The history of the application of laws designed to suppress the obscene demonstrates convincingly that the power of government can be invoked under them against great art or literature, scientific treatises, or works exciting social controversy. Mistakes of the past prove that there is a strong countervailing interest to be considered in the freedoms guaranteed by the First and Fourteenth Amendments."

And Mr. Justice Harlan, dissenting, also deeply concerned, had this to say (pp. 497, 498):

> "° ° ° The suppression of a particular writing or other tangible form of expression is ° ° ° an *individual* matter, and in the nature of things every such suppression raises an individual constitutional problem, in which a reviewing court must determine for *itself* whether the attacked expression is suppressible within constitutional standards. Since those standards do not readily lend themselves to generalized definitions, the constitutional problem in the last analysis becomes one of particularized judgments which appellate courts must make for themselves.
>
> "I do not think that reviewing courts can escape this responsibility by saying that the trier of the facts, be it a jury or a judge, has labeled the questioned matter as 'obscene', for, if 'obscenity' is to be suppressed, the question whether a particular work is of that character in-

volves not really an issue of fact but a question of constitutional *judgment* of the most sensitive and delicate kind."

Mr. Justice Frankfurter, concurring in *Kingsley International Pictures Corp.* v. *Regents,* decided on June 29, 1959, expressed a similar view. He pointed out that in determining whether particular works are entitled to the constitutional protections of freedom of expression "We cannot escape such instance by instance, case by case * * * [constitutional adjudication] in all the variety of situations that come before this Court." And Mr. Justice Harlan, in the same case, also concurring in the result, speaks of "the necessity for individualized adjudication. In the very nature of things the problems in this area are ones of individual cases * * *."

These views are not inconsistent with the decisions of the majority determining both *Roth* and *Kingsley* upon broader constitutional grounds.

It would seem that the Court itself made such "individualized" or "case by case" adjudications as to the obscenity of specific material in at least two cases following *Roth*. In *One, Inc.* v. *Olesen,* and *Sunshine Book Co.* v. *Summerfield,* the courts below had found in no uncertain terms that the material was obscene within the meaning of Section 1461. In each case the Supreme Court in a one sentence per curiam opinion granted certiorari and reversed on the authority of *Roth*.

One, Inc. v. *Olesen,* and *Sunshine Book Co.* v. *Summerfield,* involved determinations by the Post Office barring material from the mails on the ground that it was obscene. In both the District Court had found that the publication was obscene and that the determination of the Post Office should be upheld. In both the Court of Appeals had affirmed the findings of the District Court.

Yet in each the Supreme Court, without discussion, summarily reversed on the authority of *Roth*. As Judge Desmond of the New York Court of Appeals said of these cases—"Presumably, the court having looked at those books simply held them not to be obscene."

It is no less the duty of this court in the case at bar to

scrutinize the book with great care and to determine for itself whether it is within the constitutional protections afforded by the First Amendment, or whether it may be excluded from those protections because it is obscene under the *Roth* tests.

(2) Such review is quite consistent with the Administrative Procedure Act, assuming that the act is applicable here.

This is not a case where the agency determination under review is dependent on "a fair estimate of the worth of the testimony of witnesses or its informed judgment on matters within its special competence or both. . . ."

There were no disputed facts before the Postmaster General. The facts as to the mailings and the detainer were stipulated and the only issue before him was whether "Lady Chatterley's Lover" was obscene.

The complainant relied on the text of the novel and nothing more to establish obscenity. Respondents' evidence was wholly uncontradicted, and, except for the opinions of the critics Cowley and Kazin as to the effect of the book upon its readers, it scarcely could have been. The complainant conceded that the book had literary merit. The views of the critics as to the place of the novel and its author in twentieth century English literature have not been questioned.

As the Postmaster General said, he attempted to apply to the book "the tests which, it is my understanding, the courts have established for determining questions of obscenity." Thus, all he did was to apply the statute, as he interpreted it in the light of the decisions, to the book. His interpretation and application of the statute involved questions of law, not questions of fact.

The Postmaster General has no special competence or technical knowledge on this subject which qualifies him to render an informed judgment entitled to special weight in the courts. There is no parallel here to determinations of such agencies as the Interstate Commerce Commission, the Securities and Exchange Commission, the National Labor Relations Board, the Federal Communications Commission, the Federal Power Commission, or many others on highly technical and complicated subject matter upon which they have specialized knowledge and are particularly qualified to speak.

No doubt the Postmaster General has similar qualifications on many questions involving the administration of the Post Office Department, the handling of the mails, postal rates and other matters. See *Bates & Guild Co.* v. *Payne,* . . . But he has no special competence to determine what constitutes obscenity within the meaning of Section 1461, or that "contemporary community standards are not such that this book should be allowed to be transmitted in the mails" or that the literary merit of the book is outweighed by its pornographic features, as he found. Such questions involve interpretation of a statute, which also imposes criminal penalties, and its application to the allegedly offending material. The determination of such questions is peculiarly for the courts, particularly in the light of the constitutional questions implicit in each case.

It has been suggested that the court cannot interfere with the order of the Postmaster General unless it finds that he abused his discretion. But it does not appear that the Postmaster General has been vested with "discretion" finally to determine whether a book is obscene within the meaning of the statute.

It is unnecessary to pass on the questions posed by the plaintiffs as to whether the Postmaster General has any power to impose prior restraints upon the mailing of matter allegedly obscene and whether the enforcement of the statute is limited to criminal proceedings, though it seems to me that these questions are not free from doubt.

Assuming power in the Postmaster General to withhold obscene matter from dispatch in the mails temporarily, a grant of discretion to make a final determination as to whether a book is obscene and should be denied to the public should certainly not be inferred in the absence of a clear and direct mandate. As the Supreme Court pointed out under comparable circumstances in *Hannegan* v. *Esquire, Inc.,* to vest such power in the Postmaster General would, in effect, give him the power of censorship and that "is so abhorrent to our traditions that a purpose to grant it should not be easily inferred."

No such grant of power to the Postmaster General has been called to my attention and I have found none. Whatever administrative functions the Postmaster General has go no further than closing the mails to material which is obscene within the meaning of the statute. This is not an area in which the Postmaster General has any "discretion" which is entitled to be given special weight by the courts.

The Administrative Procedure Act makes the reviewing court responsible for determining all relevant questions of law, for interpreting and applying all constitutional and statutory provisions and for setting aside agency action not in accordance with law. The question presented here falls within this framework.

Thus, the question presented for decision is whether "Lady Chatterley's Lover" is obscene within the meaning of the statute and thus excludable from constitutional protections. I will now consider that question.

II

This unexpurgated edition of "Lady Chatterley's Lover" has never before been published either in the United States or England, though comparatively small editions were published by Lawrence himself in Italy and authorized for publication in France, and a number of pirated copies found their way to this country.

Grove Press is a reputable publisher with a good list which includes a number of distinguished writers and serious works. Before publishing this edition Grove consulted recognized literary critics and authorities on English literature as to the advisability of publication. All were of the view that the work was of major literary importance and should be made available to the American public.

No one is naive enough to think that Grove Press did not expect to profit from the book. Nevertheless the format and composition of the volume, the advertising and promotional material and the whole approach to publication, treat the book as a serious work of literature. The book is distributed through leading bookstores throughout the country. There has been no attempt by the publisher to appeal to prurience or the prurient minded.

The Grove edition has a preface by Archibald MacLeish,

former Librarian of Congress, Pulitzer Prize winner, and one of this country's most distinguished poets and literary figures, giving his appraisal of the novel. There follows an introduction by Mark Schorer, Professor of English Literature at the University of California, a leading scholar of D. H. Lawrence and his work. The introduction is a critique of the novel against the background of Lawrence's life, work and philosophy. At the end of the novel there is a biographical note as to the circumstances under which it was written and first published. Thus, the novel is placed in a setting which emphasizes its literary qualities and its place as a significant work of a major English novelist.

Readers' Subscription has handled the book in the same vein. The relatively small number of Readers' Subscription subscribers is composed largely of people in academic, literary and scholarly fields. Its list of books includes works of high literary merit, including books by and about D. H. Lawrence.

There is nothing of "the leer of the sensualist" in the promotion or methods of distribution of this book. There is no suggestion of any attempt to pander to the lewd and lascivious minded for profit. The facts are all to the contrary.

Publication met with unanimous critical approval. The book was favorably received by the literary critics of such diverse publications as the New York Times, the Chicago Tribune, the San Francisco Call Bulletin, the New York Post, the New York Herald Tribune, Harpers and Time, to mention only some. The critics were not agreed upon their appraisal. Critical comment ranged from acclaim on the one hand to more restrained views that this was not the best of Lawrence's writing, and was dated and in parts "wooden." But as MacLeish says in the preface,

"* * * in spite of these reservations no responsible critic would deny the book a place as one of the most important works of fiction of the century, and no reader of any kind could undertake to express an opinion about the literature of the time or about the spiritual history that literature expresses without making his peace in one way or another with D. H. Lawrence and with this work."

Publication of the Grove edition was a major literary event. It was greeted by editorials in leading newspapers throughout the country unanimously approving the publication and viewing with alarm possible attempts to ban the book.

It was against this background that the New York Postmaster impounded the book and the Postmaster General barred it. The decision of the Postmaster General, in a brief four pages, relied on three cases, *Roth* v. *United States, supra, United States* v. *One Book Called "Ulysses"*, . . . and *Besig* v. *United States*, . . . While he quotes from *Roth* the Postmaster General relies principally on *Besig*, which was not reviewed by the Supreme Court. It may be noted that the Ninth Circuit relied heavily on *Besig* in *One Book, Inc.* v. *Olesen, supra*, which was summarily reversed by the Supreme Court on the authority of *Roth*.

He refers to the book as "currently withheld from the mails in the United States and barred from the mails by several other major nations." His only discussion of its content is as follows:

> "The contemporary community standards are not such that this book should be allowed to be transmitted in the mails.
>
> "The book is replete with descriptions in minute detail of sexual acts engaged in or discussed by the book's principal characters. These descriptions utilize filthy, offensive and degrading words and terms. Any literary merit the book may have is far outweighed by the pornographic and smutty passages and words, so that the book, taken as a whole, is an obscene and filthy work.
>
> "I therefore see no need to modify or reverse the prior rulings of this Department and the Department of the Treasury with respect to this edition of this book."

This seems to be the first time since the notable opinions of Judge Woolsey and Judge Augustus Hand in *United States* v. *One Book Called "Ulysses", supra*, in 1934 that a book of comparable literary stature has come before the federal courts charged with violating the federal obscenity statutes. That case held that James Joyce's "Ulysses" which had been seized by the Customs under Section 305 of the Tariff Act of 1930 was not obscene within the meaning of that statute. It thoroughly discussed the standards to be applied in determining this question.

The essence of the *Ulysses* holding is that a work of literary merit is not obscene under federal law merely because it contains passages and language dealing with sex in a most candid and realistic fashion and uses many four-letter Anglo-Saxon words. Where a book is written with honesty and seriousness of purpose, and the portions which might be considered obscene are relevant to the theme, it is not condemned by the statute even though "it justly may offend many." "Ulysses" contains numerous passages dealing very frankly with sex and the sex act and is free in its use of four-letter Anglo-Saxon words. Yet both Judge Woolsey in the District Court, and Judge Hand in the Court of Appeals, found that it was a sincere and honest book which was not in any sense "dirt for dirt's sake." They both concluded that "Ulysses" was a work of high literary merit, written by a gifted and serious writer, which did not have the dominant effect of promoting lust or prurience and therefore did not fall within the interdiction of the statute.

Roth v. *United States, supra,* decided by the Supreme Court in 1957, twenty-three years later, unlike the *Ulysses* case, did not deal with the application of the obscenity statutes to specific material. It laid down general tests circumscribing the area in which matter is excludable from constitutional protections because it is obscene, so as to avoid impingement on First Amendment guarantees.

The court distilled from the prior cases (including the *Ulysses* case, which it cited with approval) the standards to be applied—"whether to the average person, applying contemporary community standards, the dominant theme of the material taken as a whole appeals to prurient interest."

The court saw no significant difference between this expression of the standards and those in the American Law Institute Model Penal Code to the effect that

"° ° °A thing is obscene if, considered as a whole, its predominant appeal is to prurient interest, i. e., a shameful or morbid interest in nudity, sex, or excretion, and if it goes substantially beyond customary limits of candor in description or representation of such matters * * *."

These standards are not materially different from those applied in *Ulysses* to the literary work considered there. Since the *Roth* case dealt with these standards for judging obscenity in general terms and the *Ulysses* case dealt with application of such standards to a work of recognized literary stature, the two should be read together.

A number of factors are involved in the application of these tests.

As Mr. Justice Brennan pointed out in *Roth*, sex and obscenity are by no means synonymous and "[t]he portrayal of sex, e. g., in art, literature and scientific works, is not in itself sufficient reason to deny material the constitutional protection of freedom of speech and press." As he said, sex has been "a subject of absorbing interest to mankind through the ages; it is one of the vital problems of human interest and public concern." The subject may be discussed publicly and truthfully without previous restraint or fear of subsequent punishment as long as it does not fall within the narrowly circumscribed interdicted area.

Both cases held that, to be obscene, the dominant effect of the book must be an appeal to prurient interest—that is to say, shameful or morbid interest in sex. Such a theme must so predominate as to submerge any ideas of "redeeming social importance" which the publication contains.

It is not the effect upon the irresponsible, the immature or the sensually minded which is controlling. The material must be judged in terms of its effect on those it is likely to reach who are conceived of as the average man of normal sensual impulses, or, as Judge Woolsey says, "what the French would call l'homme moyen sensuel."

The material must also exceed the limits of tolerance imposed by current standards of the community with respect to freedom of expression in matters concerning sex and sex relations. Moreover, a book is not to be judged by excerpts or individual passages but must be judged as a whole.

All of these factors must be present before a book can be held obscene and thus outside constitutional protections.

Judged by these standards, "Lady Chatterley's Lover" is not obscene. The decision of the Postmaster General that it is obscene and therefore non-mailable is contrary to law and clearly erroneous. This is emphasized when the book is considered against its background and in the light of its stature as a significant work of a distinguished English novelist.

D. H. Lawrence is one of the most important novelists writing in the English language in this century. Whether he is, as some authorities say, the greatest English novelist since Joseph Conrad, or one of a number of major figures, makes little difference. He was a writer of great gifts and of undoubted artistic integrity.

The text of this edition of "Lady Chatterley's Lover" was written by Lawrence toward the close of his life and was his third version of the novel, originally called "Tenderness."

The book is almost as much a polemic as a novel.

In it Lawrence was expressing his deep and bitter dissatisfaction with what he believed were the stultifying effects of advancing industralization and his own somewhat obscure philosophic remedy of a return to "naturalness." He attacks what he considered to be the evil effects of industrialization upon the wholesome and natural life of all classes in England. In his view this was having disastrous consequences on English society and on the English countryside. It had resulted in devitalization of the upper classes of society and debasement of the lower classes. One result, as he saw it, was the corrosion of both the emotional and physical sides of man as expressed in his sexual relationships which had become increasingly artificial and unwholesome.

The novel develops the contrasts and conflicts in characters under these influences.

The plot is relatively simple.

Constance Chatterley is married to a baronet, returned from the first World War paralyzed from the waist down. She is physically frustrated and dissatisfied with the artificiality and sterility of her life and of the society in which she moves. Her husband, immersed in himself, seeks compensation for his own

frustrations in the writing of superficial and brittle fiction and
in the exploitation of his coal mining properties, a symbol of
the creeping industrial blight. Failing to find satisfaction in
an affair with a man in her husband's circle, Constance Chatterley finds herself increasingly restless and unhappy. Her husband half-heartedly urges her to have a child by another man
whom he will treat as his heir. Repelled by the suggestion that
she casually beget a child, she is drawn to Mellors, the gamekeeper, sprung from the working class who, having achieved
a measure of spiritual and intellectual independence, is a
prototype of Lawrence's natural man. They establish a deeply
passionate and tender relationship which is described at length
and in detail. At the conclusion she is pregnant and plans to
obtain a divorce and marry the gamekeeper.

This plot serves as a vehicle through which Lawrence develops his basic theme of contrast between his own philosophy
and the sterile and debased society which he attacks. Most of
the characters are prototypes. The plot and theme are meticu-
lously worked out with honesty and sincerity.

The book is replete with fine writing and with descriptive
passages of rare beauty. There is no doubt of its literary merit.

It contains a number of passages describing sexual intercourse in great detail with complete candor and realism. Four
letter Anglo-Saxon words are used with some frequency.

These passages and this language understandably will shock
the sensitive minded. Be that as it may, these passages are
relevant to the plot and to the development of the characters
and of their lives as Lawrence unfolds them. The language
which shocks, except in a rare instance or two, is not inconsistent with character, situation or theme.

Even if it be assumed that these passages and this language
taken in isolation tend to arouse shameful, morbid and lustful
sexual desires in the average reader, they are an integral, and
to the author a necessary part of the development of theme,
plot and character. The dominant theme, purpose and effect
of the book as a whole is not an appeal to prurience or the
prurient minded. The book is not "dirt for dirt's sake." Nor do
these passages and this language submerge the dominant

theme so as to make the book obscene even if they could be considered and found to be obscene in isolation.

What the Postmaster General seems to have done is precisely what the Supreme Court in *Roth* and the courts in the *Ulysses* case said ought not to be done. He has lifted from the novel individual passages and language, found them to be obscene in isolation and therefore condemned the book as a whole. He has disregarded the dominant theme and effect of the book and has read these passages and this language as if they were separable and could be taken out of context. Thus he has "weighed" the isolated passages which he considered obscene against the remainder of the book and concluded that the work as a whole must be condemned.

Writing about sex is not in itself pornographic, as the Postmaster General recognized. Nor does the fact that sex is a major theme of a book condemn the book as obscene. Neither does the use of "four letter" words, despite the offense they may give. "Ulysses" was found not to be obscene despite long passages containing similar descriptions and language. As Judge Woolsey said there:

"The words which are criticized as dirty are old Saxon words known to almost all men and, I venture, to many women, and are such words as would be naturally and habitually used, I believe, by the types of folk whose life, physical and mental, Joyce is seeking to describe."

Such words "are, almost without exception of honest Anglo-Saxon ancestry and were not invented for purely scatological effect."

The tests of obscenity are not whether the book or passages from it are in bad taste or shock or offend the sensibilities of an individual, or even of a substantial segment of the community. Nor are we concerned with whether the community would approve of Constance Chatterley's morals. The statute does not purport to regulate the morals portrayed or the ideas expressed in a novel, whether or not they are contrary to the accepted moral code, nor could it constitutionally do so.

Plainly "Lady Chatterley's Lover" is offensive to the Postmaster General, and I respect his personal views. As a matter of personal opinion I disagree with him for I do not personally find the book offensive.

But the personal views of neither of us are controlling here. The standards for determining what constitutes obscenity under this statute have been laid down. These standards must be objectively applied regardless of personal predilections.

There has been much discussion of the intent and purpose of Lawrence in writing Lady Chatterley. It is suggested that the intent and purpose of the author has no relevance to the question as to whether his work is obscene and must be disregarded.

No doubt an author may write a clearly obscene book in the mistaken belief that he is serving a high moral purpose. The fact that this is the author's purpose does not redeem the book from obscenity.

But the sincerity and honesty of purpose of an author as expressed in the manner in which a book is written and in which his theme and ideas are developed has a great deal to do with whether it is of literary and intellectual merit. Here, as in the *Ulysses* case, there is no question about Lawrence's honesty and sincerity of purpose, artistic integrity and lack of intention to appeal to prurient interest.

Thus, this is an honest and sincere novel of literary merit and its dominant theme and effect, taken as a whole, is not an appeal to the prurient interest of the average reader.

This would seem to end the matter. However, the Postmaster General's finding that the book is non-mailable because it offends contemporary community standards bears some discussion.

I am unable to ascertain upon what the Postmaster General based this conclusion. The record before him indicates general acceptance of the book throughout the country and nothing was shown to the contrary. The critics were unanimous. Editorial comment by leading journals of opinion welcomed the publication and decried any attempts to ban it.

It is true that the editorial comment was excluded by the Judicial Officer at the hearing. But it seems to me that this was error. These expressions were relevant and material on the question of whether the book exceeded the limits of freedom of expression in matters involving sex and sex relations tolerated by the community at large in these times.

The contemporary standards of the community and the limits of its tolerance cannot be measured or ascertained accurately. There is no poll available to determine such questions. Surely expressions by leading newspapers, with circulations of millions, are some evidence at least as to what the limits of tolerance by present day community standards are, if we must embark upon a journey of exploration into such uncharted territory.

Quite apart from this, the broadening of freedom of expression and of the frankness with which sex and sex relations are dealt with at the present time require no discussion. In one best selling novel after another frank descriptions of the sex act and "four-letter" words appear with frequency. These trends appear in all media of public expression, in the kind of language used and the subjects discussed in polite society, in pictures, advertisements and dress, and in other ways familiar to all. Much of what is now accepted would have shocked the community to the core a generation ago. Today such things are generally tolerated whether we approve or not.

I hold that, at this stage in the development of our society, this major English novel, does not exceed the outer limits of the tolerance which the community as a whole gives to writing about sex and sex relations.

One final word about the constitutional problem implicit here.

It is essential to the maintenance of a free society that the severest restrictions be placed upon restraints which may tend to prevent the dissemination of ideas. It matters not whether such ideas be expressed in political pamphlets or works of political, economic or social theory or criticism, or through artistic media. All such expressions must be freely available.

A work of literature published and distributed through normal channels by a reputable publisher stands on quite a different footing from hard core pornography furtively sold for the purpose of profiting by the titillation of the dirty minded. The courts have been deeply and properly concerned about the use of obscenity statutes to suppress great works of art or literature. As Judge Augustus Hand said in *Ulysses:*

> "* * * The foolish judgments of Lord Eldon about one hundred years ago, proscribing the works of Byron and Southey, and the finding by the jury under a charge by Lord Denman that the publication of Shelley's 'Queen Mab' was an indictable offense are a warning to all who have to determine the limits of the field within which authors may exercise themselves."

To exclude this book from the mails on the grounds of obscenity would fashion a rule which could be applied to a substantial portion of the classics of our literature. Such a rule would be inimical to a free society. To interpret the obscenity statute so as to bar "Lady Chatterley's Lover" from the mails would render the statute unconstitutional in its application, in violation of the guarantees of freedom of speech and the press contained in the First Amendment.

It may be, as the plaintiffs urge, that if a work is found to be of literary stature, and not "hard core" pornography, it is *a fortiori* within the protections of the First Amendment. But I do not reach that question here. For I find that "Lady Chatterley's Lover" is not obscene within the meaning of 18 U. S. C. § 1461, and is entitled to the protections guaranteed to freedoms of speech and press by the First Amendment. I therefore hold that the order of the Postmaster General is illegal and void and violates plaintiffs' rights in contravention of the Constitution.

Defendant's motion for summary judgment is denied. Plaintiffs' cross-motions for summary judgment are granted. An order will issue permanently restraining the defendant from denying the mails to this book or to the circulars announcing its availability.

Settle order on notice.

Dated, New York, N. Y.
July 21, 1959

FREDERICK vanPELT BRYAN
U. S. D. J.

COMMENT: On Political Influence and the Writer

Besides restraints against obscenity, the modern writer is often restrained by political influence. This may be no more than political utilitarianism which asks of the poet, "What is it for?"; "What good does it do?" Or it may be simply a question of national prestige which uses a writer as an ambassador of sorts. Or it may be the Communist writer's inability to work except with social intentions.

The origins of the modern writer's political involvement were found by Julien Benda, in *La Trahison des Clercs*, about the beginning of this century, when intellectuals (particularly writers) began to identify themselves with political interests, particularly national interests or class interests, and by doing so compromised themselves as artists and thinkers and damaged their work. Where an author displays partiality toward his own nation, "there is a two-fold evil," Benda says. ". . . Not only does it considerably inflame political passion in the breast of the reader, but it deprives him of one of the most eminently civilizing effects of all works of art, i.e. that self-examination to which every spectator is impelled by a representation of human beings which he feels to be true and solely pre-occupied with truth. From the point of view of the artist and of the value of his activity alone, this partiality indicates a great degradation. The value of the artist, the thing which makes him the world's high ornament, is that he *plays* human passions instead of living them, and that he discovers in this 'play' emotion the same source of desires, joys and sufferings as ordinary men find in the pursuit of real things."

Here is a parallel to the scientist who works for a national cause rather than for the cause of science. The degradation of

the artist in the wholly authoritarian state involves compromise
of the most insidious and dreadful sort, as appears in the following passage. The author once worked for the government
of the Polish People's Democracy.

TEXT: "Ketman" from *The Captive Mind* by Czeslaw Milosz [*translated by Jane Zielonko*]

Officially, contradictions do not exist in the minds of the citizens in the people's democracies. Nobody dares to reveal them publicly. And yet the question of how to deal with them is posed in real life. More than others, the members of the intellectual elite are aware of this problem. They solve it by becoming actors.

It is hard to define the type of relationship that prevails between people in the East otherwise than as acting, with the exception that one does not perform on a theater stage but in the street, office, factory, meeting hall, or even the room one lives in. Such acting is a highly developed craft that places a premium upon mental alertness. Before it leaves the lips, every word must be evaluated as to its consequences. A smile that appears at the wrong moment, a glance that is not all it should be can occasion dangerous suspicions and accusations. Even one's gestures, tone of voice, or preference for certain kinds of neckties are interpreted as signs of one's political tendencies.

A visitor from the Imperium is shocked on coming to the West. In his contacts with others, beginning with porters or taxi drivers, he encounters no resistance. The people he meets are completely relaxed. They lack that internal concentration which betrays itself in a lowered head or in restlessly moving eyes. They say whatever words come to their tongues; they laugh aloud. Is it possible that human relations can be so direct?

Acting in daily life differs from acting in the theater in that

everyone plays to everyone else, and everyone is fully aware
that this is so. The fact that a man acts is not to his prejudice,
is no proof of unorthodoxy. But he must act well, for his ability
to enter into his role skillfully proves that he has built his
characterization upon an adequate foundation. If he makes a
passionate speech against the West, he demonstrates that he
has at least 10 per cent of the hatred he so loudly proclaims.
If he condemns Western culture lukewarmly, then he must be
attached to it in reality. Of course, all human behavior contains a significant amount of acting. A man reacts to his environment and is molded by it even in his gestures. Nevertheless, what we find in the people's democracies is a conscious
mass play rather than automatic imitation. Conscious acting,
if one practices it long enough, develops those traits which one
uses most in one's role, just as a man who became a runner
because he had good legs develops his legs even more in training. After long acquaintance with his role, a man grows into
it so closely that he can no longer differentiate his true self
from the self he simulates, so that even the most intimate of
individuals speak to each other in Party slogans. To identify
one's self with the role one is obliged to play brings relief and
permits a relaxation of one's vigilance. Proper reflexes at the
proper moment become truly automatic.

This happens in literature as well. A poet writing a piece of
propaganda does not confine himself to a purely rationalistic
approach. Imbued with the thought that poetry ideally should
be suited to recitation in chorus at a meeting, he begins by
tuning himself to an appropriate pitch of collective emotion
before he can release himself in words. In the theater, the
actor who plays the Cid, for example, *is* the Cid on stage. Yet
not every actor, even if he is young and well-built, can play
the Cid; he must have an inborn capacity to release himself
emotionally in that role. Poetry as we have known it can be
defined as the individual temperament refracted through social convention. The poetry of the New Faith can, on the contrary, be defined as social convention refracted through the individual temperament. That is why the poets who are most
adapted to the new situation are those endowed with dramatic
talent. The poet creates the character of an ideal revolutionary

and writes his verses as the monologue of this character. He does not speak for himself but for the ideal citizen. His results are reminiscent of songs written to be sung on the march since the aim is the same—the forging of the fetters of collectivity that bind together an advancing column of soldiers. The best examples of such song-slogans are certain verses of the German poet, Berthold Brecht, which are superior to the works of other Eastern poets because Brecht is fully conscious of the histrionic process involved.

Even though the identification of the play with private thought-property is carried very far, a large residue of unassimilated matter remains which forces one to keep alert. A constant and universal masquerade creates an aura that is hard to bear, yet it grants the performers certain not inconsiderable satisfactions. To say something is white when one thinks it black, to smile inwardly when one is outwardly solemn, to hate when one manifests love, to know when one pretends not to know, and thus to play one's adversary for a fool (even as he is playing you for one)—these actions lead one to prize one's own cunning above all else. Success in the game becomes a source of satisfaction. Simultaneously, that which we protect from prying eyes takes on a special value because it is never clearly formulated in words and hence has the irrational charm of things purely emotional. Man takes refuge in an inner sanctuary which is the more precious the greater the price he pays in order to bar others from access to it.

Acting on a comparable scale has not occurred often in the history of the human race. Yet in trying to describe these new mores, we happen across a striking analogy in the Islamic civilization of the Middle East. Not only was the game played in defense of one's thoughts and feelings well-known there, but indeed it was transformed into a permanent institution and graced with the name of Ketman.

What is Ketman? I found its description in a book by Gobineau entitled *Religions and Philosophies of Central Asia*. Gobineau spent many years in Persia (from 1855 to 1858 he was a secretary in the French legation, from 1861 to 1863 he was French minister), and we cannot deny his gift for keen observation, even though we need not necessarily agree with the conclusions of this rather dangerous writer. The similarities between Ketman and the customs cultivated in the countries of the New Faith are so striking that I shall permit myself to quote at length.

The people of the Mussulman East believe that "He who is in possession of truth must not expose his person, his relatives or his reputation to the blindness, the folly, the perversity of those whom it has pleased God to place and maintain in error." One must, therefore, keep silent about one's true convictions if possible.

"Nevertheless," says Gobineau, "there are occasions when silence no longer suffices, when it may pass as an avowal. Then one must not hesitate. Not only must one deny one's true opinion, but one is commanded to resort to all ruses in order to deceive one's adversary. One makes all the protestations of faith that can please him, one performs all the rites one recognizes to be the most vain, one falsifies one's own books, one exhausts all possible means of deceit. Thus one acquires the multiple satisfactions and merits of having placed oneself and one's relatives under cover, of not having exposed a venerable faith to the horrible contact of the infidel, and finally of having, in cheating the latter and confirming him in his error, imposed on him the shame and spiritual misery that he deserves.

"Ketman fills the man who practices it with pride. Thanks to it, a believer raises himself to a permanent state of superiority over the man he deceives, be he a minister of state or a powerful king; to him who uses Ketman, the other is a miserable blind man whom one shuts off from the true path whose existence he does not suspect; while you, tattered and dying of hunger, trembling externally at the feet of duped force, your eyes are filled with light, you walk in brightness before your enemies. It is an unintelligent being that you make sport of; it is a dangerous beast that you disarm. What a wealth of pleasures!"

How far Ketman can go is demonstrated by the founder of one sect, Hadzhi-Sheikh-Ahmed. "Although he left behind many works of theology, he never openly advanced in his books, as even his most passionate disciples avow, anything which could place the reader on the path of the ideas attributed to him today. But everyone affirms he practiced Ketman and that in private he was extremely daring and precise in establishing order in the doctrines which bear his name today." We cannot wonder, therefore, that, as a certain Persian admitted in conversation with Gobineau, "there is not a single true Moslem in Persia."

Not everyone was as careful as Hadzhi-Sheikh-Ahmed. To some, Ketman was useful in the preparatory period, but when they felt themselves sufficiently strong, they proclaimed their heresy openly. Here, for example, is the description of the itinerant preachings of Sadra, the disciple of Avicenna.

"He too was afraid of the mullahs. To incite their distrust was inevitable, but to provide a solid basis, furnish proof for their accusations, that would have been to expose himself to endless persecutions, and to compromise at the same time the future of the philosophical restoration he meditated. Therefore he conformed to the demands of his times and resorted to the great and splendid expedient of Ketman. When he arrived in a city he was careful to present himself humbly to all the moudjteheds or doctors of the region. He sat in a corner of their salons, their talars, remained silent usually, spoke modestly, approved each word that escaped their venerable lips. He was questioned about his knowledge; he expressed only ideas borrowed from the strictest Shiite theology and in no way indicated that he concerned himself with philosophy. After several days, seeing him so meek, the moudjteheds themselves engaged him to give public lessons. He set to work immediately, took as his text the doctrine of ablution or some similar point, and split hairs over the prescriptions and inner doubts of the subtlest theoreticians. This behavior delighted the mullahs. They lauded him to the skies; they forgot to keep an eye on him. They themselves wanted to see him lead their imaginations through less placid questions. He did not refuse. From the doctrine of ablution he passed to that of prayer; from the doctrine of prayer, to that of revelation; from revelation, to divine unity and there, with marvels of ingenuity, reticence, confidences to the most advanced pupils, self-contradiction, ambiguous propositions, fallacious syllogisms out of which only the initiated could see their way, the whole heavily seasoned with unimpeachable professions of faith, he succeeded in spreading Avicennism throughout the entire lettered class; and when at last he believed he could reveal himself completely, he drew aside the veils, repudiated Islam, and showed himself the logician, the metaphysician that he really was."

Islamic Ketman and the Ketman of the twentieth century in Europe seem to differ only in that the boldness Sadra permitted himself would instantly have brought him to a sad end in Europe. Nevertheless, Ketman in its narrowest and severest forms is widely practiced in the people's democracies. As in Islam, the feeling of superiority over those who are unworthy of attaining truth constitutes one of the chief joys of people whose lives do not in general abound in pleasures. "Deviations," the tracing of which creates so many troubles for the rulers, are not an illusion. They are cases of accidental unmaskings of Ketman; and those who are most helpful in detecting deviations are those who themselves practice a similar form of Ketman. Recognizing in other acrobats the tricks they themselves employ, they take advantage of the first occasion to down an opponent or friend. Thus they protect themselves; and the measure of dexterity is to anticipate by at least one day the similar accusation which could be leveled against them by the man they denounce. Since the number of varieties of Ketman is practically unlimited, the naming of deviations cannot keep pace with the weeding of a garden so full of unexpected specimens of heresy. Every new commentary on the precepts of the New Faith proclaimed by the Center multiplies the internal reservations of those who are externally the most faithful. It is impossible to enumerate all the forms of Ketman that one can discover in the people's democracies. I shall try, however, to proceed somewhat in the manner of a naturalist determining major groups and families.

National Ketman is broadly diffused throughout the masses, and even the upper brackets of the Party in the various dependent states are not free of it. Because Tito, like Sadra, announced his heresy to all the world, millions of human beings in the people's democracies must employ exceedingly ingenious means of masking themselves. Instructive displays of condemnation of those who wished to follow the national road to socialism in individual Eastern capitals taught the public what kind of phrases and reflexes can expose one to reproach for harboring this fatal tendency. The surest safeguard is to manifest loudly one's awe at Russia's achievements in every field of endeavor, to carry Russian books under one's arm, to hum Russian songs, to applaud Russian actors and musicians enthusiastically, etc. A writer who has not consecrated a single work to outstanding Russian figures or to Russian life, but has confined himself to national themes, cannot consider himself entirely safe. The chief characteristic of the people who practice this Ketman is an unbounded contempt for Russia as a barbaric country. Among the workers and peasants it is most often purely emotional, and based on observation of either the soldiers of the liberating army, or (since during the war a great many were in areas directly administered by the Russians) of Russians in their daily life.

Because until now the living standard of the masses in Russia was so much lower than that of the so-called people's democracies, national Ketman finds abundant nourishment. It cannot be defined simply as nationalism. For many centuries hatred existed between the Central European Slavs and the Germans, still it was colored among the Slavs by a respect for Germany's material achievements. On the other hand, perceiving by comparison the greater refinement of his own customs, his greater organizational ability (be it only in respect to transportation or the handling of machinery), the Central European would express his attitude toward Russia, if he could, by a disdainful shrug of his shoulders—which, however, doesn't prevent him from shuddering in fear before the countless hordes pouring out of the Euro-Asian continent.

But this Ketman is not exclusively emotional in its appeal. Amid the young intelligentsia of working-class origin the overwhelming opinion can be summed up shortly as "Socialism—yes, Russia—no"; and this is where the subtleties of doctrinal differences arise. The countries of Europe, this line of reasoning begins, are infinitely more prepared to realize socialism than Russia. Their population is more intelligent; most of their land is under cultivation; their systems of communication and their industry are more highly developed. Measures based on absolute cruelty are unnecessary and even pointless since there exists a greater degree of social discipline. Nevertheless, "the national road to socialism" has been condemned and many efforts made to prove that whoever is opposed to total adaptation to Russian models and to surrendering to Russian dictatorship is a traitor who must share the fate of Tito—that is, must come out against the Center and thus weaken its war potential without which there can be no revolution on a world scale. To pronounce oneself against this thesis would be to deny the New Faith and to introduce in its place a different faith, for example one directly linked to Marx and Engels. Many do so. Others, seeing in the alliance between Tito and the West an example of historical fatality, and rejecting the idea that this fatality may be due simply to the Center's policy toward dependent nations, shut themselves up in a Ketman which does not hamper the Center in its external acts. A true Moslem, even though he be deeply attached to his Ketman, never seeks to injure Islam in those areas where it is fighting for its life against unbelievers. Such Ketman expresses itself only in practical moves which do no harm in the world struggle, but which on the other hand safeguard national interests whenever possible.

The Ketman of Revolutionary Purity is a rare variety, more common in the large cities of Russia than in the people's democracies. It is based on a belief in the "sacred fire of the revolutionary epoch of Lenin" which burns in such a poet as Mayakovski. Mayakovski's suicide in 1930 marked the end of an era distinguished by the flowering of literature, the theater, and music. The "sacred fire" was dampened, collectivization was introduced mercilessly, millions of Soviet citizens perished in slave labor camps, a ruthless policy toward non-Russian nations was established. Literature became flat and colorless under the influence of imposed theories; Russian painting was destroyed; Russian theater, then the foremost in the world, was deprived of freedom to experiment; science was subjected to directives from Party chiefs. A man who reasons thus hates Him with all his heart, holding Him responsible for the terrible lot of the Russian people and for the hatred they inspire in other nations.

Still, he is not altogether sure whether He is necessary or not. Perhaps in extraordinary periods such as the present the appearance of a tyrant must be considered desirable. Mass purges in which so many good communists died, the lowering of the living standard of the citizens, the reduction of artists and scholars to the status of yes-men, the extermination of entire national groups—what other man would dare undertake such measures? After all, Russia stood firm against Hitler; the Revolution weathered the attack of enemy armies. In this perspective, His acts seem effective and even justified, perhaps, by an exceptional historical situation. If He had not instituted an exceptional terror in the year 1937, wouldn't there have been more people willing to help Hitler than there actually were? For example, doesn't the present-day line in scholarship and art, no matter how at odds it may be at times with common sense, effectually raise Russian morale in the face of the war that threatens? He is an infamous blot on the bright New Faith, but a blemish we must tolerate for the moment. And indeed we must even support Him. The "sacred fire" has not gone out. When victory is achieved, it will burst forth again with its old strength, the bonds He imposed will fall away, and relations between nations will operate on new and better principles. This variety of Ketman was widespread if not universal in Russia during the Second World War, and its present form is a rebirth of an already once-deceived hope.

Aesthetic Ketman is born of the disparity between man's longings and the sense-satisfactions the New Faith offers. A man of taste cannot approve the results of official pressure in the realm of culture no matter how much he applauds the latest verses, how many flattering reviews he writes of current art expositions, nor how studiously he pretends that the gloomy new buildings coincide with his personal preferences in architecture. He changes completely within the four walls of his home. There one finds (if he is a well-situated intellectual) reproductions of works of art officially condemned as bourgeois, records of modern music, and a rich collection of ancient authors in various languages. This luxury of splendid

isolation is pardoned him so long as his creative work is effective propaganda. To protect his position and his apartment
(which he has by the grace of the State), the intellectual is
prepared to make any sacrifice or compromise; for the value
of privacy in a society that affords little if any isolation is
greater than the saying "my home is my castle" can lead one
to surmise. Two-way television screens installed in private
homes to observe the behavior of citizens in seclusion belong
as yet to the future. Hence, by listening to foreign radio stations and reading good books, he profits from a moment of
relaxation; that is, of course, if he is alone, for as soon as guests
arrive the play begins anew.

Never has there been a close study of how necessary to a
man are the experiences which we clumsily call aesthetic. Such
experiences are associated with works of art for only an insig-
nificant number of individuals. The majority find pleasure of
an aesthetic nature in the mere fact of their existence within
the stream of life. In the cities, the eye meets colorful store
displays, the diversity of human types. Looking at passers-by,
one can guess from their faces the story of their lives. This
movement of the imagination when a man is walking through
a crowd has an erotic tinge; his emotions are very close to
physiological sensations. He rejoices in dresses, in the flash of
lights; while, for instance, Parisian markets with their heaps of
vegetables and flowers, fish of every shape and hue, fruits,
sides of meat dripping with every shade of red offer delights,
he need not go seeking them in Dutch or Impressionist painting. He hears snatches of arias, the throbbing of motors mixed
with the warble of birds, called greetings, laughter. His nose
is assailed by changing odors: coffee, gasoline, oranges, ozone,
roasting nuts, perfumes.

Those who have sung of the large cities have consecrated
many pages to the description of this joyous immersion in the
reservoir of universal life. The swimmer who trusts himself to
the wave, and senses the immensity of the element that surrounds him lives through a like emotion. I am thinking of such
great singers of the city as Balzac, Baudelaire, and Whitman.
It would seem that the exciting and invigorating power of this
participation in mass life springs from the feeling of *potential-*

ity, of constant unexpectedness, of a mystery one ever pursues.

Even the life of the peasants, though it be dulled by brutalizing hand labor, allows for aesthetic expression in the rhythm of custom, the rites of the church, holy pictures, country fairs, native costumes, paper flower decorations, folk sculptures, music, and dances.

In the countries of the New Faith the cities lose their former aspect. The liquidation of small private enterprises gives the streets a stiff and institutional look. The chronic lack of consumer goods renders the crowds uniformly gray and uniformly indigent. When consumer products do appear, they are of a single second-rate quality. Fear paralyzes individuality and makes people adjust themselves as much as possible to the average type in their gestures, clothing, and facial expressions. Cities become filled with the racial type well-regarded by the rulers: short, square men and women, with short legs and wide hips. This is the proletarian type, cultivated to an extreme, thanks to binding aesthetic standards. (We know that these same dumpy women and stocky men could change completely under the influence of films, painting, and fashion, for America has proved that mass communication is at least as important as diet in determining physical appearance.) Streets, factories, and meeting places sport the inevitable red flags and painted slogans. The new buildings are monumental and oppressive, lightness and charm in architecture being condemned as formalistic. The number of aesthetic experiences accessible to a city-dweller in the countries of the New Faith is uncommonly limited. The only place of magic is the theater, for the spell of the theater exists even though confined by the commands of socialist realism which define both the contents of a play and stage décor. The tremendous popular success of authors like Shakespeare is due to the fact that their fantasy triumphs even within the bounds of naturalistic stage setting. The hunger for *strangeness* that is so great inside the Imperium should give the rulers pause; yet in all probability it does not, for they consider such longings derelicts from the past.

In the villages, where the entire former pattern of custom is to be abolished through the transformation of peasants into agricultural workers, there still remain survivals of the individual peasant cultures which slowly stratified over the centuries. Still, let us speak frankly, the main supports of this culture were usually the wealthier peasants. The battle against them, and their subsequent need to hide, must lead to the atrophy of peasant dress, decoration of huts, cultivation of private gardens, etc. There is a definite contradiction between the official protection of folklore (as a harmless form of national culture designed to satisfy patriotic tendencies) and the necessities of the new economic structure.

In these conditions aesthetic Ketman has every possibility of spreading. It is expressed not only in that unconscious longing for strangeness which is channeled toward controlled amusements like theater, film, and folk festivals, but also into various forms of escapism. Writers burrow into ancient texts, comment upon and re-edit ancient authors. They write children's books so that their fancy may have slightly freer play. Many choose university careers because research into literary history offers a safe pretext for plunging into the past and for converse with works of great aesthetic value. The number of translators of former prose and poetry multiplies. Painters seek an outlet for their interests in illustrations for children's books, where the choice of gaudy colors can be justified by an appeal to the "naïve" imagination of children. Stage managers, doing their duty by presenting bad contemporary works, endeavor to introduce into their repertoires the plays of Lope de Vega or Shakespeare—that is, those of their plays which are approved by the Center.

Some representatives of the plastic arts are so daring that they reveal their Ketman to no small degree by proclaiming the need of an aesthetic of everyday life, and by establishing special institutes to design fabrics, furniture, glass, and ceramics for industry. There is money for such enterprises, and they find support among the most intelligent dialecticians of the upper circles of the Party. Such efforts deserve respect when one considers that before the Second World War Poland and Czechoslovakia were, aside from Sweden and Finland, the leading countries in interior decoration. Nevertheless, there is no reason why that which passes as formalism in painting and architecture should be tolerated for any length of time in the applied arts.

The rationalization of aesthetic Ketman is obvious: since everything is planned in a socialist economy, why not proceed to a planned satisfaction of the aesthetic needs of human beings? Here, however, we trespass upon the treacherous territory of the demon, Psychology. To admit that a man's eye has need of exultant colors, harmonious forms, or light sunny architecture is to affirm that the taste of the Center is bad. However, even there one can see some progress. They are already erecting skyscrapers patterned after the buildings raised in Chicago about the year 1900. It is possible that in the year 2000 they will officially introduce art forms that today are considered modern in the West. But how can one still the thought that aesthetic experiences arise out of something organic, and that the union of color and harmony with fear is as difficult to imagine as brilliant plumage on birds living in the northern tundras?

Professional Ketman is reasoned thus: since I find myself in circumstances over which I have no control, and since I have but one life and that is fleeting, I should strive to do my best. I am like a crustacean attached to a crag on the bottom of the sea. Over me storms rage and huge ships sail; but my entire effort is concentrated upon clinging to the rock, for otherwise I will be carried off by the waters and perish, leaving no trace behind. If I am a scientist I attend congresses at which I deliver reports strictly adhering to the Party line. But in the laboratory I pursue my research according to scientific methods, and in that alone lies the aim of life. If my work is successful, it matters little how it will be presented and toward whose glory. Discoveries made in the name of a disinterested search for truth are lasting, whereas the shrieks of politicians pass. I must do all they demand, they may use my name as they wish, as long as I have access to a laboratory and money for the purchase of scientific instruments.

If I am a writer, I take pride in my literary achievements. Here, for example, is my treatise on Swift, a Marxist analysis. This type of analysis, which is not synonymous with the Method or the New Faith, makes possible a keen penetration into historical events. Marx had a genius for observation. In following him one is secure against attack, for he is, after all, the prophet; and one can proclaim one's belief in the Method and the New Faith in a preface fulfilling much the same function as dedications to kings or tsars in times past. Here is my translation of a sixteenth-century poem, or my novel whose scene is laid in the distant past. Aren't they of permanent value? Here are my translations from Russian. They are viewed with approbation and have brought me a large sum of money, but certainly Pushkin is a great poet, and his worth is not altered by the fact that today his poems serve Him as a means of propaganda. Obviously I must pay for the right to practice my profession with a certain number of articles and odes in the way of tribute. Still one's life on earth is not judged by transitory panegyrics written out of necessity.

These two examples of professional Ketman should demonstrate how little discomfort it creates for the rulers. It is the source of considerable dynamic force and one cause of the tremendous impetus toward education. The object is to establish some special field in which one can release one's energies, exploit one's knowledge and sensibility, and at the same time escape the fate of a functionary entirely at the mercy of political fluctuations. The son of a worker who becomes a chemist makes a *permanent* advance. The son of a worker who becomes a member of the security police rises to the surface, where large ships sail but where the sea is changeable and stormy. But most important of all, chemical experiments, bridges, translations of poetry, and medical care are exceptionally free of falsity. The State, in its turn, takes advantage of this Ketman because it needs chemists, engineers, and doctors. From time to time, it is true, there come from above muffled grumbles of hatred against those who practice Ketman in the realm of humanistic studies. Fadeyev, Moscow's literary overseer, attacked the University of Leningrad because one of its students had written a dissertation on the English poet, Walter Savage Landor. "Who needs Landor? Who ever heard of him?" cried Fadeyev. So it would seem that moderation and watchfulness are indicated for those who espouse this form of Ketman.

Sceptical Ketman is widely disseminated throughout intellectual circles. One argues that humanity does not know how to handle its knowledge or how to resolve the problems of production and division of goods. The first scientific attempts to solve social problems, made in the nineteenth century, are interesting but not precise enough. They happened, however, into the hands of the Russians who, unable to think otherwise than dogmatically, raised these first attempts to the dignity of dogma. What is happening in Russia and the countries dependent upon her bespeaks a kind of insanity, but it is not impossible that Russia will manage to impose her insanity upon the whole world and that the return to reason will occur only after two or three hundred years. Finding oneself in the very midst of an historical cyclone, one must behave as prudently as possible, yielding externally to forces capable of destroying all adversaries. This does not prevent one from taking pleasure in one's observations, since what one beholds is indeed unprecedented. Surely man has never before been subjected to such pressure, never has he had to writhe and wriggle so to adapt himself to forms constructed according to the books but obviously not to his size. All his intellectual and emotional capacities are put to the test.

Whoever contemplates this daily sight of repudiation and humiliation knows more about man than an inhabitant of the West who feels no pressure other than that of money. The accumulating of this store of observations is the activity of a miser who counts his treasure in secret. Since this Ketman is based on a total lack of belief in the Method, it helps one conform externally to the obligatory line by allowing for complete cynicism, and therefore for elasticity in adjusting oneself to changing tactics.

Metaphysical Ketman occurs generally in countries with a Catholic past. Most examples of it within the Imperium are found in Poland. This Ketman depends upon a *suspended* belief in a metaphysical principle of the world. A man attached to this Ketman regards the epoch in which he lives as antimetaphysical, and hence as one in which no metaphysical faith can emerge. Humanity is learning to think in rationalistic and materialistic categories; it is burdened with immediate problems and entangled in a class war. Other-worldly religions are crumbling, living through a period of crisis and, what is worse, serving to defend the obsolete order. This does not mean that mankind will not return to a better and purified religion in the future. Perhaps the New Faith is an indispensable purgatory; perhaps God's purpose is being accomplished through the barbarians, i.e. the Center, who are forcing the masses to awaken out of their lethargy. The spiritual fare these masses receive from the New Faith is inferior and insufficient. Still one must commend the Center for breaking new ground and for demolishing externally splendid but internally rotten façades. One should cooperate in this task without betraying one's attachment to the Mystery. All the more so because the Mystery has no possibility of appearing in literature, for example, and because neither the language nor the ideas at the disposal of contemporary man are ripe enough to express it.

This metaphysical Ketman in its turn has a number of varieties. Certain practicing Catholics serve even in the security police, and *suspend* their Catholicism in executing their inhumane work. Others, trying to maintain a Christian community in the bosom of the New Faith, come out publicly as Catholics. They often succeed in preserving Catholic institutions, because the dialecticians are ready to accept so-called "progressive" and "patriotic" Catholics who comply in political matters. The mutual game is rather ambiguous. The rulers tolerate such Catholics as a temporary and necessary evil, reasoning that the stage has not yet arrived at which one can utterly wipe out religion, and that it is better to deal with accommodating bigots than with refractory ones. "Progressive Catholics" are, however, conscious of being relegated to a not particularly honorable place, that of shamans or witch-doctors from savage tribes whom one humors until one can dress them in trousers and send them to school. They appear in various state spectacles and are even sent abroad as shining testimonials to the Center's tolerance toward uncivilized races. One can compare their function to that of "noble savages" imported to the metropolis by colonial powers for state occasions. Their defense against total degradation is metaphysical Ketman: they swindle the devil who thinks he is swindling them. But the devil knows what they think and is satisfied.

What holds for such Catholics can be applied to members of other religions, as well as to persons outside any denomination. One of the most ominous reproaches leveled against writers is the suspicion that their verses, plays, or novels contain a "metaphysical residue." Since a writer is a civilizer who dares not be a shaman or a sorcerer, the slightest signs of a metaphysical tendency in him are unforgivable. The literature of the countries which, until the Second World War, were free from Moscow's domination betrayed especially strong inclinations in that direction, so that metaphysical deviation is of constant and imperative concern to the rulers. For instance, a play that introduces "strangeness," revealing the author's interest in the tragedy of life, has no chance of being produced because the tragedy of human fate leads to thoughts about the mystery of human destiny. One forgives certain writers like Shakespeare these predispositions, but there is no question of permitting any contemporary author to harbor them. It is for this reason that Greek tragedies are not deemed suitable for theater repertoires. Marx loved the Greek tragedians, but let us not forget that the connection between the New Faith and Marx is rather superficial.

The New Faith is a Russian creation, and the Russian intelligentsia which shaped it had developed the deepest contempt for all art that does not serve social ends directly. Other social functions of art, probably the most important ones, consistently escaped its understanding. As for poetry, since its sources are hard to differentiate from the sources of all religion, it is singularly exposed to persecution. True, the poet is free to describe hills, trees, and flowers, but if he should feel that boundless exaltation in the face of nature that seized Wordsworth on his visit to Tintern Abbey, he is at once suspect. This is an excellent means of eliminating the legions of bad poets who like to confess their pantheistic flights publicly, but it is also a means of exterminating poetry as a whole and replacing it by jingles little better than the singing commercials broadcast over the radio in America. A painter, in turn, may be attacked quite as easily for using abbreviated and synthesized forms (formalism), as for an excessive love of the beauty of the world, i.e. a contemplative attitude which signifies that he is a metaphysicist by temperament. A musician should see to it that his compositions are easy to translate into the language of common activities (enthusiasm for work, folk festivities, etc.), and that no element remains which is difficult to grasp and hence dangerous. If metaphysical Ketman is tolerated in the "savages," i.e. those who profess the Christian religion, in the artists who are considered the educators of society, it is severely punished.

Ethical Ketman results from opposition to the ethics of the New Faith, which is based on the principle that good and evil are definable solely in terms of service or harm to the interests of the Revolution. Since exemplary behavior of citizens in their interrelations aids the cause of socialism, great emphasis is placed upon individual morality.

"The development of a new man" is the key point in the New Faith's program. Demands made upon Party members are exceedingly harsh. One exacts of them no small degree of abstinence. As a result, admission to the Party is not unlike entrance into a religious order; and the literature of the New Faith treats this act with a gravity equal to that with which Catholic literature speaks of the vows of young nuns. The higher one stands in the Party hierarchy, the more attentively is one's private life supervised. Love of money, drunkenness, or a confused love-life disqualify a Party member from holding important offices. Hence the upper brackets of the Party are filled by ascetics devoted to the single cause of Revolution. As for certain human tools, deprived of real influence but useful because of their names, even if they belong to the Party one tolerates or sometimes encourages their weaknesses, for they constitute a guarantee of obedience. The general ethical ideal of the New Faith is puritanical. If it were feasible to lodge all the citizens in cells and release them only for work or for political meetings, that would undoubtedly be most desirable. But alas, one must make concessions to human nature. Procreation is possible only as a result of sexual relations between men and women, and one must take this inconvenience into account.

The "new man" is conditioned to acknowledge the good of the whole as the sole norm of his behavior. He thinks and reacts like others; is modest, industrious, satisfied with what the state gives him; limits his private life to nights spent at home, and passes all the rest of his time amidst his companions at work or at play, observing them carefully and reporting their actions and opinions to the authorities. Informing was and is known in many civilizations, but the New Faith declares it a cardinal virtue of the good citizen (though the name itself is carefully avoided). It is the basis of each man's fear of his fellow-men. Work in an office or factory is hard not only because of the amount of labor required, but even more because of the need to be on guard against omnipresent and vigilant eyes and ears. After work one goes to political meetings or special lectures, thus lengthening a day that is without a moment of relaxation or spontaneity. The people one talks with may seem relaxed and careless, sympathetic and indignant, but if they appear so, it is only to arouse corresponding attitudes and to extract confidences which they can report to their superiors.

In effect this cult of the community produces something which poisons the community itself. The mentality of the Party's sages is, indeed, rather strange. They make concessions to physiological human weaknesses, but they refuse to admit that man has other foibles as well: that he feels fine when he can relax, and unhappy when he is afraid, that lying is bad for him because it creates internal tension. These weaknesses, together with others like the desire to better one's own lot at the expense of one's fellow-men, transform the ethic which was originally founded on cooperation and brotherhood into an ethic of a war pitting all men against all others, and granting the greatest chances of survival to the craftiest. Victory in this new struggle seems to belong to a breed different from that which was favored to win in the battle for money in the early days of industrial capitalism. If biting dogs can be divided into two main categories, noisy and brutal, or silent and slyly vicious, then the second variety would seem most privileged in the countries of the New Faith. Forty or fifty years of education in these new ethical maxims must create a new and irretrievable species of mankind. The "new man" is not merely a postulate. He is beginning to become a reality.

Ethical Ketman is not rare among highly placed figures in

the Party. These persons, no matter how capable they are of murdering millions of people in the name of Communism, try to compensate for their professional severity and are often more honorable in their personal relations than people who affect individualistic ethics. Their capacity to sympathize and help is almost unlimited. Indeed this very feeling of compassion pushed them onto the road of revolution in their youth, and in this they reiterated the experience of Marx himself. One finds this Ketman chiefly among the old Communists. Conflicts between friendship and the interests of the Revolution are matters they weigh at length in their conscience; and they are pitiless only when completely convinced that, in shielding a friend or in refraining from denouncing him, they are injuring that cause which is most precious to them. Though they are usually esteemed as people of crystalline righteousness, they are not safe from frequent accusations of "intellectuality," a contemptuous epithet for those who are blameless as theoreticians, but hampered in action by an oversensitivity to ethical considerations. A revolutionary should be without scruples. It is better to cut down human trees blindly than to wonder which among them are really rotten.

This variety of Ketman is one of the most prevalent in the people's democracies because the new ethic is of recent inculcation, whereas the ethic vanquished by the New Faith was ensconced there for centuries. One can never foresee when and in whom this Ketman will appear, which makes for an element of surprise. Individuals who give one every reason to suppose that they do not denounce others turn out to be inveterate informers; individuals who are apparently most indifferent to "prejudices," show themselves inexplicably loyal toward their friends and even toward strangers. Since this Ketman augments the difficulties of controlling the citizens' thoughts, it is diligently sought out and penalized; yet the number of situations to which it can be applied is so great that it often eludes all manner of pressure.

The inhabitants of Western countries little realize that millions of their fellow-men, who seem superficially more or less similar to them, live in a world as fantastic as that of the men from Mars. They are unaware of the perspectives on human nature that Ketman opens. Life in constant internal tension develops talents which are latent in man. He does not even suspect to what heights of cleverness and psychological perspicacity he can rise when he is cornered and must either be skillful or perish. The survival of those best adapted to mental acrobatics creates a human type that has been rare until now. The necessities which drive men to Ketman sharpen the intellect.

Whoever would take the measure of intellectual life in the countries of Central or Eastern Europe from the monotonous articles appearing in the press or the stereotyped speeches pronounced there, would be making a grave error. Just as theologians in periods of strict orthodoxy expressed their views in the rigorous language of the Church, so the writers of the people's democracies make use of an accepted special style, terminology, and linguistic ritual. What is important is not what someone said but what he wanted to say, disguising his thought by removing a comma, inserting an "and," establishing this rather than another sequence in the problems discussed. Unless one has lived there one cannot know how many titanic battles are being fought, how the heroes of Ketman are falling, what this warfare is being waged over. Obviously, people caught up in this daily struggle are rather contemptuous of their compatriot political émigrés. A surgeon cannot consider a butcher his equal in dexterity; just so a Pole, Czech, or Hungarian practiced in the art of dissimulation smiles when he learns that someone in the emigration has called him a traitor (or a swine) at the very moment when this traitor (or swine) is engaged in a match of philosophical chess on whose outcome the fate of fifteen laboratories or twenty ateliers depends. They do not know how one pays—those abroad do not know. They do not know what one buys, and at what price.

Ketman as a social institution is not entirely devoid of advantages. In order to evaluate them, one need only look at life in the West. Westerners, and especially Western intellectuals, suffer from a special variety of *taedium vitae;* their emotional and intellectual life is too dispersed. Everything they think and feel evaporates like steam in an open expanse. Freedom is a burden to them. No conclusions they arrive at are binding: it may be so, then again it may not. The result is a constant uneasiness. The happiest of them seem to be those who become Communists. They live within a wall which they batter themselves against, but which provides them with a resistance that helps them define themselves. Steam that once evaporated into the air becomes a force under pressure. An even greater energy is generated in those who must hide their Communist convictions, that is, who must practice Ketman, a custom which is, after all, not unknown in the countries of the West.

In short, Ketman means self-realization *against* something. He who practices Ketman suffers because of the obstacles he meets; but if these obstacles were suddenly to be removed, he would find himself in a void which might perhaps prove much more painful. Internal revolt is sometimes essential to spiritual health, and can create a particular form of happiness. What can be said openly is often much less interesting than the emotional magic of defending one's private sanctuary. For most people the necessity of living in constant tension and watchfulness is a torture, but many intellectuals accept this necessity with masochistic pleasure.

He who practices Ketman lies. But would he be less dishonest if he could speak the truth? A painter who tries to smuggle illicit ("metaphysical") delight in the beauty of the world into his picture of life on a collective farm would be lost if he were given complete freedom, for the beauty of the world seems greater to him the less free he is to depict it. A poet muses over what he would write if he were not bound by his political responsibilities, but could he realize his visions if he were at liberty to do so? Ketman brings comfort, fostering dreams of what might be, and even the enclosing fence affords the solace of reverie.

Who knows whether it is not in man's lack of an internal *core* that the mysterious success of the New Faith and its charm for the intellectual lie? By subjecting man to pressure, the New Faith creates this core, or in any case the feeling that it exists. Fear of freedom is nothing more than fear of the void. "There is nothing in man," said a friend of mine, a dialectician. "He will never extract anything out of himself, because there is nothing there. You can't leave the people and write in a wilderness. Remember that man is a function of social forces. Whoever wants to be alone will perish." This is probably true, but I doubt if it can be called anything more than the law of our times. Feeling that there was *nothing* in him, Dante could not have written his *Divine Comedy* or Montaigne his *Essays,* nor could Chardin have painted a single still-life. Today man believes there is *nothing* in him, so he accepts *anything,* even if he knows it to be bad, in order to find himself at one with others, in order not to be alone. As long as he believes this, there is little one can reproach in his behavior. Perhaps it is better for him to breed a full-grown Ketman, to submit to pressure and thus feel that he *is,* than to take a chance on the wisdom of past ages which maintains that man is a creature of God.

But suppose one should try to live without Ketman, to challenge fate, to say: "If I lose, I shall not pity myself." Suppose one can live without outside pressure, suppose one can create one's own inner tension—then it is not true that there is nothing in man. To take this risk would be an act of faith.

COMMENT: On Political Persecution
of Writers

Hundreds of writers have fallen foul of the state for outraging
the public sense of decency on private or public grounds. Ovid
managed to combine both reasons—exiled ostensibly for his
Ars Amoris, he was said really to have offended Caesar politically. Jean Gênet, on the other hand, was tried not for his
brand of diabolism but for larceny; he went free after eminent
men had pleaded for him on account of his genius as a writer.
Büchner, Silone, Brecht, Mann, Pasternak, Joyce, Zola, Baudelaire—such men are all the more famous for surviving censorship. More, we must suppose, did not survive. One of the
strange effects of censorship on men of letters is to visit sterility
on concealment. After the defeat of the Nazi regime, some supposed that all kinds of writing would be pulled out of German
bottom drawers where it had lain hidden for up to a dozen
years. But in fact the bottom drawers were empty; writers
had stopped writing, and for years after the German defeat
there was very little that German writers had to say.

Among the famous cases of writers versus the state, none is
succincter or less gloomy than Mme. de Staël v. the censor of
Napoleon. *De l'Allemagne*, partly the work of Mme. de Staël's
friend A. W. Schlegel, was aimed at the French rather than
the Germans, though the criticism was only implied and the
praises of the Germans were convincing enough in themselves
to bolster German nationalism and alarm the French police.
By defying Napoleon's strict new censorship laws of 1810,
Mme. de Staël leaned too heavily on her wealth, influence,
character, and charm. Till 1808 Napoleon considered her tire-
some but harmless so long as she kept out of Paris; then
increasing nationalism abroad and unrest in France brought

about the inauguration of the new censorship office, where a publisher would submit proofs before final publication. Before the printing of the last volume of *De l'Allemagne,* rumors of the daring new work circulated through Paris, and the censor, who had passed the earlier volumes conditionally, took fright. Mme. de Staël applied to see the Emperor himself: but it was too late; Napoleon had already examined the book, flung it, some say, into the fireplace, and ordered the exile of the author. The first edition at the printer's was destroyed, but some copies and a set of proofs were missing—which Schlegel had safe in Berne. Mme. de Staël prudently removed herself to Geneva. Her publisher went bankrupt. In 1813, however, John Murray published the book in London, and Mme. de Staël prefaced future editions with the following account of her trials.

TEXT: Preface to *De l'Allemagne* by Germaine de Staël

[contemporary anonymous translation]

1st October, 1818.

In 1810, I put the manuscript of this work, on Germany, into the hands of the bookseller, who had published Corinne. As I maintained in it the same opinions, and preserved the same silence respecting the present government of the French, as in my former writings, I flattered myself that I should be permitted to publish this work also: yet, a few days after I had dispatched my manuscript, a decree of a very singular description appeared on the subject of the liberty of the press; it declared "that no work could be printed without having been examined by censors." Very well; it was usual in France, under the old *régime,* for literary works to be submitted to the examination of a censorship; the tendency of public opinion was then towards the feeling of liberty, which rendered such a restraint a matter very little to be dreaded; a little article, however, at the end of the new regulation declared, "that when the censors should have examined a work and permitted its publication, booksellers should be authorized to publish it, but that the Minister of the Police should still have a right to suppress it altogether, if he should think fit so to do." The meaning of which is, that such and such forms should be adopted until it should be thought fit no longer to abide by them: a law was not necessary to decree what was in fact the absence of all law; it would have been better to have relied simply upon the exercise of absolute power.

My bookseller, however, took upon himself the responsibility of the publication of my book, after submitting it to the censors, and thus our contract was made. I came to reside within forty leagues of Paris, to superintend the printing of the work, and it was upon this occasion that, for the last time, I breathed the air of France. I had, however, abstained in this book, as will be seen, from making any reflections on the political state of Germany: I supposed myself to be writing at the distance of fifty years from the present time; but the present time will not suffer itself to be forgotten. Several of the censors examined my manuscript; they suppressed the different passages which I have now restored and pointed out by notes. With the exception, however, of these passages, they allowed the work to be printed, as I now publish it, for I have thought it my duty to make no alteration in it. It appears to me a curious thing to show what the work is, which is capable even now in France, of drawing down the most cruel persecution on the head of its author.

At the moment when this work was about to appear, and when the ten thousand copies of the first edition had been actually printed off, the Minister of the Police, known under the name of General Savary, sent his gensdarmes to the house of the bookseller, with orders to tear the whole edition in pieces, and to place sentinels at the different entrances to the warehouses, for fear a single copy of this dangerous writing should escape. A commissary of police was charged with the superintendence of this expedition, in which General Savary easily obtained the victory; and the poor commissary, it is said, died of the fatigue he underwent in too minutely assuring himself of the destruction of so great a number of volumes, or rather in seeing them transformed into paper perfectly white, upon which no trace of human reason remained; the price of the paper, valued at twenty louis by the police, was the only indemnification which the bookseller obtained from the minister.

At the same time that the destruction of my work was going on at Paris, I received in the country an order to deliver up the copy from which it had been printed, and to quit France in four-and-twenty hours. The conscripts are almost the only persons I know for whom four-and-twenty hours are considered a sufficient time to prepare for a journey; I wrote, therefore, to the Minister of the Police that I should require eight days to procure money and my carriage. The following is the letter which he sent me in answer:

GENERAL POLICE, Minister's Office,
Paris, 3d October, 1810.

"I received, Madam, the letter that you did me the honor to write me. Your son will have apprised you, that I had no objection to your postponing your departure for seven or eight days. I beg you will make that time sufficient for the arrangements you still have to make, because I cannot grant you more.

"The cause of the order which I have signified to you, is not to be looked for in the silence you have preserved with respect to the Emperor in your last work; that would be a mistake; no place could be found in it worthy of him; but your banishment is a natural consequence of the course you have constantly pursued for some years past. It appeared to me, that the air of this country did not agree with you, and we are not yet reduced to seek for models among the people you admire.

"Your last work is not French; it is I who have put a stop to the publication of it. I am sorry for the loss the bookseller must sustain, but it is not possible for me to suffer it to appear.

"You know, Madam, that you were only permitted to quit Coppet, because you had expressed a desire to go to America. If my predecessor suffered you to remain in the department of Loire-et-Cher, you were not to look upon that indulgence as a revocation of the orders which had been given with respect to you. At present, you oblige me to cause them to be strictly executed, and you have only yourself to accuse for it.

"I desire M. Corbigny to suspend the execution of the order I had given him, until the expiration of the time I now grant you.

"I regret, Madam, that you have obliged me to commence my correspondence with you by a measure of severity; it would have been more agreeable to me to have had only to offer you the testimonies of the high consideration with which I have the honor to be, Madam, your very humble and very obedient servant,

(Signed) "THE DUKE DE ROVIGO."
"MAD. DE STAEL.

"P. S. I have reasons, Madam, for mentioning to you the ports of Lorient, la Rochelle, Bourdeaux, and Rochefort, as being the only ports at which you can embark; I beg you will let me know which of them you choose."*

I shall add some reflections upon this letter, although it appears to me curious enough in itself. "It appeared to me," said General Savary, "that *the air of this country did not agree with you;*" what a gracious manner of announcing to a woman, then, alas! the mother of three children, the daughter of a man who had served France with so much fidelity, that she was banished forever from the place of her birth, without being suffered, in any manner, to protest against a punishment, esteemed the next in severity to death! There is a French vaudeville, in which a bailiff, boasting of his politeness towards those persons whom he takes to prison, says,

"Aussi je suis aimé de tout ceux que j'arrête."†

I know not whether such was the intention of General Savary.

He adds, that *the French are not reduced to seek for models among the people I admire.* These people are the English first, and in many respects the Germans. At all events, I think I cannot be accused of not loving France. I have shown but too much sensibility in being exiled from a country where I have so many objects of affection, and where those who are dear to me delight me so much! But, notwithstanding this attachment, perhaps too lively, for so brilliant a country, and its spiritual inhabitants, it did not follow that I was to be forbidden to admire England. She has been seen like a knight armed for the defence of social order, preserving Europe during ten years of anarchy, and ten years more of despotism. Her happy

* The object of this Postscript was to forbid me the Ports of the Channel.
† "So I am loved by all I arrest."

constitution was, at the beginning of the Revolution, the object of the hopes and the efforts of the French; my mind still remains where theirs was then.

On my return to the estate of my father, the Préfet of Geneva forbade me to go to a greater distance than four leagues from it. I suffered myself one day to go as far as ten leagues, merely for an airing: the gensdarmes immediately pursued me, the postmasters were forbidden to supply me with horses, and it would have appeared as if the safety of the State depended on such a weak being as myself. However, I still submitted to this imprisonment in all its severity, when a last blow rendered it quite insupportable to me. Some of my friends were banished, because they had had the generosity to come and see me; this was too much: to carry with us the contagion of misfortune, not to dare to associate with those we love, to be afraid to write to them, or pronounce their names, to be the object by turns, either of affectionate attentions which make us tremble for those who show them, or of those refinements of baseness which terror inspires, is a situation from which every one, who still values life, would withdraw!

I was told, as a means of softening my grief, that these continual persecutions were a proof of the importance that was attached to me; I could have answered that I had not deserved

"Ni cet excés d'honeur, ni cette indignité;"*

but I never suffered myself to look to consolations addressed to my vanity; for I knew that there was no one then in France, from the highest to the lowest, who might not have been found worthy of being made unhappy. I was tormented in all the concerns of my life, in all the tender points of my character, and power condescended to take the trouble of becoming well acquainted with me, in order the more effectually to enchance my sufferings. Not being able then to disarm that power by the simple sacrifice of my talents, and resolved not to employ them in its service, I seemed to feel, to the bottom of my heart, the advice my father had given me, and I left my paternal home.

* "Neither this excess of honor, nor this indignity."

I think it my duty to make this calumniated book known to the public—this book, the source of so many troubles; and, though General Savary told me in his letter that my work *was not French*, as I certainly do not consider him to be the representative of France, it is to Frenchmen such as I have known them, that I should with confidence address a production, in which I have endeavored, to the best of my abilities, to heighten the glory of the works of the human mind. . . .

COMMENT: On Literature and Nationalism

Much of this anthology has been taken up with pieces that labor the obvious. Yet we have only to look about us to see how deeply our freedoms of speech and the printed word have been whittled away. The arrival of Napoleon ended the long struggle for these freedoms, which in modern times have been based on the notion that they are *rights*. The long disaster of the Napoleonic wars and the disillusion with the spirit of the French Revolution which accompanied them soon exposed the fact that freedom was no longer a self-sustaining idea. Universal wars have recently made us used to giving ourselves unconditionally to the service of our different nations in the belief that if they perish, our rights will be forfeit. Without such rights, we have declared, life is not worth living. Yet when the wars finish, we find that our rights, which have created the national image for us, and for which we believed we fought, have seeped away—and the national image has imperceptibly swollen in their place. Because people do not fully realize how much has been given up, they tend to assume that all is as it was. Nevertheless there is a very strong body of opinion which now leans its weight *against* freedom of expression by declaring that such freedom is not a right but a privilege. The following essay, which was written just after the Second World War, draws attention to the basic principles stated in *Areopagitica* and puts it in historical perspective.

TEXT: "The Prevention of Literature" by George Orwell

About a year ago I attended a meeting of the P.E.N. Club, the occasion being the tercentenary of Milton's *Areopagitica*— a pamphlet, it may be remembered, in defence of freedom of the Press. Milton's famous phrase about the sin of "killing" a book was printed on the leaflets advertising the meeting which had been circulated beforehand.

There were four speakers on the platform. One of them delivered a speech which did deal with the freedom of the Press, but only in relation to India; another said, hesitantly, and in very general terms, that liberty was a good thing; a third delivered an attack on the laws relating to obscenity in literature. The fourth devoted most of his speech to a defence of the Russian purges. Of the speeches from the body of the hall, some reverted to the question of obscenity and the laws that deal with it, others were simply eulogies of Soviet Russia. Moral liberty—the liberty to discuss sex questions frankly in print— seemed to be generally approved, but political liberty was not mentioned. Out of this concourse of several hundred people, perhaps half of whom were directly connected with the writing trade, there was not a single one who could point out that freedom of the Press, if it means anything at all, means the freedom to criticize and oppose. Significantly, no speaker quoted from the pamphlet which was ostensibly being commemorated. Nor was there any mention of the various books that have been "killed" in England and the United States during the war. In its net effect the meeting was a demonstration in favor of censorship.*

* "It is fair to say that the P.E.N. Club celebrations, which lasted a week or more, did not always stick at quite the same level. I

There was nothing particularly surprising in this. In our age, the idea of intellectual liberty is under attack from two directions. On the one side are its theoretical enemies, the apologists of totalitarianism, and on the other its immediate, practical enemies, monopoly and bureaucracy. Any writer or journalist who wants to retain his integrity finds himself thwarted by the general drift of society rather than by active persecution. The sort of things that are working against him are the concentration of the Press in the hands of a few rich men, the grip of monopoly on radio and the films, the unwillingness of the public to spend money on books, making it necessary for nearly every writer to earn part of his living by hackwork, the encroachment of official bodies like the M.O.I. and the British Council, which help the writer to keep alive but also waste his time and dictate his opinions, and the continuous war atmosphere of the past ten years, whose distorting effects no one has been able to escape. Everything in our age conspires to turn the writer, and every other kind of artist as well, into a minor official, working on themes handed down from above and never telling what seems to him the whole of the truth. But in struggling against this fate he gets no help from his own side: that is, there is no large body of opinion which will assure him that he is in the right. In the past, at any rate throughout the Protestant centuries, the idea of rebellion and the idea of intellectual integrity were mixed up. A heretic—political, moral, religious, or aesthetic—was one who refused to outrage his own conscience. His outlook was summed up in the words of the Revivalist hymn:

> Dare to be a Daniel,
> Dare to stand alone;
> Dare to have a purpose firm,
> Dare to make it known.

---

happened to strike a bad day. But an examination of the speeches (printed under the title *Freedom of Expression*) shows that almost nobody in our own day is able to speak out as roundly in favor of intellectual liberty as Milton could do 300 years ago—and this in spite of the fact Milton was writing in a period of civil war." [Orwell's note.]

To bring this hymn up to date one would have to add a "Don't"
at the beginning of each line. For it is the peculiarity of our
age that the rebels against the existing order, at any rate the
most numerous and characteristic of them, are also rebelling
against the idea of individual integrity. "Daring to stand
alone" is ideologically criminal as well as practically dangerous.
The independence of the writer and the artist is eaten away by
vague economic forces, and at the same time it is undermined
by those who should be its defenders. It is with the second
process that I am concerned here.

Freedom of thought and of the Press are usually attacked
by arguments which are not worth bothering about. Anyone
who has experience of lecturing and debating knows them off
backwards. Here I am not trying to deal with the familiar
claim that freedom is an illusion, or with the claim that there
is more freedom in totalitarian countries than in democratic
ones, but with the much more tenable and dangerous proposition that freedom is *undesirable* and that intellectual honesty
is a form of anti-social selfishness. Although other aspects of
the question are usually in the foreground, the controversy
over freedom of speech and of the Press is at bottom a controversy over the desirability, or otherwise, of telling lies. What
is really at issue is the right to report contemporary events
truthfully, or as truthfully as is consistent with the ignorance,
bias and self-deception from which every observer necessarily
suffers. In saying this I may seem to be saying that straightforward "reportage" is the only branch of literature that matters:
but I will try to show later that at every literary level, and
probably in every one of the arts, the same issue arises in more
or less subtilized forms. Meanwhile, it is necessary to strip
away the irrelevancies in which this controversy is usually
wrapped up.

The enemies of intellectual liberty always try to present
their case as a plea for discipline versus individualism. The issue truth-versus-untruth is as far as possible kept in the background. Although the point of emphasis may vary, the writer
who refuses to sell his opinions is always branded as a mere
egoist. He is accused, that is, either of wanting to shut himself up in an ivory tower, or of making an exhibitionist display

of his own personality, or of resisting the inevitable current of history in an attempt to cling to unjustified privileges. The Catholic and the Communist are alike in assuming that an opponent cannot be both honest and intelligent. Each of them tacitly claims that "the truth" has already been revealed, and that the heretic, if he is not simply a fool, is secretly aware of "the truth" and merely resists it out of selfish motives. In Communist literature the attack on intellectual liberty is usually masked by oratory about "petty-bourgeois individualism," "the illusions of nineteenth-century liberalism," etc., and backed up by words of abuse such as "romantic" and "sentimental," which, since they do not have any agreed meaning, are difficult to answer. In this way the controversy is maneuvered away from its real issue. One can accept, and most enlightened people would accept, the Communist thesis that pure freedom will only exist in a classless society, and that one is most nearly free when one is working to bring such a society about. But slipped in with this is the quite unfounded claim that the Communist party is itself aiming at the establishment of the classless society, and that in the U.S.S.R. this aim is actually on the way to being realized. If the first claim is allowed to entail the second, there is almost no assault on common sense and common decency that cannot be justified. But meanwhile, the real point has been dodged. Freedom of the intellect means the freedom to report what one has seen, heard, and felt, and not to be obliged to fabricate imaginary facts and feelings. The familiar tirades against "escapism," and "individualism," "romanticism" and so forth, are merely a forensic device, the aim of which is to make the perversion of history seem respectable.

Fifteen years ago, when one defended the freedom of the intellect, one had to defend it against Conservatives, against Catholics, and to some extent—for they were not of great importance in England—against Fascists. Today one has to defend it against Communists and "fellow-travellers." One ought not to exaggerate the direct influence of the small English Communist party, but there can be no question about the poisonous effect of the Russian *mythos* on English intellectual life. Because of it known facts are suppressed and distorted to such an extent as to make it doubtful whether a true history of our times can ever be written. Let me give just one instance out of the hundreds that could be cited. When Germany collapsed, it was found that very large numbers of Soviet Russians—mostly, no doubt, from non political motives had changed sides and were fighting for the Germans. Also, a small but not negligible proportion of the Russian prisoners and Displaced Persons refused to go back to the U.S.S.R., and some of them, at least, were repatriated against their will. These facts, known to many journalists on the spot, went almost unmentioned in the British Press, while at the same time Russophile publicists in England continued to justify the purges and deportations of 1936–38 by claiming that the U.S.S.R. "had no quislings." The fog of lies and misinformation that surrounds such subjects as the Ukraine famine, the Spanish civil war, Russian policy in Poland, and so forth, is not due entirely to conscious dishonesty, but any writer or journalist who is fully sympathetic to the U.S.S.R.—sympathetic, that is, in the way the Russians themselves would want him to be—does have to acquiesce in deliberate falsification on important issues. I have before me what must be a very rare pamphlet, written by Maxim Litvinoff in 1918 and outlining the recent events in the Russian Revolution. It makes no mention of Stalin, but gives high praise to Trotsky, and also to Zinoviev, Kamenev, and others. What could be the attitude of even the most intellectually scrupulous Communist towards such a pamphlet? At best, the obscurantist attitude of saying that it is an undesirable document and better suppressed. And if for some reason it were decided to issue a garbled version of the pamphlet, denigrating Trotsky and inserting references to Stalin, no Communist who remained faithful to his party could protest. Forgeries almost as gross as this have been committed in recent years. But the significant thing is not that they happen, but that, even when they are known about, they provoke no reaction from the Left-wing intelligentsia as a whole. The argument that to tell the truth would be "inopportune" or would "play into the hands of" somebody or other is felt to be unanswerable, and few people are bothered by the prospect of the lies which they condone getting out of the newspapers and into the history books.

The organized lying practised by totalitarian states is not, as is sometimes claimed, a temporary expedient of the same nature as military deception. It is something integral to totalitarianism, something that would still continue even if concentration camps and secret police forces had ceased to be necessary. Among intelligent Communists there is an underground legend to the effect that although the Russian government is obliged *now* to deal in lying propaganda, frame-up trials, and so forth, it is secretly recording the true facts and will publish them at some future time. We can, I believe, be quite certain that this is not the case, because the mentality implied by such an action is that of a liberal historian who believes that the past cannot be altered and that a correct knowledge of history is valuable as a matter of course. From the totalitarian point of view history is something to be created rather than learned. A totalitarian state is in effect a theocracy, and its ruling caste, in order to keep its position, has to be thought of as infallible. But since, in practice, no one is infallible, it is frequently necessary to rearrange past events in order to show that this or that mistake was not made, or that this or that imaginary triumph actually happened. Then, again, every major change in policy demands a corresponding change of doctrine and a revaluation of prominent historical figures. This kind of thing happens everywhere, but is clearly likelier to lead to outright falsification in societies where only *one* opinion is permissible at any given moment. Totalitarianism demands, in fact, the continuous alteration of the past, and in the long run probably demands a disbelief in the very existence of objective truth. The friends of totalitarianism in this country usually tend to argue that since absolute truth is not attainable, a big lie is no worse than a little lie. It is pointed out that *all* historical records are biased and inaccurate, or, on the other hand, that modern physics has proved that what seems to us the real world is an illusion, so that to believe in the evidence of one's senses is simply vulgar philistinism. A totalitarian society which succeeded in perpetuating itself would probably set up a schizophrenic system of thought, in which the laws of common sense held good in everyday life and in certain exact sciences, but could be disregarded by the politician, the

historian, and the sociologist. Already there are countless people who would think it scandalous to falsify a scientific text-
book, but would see nothing wrong in falsifying an historical
fact. It is at the point where literature and politics cross that
totalitarianism exerts its greatest pressure on the intellectual.
The exact sciences are not, at this date, menaced to anything
like the same extent. This partly accounts for the fact that in
all countries it is easier for the scientists than for the writers
to line up behind their respective governments.

To keep the matter in perspective, let me repeat what I
said at the beginning of this essay: that in England the *immediate* enemies of truthfulness, and hence of freedom of
thought, are the Press lords, the film magnates, and the
bureaucrats, but that on a long view the weakening of the desire for liberty among the intellectuals themselves is the most
serious symptom of all. It may seem that all this time I have
been talking about the effects of censorship, not on literature
as a whole, but merely on one department of political journalism. Granted that Soviet Russia constitutes a sort of forbidden
area in the British Press, granted that issues like Poland, the
Spanish civil war, the Russo-German pact, and so forth, are
debarred from serious discussion, and that if you possess information that conflicts with the prevailing orthodoxy you are
expected either to distort it or keep quiet about it—granted all
this, why should literature in the wider sense be affected? Is
every writer a politician, and is every book necessarily a work
of straightforward "reportage"? Even under the tightest dictatorship, cannot the individual writer remain free inside his
own mind and distil or disguise his unorthodox ideas in such
a way that the authorities will be too stupid to recognize them?
And in any case, if the writer himself is in agreement with
the prevailing orthodoxy, why should it have a cramping effect on him? Is not literature, or any of the arts, likeliest to
flourish in societies in which there are no major conflicts of
opinion and no sharp distinction between the artist and his
audience? Does one have to assume that every writer is a rebel,
or even that a writer as such is an exceptional person?

Whenever one attempts to defend intellectual liberty
against the claims of totalitarianism, one meets with these ar-

guments in one form or another. They are based on a complete
misunderstanding of what literature is, and how—one should
perhaps rather say *why*—it comes into being. They assume that
a writer is either a mere entertainer or else a venal hack who
can switch from one line of propaganda to another as easily
as an organ grinder changing tunes. But after all, how is it
that books ever come to be written? Above a quite low level,
literature is an attempt to influence the viewpoint of one's contemporaries by recording experience. And so far as freedom of
expression is concerned, there is not much difference between
a mere journalist and the most "unpolitical" imaginative writer.
The journalist is unfree, and is conscious of unfreedom, when
he is forced to write lies or suppress what seems to him important news: the imaginative writer is unfree when he has
to falsify his subjective feelings, which from his point of view
are facts. He may distort and caricature reality in order to
make his meaning clearer, but he cannot misrepresent the
scenery of his own mind: he cannot say with any conviction
that he likes what he dislikes, or believes what he disbelieves.
If he is forced to do so, the only result is that his creative faculties dry up. Nor can he solve the problem by keeping away
from controversial topics. There is no such thing as genuinely
non-political literature, and least of all in an age like our own,
when fears, hatreds, and loyalties of a directly political kind
are near to the surface of everyone's consciousness. Even a
single taboo can have an all-round crippling effect upon the
mind, because there is always the danger that any thought
which is freely followed up may lead to the forbidden thought.
It follows that the atmosphere of totalitarianism is deadly to
any kind of prose writer, though a poet, at any rate a lyric
poet, might possibly find it breathable. And in any totalitarian
society that survives for more than a couple of generations, it
is probable that prose literature, of the kind that has existed
during the past four hundred years must actually *come to an
end*.

Literature has sometimes flourished under despotic régimes,
but, as has often been pointed out, the despotisms of the past
were not totalitarian. Their repressive apparatus was always
inefficient, their ruling classes were usually either corrupt or

apathetic or half-liberal in outlook, and the prevailing religious doctrines usually worked against perfectionism and the notion of human infallibility. Even so it is broadly true that prose literature has reached its highest levels in periods of democracy and free speculation. What is new in totalitarianism is that its doctrines are not only unchallengeable but also unstable. They have to be accepted on pain of damnation, but on the other hand they are always liable to be altered at a moment's notice. Consider, for example, the various attitudes, completely incompatible with one another, which an English Communist or "fellow-traveller" has had to adopt towards the war between Britain and Germany. For years before September, 1939, he was expected to be in a continuous stew about "the horrors of Nazism" and to twist everything he wrote into a denunciation of Hitler: after September, 1939, for twenty months, he had to believe that Germany was more sinned against than sinning, and the word "Nazi," at least as far as print went, had to drop right out of his vocabulary. Immediately after hearing the 8 o'clock news bulletin on the morning of 22nd June, 1941, he had to start believing once again that Nazism was the most hideous evil the world had ever seen. Now, it is easy for a politician to make such changes: for a writer the case is somewhat different. If he is to switch his allegiance at exactly the right moment, he must either tell lies about his subjective feelings, or else suppress them altogether. In either case he has destroyed his dynamo. Not only will ideas refuse to come to him, but the very words he uses will seem to stiffen under his touch. Political writing in our time consists almost entirely of prefabricated phrases bolted together like the pieces of a child's Meccano set. It is the unavoidable result of self-censorship. To write in plain, vigorous language one has to think fearlessly, and if one thinks fearlessly one cannot be politically orthodox. It might be otherwise in an "age of faith," when the prevailing orthodoxy has been long established and is not taken too seriously. In that case it would be possible, or might be possible, for large areas of one's mind to remain unaffected by what one officially believed. Even so, it is worth noticing that prose literature almost disappeared during the only age of faith that Europe has ever enjoyed. Throughout the whole of

the Middle Ages there was almost no imaginative prose literature and very little in the way of historical writing: and the
intellectual leaders of society expressed their most serious
thoughts in a dead language which barely altered during a
thousand years.

Totalitarianism, however, does not so much promise an age
of faith as an age of schizophrenia. A society becomes totalitarian when its structure becomes flagrantly artificial: that is,
when its ruling class has lost its function but succeeds in clinging to power by force or fraud. Such a society, no matter how
long it persists, can never afford to become either tolerant or
intellectually stable. It can never permit either the truthful recording of facts, or the emotional sincerity, that literary creation demands. But to be corrupted by totalitarianism one does
not have to live in a totalitarian country. The mere prevalence
of certain ideas can spread a kind of poison that makes one
subject after another impossible for literary purposes. Where-
ever there is an enforced orthodoxy—or even two orthodoxies,
as often happens—good writing stops. This was well illustrated
by the Spanish civil war. To many English intellectuals the
war was a deeply moving experience, but not an experience
about which they could write sincerely. There were only two
things that you were allowed to say, and both of them were
palpable lies: as a result, the war produced acres of print but
almost nothing worth reading.

It is not certain whether the effects of totalitarianism upon
verse need be so deadly as its effects on prose. There is a whole
series of converging reasons why it is somewhat easier for a
poet than for a prose writer to feel at home in an authoritarian
society. To begin with, bureaucrats and other "practical" men
usually despise the poet too deeply to be much interested in
what he is saying. Secondly, what the poet is saying—that is,
what his poem "means" if translated into prose—is relatively
unimportant even to himself. The thought contained in a poem
is always simple, and is no more the primary purpose of the
poem than the anecdote is the primary purpose of the picture.
A poem is an arrangement of sounds and associations, as a
painting is an arrangement of brushmarks. For short snatches,
indeed, as in the refrain of a song, poetry can even dispense

with meaning altogether. It is therefore fairly easy for a poet to keep away from dangerous subjects and avoid uttering heresies: and even when he does utter them, they may escape notice. But above all, good verse, unlike good prose, is not necessarily an individual product. Certain kinds of poems, such as ballads, or, on the other hand, very artificial verse forms, can be composed co-operatively by groups of people. Whether the ancient English and Scottish ballads were originally produced by individuals, or by the people at large, is disputed; but at any rate they are non-individual in the sense that they constantly change in passing from mouth to mouth. Even in print no two versions of a ballad are ever quite the same. Many primitive peoples compose verse communally. Someone begins to improvise, probably accompanying himself on a musical instrument, somebody else chips in with a line or a rhyme when the first singer breaks down, and so the process continues until there exists a whole song or ballad which has no identifiable author.

In prose, this kind of intimate collaboration is quite impossible. Serious prose, in any case, has to be composed in solitude, whereas the excitement of being part of a group is actually an aid to certain kinds of versification. Verse—and perhaps good verse of its kind, though it would not be the highest kind—might survive under even the most inquisitorial régime. Even in a society where liberty and individuality had been extinguished, there would still be need either for patriotic songs and heroic ballads celebrating victories, or for elaborate exercises in flattery: and these are the kinds of poem that can be written to order, or composed communally, without necessarily lacking artistic value. Prose is a different matter, since the prose writer cannot narrow the range of his thoughts without killing his inventiveness. But the history of totalitarian societies, or of groups of people who have adopted the totalitarian outlook, suggests that loss of liberty is inimical to *all* forms of literature. German literature almost disappeared during the Hitler régime, and the case was not much better in Italy. Russian literature, so far as one can judge by translations, has deteriorated markedly since the early days of the Revolution, though some of the verse appears to be better than the prose. Few if any Russian novels that it is possible to take seriously have been translated for about fifteen years. In western Europe and America large sections of the literary intelligentsia have either passed through the Communist party or have been warmly sympathetic to it, but this whole leftward movement has produced extraordinarily few books worth reading. Orthodox Catholicism, again, seems to have a crushing effect upon certain literary forms, especially the novel. During a period of three hundred years, how many people have been at once good novelists and good Catholics? The fact is that certain themes cannot be celebrated in words and tyranny is one of them. No one ever wrote a good book in praise of the Inquisition. Poetry *might* survive in a totalitarian age, and certain arts or half-arts, such as architecture, might even find tyranny beneficial, but the prose writer would have no choice between silence and death. Prose literature as we know it is the product of rationalism, of the Protestant centuries, of the autonomous individual. And the destruction of intellectual liberty cripples the journalist, the sociological writer, the historian, the novelist, the critic, and the poet, in that order. In the future it is possible that a new kind of literature, not involving individual feeling or truthful observation, may arise, but no such thing is at present imaginable. It seems much likelier that if the liberal culture that we have lived in since the Renaissance actually comes to an end, the literary art will perish with it.

Of course, print will continue to be used, and it is interesting to speculate what kinds of reading matter would survive in a rigidly totalitarian society. Newspapers will presumably continue until television technique reaches a higher level, but apart from newspapers it is doubtful even now whether the great mass of people in the industrialized countries feel the need for any kind of literature. They are unwilling, at any rate, to spend anywhere near as much on reading matter as they spend on several other recreations. Probably novels and stories will be completely superseded by film and radio productions. Or perhaps some kind of low-grade sensational fiction will survive, produced by a sort of conveyor-belt process that reduces human initiative to the minimum.

It would probably not be beyond human ingenuity to write books by machinery. But a sort of mechanizing process can already be seen at work in the film and radio, in publicity and propaganda, and in the lower reaches of journalism. The Disney films, for instance, are produced by what is essentially a factory process, the work being done partly mechanically and partly by teams of artists who have to subordinate their individual style. Radio features are commonly written by tired hacks to whom the subject and the manner of treatment are dictated beforehand: even so, what they write is merely a kind of raw material to be chopped into shape by producers and censors. So also with the innumerable books and pamphlets commissioned by government departments. Even more machine-like is the production of short stories, serials, and poems for the very cheap magazines. Papers such as the *Writer* abound with advertisements of literary schools, all of them offering you ready-made plots at a few shillings a time. Some, together with the plot, supply the opening and closing sentences of each chapter. Others furnish you with a sort of algebraical formula by the use of which you can construct your plots for yourself. Others offer packs of cards marked with characters and situations, which have only to be shuffled and dealt in order to produce ingenious stories automatically. It is probably in some such way that the literature of a totalitarian society would be produced, if literature were still felt to be necessary. Imagination—even consciousness, so far as possible —would be eliminated from the process of writing. Books would be planned in their broad lines by bureaucrats, and would pass through so many hands that when finished they would be no more an individual product than a Ford car at the end of the assembly line. It goes without saying that anything so produced would be rubbish; but anything that was *not* rubbish would endanger the structure of the state. As for the surviving literature of the past, it would have to be suppressed or at least elaborately rewritten.

Meanwhile totalitarianism has not fully triumphed anywhere. Our own society is still, broadly speaking, liberal. To exercise your right of free speech you have to fight against economic pressure and against strong sections of public opinion, but not, as yet, against a secret police force. You can say or print almost anything so long as you are willing to do it in a hole-and-corner way. But what is sinister, as I said at the beginning of this essay, is that the conscious enemies of liberty are those to whom liberty ought to mean most. The big public do not care about the matter one way or the other. They are not in favor of persecuting the heretic, and they will not exert themselves to defend him. They are at once too sane and too stupid to acquire the totalitarian outlook. The direct, conscious attack on intellectual decency comes from the intellectuals themselves.

It is possible that the Russophile intelligentsia, if they had not succumbed to that particular myth, would have succumbed to another of much the same kind. But at any rate the Russian myth is there, and the corruption it causes stinks. When one sees highly educated men looking on indifferently at oppression and persecution, one wonders which to despise more, their cynicism or their short-sightedness. Many scientists, for example, are the uncritical admirers of the U.S.S.R. They appear to think that the destruction of liberty is of no importance so long as their own line of work is for the moment unaffected. The U.S.S.R. is a large, rapidly developing country which has acute need of scientific workers and, consequently, treats them generously. Provided that they steer clear of dangerous subjects such as psychology, scientists are privileged persons. Writers, on the other hand, are viciously persecuted. It is true that literary prostitutes like Ilya Ehrenburg or Alexei Tolstoy are paid huge sums of money, but the only thing which is of any value to the writer as such—his freedom of expression—is taken away from him. Some, at least, of the English scientists who speak so enthusiastically of the opportunities enjoyed by scientists in Russia are capable of understanding this. But their reflection appears to be: "Writers are persecuted in Russia. So what? I am not a writer." They do not see that any attack on intellectual liberty, and on the concept of objective truth, threatens in the long run every department of thought.

For the moment the totalitarian state tolerates the scientist because it needs him. Even in Nazi Germany, scientists, other than Jews, were relatively well treated and the German scientific community, as a whole, offered no resistance to Hitler. At this stage of history, even the most autocratic ruler is forced to take account of physical reality, partly because of the lingering-on of liberal habits of thought, partly because of the need to prepare for war. So long as physical reality cannot be altogether ignored, so long as two and two have to make four when you are, for example, drawing the blueprint of an aeroplane, the scientist has his function, and can even be allowed a measure of liberty. His awakening will come later, when the totalitarian state is firmly established. Meanwhile, if he wants to safeguard the integrity of science, it is his job to develop some kind of solidarity with his literary colleagues and not regard it as a matter of indifference when writers are silenced or driven to suicide, and newspapers systematically falsified.

But however it may be with the physical sciences, or with music, painting, and architecture, it is—as I have tried to show—certain that literature is doomed if liberty of thought perishes. Not only is it doomed in any country which retains a totalitarian structure; but any writer who adopts the totalitarian outlook, who finds excuses for persecution and the falsification of reality, thereby destroys himself as a writer. There is no way out of this. No tirades against "individualism" and "the ivory tower," no pious platitudes to the effect that "true individuality is only attained through identification with the community," can get over the fact that a bought mind is a spoiled mind. Unless spontaneity enters at some point or another, literary creation is impossible, and language itself becomes ossified. At some time in the future, if the human mind becomes something totally different from what it now is, we may learn to separate literary creation from intellectual honesty. At present we know only that the imagination, like certain wild animals, will not breed in captivity. Any writer or journalist who denies that fact—and nearly all the current praise of the Soviet Union contains or implies such a denial—is, in effect, demanding his own destruction.

II. CENSORSHIP and the THEATRE

COMMENT

The theatre's close relationship with both public opinion and official patronage has kept drama under narrower surveillance than any of the other arts. Politics has been a proper subject of drama more than of any other art, and, in return, political censorship has been eager to direct and proscribe at all times the whole area of the theatre. The essay by Rousseau which follows approaches the drama from the point of view of society. There is no reflection in it of the value the author himself places elsewhere on the confession, or on human relationships for themselves, nor does Rousseau refer here to the value of the "anatomy," or the literary portrait, or the "character" that was beginning to obtain in the novel and other forms of literature. Society, that is to say, was certainly stable enough for work of a reflective, personal, even extraordinarily intimate kind, which the reading public was anxious to take up, and which had no immediate utility whatever; but where the theatre was concerned, the question of morality easily superseded the question of human nature which Rousseau himself so often proposed in other of his writings.

The obvious perversity revealed in a comparison between Rousseau's tastes—for the theatre itself, or for women, for example—and his dicta on the subjects of those tastes when he was addressing other people, reveals a sociologist rather than a man of letters. His design in the following essay was to preserve the goodness of others on the grounds of social good, when that good existed in a simple natural state. Milton's virtue, hardy and adventurous, is very different from the pastoral virtue of Rousseau. The chief difference is that, even allowing for the fact that Rousseau is discussing the theatre rather than books, he is thinking all the time about societies of various kinds. Milton, on the other hand, is thinking about a generalized Man, or else about the English Republic of 1643. The fact that Rousseau refers to *civic* virtue, rather than (like Milton) virtue *sub specie aeternitatis* (albeit in one historical moment), limits his criticism of the art of the drama to the political effect of that art. In fact, insofar as his criticism of the drama has force at all, it reveals the limits of the drama as art. After reading the essay we have to admit that with all the changes that have taken place in the drama since 1753, the dramatic limitations have shown up more than ever in the sort of society we live in today. The interesting thing is that the miserable degeneracy of the stage that we suffer from today invites exactly the sort of criticism that Rousseau goes in for here. Moreover, the republicanism of Rousseau's day shares with our own the implicit belief in social amelioration, the seeds of improvement being within the society rather than outside it or in any hope in the world to come. However, improvement is far from inevitable, Rousseau says. Contrary to Milton's belief, the exercise of reason alone will not result in right choice. Better, Rousseau declares, to have no drama than the presentation to a simple, busy, innocent society of entertainments foreign to them and in effect only deleterious. As for a more urbane and polished society, the theatre can do little harm, but it will do morals no good.

Rousseau's declaration that the effect of the theatre on society is essentially a leveling one was directly opposed to the beliefs of the group represented by d'Alembert. The article which provoked Rousseau's essay was on Geneva and was intended to fill a place in the Encyclopedia, which, Voltaire and others believed, would lead to social amelioration through the spread of knowledge and the softening of barbarities. The clergy of Geneva had forbidden plays; the Encyclopedia article advocated the foundation of theatres in a city otherwise charming. In defending his native city, Rousseau was advocat-

ing not so much censorship as the banishment of this one art
as a social institution. It is doubtful whether his strictures apply to the other arts, as their social influence is far more dispersed and indirect. Spartan discipline among citizens appealed to Rousseau just as it did to Plato when he wrote the
Republic. Rousseau's representation of the function of drama
in classical times suggests, however, that he made no distinction between modern civic liberty and the liberty of the *polis*
to which every citizen of classical times was wholly pledged.
We have already discussed the latter kind of liberty (page
35 ff.) and seen how for us it has come to represent a model
for totalitarian regimes. Rousseau, of course, admired the
Spartan heroic simplicity, without having any reason to fear
the Spartan mindlessness, but it is hard to see how he could
criticize the *aesthetics* of classical dramatists without taking
into account the fact that the conception of liberty had
changed, not merely the conceptions of taste, and that while
under the old conception of liberty the public morale was desperately important, what was important under the modern
conception of liberty was some representation of the solitude
in which a man dwelt with his conscience. "Beings so enormous, so bloated, so chimerical, that the example of their vices
is hardly more contagious than that of their virtues . . ."—such
a description may justly castigate some bad tragedies of Rousseau's time, but it is pointless criticism of the monster Mac-
beth, the chimeras that drove Lear, or the bloatedness of Mark
Antony.

A didactic critic must be read with unusual regard to his
historical context. In some ways Rousseau was using the drama
as a stalking horse in his battle for social conscience against
the self-indulgent Encyclopedists; however, his criticism of the
drama as such is still very much to the point today.

His style is highly rhetorical and we have pared the essay
to the central issue. The translator has rendered *moeurs* by
both "morals" and "manners," since the French contains both
English meanings and Rousseau dwells constantly on the full
meaning of the French.

TEXT: From "Letter to M. d'Alembert" by J.-J. Rousseau
[translated by Alan Bloom]

. . . I hasten to turn to . . . the project to establish a theatre for the drama at Geneva. I shall not expound here my conjectures about the motives which might have brought you to propose an establishment so contrary to our maxims. Whatever your reasons, I have here to do only with ours; and all that I shall permit myself to say with respect to you is that you will surely be the first philosopher who ever encouraged a free people, a small city, and a poor state to burden itself with a public theatre.

How many questions I find to discuss in what you appear to have settled! Whether the theatre is good or bad in itself? Whether it can be united with morals [manners]? Whether it is in conformity with republican austerity? Whether it ought to be tolerated in a little city? Whether the actor's profession can be a decent one? Whether actresses can be as well behaved as other women? Whether good laws suffice for repressing the abuses? Whether these laws can be well observed? etc. Everything is still problematic concerning the real effects of the theatre; for, since the disputes that it occasions are solely between the men of the church and the men of the world, each side views the problem only through its prejudices. Here, Sir, are studies that would not be unworthy of your pen. As for me, without believing that what I might do could serve as a substitute for your efforts, I shall limit myself in this essay to seeking those clarifications that you have made necessary. I beg you to take into consideration that in speaking my opinion in imitation of your example, I am fulfilling a duty toward my country, and that, if my sentiments are mistaken, at least this error can hurt no one.

At the first glance given to these institutions I see immediately that the theatre is a form of amusement; and if it is true that amusements are necessary to man, you will at least admit that they are only permissible insofar as they are necessary, and that every useless amusement is an evil for a being whose life is so short and whose time is so precious. The state of man has its pleasures which are derived from his nature and are born of his labors, his relations, and his needs. And these pleasures, sweeter to the one who tastes them in the measure that his soul is healthier, make whoever is capable of participating in them indifferent to all others. A father, a son, a husband, and a citizen have such cherished duties to fulfil that they are left nothing to give to boredom. The good use of time makes time even more precious, and the better one puts it to use, the less one can find to lose. Thus it is constantly seen that the habit of work renders inactivity intolerable and that a good conscience extinguishes the taste for frivolous pleasures. But it is discontent with one's self, the burden of idleness, the neglect of simple and natural tastes, that makes foreign amusement so necessary. I do not like the need to occupy the heart constantly with the stage as if it were ill at ease inside of us. Nature itself dictated the response of that barbarian to whom were vaunted the magnificences of the circus and the games established at Rome. "Don't the Romans," asked this fellow, "have wives or children?" The barbarian was right. People think they come together in the theatre, and it is there that they are isolated. It is there that they go to forget their friends, neighbors, and relations in order to concern themselves with fables, in order to cry for the misfortunes of the dead, or to laugh at the expense of the living. But I should have sensed that this language is no longer seasonable in our times. Let us try to find another which is better understood.

To ask if the theatre is good or bad in itself is to pose too vague a question; it is to examine a relation before having defined the terms. The theatre is made for the people, and it is only by its effects on the people that one can determine its absolute qualities. There can be all sorts of entertainment.

There is, from people to people, a prodigious diversity of morals [manners], temperaments, and characters. Man is one; I admit it! But man modified by religions, governments, laws, customs, prejudices, and climates becomes so different from himself that one ought not to seek among us for what is good for men in general, but only what is good for them in this time or that country. Thus the plays of Menander, made for the Athenian theatre, were out of place in Rome's. Thus the gladiatorial combats which, during the republic, animated the courage and valor of the Romans, only inspired the population of Rome, under the emperors, with the love of blood and cruelty. The same object offered to the same people at different times taught men at first to despise their own lives and, later, to make sport of the lives of others.

The sorts of entertainment are determined necessarily by the pleasure they give and not by their utility. If utility is there too, so much the better. But the principal object is to please; and, provided that the people enjoy themselves, this object is sufficiently attained. This alone will always prevent our being able to give these sorts of institutions all the advantages they are susceptible of; and it is a gross self-deception to form an idea of perfection for them that could not be put into practice without putting off those whom one wants to instruct. It is from this that is born the diversity of entertainments according to the diverse tastes of nations. An intrepid and grave people wants deadly and perilous festivals in which valor and composure shine. A ferocious and intense people wants blood, combat, and terrible passions. A voluptuous people wants music and dances. A gallant people wants love and civility. A frivolous people wants joking and ridicule. *Trahit sua quemque voluptas.*[1] To please them, there must be entertainments which promote their penchants, whereas what is needed are entertainments which would moderate them.

The stage is, in general, a painting of the human passions, the original of which is in every heart. But if the painter neglected to flatter these passions, the spectators would soon be repelled and would not want to see themselves in a light which made them despise themselves. So that, if he gives an odious coloring to some passions, it is only to those that are not general and are naturally hated. Hence the author, in this respect, only follows public sentiment. And then, these repulsive passions are always used to set off others, if not more legitimate, at least more to the liking of the spectators. It is only reason that is good for nothing on the stage. A man without passions or who always mastered them could not attract anyone. And it has already been observed that a Stoic in tragedy would be an insufferable figure. In comedy he would, at most, cause laughter.

Let no one then attribute to the theatre the power to change sentiments or morals [manners], which it can only follow and embellish. An author who would brave the general taste would soon write for himself alone. When Molière transformed the comic stage, he attacked modes and ridiculous traits. But, for all of that, he did not shock the public's taste. He followed or expanded on it, just as Corneille, on his part, did. It was the old theatre which was beginning to shock this taste, because, in an age grown more refined, the theatre preserved its initial coarseness. So, also, the general taste having changed since the time of these two authors, if their masterpieces were now to be presented for the first time, they would inevitably fail. The connoisseurs can very well admire them forever; if the public still admires them, it is more for shame at recanting than from a real sentiment for their beauties. It is said that a good play never fails. Indeed, I believe it; this is because a good play never shocks the morals [manners] of its time. Who doubts that the best play of Sophocles would fall flat in our theatre? We would be unable to put ourselves in the places of men who are totally dissimilar to us.

Any author who wants to depict alien morals [manners] for us nevertheless takes great pains to make his play correspond to our morals [manners]. Without this precaution, one never succeeds, and even the success of those who have taken it often has grounds very different from those supposed by a superficial observer. If the *Arlequin sauvage*[2] is so well received by audiences, is it thought that this is a result of their taste for the character's sense and simplicity, or that a single one of them would want to resemble him? It is, all to the contrary, that this play appeals to their turn of mind, which is to love and seek out new and singular ideas. Now there is nothing newer for them than what has to do with nature. It is precisely their aversion for the ordinary which sometimes leads them back to the simple things.

It follows from these first observations that the general effect of the theatre is to strengthen the national character, to augment the natural inclinations, and to give a new energy to all the passions. In this sense it would seem that, its effect being limited to intensifying and not changing the established morals [manners], the drama would be good for the good and bad for the vicious. Even in the first case it would remain to be seen if the passions did not degenerate into vices from being too much excited. I know that the poetic theatre claims to do exactly the opposite and to purge the passions in exciting them. But I have difficulty understanding this rule. Is it possible that in order to become temperate and prudent we must begin by being intemperate and mad?

"Oh no! It is not that," say the partisans of the theatre. "Tragedy certainly intends that all the passions which it portrays move us; but it does not always want our emotion to be the same as that of the character tormented by a passion. More often, on the contrary, its purpose is to excite sentiments in us opposed to those it lends its characters." They say, moreover, that if authors abuse their power of moving hearts to excite an inappropriate interest, this fault ought to be attributed to the ignorance and depravity of the artists and not to the art. They say, finally, that the faithful depiction of the passions and of the sufferings which accompany them suffices in itself to make us avoid them with all the care of which we are capable.

To become aware of the bad faith of all these responses, one need only consult his own heart at the end of a tragedy. Do the emotion, the disturbance, and the softening which are felt within oneself and which continue after the play give indication of an immediate disposition to master and regulate our passions? Are the lively and touching impressions to which we become accustomed and which return so often, quite the means to moderate our sentiments in the case of need? Why should the image of the sufferings born of the passions efface

that of the transports of pleasure and joy which are also seen
to be born of them and which the authors are careful to adorn
even more in order to render their plays more enjoyable? Do
we not know that all the passions are sisters and that one alone
suffices for arousing a thousand, and that to combat one by
the other is only the way to make the heart sensitive to them
all? The only instrument which serves to purge them is reason, and I have already said that reason has no effect in the
theatre. It is true that we do not share the feelings of all the
characters; for, since their interests are opposed, the author
must indeed make us prefer one of them; otherwise we would
have no contact at all with the play. But far from choosing,
for that reason, the passions which he wants to make us like,
he is forced to choose those which we like already. What I
have said of the sorts of entertainment ought to be understood
even more of the interest which is made dominant in them.
At London a drama is interesting when it causes the French
to be hated; at Tunis, the noble passion would be piracy; at
Messina, a delicious revenge; at Goa, the honor of burning
Jews. If an author shocks these maxims, he will write a very
fine play to which no one will go. And then this author must
be taxed with ignorance, with having failed in the first law of
his art, in the one which serves as the basis for all the others,
which is, to succeed. Thus the theatre purges the passions that
one does not have and foments those that one does. Is that a
well-administered remedy?

Hence, there is a combination of general and particular
causes which keeps the theatre from being given that perfection of which it is thought to be susceptible and from producing the advantageous effects that seem to be expected from
it. Even if this perfection is supposed to be as great as it can
be, and the people as well disposed as could be wished, nevertheless these effects would be reduced to nothing for want of
means to make them felt. I know of only three instruments
with which the morals [manners] of a people can be acted
upon: the force of the laws, the empire of opinion, and the
appeal of pleasure. Now the laws have no access to the theatre where the least constraint would make it a pain and not
an amusement. Opinion does not depend on the theatre, since,

rather than giving the law to the public, the theatre receives
the law from it. And, as to the pleasure that can be had in the
theatre, its whole effect is to bring us back more often . . .

I hear it said that tragedy leads to pity through fear. So it
does; but what is this pity? A fleeting and vain emotion which
lasts no longer than the illusion which produced it; a vestige
of natural sentiment soon stifled by the passions; a sterile pity
which feeds on a few tears and which has never produced the
slightest act of humanity . . . In the final accounting, when
a man has gone to admire fine actions in stories and to cry
for imaginary miseries, what more can be asked of him? Is he
not satisfied with himself? Does he not applaud his fine soul?
Has he not acquitted himself of all that he owes to virtue by
the homage which he has just rendered it? What more could
one want of him? That he practice it himself? He has no role
to play; he is no actor.

The more I think about it, the more I find that everything
that is played in the theatre is not brought nearer to us but
made more distant . . . The theatre has rules, principles, and
a morality apart, just as it has a language and a style of dress
that is its own. We say to ourselves that none of this is suitable
for us, and that we should think ourselves as ridiculous to
adopt the virtues of its heroes as it would be to speak in verse
or to put on Roman clothing. This is pretty nearly the use of
all these great sentiments and of all these brilliant maxims that
are vaunted with so much emphasis—to relegate them forever
to the stage, and to present virtue to us as a theatrical game,
good for amusing the public but which it would be folly seriously to attempt introducing into society. Thus the most advantageous impression of the best tragedies is to reduce all the
duties of man to some passing and sterile emotions that have
no consequences, to make us applaud our courage in praising
that of others, our humanity in pitying the ills that we could
have cured, our charity in saying to the poor, God will help
you!

To be sure, a simpler style can be adopted on the stage, and
the tone of the theatre can be reconciled in the drama with
that of the world. But in this way, morals [manners] are not
corrected; they are depicted, and an ugly face does not ap-

pear ugly to him who wears it. If we wish to correct them by caricaturing them, we leave the realm of probability and nature, and the picture no longer produces an effect. Caricature does not render objects hateful; it only renders them ridiculous. And out of this arises a very great difficulty; afraid of being ridiculous, men are no longer afraid of being vicious. The former cannot be remedied without promoting the latter. Why, you will ask, must I suppose this to be a necessary opposition? Why, Sir? Because the good do not make evil men objects of derision, but crush them with their contempt, and nothing is less funny or laughable than virtue's indignation. Ridicule, on the other hand, is the favorite arm of vice. With it, the respect that the heart owes to virtue is attacked at its root, and the love that is felt for it is finally extinguished.

Thus everything compels us to abandon this vain idea that some wish to give us of the perfection of a form of theatre directed toward public utility. It is an error, said the grave Muralt, to hope that the true relations of things will be faithfully presented in the theatre. For, in general, the poet can only alter these relations in order to accommodate them to the taste of the public. In the comic, he diminishes them and sets them beneath man; in the tragic, he extends them to render them heroic and sets them above humanity. Thus they are never to his measure, and we always see beings other than our own kind in the theatre . . .

I believe I can assert as a truth easy to prove, on the basis of those mentioned above, that the French theatre, with all of its faults, is nevertheless pretty nearly as perfect as it can be, whether from the point of view of pleasure or that of utility, and that these two advantages are in a relation that cannot be disturbed without taking from one more than would be given the other, which would make the theatre even less perfect. This is not to say that a man of genius could not invent a kind of play preferable to those which are established. But this new kind, needing the talents of the author to sustain itself, will necessarily die with him. And his successors, lacking the same resources, will always be forced to return to the common means of interesting and of pleasing. What are these means in our theatre? Celebrated actions, great names, great virtues, in tragedy; comic situations and the amusing in comedy; and always love in both. I ask in what way morals [manners] can profit from all this?

I will be told that in these plays crime is always punished and virtue always rewarded. I answer that, even if this were so, most tragic actions are only pure fables, events known to be inventions of the poet, and so do not make a strong impression on the audience; as a result of showing them that we want to instruct them, we no longer instruct them. I answer, moreover, that these punishments and rewards are always effected by such extraordinary means that nothing similar is expected in the natural course of human things. Finally, I answer by denying the fact. It is not, nor can it be, generally true. For, since this end is not the one toward which authors direct their plays, they are likely to attain it rarely; and often it would be an obstacle to success. Vice or virtue?—what is the difference, provided that the public is overawed by an impression of greatness? . . . What do we learn from *Phèdre* and *Oedipe* other than that man is not free and that heaven punishes him for crimes that it makes him commit? What do we learn in *Médée* other than how cruel and unnatural a mother can be made by the rage of jealousy? Look at most of the plays in the French theatre; in practically all of them you will find abominable monsters and atrocious actions, useful, if you please, in making the plays interesting and in giving exercise to the virtues; but they are certainly dangerous in that they accustom the eyes of the people to horrors that they ought not even to know and to crimes they ought not to suppose possible. It is not even true that murder and parricide are always hateful in the theatre. With the help of some easy suppositions, they are rendered permissible or pardonable. . . .

If the Greeks tolerated such theatre it was because it represented for them national traditions which were always common among the people, which they had reasons to recall constantly; and even its hateful aspects were part of its intention. Deprived of the same motives and the same concern, how can the same tragedy find, in your country, spectators capable of enduring the depictions it presents to them and the characters which are given life in it? One kills his father, marries his

mother, and finds himself the brother of his children; another
forces a son to slay his father; a third makes a father drink
the blood of his son. We shudder at the very idea of the horrors with which the French stage is decked out for the
amusement of the gentlest and the most humane people on
earth. . . .

Happily, the tragedy such as it exists is so far from us, it
presents beings so enormous, so bloated, so chimerical, that
the example of their vices is hardly more contagious than that
of their virtues is useful; and, to the extent it wants to instruct
us less, it does us also less harm. But it is not so with comedy,
the morals [manners] of which have a more immediate relationship with ours, and whose characters resemble men more.
It is all bad and pernicious; every aspect strikes home with
the audience. And since the very pleasure of the comic is
founded on a vice of the human heart, it is a consequence of
this principle that the more the comedy is amusing and perfect, the more its effect is disastrous for morals [manners]. . . .

It is agreed, and it is more clearly grasped every day, that
Molière is the most perfect comic author whose words are
known to us. But who can deny also that the theatre of this
same Molière, of whose talents I am a greater admirer than
anyone, is a school of vices and bad morals [manners] even
more dangerous than the very books which profess to teach
them? His greatest care is to ridicule goodness and simplicity
and to present treachery and falsehood so that they arouse our
interest and sympathy. His decent people only talk; his vicious
characters act, and the most brilliant successes accompany
them most of the time. Finally, the honor of applause is re-
served rarely for those who are the most respectable, and goes
almost always to the cleverest. . . .

[*Rousseau now closely analyzes some of Molière's plays,
and then turns to Molière's successors.*]

. . . It is unbelievable that, with the accord of the police, a
comedy is publicly played right in Paris in which a nephew,
the hero of the play, along with his worthy attendants, in the
apartment of his uncle whom he has just witnessed dying,
busies himself with activities which the law punishes with the

rope; and that, instead of shedding the tears which simple humanity elicits from even the indifferent under such circumstances, they vie with one another to lighten the sad rites of death with barbarous jokes. The most sacred rights, the most touching sentiments of nature, are played upon in this dreadful scene. The most criminal acts are wantonly gathered together here with a playfulness which makes all this pass for nicety. Counterfeiting, forgery, theft, imposture, lying, cruelty; everything is there, everything is applauded. When the dead man takes it into his head to rise again, to the great displeasure of his dear nephew, and is not willing to ratify what has been done in his name, the means are found to extract his consent by force, and everything comes out to the satisfaction of the actors and the spectators. In spite of themselves, the latter have identified with these wretches, and leave the play with the edifying reminiscence of having been, in the depths of their hearts, accomplices of the crimes they have seen committed.

Let us dare to say it without being roundabout. Which of us is sure enough of himself to bear the performance of such a comedy without halfway taking part in the deeds which are played in it? Who would not be a bit distressed if the thief were to be taken by surprise or fail in his attempt? Who does not himself become a thief for a minute in being concerned about him? For is being concerned about someone anything other than putting oneself in his place? A fine instruction for the youth, one in which grown men have difficulty protecting themselves from the seductions of vice! Is that to say that it is never permissible to show blamable actions in the theatre? No; but, in truth, to know how to put a rascal on the stage, a very good man must be the author.

These failings are so inherent to our theatre that, in wanting to remove them, it is disfigured. Our contemporary authors, guided by the best of intentions, write more refined plays. But what happens then? They are no longer really comic and produce no effect. They are very instructive, if you please; but they are even more boring. One might as well go to a sermon.

In this decadence of the theatre, we are constrained to substitute for the true beauties, now eclipsed, little pleasurable accessories capable of impressing the multitude. No longer able to maintain the strength of comic situations and character, the love interest has been reinforced. The same has been done in tragedy to take the place of situations drawn from political concerns we no longer have, and of simple and natural sentiments which no longer move anyone. The authors, in the public interest, contest with one another to give a new energy and a new coloring to this dangerous passion; and, since Molière and Corneille, only romances, under the name of dramatic plays, succeed in the theatre.

Love is the realm of women. It is they who necessarily give the law in it, because, according to the order of nature, resistance belongs to them, and men can conquer this resistance only at the expense of their liberty. Hence, a natural effect of this sort of play is to extend the empire of the fair sex, to make women and girls the preceptors of the public, and to give them the same power over the audience that they have over their lovers. . . .

However love is depicted for us, it seduces or it is not love. If it is badly depicted, the play is bad. If it is well depicted, it overshadows everything that accompanies it. Its combats, its troubles, its sufferings, make it still more touching than if it had no resistance to overcome. Far from its sad effects putting us off, love becomes only more appealing by its very misfortunes. We say, in spite of ourselves, that such a delicious sentiment makes up for everything. So sweet an image softens the heart without its being noticed. We take from the passion that part which leads to pleasure, and put aside that which torments. No one thinks he is obliged to be a hero; and it is thus that in admiring decent love one abandons oneself to criminal love. . . .

Beyond these effects of the theatre, which are relative to what is performed, there are others no less necessary which relate directly to the stage and to the persons who perform; and it is to them that the previously mentioned Genevans attribute the taste for luxury, adornment, and dissipation, whose introduction among us they rightly fear. It is not only the frequenting of actors, but also the frequenting of the theatre, which, because of the costumes and jewelry of the players, can

introduce this taste. If the theatre had no other effect than
to interrupt the course of civil and domestic affairs at certain
hours and to offer an assured resource to idleness, it is impossible that the opportunity of going every day to the same
place to forget oneself and becoming involved with foreign
objects should not give other habits to the citizen and form
new morals [manners] for him. But will these changes be advantageous or harmful? This is a question that depends less
on the consideration of the theatre than on that of the spectators. It is certain that these changes will bring them all pretty
nearly to the same point. It is, then, from the situation of
each at the beginning that the differences must be estimated.

When amusements are by their nature indifferent (and I am
willing to consider the theatre as such for now), it is the nature
of the occupations which they interrupt that cause them to
be judged good or bad, especially when the amusements are
engaging enough to become occupations themselves and to
substitute the taste for them in place of that for work. . . .
In a big city, full of scheming, idle people without religion
or principle, whose imagination, depraved by sloth, inactivity,
the love of pleasure, and great needs, engenders only monsters
and inspires only crimes; in a big city, where morals [manners]
and honor are nothing because each, easily hiding his conduct from the public eye, shows himself only by his reputation and is esteemed only for his riches; in a big city, I say,
the police can never increase the number of pleasures permitted too much or apply itself too much to making them
agreeable in order to deprive individuals of the temptation of
seeking more dangerous ones . . . But in small cities, in less
populated places where individuals, always in the public eye,
are born censors of one another and where the police can easily
watch everyone, contrary maxims must be followed. If there
are industry, arts, and manufactures, care must be taken
against offering distractions which relax the greedy interest
that finds its pleasures in its efforts and enriches the prince
from the avarice of his subjects. If the country, without commerce, nourishes its inhabitants in inaction, far from fomenting
idleness in them, to which they are already only too susceptible because of their simple and easy life, their life must be

rendered insufferable in constraining them, by dint of boredom, to employ time usefully which they could not abuse. I see that in Paris, where everything is judged by appearances because there is no leisure to examine anything, it is believed, on the basis of the apparent inactivity and listlessness which strikes one at first glance in provincial towns, that the inhabitants, plunged in a stupid inactivity, either simply vegetate or only pester one another and quarrel. This is an error which could easily be corrected if it were remembered that most of the literary men who shine in Paris and most of the useful discoveries and new inventions come from these despised provinces. Stay some time in a little town where you had at first believed you would find only automatons; not only will you soon see there men a great deal more sensible than your big-city monkeys, but you will rarely fail to discover in obscurity there some ingenious man who will surprise you by his talents and his works, who you will surprise even more in admiring them, and who, in showing you prodigies of work, patience, and industry, will think he is showing you only what is ordinary at Paris. Such is the simplicity of true genius. . . .

. . . Even if it were true that the theatre is not bad in itself, it would remain to be investigated if it does not become so in respect to the people for which it is destined. In certain places it will be useful for attracting foreigners, for increasing the circulation of money; for stimulating artists; for varying the fashions; for occupying those who are too rich or aspire to be so; for making them less mischievous; for distracting the people from its miseries; for making it forget its leaders in seeing its buffoons; for maintaining and perfecting taste when decency is lost; for covering the ugliness of vice with the polish of forms; in a word, for preventing bad morals [manners] from degenerating into brigandage. In other places it would only serve to destroy the love of work; to discourage industry, to ruin individuals; to inspire them with the taste for idleness; to make them seek for the means of subsistence without doing anything; to render a people inactive and slack; to prevent it from seeing the public and private goals with which it ought to busy itself; to turn prudence to ridicule; to substitute a theatrical jargon for the practice of the virtues; to make metaphysic of all morality; to turn citizens into wits, housewives into bluestockings, and daughters into sweethearts out of the drama. The general effect will be the same on all men; but the men thus changed will suit their country more or less. In becoming equals, the bad will gain and the good will lose still more; all will contract a soft disposition and a spirit of inaction which will deprive the good of great virtues but will keep the bad from meditating great crimes.

From these new reflections results a consequence directly opposed to the one I drew from the first, namely, that when the people is corrupted, the theatre is good for it, and bad for it when it is itself good. It would, hence, seem that these two contrary effects would destroy one another and the theatre remain indifferent to both. But there is this difference: the effect which reinforces the good and the bad, since it is drawn from the spirit of the plays, is subject, as are they, to countless modifications which reduce it to practically nothing, while the effect which changes the good into bad and the bad into good, resulting from the very existence of a theatre, is a real, constant one which returns every day and must finally prevail.

It follows from this that, in order to decide if it is proper or not to establish a theatre in a certain town, we must know in the first place if the morals [manners] are good or bad there, a question concerning which it is perhaps not for me to answer with regard to us. However that may be, all that I can admit about this is that it is true that the drama will not harm us if nothing at all can harm us any more.

COMMENT: On the Theatre as a Forum

Rousseau's essay concerned itself with the influence of the theatre on the behavior of man in society. The next piece deals with the control of the theatre. Lord Chesterfield, who wrote it for delivery in the House of Lords in 1737 (though he apparently never actually gave it), is the most famous advocate of manners as opposed to morals. On the occasion of the following piece, however, Chesterfield is making a stand against the political opportunism of the Government Bill for censorship, and his stance is on ostensibly moral grounds, though his argument proceeds on utilitarian lines. Thus in a minor key, and paying attention to actualities rather than to the philosophy of politics and the arts, Chesterfield goes over much the same ground that Rousseau was to cover a few years later.

The Bill Chesterfield opposed was introduced by Sir Robert Walpole's Government after the performance of a lewd play, *The Golden Rump*. The scandal which attended this play provided the government with a useful opportunity to defend its own corrupt administration from such attacks as that contained in John Gay's famous *Beggar's Opera* and its sequel, *Polly*. *Polly* did not enjoy the tremendous success of the *Beggar's Opera*, for it came in for the attention of the Lord Chamberlain after the prompting of the Government which had been so sorely attacked. Its suppression on the stage gave rise to an immensely profitable printing (1729) and netted Gay more than £1000. It is significant, however, that the Government had to wait for a pretext of obscenity before introducing a new censorship of the theatre bill. Profanity seems to have been associated with the theatre since classical times, and the step from profanity to satire is a short one. It is no accident that attempts to "purify" the theatre crop up in times of lively political criticism.

TEXT: Speech Against Licensing the Stage by the Earl of Chesterfield

My Lords,

The Bill now before you I apprehend to be of a very extraordinary, a very dangerous Nature. It seems designed not only as a Restraint on the Licentiousness of the Stage, but it will prove a most arbitrary Restraint on the Liberty of the Stage; and, I fear, it looks yet farther, I fear, it tends towards a Restraint on the Liberty of the Press, which will be a long Stride towards the Destruction of Liberty itself. It is not only a Bill, my Lords, of a very extraordinary Nature, but it has been brought in at a very extraordinary Season, and pushed with most extraordinary Dispatch. When I consider how near it was to the End of the Session, and how long this Session had been protracted beyond the usual Time of the Year; when I considered that this Bill passed through the other House with so much Precipitancy, as even to get the Start of a Bill which deserved all the Respect, and all the Dispatch, the Forms of either House of Parliament could admit of, it set me upon enquiring, what could be the Reason for introducing this Bill at so unseasonable a Time, and pressing it forward in a Manner so very singular and uncommon. I have made all possible Inquiry, and as yet, I must confess, I am at a loss to find out the great Occasion. I have, it is true, learned from common Report without Doors, that a most seditious, a most heinous Farce had been offered to one of the Theatres, a Farce for which the Authors ought to be punished in the most exemplary Manner: But what was the Consequence? the Master of that Theatre behaved as he was in Duty bound, and as common Prudence directed: He not only refused to bring it upon the Stage, but carried it to a certain honourable Gentleman in the

Administration, as the surest Method of having it absolutely suppressed. Could this be the Occasion of introducing such an extraordinary Bill, at such an extraordinary Season, and pushing it in so extraordinary a Manner? Surely no;—The dutiful Behaviour of the Players, the prudent Caution they shewed upon that Occasion, can never be a Reason for subjecting them to such an arbitrary Restraint: It is an Argument in their Favour, and a material one, in my Opinion, against the Bill. Nay farther, if we consider all Circumstances, it is to me a full Proof that the Laws now in being are sufficient for punishing those Players who shall venture to bring any seditious Libel upon the Stage, and consequently sufficient for deterring all Players from acting any thing that may have the least Tendency towards giving a reasonable Offence.

I do not, my Lords, pretend to be a Lawyer, I do not pretend to know perfectly the Power and Extent of our Laws, but I have conversed with those that do, and by them I have been told, that our Laws are sufficient for punishing any Person that shall dare to represent upon the Stage what may appear, either by the Words or the Representation, to be blasphemous, seditious, or immoral. I must own, indeed, I have observed of late a remarkable Licentiousness in the Stage. There have but very lately been two Plays acted, which, one would have thought, should have given the greatest Offence, and yet both were suffered to be often represented without Disturbance, without Censure. In one, the Author thought fit to represent the three great Professions, Religion, Physick, and the Law, as inconsistent with Common Sense: In the other, a most tragical Story was brought upon the Stage, a Catastrophe too recent, too melancholy, and of too solemn a Nature, to be heard of any where but from the Pulpit. How these Pieces came to pass unpunished, I do not know: If I am rightly informed, it was not for want of Law, but for want of Prosecution, without which no Law can be made effectual: But if there was any Neglect in this Case, I am convinced it was not with a Design to prepare the Minds of the People, and to make them think a new Law necessary.

Our Stage ought certainly, my Lords, to be kept within

Bounds; but for this, our Laws as they stand at present are
sufficient: If our Stage-players at any Time exceed those
Bounds, they ought to be prosecuted, they may be punished: We have Precedents, we have Examples of Persons
having been punished for Things less criminal than either of
the two Pieces I have mentioned. A new Law must therefore
be unnecessary, and in the present Case it cannot be unnecessary without being dangerous: Every unnecessary Restraint
on Licentiousness is a Fetter upon the Legs, is a Shackle
upon the Hands of Liberty. One of the greatest Blessings we
enjoy, one of the greatest Blessings a People, my Lords, can
enjoy, is Liberty;—but every Good in this Life has its Allay
of Evil:—Licentiousness is the Allay of Liberty; it is an
Ebullition, an Excrescence;—it is a Speck upon the Eye of
the Political Body, which I can never touch but with a
gentle,—with a trembling Hand, lest I destroy the Body,
lest I injure the Eye upon which it is apt to appear. If the
Stage becomes at any Time licentious; if a Play appears to be
a Libel upon the Government, or upon any particular Man,
the Kings Courts are open, the Laws are sufficient for punishing the Offender; and in this Case the Person injured has a
singular Advantage; he can be under no Difficulty to prove
who is the Publisher; the Players themselves are the Publishers, and there can be no want of Evidence to convict them.

But, my Lords, suppose it true, that the Laws now in being are not sufficient for putting a Check to or preventing the
licentiousness of the Stage; suppose it absolutely necessary
some new Law should be made for that purpose; yet it must
be granted that such a Law ought to be maturely considered, and every Clause, every Sentence, nay every Word of
it well weighed and examined, lest under some of those
Methods, presumed or pretended to be necessary for restraining licentiousness, a Power should lie concealed, which
might be afterwards made Use of for giving a dangerous
Wound to Liberty. Such a Law ought not to be introduced
at the Close of a Session, nor ought we, in the passing of
such a Law, to depart from any of the Forms prescribed
by our Ancestors for preventing Deceit and Surprize. There
is such a Connection between licentiousness and Liberty,

that it is not easy to correct the one, without dangerously wounding the other: It is extremely hard to distinguish the true limit between them: like a changeable Silk, we can easily see there are too different Colours, but we cannot easily discover where the one ends, or where the other begins.—— There can be no great and immediate Danger from the licentiousness of the Stage: I hope it will not be pretended that our Government may, before next Winter, be overturned by such licentiousness, even though our Stage were at present under no sort of legal Controul. Why then may we not delay till next Session passing any Law against the licentiousness of the Stage? Neither our Government can be altered, nor our Constitution overturned by such a Delay; but by passing a Law rashly and unadvisedly, our Constitution may at once be destroyed, and our Government rendered arbitrary. Can we then put a small, a short-lived inconvenience in the Ballance with perpetual Slavery? Can it be supposed that a Parliament of *Great Britain* will so much as risque the latter, for the sake of avoiding the former?

Surely, my Lords, this is not to be expected, were the licentiousness of the stage much greater than it is, were the insufficiency of our Laws more obvious than can be pretended; but when we complain of the licentiousness of the Stage, and of the insufficiency of our Laws, I fear we have more Reason to complain of bad measures in our Polity, and a general Decay of Virtue and Morality among the People. In publick as well as private Life, the only way to prevent being ridiculed or censured, is to avoid all ridiculous or wicked Measures, and to pursue such only as are virtuous and worthy. The People never endeavour to ridicule those they love and esteem, nor will they suffer them to be ridiculed: If any one attempts it, the Ridicule returns upon the Author: he makes himself only the Object of publick Hatred and Contempt. The Actions or Behaviour of a private Man may pass unobserved, and consequently unapplauded, uncensured; but the Actions of those in high Stations, can neither pass without Notice, nor without censure or Applause; and therefore an Administration without Esteem, without Authority among the People, let their Power be never so great, let their

Power be never so arbitrary, they will be ridiculed: The severest Edicts, the most terrible Punishments, cannot entirely prevent it. If any Man therefore thinks he has been censured; if any Man thinks he has been ridiculed upon any of our publick Theatres, let him examine his Actions he will find the Cause, let him alter his Conduct he will find a Remedy. As no Man is perfect, as no Man is infallible, the greatest may err, the most circumspect may be guilty of some piece of ridiculous Behaviour. It is not Licentiousness, it is an useful Liberty always indulged the Stage in a free Country, that some great Men may there meet with a just Reproof, which none of their Friends will be free enough or rather faithful enough to give them. Of this we have a famous instance in the *Roman* History. The great *Pompey,* after the many Victories he had obtained, and the great Conquests he had made, had certainly a good Title to the Esteem of the People of *Rome;* yet that great Man, by some Error in his Conduct, became an Object of general Dislike; and therefore, in the Representation of an old Play, when *Diphilus* the Actor, came to repeat these Words, *Nostra Miseria tu es Magnus,* the Audience immediately applied them to *Pompey,* who at that Time was as well known by the Name *Magnus,* as by the Name *Pompey,* and were so highly pleased with the Satyr, that, as *Cicero* says, they made the Actor repeat the Words an hundred Times over: An Account of this was immediately sent to *Pompey,* who, instead of resenting it as an Injury, was so wise as to take it for a just Reproof: He examined his Conduct, he altered his Measures, he regained by degrees the Esteem of the People, and then he neither feared the Wit, nor felt the Satyr of the Stage. This is an Example which ought to be followed by great Men in all Countries. Such Accidents will often happen in every free Country, and many such would probably have afterwards happened at *Rome,* if they had continued to enjoy their Liberty; but this sort of Liberty in the Stage, came soon after, I suppose, to be called Licentiousness; for we are told that *Augustus,* after having established his Empire, restored Order to *Rome* by restraining Licentiousness. God forbid! we should in this Country have Order restored, or Licentiousness restrained, at so dear a Rate as the People of *Rome* paid for it to *Augustus.*

In the Case I have mentioned, my Lords, it was not the Poet that wrote, for it was an old Play, nor the Players that acted, for they only repeated the Words of the Play; it was the People who pointed the Satyr; and the Case will always be the same: When a Man has the Misfortune to incur the Hatred or Contempt of the People, when public Measures are despised, the Audience will apply what never was, what could not be designed as a Satyr on the present Times. Nay, even tho' the People should not apply, those who are conscious of Guilt, those who are conscious of the Wickedness or Weakness of their own Conduct, will take to themselves what the Author never designed. A public Thief is as apt to take the Satyr as he is apt to take the Money, which was never designed for him. We have an Instance of this in the Case of a famous Comedian of the last Age; a Comedian who was not only a good Poet, but an honest Man, and a quiet and good Subject: The famous *Moliere* when he wrote his *Tartuffe,* which is certainly an excellent and a good moral Comedy, did not design to satirize any great Man of that Age; yet a great Man in *France* at that Time took it to himself, and fancied the Author had taken him as a Model for one of the principal and one of the worst Characters in that Comedy: By good Luck he was not the Licenser, otherwise the Kingdom of *France* had never had the Pleasure, the Happiness, I may say, of seeing that Play acted; but when the Players first proposed to act it at *Paris,* he had Interest enough to get it forbid. *Moliere,* who knew himself innocent of what was laid to his Charge, complained to his Patron the Prince of *Conti,* that as his Play was designed only to expose Hypocrisy, and a false Pretence to Religion, it was very hard it should be forbid being acted, when at the same Time they were suffered to expose Religion itself every Night publickly upon the *Italian* Stage. To which the Prince wittily answered, *'Tis true,* Moliere, *Harlequin ridicules Heaven, and exposes Religion; but you have done much worse—you have ridiculed the first Minister of Religion.*

I am as much for restraining the Licentiousness of the

Stage, and every other sort of Licentiousness, as any of your Lordships can be; but, my Lords, I am, I shall always be extremely cautious and fearful of making the least Encroachment upon Liberty; and therefore, when a new Law is proposed against Licentiousness, I shall always be for considering it deliberately and maturely, before I venture to give my Consent to its being passed. This is a sufficient Reason for my being against passing this Bill at so unseasonable a Time, and in so extraordinary a Manner; but I have my Reasons for being against the Bill itself, some of which I shall beg leave to explain to your Lordships. The Bill, my Lords, at first View, may seem to be designed only against the Stage, but to me it plainly appears to point somewhere else. It is an Arrow that does but glance upon the Stage, the mortal Wound seems designed against the Liberty of the Press. By this Bill you prevent a Play's being acted, but you do not prevent its being printed; therefore, if a License should be refused for its being acted, we may depend on it the Play will be printed. It will be printed and published, my Lords, with the refusal in capital Letters on the Title Page. People are always fond of what is forbidden. *Libri prohibiti* are in all Countries diligently and generally sought after. It will be much easier to procure a Refusal, than it ever was to procure a good House, or a good Sale: Therefore we may expect, that Plays will be wrote on purpose to have a Refusal: This will certainly procure a good Sale: Thus will Satyrs be spread and dispersed through the whole Nation, and thus every Man in the Kingdom may and probably will, read for Sixpence, what a few only could have seen acted and that not under the expence of half a Crown. We shall then be told, What! Will you allow an infamous Libel to be printed and dispersed, which you would not allow to be acted? You have agreed to a Law for preventing its being acted, can you refuse your Assent to a Law for preventing its being printed and published? I should really, my Lords, be glad to hear what Excuse, what Reason one could give for being against the latter, after having agreed to the former; for, I protest I cannot suggest to myself the least Shadow of an Excuse. If we agree to the Bill now before

us, we must perhaps next Session, agree to a Bill for preventing any Play's being printed without a Licence. Then
Satyrs will be wrote by way of Novels, secret Histories,
Dialogues, or under some such Title; and thereupon we
shall be told, What! will you allow an infamous Libel to
be printed and dispersed, only because it does not bear the
Title of a Play? Thus, my Lords, from the Precedent now
before us, we shall be induced, nay we can find no Reason
for refusing to lay the Press under a general Licence, and then
we may bid adieu to the Liberties of *Great-Britain.*

But suppose, my Lords, it were necessary to make a new
Law for the restraining the Licentiousness of the Stage,
which I am very far from granting, yet I shall never be for
establishing such a Power as is proposed by this Bill. If
Poets and Players are to be restrained, let them be restrained
as other Subjects are, by the known Laws of their Country;
if they offend, let them be tried as every *Englishman* ought
to be, by God and their Country. Do not let us subject them
to the arbitrary Will and Pleasure of any one Man. A
Power lodged in the Hands of one single Man, to judge and
determine, without any Limitation, without any Controul or
Appeal, is a sort of Power unknown to our Laws, inconsistent
with our Constitution. It is a higher, a more absolute Power
than we trust even to the King himself; and therefore I must
think, we ought not to vest any such Power in his Majesty's
Lord Chamberlain. When I say this, I am sure I do not mean
to give the least, the most distant Offence to the noble Duke
who now fills the Post of Lord Chamberlain: His natural
Candour and Love of Justice, would not, I know, permit him
to exercise any Power but with the strictest regard to the
Rules of Justice and Humanity. Were we sure his Successors
in that high Office would always be Persons of such distinguished Merit, even the Power to be established by this Bill
could give me no farther Alarm, than lest it should be made a
Precedent for introducing other new Powers of the same
Nature. This, indeed, is an Alarm which cannot be avoided,
which cannot be prevented by any Hope, by any Consideration; it is an Alarm which, I think, every Man must take,

who has a due Regard to the Constitution and Liberties of his Country.

I shall admit, my Lords, that the Stage ought not upon any Occasion to meddle with Politics, and for this very Reason, among the rest, I am against the Bill now before us: This Bill will be so far from preventing the Stage's meddling with Politics, that I fear it will be the Occasion of its meddling with nothing else; but then it will be a political Stage *ex parte*. It will be made subservient to the Politics and Schemes of the Court only. The Licentiousness of the Stage will be encouraged instead of being restrained; but, like Court-Journalists, it will be licentious only against the Patrons of Liberty, and the Protectors of the People. Whatever Man, whatever Party opposes the Court in any of their most destructive Schemes, will, upon the Stage be represented in the most ridiculous Light the Hirelings of a Court can contrive. True Patriotism and Love of Public Good will be represented as Madness, or as a Cloak for Envy, Disappointment and Malice; while the most flagitious Crimes, the most extravagant Vices and Follies, if they are fashionable at Court, will be disguised and dressed up in the Habit of the most amiable Virtues. This has formerly been the Case:—In King *Charles* IId's Days the Play-house was under a Licence. What was the Consequence?—The Play-house retaled nothing but the Politics, the Vices, and the Follies of the Court: Not to expose them; no—but to recommend them; tho' it must be granted their Politics were often as bad as their Vices, and much more pernicious than their other Follies. 'Tis true, the Court had, at that Time, a great deal of Wit; it was then indeed full of Men of true Wit and great Humour; but it was the more dangerous; for the Courtiers did then, as thorough-paced Courtiers always will do, they sacrificed their Honour, by making their Wit and their Humour subservient to the Court only; and what made it still more dangerous, no Man could appear upon the Stage against them. We know that *Dryden*, the Poet Laureat of that Reign, always represents the Cavaliers as honest, brave, merry Fellows, and fine Gentlemen: Indeed his fine Gentleman, as he generally draws him, is an atheistical, lewd, abandoned Fellow, which was at that Time, it seems, the fashionable Character at Court. On the other Hand, he always represents the Dissenters as hypocritical, dissembling Rogues, or stupid senseless Boobies—When the Court had a Mind to fall out with the *Dutch,* he wrote his *Amboyna,* in which he represents the *Dutch* as a Pack of avaritious, cruel, ungrateful Rascals.— And when the Exclusion Bill was moved in Parliament, he wrote his *Duke of Guise,* in which those who were for preserving and securing the Religion of their Country, were exposed under the Character of the Duke of *Guise* and his Party, who leagued together, for excluding *Henry* IV. of *France* from the Throne, on account of his Religion.—The City of *London* too, was made to feel the partial and mercenary Licentiousness of the Stage at that Time; for the Citizens having at that Time, as well as now, a great deal of Property, they had a Mind to preserve that Property, and therefore they opposed some of the arbitrary Measures which were then begun, but pursued more openly in the following Reign; for which Reason they were then always represented upon the Stage, as a Parcel of designing Knaves, dissembling Hypocrites, griping Usurers, and—Cuckolds into the Bargain.

My Lords, the proper Business of the Stage, and that for which only it is useful, is to expose those Vices and Follies, which the Laws cannot lay hold of, and to recommend those Beauties and Virtues, which Ministers and Courtiers seldom either imitate or reward; but by laying it under a Licence, and under an arbitrary Court-licence too, you will, in my Opinion, intirely pervert its Use; for tho' I have the greatest Esteem for that noble Duke, in whose Hands this Power is at present designed to fall, tho' I have an intire Confidence in his Judgment and Impartiality; yet I may suppose that a leaning towards the Fashions of a Court is sometimes hard to be avoided.—It may be very difficult to make one who is every Day at Court believe that to be a Vice or Folly, which he sees daily practised by those he loves and esteems. —By Custom even Deformity itself becomes familiar, and at last agreeable.—To such a Person, let his natural Impartiality be never so great, that may appear a Libel against the Court, which is only a most just and a most necessary

Satyr upon the fashionable Vices and Follies of the Court. Courtiers, my Lords, are too polite to reprove one another; the only Place where they can meet with any just Reproof, is a free, tho' not a licentious Stage; and as every sort of Vice and Folly, generally in all Countries, begins at Court, and from thence spreads thro' the Country, by laying the Stage under an arbitrary Court-licence, instead of leaving it what it is, and always ought to be, a gentle Scourge for the Vices of Great Men and Courtiers, you will make it a Canal for propagating and conveying their Vices and Follies thro' the whole Kingdom.

From hence, my Lords, I think it must appear, that the Bill now before us cannot so properly be called a Bill for restraining the Licentiousness, as it may be called a Bill for restraining the Liberty of the Stage, and for restraining it too in that Branch which in all Countries has been the most useful; therefore I must look upon the Bill as a most dangerous Encroachment upon Liberty in general. Nay farther, my Lords, it is not only an Encroachment upon Liberty, but it is likewise an Encroachment on Property. Wit, my Lords, is a Sort of Property: It is the Property of those that have it, and too often the only Property they have to depend on. It is, indeed, but a precarious Dependance. Thank God! We—my Lords, have a Dependance of another Kind, we have a much less precarious Support, and therefore, cannot feel the Inconveniences of the Bill now before us; but it is our Duty to encourage and protect Wit, whosoever's Property it may be. Those Gentlemen who have any such Property, are all, I hope, our Friends: Do not let us subject them to any unnecessary or arbitrary Restraint. I must own, I cannot easily agree to the laying of any tax upon Wit; but by this Bill it is to be heavily taxed,—it is to be excised;— for if this Bill passes, it cannot be retaled in a proper Way without a Permit; and the Lord Chamberlain is to have the Honour of being chief Gauger, Supervisor, Commissioner, Judge and Jury: But what is still more hard, tho' the poor Author, the Proprietor I should say, cannot perhaps dine till he has found out and agreed with a Purchaser; yet before he can propose to seek for a Purchaser, he must patiently submit to have his Goods rummaged at this new Excise-office, where they may be detained for fourteen Days, and even then he may find them returned as prohibited Goods, by which his chief and best Market will be for ever shut against him; and that without any Cause, without the least Shadow of Reason, either from the Laws of his Country, or the Laws of the Stage.

These Hardships, this Hazard, which every Gentleman will be exposed to who writes any thing for the Stage, must certainly prevent every Man of a generous and free Spirit from attempting any Thing in that Way; and as the Stage has always been the proper Channel for Wit and Humour, therefore, my Lords, when I speak against this Bill, I must think I plead the Cause of Wit, I plead the Cause of Humour, I plead the Cause of the *British* Stage, and of every Gentleman of Taste in the Kingdom: But it is not, my Lords, for the Sake of Wit only; even for the Sake of his Majesty's Lord Chamberlain, I must be against this Bill. The noble Duke who has now the Honour to execute that Office, has, I am sure, as little Inclination to disoblige as any Man; but if this Bill passes, he must disoblige, he may disoblige some of his most intimate Friends. It is impossible to write a Play, but some of the Characters, or some of the Satyr, may be interpreted so as to point at some Person or other, perhaps at some Person in an eminent Station: When it comes to be acted, the People will make the Application, and the Person against whom the Application is made, will think himself injured, and will, at least privately, resent it: At present this Resentment can be directed only against the Author; but when an Author's Play appears with my Lord Chamberlain's Passport, every such Resentment will be turned from the Author, and pointed directly against the Lord Chamberlain, who by his Stamp made the Piece current. What an unthankful Office are we therefore by this Bill to put upon his Majesty's Lord Chamberlain! an Office which can no way contribute to his Honour or Profit, and yet such a one as must necessarily gain him a great deal of ill will, and create him a number of Enemies.

The last Reason I shall trouble your Lordships with for

my being against the Bill, is, that in my Opinion, it will no way answer the End proposed: I mean the End openly proposed, and, I am sure, the only End which your Lordships propose. To prevent the acting of a Play which has any Tendency to Blasphemy, Immorality, Sedition, or private Scandal, can signify nothing, unless you can likewise prevent its being printed and published. On the contrary, if you prevent its being acted, and admit of its being printed and published, you will propagate the Mischief: Your Prohibition will prove a Bellows which will blow up the Fire you intend to extinguish. This Bill can therefore be of no Use for preventing either the publick or the private Injury intended by such a Play; and consequently can be of no manner of Use, unless it be designed as a Precedent, as a leading Step towards another, for subjecting the Press likewise to a Licenser. For such a wicked Purpose it may, indeed, be of great Use; and in that Light, it may most properly be called a Step towards arbitrary Power.

Let us consider, my Lords, that arbitrary Power has seldom or never been introduced into any Country at once. It must be introduced by slow degrees, and as it were step by step, lest the people should perceive its approach. The barriers and fences of the people's liberty must be plucked up one by one, and some plausible pretences must be found for removing or hood-winking, one after another, those sentries who are posted by the constitution of every free country, for warning the people of their danger. When these preparatory Steps are once made, the People may then, indeed, with Regret see Slavery and arbitrary Power making long Strides over their Land, but it will then be too late to think of preventing or avoiding the impending Ruin. The Stage, my Lords, and the Press, are two of our Out-sentries; if we remove them,—if we hood-wink them,—if we throw them in Fetters;—the Enemy may surprize us. Therefore I must look upon the Bill now before us as a Step, and a most necessary Step too, for introducing arbitrary Power into this Kingdom: It is a Step so necessary, that, if ever any future ambitious King, or guilty Minister, should form to himself so wicked a Design, he will have Reason to thank us for having done so much of the Work to his Hand; but such Thanks, or Thanks from such a Man, I am convinced every one of your Lordships would blush to receive,—and scorn to deserve.

By this Bill, which passed both houses, all copies of Plays, Farces, or any thing wrote in the dramatic way, are to lie before his Grace the Lord Chamberlain of his Majesty's household for the time being, for his Grace's perusal and approbation, before they shall be exhibited on the stage.

COMMENT: On George Bernard
Shaw and Theatre Reform

The following extract comes from a statement which Shaw offered to the Select Committee of both Houses of Parliament which was sitting in 1909 to consider the question of the censorship of stage plays. According to Shaw, the Committee, once they had read his statement, rejected it in fright, and he consequently published it as part of the Preface to *The Shewing-Up of Blanco Posnet*. Again according to Shaw, the Committee never had any serious intentions of reforming the existing censorship; the most they had in mind was to consider it. It is plain that the complicated ironies of the rejected statement would throw the most reform-minded committee into confusion, let alone one as conservative and philistine as the one that faced Shaw.

In effect the censorship of the theatre in England has changed very little officially up to the present day, such changes of temperament as it displays being due to liberalization of the public attitude and the vagaries of individual Lord Chamberlains. Inasmuch as the statement is geared to the actual situation on the stage in fairly recent times, rather than to a moral or a legal situation as in the case of Rousseau's and Chesterfield's pieces, Shaw's must be taken as a criticism of the contemporary drama as much as an argument against censorship.

TEXT: "The Necessity of Immoral Plays" from the Preface to *The Shewing-Up of Blanco Posnet* by George Bernard Shaw

The Witness's Qualifications

I am by profession a playwright . . . I am not an ordinary playwright in general practice. I am a specialist in immoral and heretical plays. My reputation has been gained by my persistent struggle to force the public to reconsider its morals. In particular, I regard much current morality as to economic and sexual relations as disastrously wrong; and I regard certain doctrines of the Christian religion as understood in England to-day with abhorrence. I write plays with the deliberate object of converting the nation to my opinions in these matters. I have no other effectual incentive to write plays, as I am not dependent on the theatre for my livelihood. If I were prevented from producing immoral and heretical plays, I should cease to write for the theatre, and propagate my views from the platform and through books. I mention these facts to shew that I have a special interest in the achievement by my profession of those rights of liberty of speech and conscience which are matters of course in other professions. I object to censorship not merely because the existing form of it grievously injures and hinders me individually, but on public grounds.

The Definition of Immorality

In dealing with the question of the censorship, everything depends on the correct use of the word immorality, and a careful discrimination between the powers of a magistrate or judge to administer a code, and those of a censor to please himself.

Whatever is contrary to established manners and customs is immoral. An immoral act or doctrine is not necessarily a sinful one: on the contrary, every advance in thought and conduct is by definition immoral until it has converted the majority. For this reason it is of the most enormous importance that immorality should be protected jealously against the attacks of those who have no standard except the standard of custom, and who regard any attack on custom—that is, on morals—as an attack on society, on religion, and on virtue.

A censor is never intentionally a protector of immorality. He always aims at the protection of morality. Now morality is extremely valuable to society. It imposes conventional conduct on the great mass of persons who are incapable of original ethical judgment, and who would be quite lost if they were not in leading-strings devised by lawgivers, philosophers, prophets and poets for their guidance. But morality is not dependent on censorship for protection. It is already powerfully fortified by the magistracy and the whole body of law. Blasphemy, indecency, libel, treason, sedition, obscenity, profanity, and all the other evils which a censorship is supposed to avert, are punishable by the civil magistrate with all the severity of vehement prejudice. Morality has not only every engine that lawgivers can devise in full operation for its protection, but also that enormous weight of public opinion enforced by social ostracism which is stronger than all the statutes. A censor pretending to protect morality is like a child pushing the cushions of a railway carriage to give itself the sensation of making the train travel at sixty miles an hour. It is immorality, not morality, that needs protection: it is morality, not immorality, that needs restraint; for morality, with all the dead weight of human inertia and superstition to hang on the back of the pioneer, and all the malice of vulgarity and prejudice to threaten him, is responsible for many persecutions and many martyrdoms.

Persecutions and martyrdoms, however, are trifles compared to the mischief done by censorships in delaying the general march of enlightenment. This can be brought home to us by imagining what would have been the effect of applying to all literature the censorship we still apply to the stage. The works of Linnæus and the evolutionists of 1790–1830, of Darwin, Wallace, Huxley, Helmholtz, Tyndall, Spencer, Carlyle, Ruskin, and Samuel Butler, would not have been published, as they were all immoral and heretical in the very highest degree, and gave pain to many worthy and pious people. They are at present condemned by the Greek and Roman Catholic censorships as unfit for general reading. A censorship of conduct would have been equally disastrous. The disloyalty of Hampden and of Washington; the revolting immorality of Luther in not only marrying when he was a priest, but actually marrying a nun; the heterodoxy of Galileo; the shocking blasphemies and sacrileges of Mohammed against the idols whom he dethroned to make way for his conception of one god; the still more startling blasphemy of Jesus when he declared God to be the son of man and himself to be the son of God, are all examples of shocking immoralities (every immorality shocks somebody), the suppression and extinction of which would have been more disastrous than the utmost mischief that can be conceived as ensuing from the toleration of vice.

These facts, glaring as they are, are disguised by the promotion of immoralities into moralities which is constantly going on. Christianity and Mohammedanism, once thought of and dealt with exactly as Anarchism is thought of and dealt with today, have become established religions; and fresh immoralities are persecuted in their name. The truth is that the vast majority of persons professing these religions have never been anything but simple moralists. The respectable Englishman who is a Christian because he was born in Clapham would be a Mohammedan for the cognate reason if he had been born in Constantinople. He has never willingly tolerated immorality. He did not adopt any innovation until it had become moral; and then he adopted it, not on its merits, but solely because it had become moral. In doing so he never realized that it had ever been immoral: consequently its early struggles taught him no lesson; and he has opposed the next step in human progress as indignantly as if neither manners, customs, nor thought had ever changed since the beginning of the world. Toleration must be imposed on him as a mystic and painful duty by his spiritual and political leaders, or he will condemn the world to stagnation, which is the penalty of an inflexible morality.

What Toleration Means

This must be done all the more arbitrarily because it is not possible to make the ordinary moral man understand what toleration and liberty really mean. He will accept them verbally with alacrity, even with enthusiasm, because the word toleration has been moralized by eminent Whigs; but what he means by toleration is toleration of doctrines that he considers enlightened, and, by liberty, liberty to do what he considers right: that is, he does not mean toleration or liberty at all; for there is no need to tolerate what appears enlightened or to claim liberty to do what most people consider right. Toleration and liberty have no sense or use except as toleration of opinions that are considered damnable, and liberty to do what seems wrong. . . . Setting Englishmen free to marry their deceased wife's sisters is not tolerated by the people who approve of it, but by the people who regard it as incestuous. Catholic Emancipation and the admission of Jews to parliament needed no toleration from Catholics and Jews: the toleration they needed was that of the people who regarded the one measure as a facilitation of idolatry, and the other as a condonation of the crucifixion. Clearly such toleration is not clamored for by the multitude or by the press which reflects its prejudices. It is essentially one of those abnegations of passion and prejudice which the common man submits to because uncommon men whom he respects as wiser than himself assure him that it must be so, or the higher affairs of human destiny will suffer. . . .

The Case for Toleration

Accordingly, there has risen among wise and far-sighted men a perception of the need for setting certain departments of human activity entirely free from legal interference. This has nothing to do with any sympathy these liberators may themselves have with immoral views. A man with the strongest conviction of the Divine ordering of the universe and of the superiority of monarchy to all forms of government may nevertheless quite consistently and conscientiously be ready to lay down his life for the right of every man to advocate Atheism or Republicanism if he believes in them. An attack on morals may turn out to be the salvation of the race. A hundred years ago nobody foresaw that Tom Paine's centenary would be the subject of a laudatory special article in The Times; and only a few understood that the persecution of his works and the transportation of men for the felony of reading them was a mischievous mistake. Even less, perhaps, could they have guessed that Proudhon, who became notorious by his essay entitled "What is Property? It is Theft" would have received, on the like occasion and in the same paper, a respectful consideration which nobody would now dream of according to Lord Liverpool or Lord Brougham. Nevertheless there was a mass of evidence to shew that such a development was not only possible but fairly probable, and that the risks of suppressing liberty of propaganda were far greater than the risk of Paine's or Proudhon's writings wrecking civilization. Now there was no such evidence in favor of tolerating the cutting of throats and the robbing of tills. No case whatever can be made out for the statement that a nation cannot do without common thieves and homicidal ruffians. But an overwhelming case can be made out for the statement that no nation can prosper or even continue to exist without heretics and advocates of shockingly immoral doctrines. The Inquisition and the Star Chamber, which were nothing but censorships, made ruthless war on impiety and immorality. The result was once familiar to Englishmen, though of late years it seems to have been forgotten. It cost England a revolution to get rid of the Star Chamber. Spain did not get rid of the Inquisition, and paid for that omission by becoming a barely third-rate power politically, and intellectually no power at all, in the Europe she had once dominated as the mightiest of the Christian empires. . . .

Is there not something to be said for a political censorship, if not for a moral one? May not those continental governments who leave the stage practically free in every other respect, but muzzle it politically, be justified by the practical exigencies of the situation?

The Difference between Law and Censorship

The answer is that a pamphlet, a newspaper article, or a resolution moved at a political meeting can do all the mischief that a play can, and often more; yet we do not set up a permanent censorship of the press or of political meetings. Any journalist may publish an article, any demagogue may deliver a speech without giving notice to the government or obtaining its licence. The risk of such freedom is great; but as it is the price of our political liberty, we think it worth paying. We may abrogate it in emergencies by a Coercion Act, a suspension of the Habeas Corpus Act, or a proclamation of martial law, just as we stop the traffic in a street during a fire, or shoot thieves at sight if they loot after an earthquake. But when the emergency is past, liberty is restored everywhere except in the theatre. The Act of 1843 is a permanent Coercion Act for the theatre, a permanent suspension of the Habeas Corpus Act as far as plays are concerned, a permanent proclamation of martial law with a single official substituted for a court martial. It is, in fact, assumed that actors, playwrights, and theatre managers are dangerous and dissolute characters whose existence creates a chronic state of emergency, and who must be treated as earthquake looters are treated. It is not necessary now to discredit this assumption. It was broken down by the late Sir Henry Irving when he finally shamed the Government into extending to his profession the official recognition enjoyed by the other branches of fine art. To-day we have on the roll of knighthood actors, authors, and managers. The rogue and vagabond theory of the depravity of the theatre is as dead officially as it is in general society; and with it has perished the sole excuse for the Act of 1843 and for the denial to the theatre of the liberties secured, at far greater social risk, to the press and the platform.

There is no question here of giving the theatre any larger

liberties than the press and the platform, or of claiming larger powers for Shakespear to eulogize Brutus than Lord Rosebery has to eulogize Cromwell. The abolition of the censorship does not involve the abolition of the magistrate and of the whole civil and criminal code. On the contrary it would make the theatre more effectually subject to them than it is at present; for once a play now runs the gauntlet of the censorship, it is practically placed above the law. It is almost humiliating to have to demonstrate the essential difference between a censor and a magistrate or a sanitary inspector; but it is impossible to ignore the carelessness with which even distinguished critics of the theatre assume that all the arguments proper to the support of a magistracy and body of jurisprudence apply equally to a censorship.

A magistrate has laws to administer: a censor has nothing but his own opinion. A judge leaves the question of guilt to the jury: the Censor is jury and judge as well as lawgiver. A magistrate may be strongly prejudiced against an atheist or an anti-vaccinator, just as a sanitary inspector may have formed a careful opinion that drains are less healthy than cesspools; but the magistrate must allow the atheist to affirm instead of to swear, and must grant the anti-vaccinator an exemption certificate, when their demands are lawfully made; and in cities the inspector must compel the builder to make drains and must prosecute him if he makes cesspools. The law may be only the intolerance of the community; but it is a defined and limited intolerance. The limitation is sometimes carried so far that a judge cannot inflict the penalty for housebreaking on a burglar who can prove that he found the door open and therefore made only an unlawful entry. On the other hand, it is sometimes so vague, as for example in the case of the American law against obscenity, that it makes the magistrate virtually a censor. But in the main a citizen can ascertain what he may do and what he may not do; and, though no one knows better than a magistrate that a single ill-conducted family may demoralize a whole street, no magistrate can imprison or otherwise restrain its members on the ground that their immorality may corrupt their neighbors. He can prevent any citizen from carrying certain specified weapons, but not from handling pokers, table-knives, bricks or bottles of corrosive fluid, on the ground that he might use them to commit murder or inflict malicious injury. He has no general power to prevent citizens from selling unhealthy or poisonous substances, or judging for themselves what substances are unhealthy and what wholesome, what poisonous and what innocuous: what he *can* do is to prevent anybody who has not a specific qualification from selling certain specified poisons of which a schedule is kept. Nobody is forbidden to sell minerals without a licence; but everybody is forbidden to sell silver without a licence. When the law has forgotten some atrocious sin—for instance, contracting marriage whilst suffering from contagious disease—the magistrate cannot arrest or punish the wrongdoer, however he may abhor his wickedness. In short, no man is lawfully at the mercy of the magistrate's personal caprice, prejudice, ignorance, superstition, temper, stupidity, resentment, timidity, ambition, or private conviction. But a playwright's livelihood, his reputation, and his inspiration and mission are at the personal mercy of the Censor. The two do not stand, as the criminal and the judge stand, in the presence of a law that binds them both equally, and was made by neither of them, but by the deliberative collective wisdom of the community. The only law that affects them is the Act of 1843, which empowers one of them to do absolutely and finally what he likes with the other's work. And when it is remembered that the slave in this case is the man whose profession is that of Eschylus and Euripides, of Shakespear and Goethe, of Tolstoy and Ibsen, and the master the holder of a party appointment which by the nature of its duties practically excludes the possibility of its acceptance by a serious statesman or great lawyer, it will be seen that the playwrights are justified in reproaching the framers of that Act for having failed not only to appreciate the immense importance of the theatre as a most powerful instrument for teaching the nation how and what to think and feel, but even to conceive that those who make their living by the theatre are normal human beings with the common rights of English citizens. In this extremity of inconsiderateness it is not surprising that they also did not trouble themselves to study the difference between a censor and a magistrate. And it will be found that almost all the people who disinterestedly defend the censorship today are defending him on the assumption that there is no constitutional difference between him and any other functionary whose duty it is to restrain crime and disorder. . . .

Why not an Enlightened Censorship?

. . . Everyone who condemns the principle of censorship must also condemn the Lord Chamberlain's control of the drama; but those who approve of the principle do not necessarily approve of the Lord Chamberlain being the Censor *ex officio*. They may, however, be entirely opposed to popular liberties, and may conclude from what has been said, not that the stage should be made as free as the church, press, or platform, but that these institutions should be censored as strictly as the stage. It will seem obvious to them that nothing is needed to remove all objections to a censorship except the placing of its powers in better hands.

Now though the transfer of the censorship to, say, the Lord Chancellor, or the Primate, or a Cabinet Minister, would be much less humiliating to the persons immediately concerned, the inherent vices of the institution would not be appreciably less disastrous. They would even be aggravated, for reasons which do not appear on the surface, and therefore need to be followed with some attention.

It is often said that the public is the real censor. That this is to some extent true is proved by the fact that plays which are licensed and produced in London have to be expurgated for the provinces. This does not mean that the provinces are more strait-laced, but simply that in many provincial towns there is only one theatre for all classes and all tastes, whereas in London there are separate theatres for separate sections of playgoers; so that, for example, Sir Herbert Beerbohm Tree can conduct His Majesty's Theatre without the slightest regard to the tastes of the frequenters of the Gaiety Theatre; and Mr. George Edwardes can conduct the Gaiety Theatre without catering in any way for lovers of Shakespear. Thus the farcical comedy which has scandalized the critics in London by the libertinage of its jests is played to the respectable dress circle of Northampton with these same jests slurred over so as to be imperceptible by even the most prurient spectator. The public, in short, takes care that nobody shall outrage it.

But the public also takes care that nobody shall starve it, or regulate its dramatic diet as a schoolmistress regulates the reading of her pupils. Even when it wishes to be debauched, no censor can—or at least no censor does—stand out against it. If a play is irresistibly amusing, it gets licensed no matter what its moral aspect may be. A brilliant instance is the Divorçons of the late Victorien Sardou, which may not have been the naughtiest play of the 19th century, but was certainly the very naughtiest that any English manager in his senses would have ventured to produce. Nevertheless, being a very amusing play, it passed the licenser with the exception of a reference to impotence as a ground for divorce which no English actress would have ventured on in any case. Within the last few months a very amusing comedy with a strongly polygamous moral was found irresistible by the Lord Chamberlain. Plenty of fun and a happy ending will get anything licensed, because the public will have it so, and the Examiner of Plays, as the holder of the office testified before the Commission of 1892 (Report, page 330), feels with the public, and knows that his office could not survive a widespread unpopularity. In short, the support of the mob—that is, of the unreasoning, unorganized, uninstructed mass of popular sentiment—is indispensable to the censorship as it exists to-day in England. This is the explanation of the toleration by the Lord Chamberlain of coarse and vicious plays. It is not long since a judge before whom a licensed play came in the course of a lawsuit expressed his scandalized astonishment at the licensing of such a work. Eminent churchmen have made similar protests. In some plays the simulation of criminal assaults on the stage has been carried to a point at which a step further would have involved the interference of the police. Provided the treatment of the theme is gaily or hypocritically popular, and the ending happy, the indulgence of the Lord Chamberlain can be counted on. On the other hand, anything unpleasing and unpopular is rigorously censored.

VERSIONS OF CENSORSHIP

Adultery and prostitution are tolerated and even encouraged to such an extent that plays which do not deal with them are commonly said not to be plays at all. But if any of the unpleasing consequences of adultery and prostitution—for instance, an *unsuccessful* illegal operation (successful ones are tolerated) or venereal disease—are mentioned, the play is prohibited. This principle of shielding the playgoer from unpleasant reflections is carried so far that when a play was submitted for license in which the relations of a prostitute with all the male characters in the piece was described as "immoral," the Examiner of Plays objected to that passage, though he made no objection to the relations themselves. The Lord Chamberlain dare not, in short, attempt to exclude from the stage the tragedies of murder and lust, or the farces of mendacity, adultery, and dissolute gaiety in which vulgar people delight. But when these same vulgar people are threatened with an unpopular play in which dissoluteness is shown to be no laughing matter, it is prohibited at once amid the vulgar applause, the net result being that vice is made delightful and virtue banned by the very institution which is supported on the understanding that it produces exactly the opposite result. . . .

NOTES ON CENSORSHIP AND IMAGINATION

1. "Each led by his pleasure" (Virgil's *Eclogues* II. 65).
2. "A popular comedy in the eighteenth century representing a natural man, written by Delisle de la Drévetière" (Translator).

SELF-CENSORSHIP

COMMENT

"We cannot assert the innocence of anyone," says the lawyer in *The Fall*, by Albert Camus, "whereas we can state with certainty the guilt of all. Every man testifies to the crime of all the others—that is my faith and hope." And again—"When we are all guilty, that will be democracy . . . Isn't it good likewise to live like the rest of the world, and for that doesn't the rest of the world have to be like me? Threat, dishonor, police are the sacraments of that resemblance. Scorned, hunted down, compelled, I can then show what I am worth, enjoy what I am, be natural at last. . . ."

We do not have to strangle ourselves with the irony to appreciate the truth of these statements. Censorship is like guilt in that it is an ingredient of the deception we practise on ourselves as well as others, sometimes unwittingly. However, this is far from being merely an absurd situation, as Camus would have it, because it is not permanent, any more than government or people are permanent; and situations which change admit of hope. The incongruity between the hoped-for and the given caused the narrator of *The Fall* to despair: when one applies the parallel to censorship once more, one can see that the same incongruity makes censors busy men.\Censorship is, indeed, one of our attempts to make life tolerable.\But in our highly developed, ostensibly egalitarian society, it generally makes life not better but incomprehensible. The decline of ideals and of idealism and of liberalism since *Areopagitica*, and the corresponding growth in censorship (as Orwell pointed out in his essay) represent a lowering of the sights of the hoped-for. We expect less. And yet the result is not a lessening of the incongruity between the hoped-for and the given. On the contrary, along with the increase in mediocrity has come an apparent increase in deception.

The two pieces that follow deal with the problem of self-censorship, though in very different ways. The first is a revised version of lectures which Freud originally gave at the University of Vienna in 1917; when he revised them, a throat affliction had made him incapable of lecturing; the style is correspondingly more contemplative than in the unrevised version. Between the neutral morality of dream-censorship and censorship by authorities there is a clear affinity: both reveal the same stresses on self-interest, the same ambivalence over the truth of a situation, the same conservativism, and a hint that censorship may be a way of absorbing and transforming unpleasantnesses by a kind of metamorphosis of the agent. At the very least we may assume that the people who carry out censorship are limited as shames and desires limit their dreams —unless their insight is as great as their sense of responsibility, which is seldom the case.

TEXT: "Dream-Censorship" by Sigmund Freud
[*translated by W. H. J. Sprott*]

Although in dream-interpretation we are in general and predominantly dependent on the associations of the dreamer, nevertheless we treat certain elements of the content quite independently—mainly because we have to, because, as a rule,
associations refuse to come. We noticed at an early stage that
this happens always in connection with the same material;
these elements are not very numerous, and long experience
has taught us that they are to be taken as *symbols* for something else, and to be interpreted as such. In comparison with
the other elements of the dream one can give them a permanent meaning, which need not, however, be ambiguous,
and the limits of which are determined by special laws, which
are of an unusual kind. Since we understand how to translate
these symbols, while the dreamer does not, although he himself has made use of them, it may very well be that the sense
of the dream is immediately clear to us, even before we have
begun the work of dream-interpretation, as soon as we have
heard the text of the dream, while the dreamer himself is still
puzzled by it. But in the earlier lectures I have already said
so much about symbolism, about our knowledge of it, and
about the special problems to which it gives rise, that I need
not go over the same ground again to-day.

That, then, is our method of dream-interpretation. The next
and very proper question is—can we by these means interpret
every dream? And the answer is—no, not every one; but so
many that we can afford to be absolutely certain about the
utility and correctness of our procedure. But why not all? The

recent answer to this question will teach us something important, which has a bearing on the psychological conditions of dream formation. It is because the work of interpretation is carried on in the face of resistance, which may vary from an imperceptible amount to an amount so great that we cannot overcome it—at any rate with the means which are at present at our disposal. One cannot help observing the manifestation of this resistance during the interpretation. In many places the associations are given without hesitation, and the first or second of them already provides us with the explanation. In other places the patient pauses and hesitates before he utters an association, and then one often has to listen to a long chain of ideas before one gets anything which is of any use for the understanding of the dream. We are right in supposing that the longer and the more circuitous the chain of associations, the stronger is the resistance. And in the forgetting of dreams, too, we sense the same influence. Often enough it happens that, however much he may try, the patient cannot remember one of his dreams. But when, by a piece of analytical work, we have removed a difficulty which has been disturbing the patient in his relation to the analysis, the forgotten dream will come into his mind quite suddenly. Two more observations may be mentioned here. It very often happens that a piece of the dream is missing, which is eventually added as an afterthought. This is to be regarded as an attempt to forget that particular piece. Experience shows that it is this very piece of the dream which is the most valuable; we suppose that a stronger resistance stood in the way of its communication than was the case with the other parts. And, furthermore, we often find that a patient may try to combat the forgetting of his dreams by writing them down immediately after he wakes up. We may as well tell him that it is useless to do so, because the resistance from which he may have preserved the text of the dream will then transfer itself to the associations and render the manifest dream inaccessible for interpretation. This being the case, we need not be surprised if a further increase of the resistance suppresses the associations altogether, and thus frustrates the interpretation of the dream entirely.

From all this we draw the conclusion that the resistance

which we come across during the process of dream-interpretation must play some part in the formation of the dream as well. One can actually distinguish between dreams which have been formed under low pressure of resistance and those in which the resistance has been high. But this pressure also changes within the same dream from one place to another; it is responsible for the gaps, the obscurities and the confusion which may upset the coherence of the most beautiful dreams.

But what is the resistance doing here, and what is it resisting? Now for us a resistance is the sure sign of a conflict. There must be a force present which is trying to express something, and another which is striving to prevent its expression. What comes into being as the manifest dream may, therefore, be regarded as comprising all the solutions to which the battle between these two opposing forces can be reduced. At one point one of the forces may have been able to get through what it wanted to say, at another the counteracting force may have succeeded in abolishing the intended communication entirely, or may have substituted for it something which betrays no sign of it. The most usual cases, and those which are the most characteristic of the process of dream-formation, are those in which the conflict results in a compromise, so that the communicating force can indeed say what it wants to say, but not in the way it wants to say it; it is toned down, distorted and made unrecognizable. If therefore the dream does not faithfully represent the dream-thoughts, if a process of interpretation is necessary to bridge the gulf between the two, this is the result of the counteracting, inhibiting and restraining force whose existence we have inferred from perceiving the resistance in dream-interpretation. So long as we regarded the dream as an isolated phenomenon, independent of other psychological formations which are allied to it, we called this force the *dream-censor*.

You have long been familiar with the fact that this censorship is not a mechanism which is peculiar to dreams. You remember that the conflict of two psychic factors, which we—roughly—call the repressed unconscious and the conscious, dominates our lives, and that the resistance against the interpretation of dreams, the hall-mark of the dream-censorship, is none other than the repression-resistance which keeps these two factors apart. You also know that under certain conditions other psychological formations emerge from the conflict between these same factors, formations which are the result of compromises just as dreams are; and you will not require me to repeat all that is involved in my introduction to the theory of the neuroses in order to put before you what we know about the conditions under which such compromise formations come about. You will have realized that the dream is a pathological product, the first member of the series which includes the hysterical symptom, the obsession and the delusion among its members; it is differentiated from the others by its transitoriness and by the fact that it occurs under conditions which are part of normal life. For we must never forget that the dream-life is, as Aristotle has already told us, the way our mind works during sleep. The state of sleep represents a turning away from the real external world, and thus provides a necessary condition for the development of a psychosis. The most penetrating study of serious cases of psychosis will reveal no characteristic which is more typical of these pathological conditions. In psychoses, however, the turning away from reality is brought about in two ways; either because the repressed unconscious is too strong, so that it overwhelms the conscious which tries to cling on to reality, or because reality has become so unbearably painful that the threatened ego, in a despairing gesture of opposition, throws itself into the arms of the unconscious impulses. The harmless dream-psychosis is the result of a consciously willed, and only temporary, withdrawal from the external world; it ceases to operate when relations with the external world are resumed. While the sleeper is isolated, there is an alteration in the distribution of his psychic energy; part of the repressive expenditure, which is otherwise used to keep down the unconscious, can be saved, for if the unconscious makes use of its relative freedom and enters on some activity, it finds the avenue to motor expression stopped up, and only the innocent outlet of hallucinatory satisfaction open to it. It can now, therefore, form a dream, but the fact of dream-censorship shows that enough repressive resistance remains operative even during sleep.

Here we have an opportunity of answering the question whether the dream has also a function to perform, whether any useful task is entrusted to it. The condition of repose without stimuli, which the state of sleep attempts to bring about, is threatened from three sides: in a chance fashion by external stimuli during sleep, by interests of the day before which have not yet abated and, in an unavoidable manner, by the unsatisfied repressed impulses, which are ready to seize on any opportunity for expression. On account of the nightly reduction of the repressive forces, the risk is run that the repose of sleep will be broken every time the outer and inner disturbances manage to link up with one of the unconscious sources of energy. The dream-process allows the result of such a combination to discharge itself through the channel of a harmless hallucinatory experience, and thus insures the continuity of sleep. There is no contradiction of this function in the fact that the dream sometimes wakes the sleeper in a state of anxiety; it is rather a sign that the watcher regards the situation as being too dangerous, and no longer thinks he can cope with it. Quite often, indeed, while we are still asleep, we are aware of the comforting thought, which is there to prevent our waking up: "after all, it is only a dream."

That is all, ladies and gentlemen, that I wanted to say about dream-interpretation, the business of which is to trace the manifest dream back to the latent dream-thoughts. When this has been done, the interest in the dream from the point of view of practical analysis fades. The analyst links up the communication which he has received in the form of a dream with the patient's other communications and proceeds with the analysis. We, however, wish to linger a little longer over the dream; we are tempted to study the process by means of which the latent dream-thoughts are transformed into the manifest dream. We call this the dream-work. You will remember that in the previous lectures I described it in such detail that, for to-day's review of the subject, I can confine myself to the briefest summary.

The process of dream-work is something quite new and strange, the like of which has never before been known. It has given us our first glimpse into those processes which go on in our unconscious mental system, and shows us that they are quite different from what we know about our conscious thought, and that to this latter they must necessarily appear faulty and preposterous. The importance of this discovery is increased when we realise that the same mechanisms—we hardly dare call them "thought processes"—are at work in the formation of neurotic symptoms as have turned the latent dream-thoughts into the manifest dream.

In what follows I cannot avoid making my exposition a schematic one. Supposing we have before us in a given instance all the latent thoughts, more or less affectively toned, which have taken the place of the manifest dream after a complete interpretation. We shall then notice a distinction among them, and this distinction will take us a long way. Almost all these dream-thoughts will be recognised or acknowledged by the dreamer; he will admit that he thought thus at one time or another, or that he might very well have done so. But he may resist the acceptance of one single thought, it is foreign to him, perhaps even repellent; it may be that he will passionately repudiate it. Now it becomes clear to us that the other thoughts are bits of his conscious, or, more correctly, of his pre-conscious thought; they might very well have been thought during waking life, and have probably formed themselves during the day. This one rejected thought, or, better, this one impulse, is a child of the night; it belongs to the unconscious of the dreamer, and is therefore disowned and repudiated by him. It had to await the nightly relaxation of repression in order to achieve any sort of expression. In any case the expression that it obtains is enfeebled, distorted and disguised; without the work of interpretation we should never have discovered it. It is thanks to its connection with the other unobjectionable dream-thoughts that this unconscious impulse has had the opportunity of slipping past the barrier of the censorship in an unostentatious disguise; on the other hand, the pre-conscious dream-thoughts owe to the same connection their power of occupying the mental life, even during sleep. We can, indeed, have no doubt about this: the unconscious impulse is the real creator of the dream, it provides the psychic energy required for its formation. Just like any other

instinctual impulse it can do no other than seek its own satisfaction, and our experience in dream-interpretation shows us,
moreover, that this is the meaning of all dreaming. In every
dream an instinctual wish is displayed as fulfilled. The nightly
cutting-off of mental life from reality, and the regression to
primitive mechanisms which it makes possible, enable this desired instinctual satisfaction to be experienced in a hallucinatory fashion as actually happening. On account of the same
process of regression ideas are turned into visual pictures in
the dream; the latent dream-thoughts are, that is to say,
dramatized and illustrated.

From this piece of dream-work we obtain information about
some of the most striking and peculiar characteristics of the
dream. Let me repeat the stages of dream-formation. The introduction: the wish to sleep, the voluntary withdrawal from
the outside world. Two things follow from this: firstly, the
possibility for older and more primitive modes of activity to
manifest themselves, i.e. regression; and secondly, the decrease
of the repression-resistance which weighs on the unconscious.
As a result of this latter feature an opportunity for dream-
formation presents itself, which is seized upon by the factors
which are the occasion of the dream; that is to say, the internal
and external stimuli which are in activity. The dream which
thus eventuates is already a compromise-formation; it has a
double function: it is on the one hand in conformity with the
ego ("ego-syntonic"), since it subserves the wish to sleep by
draining of the stimuli which would otherwise disturb it, while
on the other hand it allows to a repressed impulse the satisfaction which is possible in these circumstances in the form of
an hallucinatory wish-fulfillment. The whole process of dream-
formation, which is permitted by the sleeping ego, is, however, under the control of the censorship, a control which is
exercised by what is left of the forces of repression. I cannot
explain the process more simply; it is not in itself simpler than
that. But now I can proceed with the description of the dream-
work.

Let us go back once more to the latent dream-thoughts.
Their dominating element is the repressed impulse, which has
obtained some kind of expression, toned down and disguised

though it may be, by associating itself with stimuli which happen to be there and by tacking itself on the residue of the day before. Just like any other impulse this one presses forward toward satisfaction in action, but the path to motor discharge is closed to it on account of the physiological characteristics of the state of sleep, and so it is forced to travel in the retrograde direction to perception, and content itself with an hallucinatory satisfaction. The latent dream-thoughts are therefore turned into a collection of sensory images and visual scenes. As they are travelling in this direction something happens to them which seems to us new and bewildering. All the verbal apparatus by means of which the more subtle thought-relations are expressed, the conjunctions and prepositions, the variations of declension and conjugation, are lacking, because the means of portraying them are absent: just as in primitive, grammarless speech, only the raw material of thought can be expressed, and the abstract is merged again in the concrete from which it sprang. What is left over may very well seem to lack coherence. It is as much the result of the archaic regression in the mental apparatus as of the demands of the censorship that so much use is made of the representation of certain objects and processes by means of symbols which have become strange to conscious thought. But of more far-reaching import are the other alterations to which the elements comprising the dream-thoughts are subjected. Such of them as have any point of contact are *condensed* into new unities. When the thoughts are translated into pictures those forms are indubitably preferred which allow of this kind of telescoping, or condensation; it is as though a force were at work which subjected the materials to a process of pressure or squeezing together. As a result of condensation one element in a manifest dream may correspond to a number of elements of the dream-thoughts; but conversely one of the elements from among the dream-thoughts may be represented by a number of pictures in the dream.

Even more remarkable is the other process of *displacement* or transference of accent, which in conscious thinking figures only as an error in thought or as a method employed in jokes. For the individual ideas which make up the dream-thoughts are not all of equal value; they have various degrees of affective-tone attached to them, and corresponding to these, they are judged as more or less important, and more or less worthy of attention. In the dream-work these ideas are separated from their affects; the affects are treated separately. They may be transferred to something else, they may remain where they were, they may undergo transformation, or they may disappear from the dream entirely. The importance of the ideas which have been shorn of their affect, reappears in the dream in the form of the sensuous vividness of the dream-pictures; but we notice that this accent, which should lie on important elements, has been transferred to unimportant ones, so that what seems to be pushed to the forefront in the dream, as the most important element in it, only plays a subsidiary rôle in the dream-thoughts, and conversely, what is important among the dream-thoughts obtains only incidental and rather indistinct representation in the dream. No other factor in the dream-work plays such an important part in rendering the dream strange and unintelligible to the dreamer. Displacement is the chief method employed in the process of *dream-distortion*, which the dream-thoughts have to undergo under the influence of the censorship.

COMMENT: On Authority and Freedom

The Legend of the Grand Inquisitor is one of the most
famous efforts in literature to present the problem of authority and human freedom. As Berdayev points out, it is
noteworthy that its "extremely powerful vindication of Christ
. . . should be put into the mouth of the atheist Ivan
Karamazov." Dostoyevsky leaves the reader to choose the
Inquisitor's version of liberty or Christ's. He gives us to
understand—as Camus did—that with either version goes
suffering that may become grotesque. Authority that seeks to
protect humanity has to assume all the human burdens;
while one who believes in the high nature of a man to
decide for himself may have to take on all the marks of
social degradation. The struggle involves the different faces,
the Janus quality, of power and love.

3 2 3. 4

Mice M

TEXT: "The Legend of the Grand Inquisitor" from *The Brothers Karamazov* by Feodor Dostoyevsky
[*translated by Constance Garnett*]

". . . My story is laid in Spain, in Seville, in the most terrible time of the Inquisition, when fires were lighted every
day to the glory of God, and 'in the splendid *auto da fé* the
wicked heretics were burnt.' Oh, of course, this was not the
coming in which He will appear according to His promise at
the end of time in all His heavenly glory, and which will
be sudden 'as lightning flashing from east to west.' No, He
visited His children only for a moment, and there where
the flames were crackling round the heretics. In His infinite
mercy He came once more among men in that human shape
in which He walked among men for three years fifteen centuries ago. He came down to the 'hot pavement' of the
southern town in which on the day before almost a hundred
heretics had, *ad majorem gloriam Dei,* been burnt by the
cardinal, the Grand Inquisitor, in a magnificent *auto da fé,* in
the presence of the king, the court, the knights, the cardinals,
the most charming ladies of the court, and the whole population of Seville.

"He came softly, unobserved, and yet, strange to say, every
one recognised Him. That might be one of the best passages
in the poem. I mean, why they recognised Him. The people
are irresistibly drawn to Him, they surround Him, they flock
about Him, follow Him. He moves silently in their midst with
a gentle smile of infinite compassion. The sun of love burns in
His heart, light and power shine from His eyes, and their

radiance, shed on the people, stirs their hearts with responsive love. He holds out His hands to them, blesses them, and a healing virtue comes from contact with Him, even with His garments. An old man in the crowd, blind from childhood, cries out, 'O Lord, heal me and I shall see Thee!' and, as it were, scales fall from his eyes and the blind man sees Him. The crowd weeps and kisses the earth under His feet. Children throw flowers before Him, sing, and cry hosannah. 'It is He—it is He!' all repeat. 'It must be He, it can be no one but Him!' He stops at the steps of the Seville cathedral at the moment when the weeping mourners are bringing in a little open white coffin. In it lies a child of seven, the only daughter of a prominent citizen. The dead child lies hidden in flowers. 'He will raise your child,' the crowd shouts to the weeping mother. The priest, coming to meet the coffin, looks perplexed, and frowns, but the mother of the dead child throws herself at His feet with a wail. 'If it is Thou, raise my child!' she cries, holding out her hands to Him. The procession halts, the coffin is laid on the steps at His feet. He looks with compassion, and His lips once more softly pronounce, 'Maiden, arise!' and the maiden arises. The little girl sits up in the coffin and looks round, smiling with wide-open wondering eyes, holding a bunch of white roses they had put in her hand.

"There are cries, sobs, confusion among the people, and at that moment the cardinal himself, the Grand Inquisitor, passes by the cathedral. He is an old man, almost ninety, tall and erect, with a withered face and sunken eyes, in which there is still a gleam of light. He is not dressed in his gorgeous cardinal's robes, as he was the day before, when he was burning the enemies of the Roman Church—at that moment he was wearing his coarse, old, monk's cassock. At a distance behind him come his gloomy assistants and slaves and the 'holy guard.' He stops at the sight of the crowd and watches it from a distance. He sees everything; he sees them set the coffin down at His feet, sees the child rise up, and his face darkens. He knits his thick grey brows and his eyes gleam with a sinister fire. He holds out his finger and bids the guards take Him. And such is his power, so completely are the people cowed into submission and trembling obedience to him, that the crowd immediately make way for the guards, and in the midst of deathlike silence they lay hands on Him and lead Him away. The crowd instantly bows down to the earth, like one man, before the old inquisitor. He blesses the people in silence and passes on. The guards lead their prisoner to the close, gloomy vaulted prison in the ancient palace of the Holy Inquisition and shut Him in it. The day passes and is followed by the dark, burning 'breathless' night of Seville. The air is 'fragrant with laurel and lemon.' In the pitch darkness the iron door of the prison is suddenly opened and the Grand Inquisitor himself comes in with a light in his hand. He is alone; the door is closed at once behind him. He stands in the doorway and for a minute or two gazes into His face. At last he goes up slowly, sets the light on the table and speaks.

"'Is it Thou? Thou?' but receiving no answer, he adds at once, 'Don't answer, be silent. What canst Thou say, indeed? I know too well what Thou wouldst say. And Thou hast no right to add anything to what Thou hadst said of old. Why, then, art Thou come to hinder us? For Thou hast come to hinder us, and Thou knowest that. But dost Thou know what will be to-morrow? I know not who Thou art and care not to know whether it is Thou or only a semblance of Him, but to-morrow I shall condemn Thee and burn Thee at the stake as the worst of heretics. And the very people who have to-day kissed Thy feet, to-morrow at the faintest sign from me will rush to heap up the embers of Thy fire. Knowest Thou that? Yes, maybe Thou knowest it,' he added with thoughtful penetration, never for a moment taking his eyes off the Prisoner."

"I don't quite understand, Ivan. What does it mean?" Alyosha, who had been listening in silence, said with a smile. "Is it simply a wild fantasy, or a mistake on the part of the old man—some impossible *quiproquo?*"

"Take it as the last," said Ivan, laughing, "if you are so corrupted by modern realism and can't stand anything fantastic. If you like it to be a case of mistaken identity, let it be so. It is true," he went on, laughing, "the old man was ninety, and he might well be crazy over his set idea. He might have been struck by the appearance of the Prisoner. It might, in fact, be simply his ravings, the delusion of an old man of ninety, over-excited by the *auto da fé* of a hundred heretics the day before. But does it matter to us after all whether it was a mistake of identity or a wild fantasy? All that matters is that the old man should speak out, should speak openly of what he has thought in silence for ninety years."

"And the Prisoner too is silent? Does He look at him and not say a word?"

"That's inevitable in any case," Ivan laughed again. "The old man has told Him He hasn't the right to add anything to what He has said of old. One may say it is the most fundamental feature of Roman Catholicism, in my opinion at least. 'All has been given by Thee to the Pope,' they say, 'and all, therefore, is still in the Pope's hands, and there is no need for Thee to come now at all. Thou must not meddle for the time, at least.' That's how they speak and write too— the Jesuits, at any rate. I have read it myself in the works of their theologians. 'Hast Thou the right to reveal to us one of the mysteries of that world from which Thou hast come?' my old man asks Him, and answers the question for Him. 'No, Thou hast not; that Thou mayest not add to what has been said of old, and mayest not take from men the freedom which Thou didst exalt when Thou wast on earth. Whatsoever Thou revealest anew will encroach on men's freedom of faith; for it will be manifest as a miracle, and the freedom of their faith was dearer to Thee than anything in those days fifteen hundred years ago. Didst Thou not often say then, "I will make you free"? But now Thou hast seen these "free" men,' the old man adds suddenly, with a pensive smile. 'Yes, we've paid dearly for it,' he goes on, looking sternly at Him, 'but at last we have completed that work in Thy name. For fifteen centuries we have been wrestling with Thy freedom, but now it is ended and over for good. Dost Thou not believe that it's over for good? Thou lookest meekly at me and deignest not even to be wroth with me. But let me tell Thee that now, to-day, people are more persuaded than ever that they have perfect freedom, yet they have brought their freedom to us and laid it humbly at our feet. But that has been our doing. Was this what Thou didst? Was this Thy freedom?'"

"I don't understand again," Alyosha broke in. "Is he ironical, is he jesting?"

"Not a bit of it! He claims it as a merit for himself and his Church that at last they have vanquished freedom and have done so to make men happy. 'For now' (he is speaking of the Inquisition, of course) 'for the first time it has become possible to think of the happiness of men. Man was created a rebel; and how can rebels be happy? Thou wast warned,' he says to Him. 'Thou hast had no lack of admonitions and warnings, but Thou didst not listen to those warnings; Thou didst reject the only way by which men might be made happy. But, fortunately, departing Thou didst hand on the work to us. Thou hast promised, Thou hast established by Thy word, Thou hast given to us the right to bind and to unbind, and now, of course, Thou canst not think of taking it away. Why, then, hast Thou come to hinder us?'"

"And what's the meaning of 'no lack of admonitions and warnings'?" asked Alyosha.

"Why, that's the chief part of what the old man must say."

"'The wise and dread spirit, the spirit of self-destruction and non-existence,' the old man goes on, 'the great spirit talked with Thee in the wilderness, and we are told in the books that he "tempted" Thee. Is that so? And could anything truer be said than what he revealed to Thee in three questions and what Thou didst reject, and what in the books is called "the temptation"? And yet if there has ever been on earth a real stupendous miracle, it took place on that day, on the day of the three temptations. The statement of those three questions was itself the miracle. If it were possible to imagine simply for the sake of argument that those three questions of the dread spirit had perished utterly from the books, and that we had to restore them and to invent them anew, and to do so had gathered together all the wise men of the earth—rulers, chief priests, learned men, philosophers, poets—and had set them the task to invent three questions, such as would not only fit the occasion, but express in three words, three human phrases, the whole future history of the world and of humanity—dost Thou believe that all the wisdom of the earth united could have invented anything in depth and force equal to the three questions which were actually put to Thee then by the wise and mighty spirit in the wilderness? From those questions alone, from the miracle of their statement, we can see that we have here to do not with the fleeting human intelligence, but with the absolute and eternal. For in those three questions the whole subsequent history of mankind is, as it were, brought together into one whole, and foretold, and in them are united all the unsolved historical contradictions of human nature. At the time it could not be so clear, since the future was unknown; but now that fifteen hundred years have passed, we see that everything in those three questions was so justly divined and foretold, and has been so truly fulfilled, that nothing can be added to them or taken from them.

"'Judge Thyself who was right—Thou or he who questioned Thee then? Remember the first question; its meaning, in other words, was this: "Thou wouldst go into the world, and art going with empty hands, with some promise of freedom which men in their simplicity and their natural unruliness cannot even understand, which they fear and dread—for nothing has ever been more insupportable for a man and a human society than freedom. But seest Thou these stones in this parched and barren wilderness? Turn them into bread, and mankind will run after Thee like a flock of sheep, grateful and obedient, though for ever trembling, lest Thou withdraw Thy hand and deny them Thy bread." But Thou wouldst not deprive man of freedom and didst reject the offer, thinking, what is that freedom worth, if obedience is bought with bread? Thou didst reply that man lives not by bread alone. But dost Thou know that for the sake of that earthly bread the spirit of the earth will rise up against Thee and will strive with Thee and overcome Thee, and all will follow him, crying, "Who can compare with this beast? He has given us fire from heaven!" Dost Thou know that the ages will pass, and humanity will proclaim by the lips of their sages that there is no crime, and therefore no sin; there is only hunger? "Feed men, and then ask of them virtue!" that's what they'll write on the banner, which they will raise against Thee, and with which they will destroy Thy temple. Where Thy temple stood will rise a new building; the terrible tower of Babel will be built again, and though, like the one of old, it will not be finished, yet Thou mightest have prevented that new tower and have cut short the sufferings of men for a thousand years; for they will come back to us after a thousand years of agony with their tower. They will seek us again, hidden underground in the catacombs, for we shall be again persecuted and tortured. They will find us and cry to us, "Feed us, for those who have promised us fire from heaven haven't given it!" And then we shall finish building their tower, for he finishes the building who feeds them. And we alone shall feed them in Thy name, declaring falsely that it is in Thy name. Oh, never, never can they feed themselves without us! No science will give them bread so long as they remain free. In the end they will lay their freedom at our feet, and say to us, "Make us your slaves, but feed us." They will understand themselves, at last, that freedom and bread enough for all are inconceivable together, for never, never will they be able to share between them! They will be convinced, too, that they can never be free, for they are weak, vicious, worthless and rebellious. Thou didst promise them the bread of Heaven, but, I repeat again, can it compare with earthly bread in the eyes of the weak, ever sinful and ignoble race of man? And if for the sake of the bread of Heaven thousands and tens of thousands shall follow Thee, what is to become of the millions and tens of thousands of millions of creatures who will not have the strength to forego the earthly bread for the sake of the heavenly? Or dost Thou care only for the tens of thousands of the great and strong, while the millions, numerous as the sands of the sea, who are weak but love Thee, must exist only for the sake of the great and strong? No, we care for the weak too. They are sinful and rebellious, but in the end they too will become obedient. They will marvel at us and look on us as gods, because we are ready to endure the freedom which they have found so dreadful and to rule over them—so awful it will seem to them to be free. But we shall tell them that we are Thy servants and

rule them in Thy name. We shall deceive them again, for
we will not let Thee come to us again. That deception will
be our suffering, for we shall be forced to lie.

" 'This is the significance of the first question in the wilderness, and this is what Thou hast rejected for the sake of that
freedom which Thou hast exalted above everything. Yet in
this question lies hid the great secret of this world. Choosing
"bread," Thou wouldst have satisfied the universal and ever-
lasting craving of humanity—to find some one to worship. So
long as man remains free he strives for nothing so incessantly
and so painfully as to find some one to worship. But man seeks
to worship what is established beyond dispute, so that all men
would agree at once to worship it. For these pitiful creatures
are concerned not only to find what one or the other can worship, but to find something that all would believe in and
worship; what is essential is that all may be *together* in it.
This craving for *community* of worship is the chief misery of
every man individually and of all humanity from the beginning of time. For the sake of common worship they've slain
each other with the sword. They have set up gods and chal-
lenged one another, "Put away your gods and come and
worship ours, or we will kill you and your gods!" And so it
will be to the end of the world, even when gods disappear
from the earth; they will fall down before idols just the same.
Thou didst know, Thou couldst not but have known, this
fundamental secret of human nature, but Thou didst reject
the one infallible banner which was offered Thee to make all
men bow down to Thee alone—the banner of earthly bread;
and Thou hast rejected it for the sake of freedom and the
bread of Heaven. Behold what Thou didst further. And all
again in the name of freedom! I tell Thee that man is tormented by no greater anxiety than to find some one quickly
to whom he can hand over that gift of freedom with which
the ill-fated creature is born. But only one who can appease
their conscience can take over their freedom. In bread there
was offered Thee an invincible banner; give bread, and man
will worship Thee, for nothing is more certain than bread.
But if some one else gains possession of his conscience—oh!
then he will cast away Thy bread and follow after him who

has ensnared his conscience. In that Thou wast right. For the secret of man's being is not only to live but to have something to live for. Without a stable conception of the object of life, man would not consent to go on living, and would rather destroy himself than remain on earth, though he had bread in abundance. That is true. But what happened? Instead of taking men's freedom from them, Thou didst make it greater than ever! Didst Thou forget that man prefers peace, and even death, to freedom of choice in the knowledge of good and evil? Nothing is more seductive for man than his freedom of conscience, but nothing is a greater cause of suffering. And behold, instead of giving a firm foundation for setting the conscience of man at rest for ever, Thou didst choose all that is exceptional, vague and enigmatic; Thou didst choose what was utterly beyond the strength of men, acting as though Thou didst not love them at all—Thou who didst come to give Thy life for them! Instead of taking possession of men's freedom, Thou didst increase it, and burdened the spiritual kingdom of mankind with its sufferings for ever. Thou didst desire man's free love, that he should follow Thee freely, enticed and taken captive by Thee. In place of the rigid ancient law, man must hereafter with free heart decide for himself what is good and what is evil, having only Thy image before him as his guide. But didst Thou not know he would at last reject even Thy image and Thy truth, if he is weighed down with the fearful burden of free choice? They will cry aloud at last that the truth is not in Thee, for they could not have been left in greater confusion and suffering than Thou hast caused, laying upon them so many cares and unanswerable problems.

" 'So that, in truth, Thou didst Thyself lay the foundation for the destruction of Thy kingdom, and no one is more to blame for it. Yet what was offered Thee? There are three powers, three powers alone, able to conquer and to hold captive for ever the conscience of these impotent rebels for their happiness—those forces are miracle, mystery and authority. Thou hast rejected all three and hast set the example for doing so. When the wise and dread spirit set Thee on the pinnacle of the temple and said to Thee, "If Thou wouldst know whether Thou art the Son of God then cast Thyself down, for it is written: the angels shall hold him up lest he fall and bruise himself, and Thou shalt know then whether Thou art the Son of God and shalt prove then how great is Thy faith in Thy Father." But Thou didst refuse and wouldst not cast Thyself down. Oh! of course, Thou didst proudly and well, like God; but the weak, unruly race of men, are they gods? Oh, Thou didst know then that in taking one step, in making one movement to cast Thyself down, Thou wouldst be tempting God and have lost all Thy faith in Him, and wouldst have been dashed to pieces against that earth which Thou didst come to save. And the wise spirit that tempted Thee would have rejoiced. But I ask again, are there many like Thee? And couldst Thou believe for one moment that men, too, could face such a temptation? Is the nature of men such, that they can reject miracle, and at the great moments of their life, the moments of their deepest, most agonising spiritual difficulties, cling only to the free verdict of the heart? Oh, Thou didst know that Thy deed would be recorded in books, would be handed down to remote times and the utmost ends of the earth, and Thou didst hope that man, following Thee, would cling to God and not ask for a miracle. But Thou didst not know that when man rejects miracle he rejects God too; for man seeks not so much God as the miraculous. And as man cannot bear to be without the miraculous, he will create new miracles of his own for himself, and will worship deeds of sorcery and witchcraft, though he might be a hundred times over a rebel, heretic and infidel. Thou didst not come down from the Cross when they shouted to Thee, mocking and reviling Thee, "Come down from the cross and we will believe that Thou art He." Thou didst not come down, for again Thou wouldst not enslave man by a miracle, and didst crave faith given freely, not based on miracle. Thou didst crave for free love and not the base raptures of the slave before the might that has overawed him for ever. But Thou didst think too highly of men therein, for they are slaves, of course, though rebellious by nature. Look round and judge; fifteen centuries have passed, look upon them. Whom hast Thou raised up to Thyself? I swear, man is weaker and baser by nature than Thou hast believed him! Can he, can he do what Thou didst? By showing him so much respect, Thou didst, as it were, cease to feel for him, for Thou didst ask far too much from him—Thou who hast loved him more than Thyself! Respecting him less, Thou wouldst have asked less of him. That would have been more like love, for his burden would have been lighter. He is weak and vile. What though he is everywhere now rebelling against our power, and proud of his rebellion? It is the pride of a child and a schoolboy. They are little children rioting and barring out the teacher at school. But their childish delight will end; it will cost them dear. They will cast down temples and drench the earth with blood. But they will see at last, the foolish children, that, though they are rebels, they are impotent rebels, unable to keep up their own rebellion. Bathed in their foolish tears, they will recognise at last that He who created them rebels must have meant to mock at them. They will say this in despair, and their utterance will be a blasphemy which will make them more unhappy still, for man's nature cannot bear blasphemy, and in the end always avenges it on itself. And so unrest, confusion and unhappiness—that is the present lot of man after Thou didst bear so much for their freedom! Thy great prophet tells in vision and in image, that he saw all those who took part in the first resurrection and that there were of each tribe twelve thousand. But if there were so many of them, they must have been not men but gods. They had borne Thy cross, they had endured scores of years in the barren, hungry wilderness, living upon locusts and roots—and Thou mayest indeed point with pride at those children of freedom, of free love, of free and splendid sacrifice for Thy name. But remember that they were only some thousands; and what of the rest? And how are the other weak ones to blame, because they could not endure what the strong have endured? How is the weak soul to blame that it is unable to receive such terrible gifts? Canst Thou have simply come to the elect and for the elect? But if so, it is a mystery and we cannot understand it. And if it is a mystery, we too have a right to preach a mystery, and to teach them that it's not the free judgment of their hearts, not love that matters, but a mystery which they must follow blindly, even against their conscience. So we have done. We have corrected Thy work and have founded it upon *miracle, mystery* and *authority*. And men rejoiced that they were again led like sheep, and that the terrible gift that had brought them such suffering, was, at last, lifted from their hearts. Were we right teaching them this? Speak! Did we not love mankind, so meekly acknowledging their feebleness, lovingly lightening their burden, and permitting their weak nature even sin with our sanction? Why hast Thou come now to hinder us? And why dost Thou look silently and searchingly at me with Thy mild eyes? Be angry. I don't want Thy love, for I love Thee not. And what use is it for me to hide anything from Thee? Don't I know to Whom I am speaking? All that I can say is known to Thee already. And is it for me to conceal from Thee our mystery? Perhaps it is Thy will to hear it from my lips. Listen, then. We are not working with Thee, but with *him*—that is our mystery. It's long—eight centuries—since we have been on *his* side and not on Thine. Just eight centuries ago, we took from him what Thou didst reject with scorn, that last gift he offered Thee, showing Thee all the kingdoms of the earth. We took from him Rome and the sword of Cæsar, and proclaimed ourselves sole rulers of the earth, though hitherto we have not been able to complete our work. But whose fault is that? Oh, the work is only beginning, but it has begun. It has long to await completion and the earth has yet much to suffer, but we shall triumph and shall be Cæsars, and then we shall plan the universal happiness of man. But Thou mightest have taken even then the sword of Cæsar. Why didst Thou reject that last gift? Hadst Thou accepted that last counsel of the mighty spirit, Thou wouldst have accomplished all that man seeks on earth—that is, some one to worship, some one to keep his conscience, and some means of uniting all in one unanimous and harmonious ant-heap, for the craving for universal unity is the third and last anguish of men. Mankind as a whole has always striven to organise a universal state. There have been many great nations with great histories, but the more highly they were developed the more unhappy they were, for they felt more acutely than other people the craving for worldwide union. The great conquerors,

SELF-CENSORSHIP 371

Timours and Ghenghis-Khans, whirled like hurricanes over
the face of the earth striving to subdue its people, and
they too were but the unconscious expression of the same
craving for universal unity. Hadst Thou taken the world and
Cæsar's purple, Thou wouldst have founded the universal
state and have given universal peace. For who can rule
men if not he who holds their conscience and their bread in
his hands? We have taken the sword of Cæsar, and in taking
it, of course, have rejected Thee and followed *him*. Oh, ages
are yet to come of the confusion of free thought, of their
science and cannibalism. For having begun to build their
tower of Babel without us, they will end, of course, with
cannibalism. But then the beast will crawl to us and lick our
feet and spatter them with tears of blood. And we shall sit
upon the beast and raise the cup, and on it will be written,
"Mystery." But then, and only then, the reign of peace and
happiness will come for men. Thou art proud of Thine elect,
but Thou hast only the elect, while we give rest to all. And
besides, how many of those elect, those mighty ones who
could become elect, have grown weary waiting for Thee,
and have transferred and will transfer the powers of their
spirit and the warmth of their heart to the other camp, and
end by raising their *free* banner against Thee. Thou didst
Thyself lift up that banner. But with us all will be happy
and will no more rebel nor destroy one another as under Thy
freedom. Oh, we shall persuade them that they will only become free when they renounce their freedom to us and submit to us. And shall we be right or shall we be lying? They
will be convinced that we are right, for they will remember
the horrors of slavery and confusion to which Thy freedom
brought them. Freedom, free thought and science, will lead
them into such straits and will bring them face to face with
such marvels and insoluble mysteries, that some of them, the
fierce and rebellious, will destroy themselves, others, rebellious
but weak, will destroy one another, while the rest, weak and
unhappy, will crawl fawning to our feet and whine to us:
"Yes, you were right, you alone possess His mystery, and we
come back to you, save us from ourselves!"

    " 'Receiving bread from us, they will see clearly that we

take the bread made by their hands from them, to give it to
them, without any miracle. They will see that we do not
change the stones to bread, but in truth they will be more
thankful for taking it from our hands than for the bread
itself! For they will remember only too well that in old days,
without our help, even the bread they made turned to stones
in their hands, while since they have come back to us, the very
stones have turned to bread in their hands. Too, too well they
know the value of complete submission! And until men know
that, they will be unhappy. Who is most to blame for their
not knowing it, speak? Who scattered the flock and sent it
astray on unknown paths? But the flock will come together
again and will submit once more, and then it will be once for
all. Then we shall give them the quiet humble happiness of
weak creatures such as they are by nature. Oh, we shall persuade them at last not to be proud, for Thou didst lift them
up and thereby taught them to be proud. We shall show them
that they are weak, that they are only pitiful children, but
that childlike happiness is the sweetest of all. They will become timid and will look to us and huddle close to us in fear,
as chicks to the hen. They will marvel at us and will be awe-
stricken before us, and will be proud at our being so powerful
and clever, that we have been able to subdue such a turbulent
flock of thousands of millions. They will tremble impotently
before our wrath, their minds will grow fearful, they will be
quick to shed tears like women and children, but they will be
just as ready at a sign from us to pass to laughter and rejoic-
ing, to happy mirth and childish song. Yes, we shall set them
to work, but in their leisure hours we shall make their life like
a child's game, with children's songs and innocent dance. Oh,
we shall allow them even sin, they are weak and helpless, and
they will love us like children because we allow them to sin.
We shall tell them that every sin will be expiated, if it is done
with our permission, that we allow them to sin because we
love them, and the punishment for these sins we take upon
ourselves. And we shall take it upon ourselves, and they will
adore us as their saviours who have taken on themselves their
sins before God. And they will have no secrets from us. We
shall allow or forbid them to live with their wives and mis-

tresses, to have or not to have children—according to whether
they have been obedient or disobedient—and they will submit
to us gladly and cheerfully. The most painful secrets of their
conscience, all, all they will bring to us, and we shall have an
answer for all. And they will be glad to believe our answer,
for it will save them from the great anxiety and terrible agony
they endure at present in making a free decision for themselves. And all will be happy, all the millions of creatures except the hundred thousand who rule over them. For only we,
we who guard the mystery, shall be unhappy. There will be
thousands of millions of happy babes, and a hundred thousand
sufferers who have taken upon themselves the curse of the
knowledge of good and evil. Peacefully they will die, peacefully they will expire in Thy name, and beyond the grave they
will find nothing but death. But we shall keep the secret, and
for their happiness we shall allure them with the reward of
heaven and eternity. Though if there were anything in the
other world, it certainly would not be for such as they. It is
prophesied that Thou wilt come again in victory, Thou wilt
come with Thy chosen, the proud and strong, but we will say
that they have only saved themselves, but we have saved all.
We are told that the harlot who sits upon the beast, and
holds in her hands the *mystery*, shall be put to shame, that
the weak will rise up again, and will rend her royal purple
and will strip naked her loathsome body. But then I will stand
up and point out to Thee the thousand millions of happy
children who have known no sin. And we who have taken
their sins upon us for their happiness will stand up before Thee
and say: "Judge us if Thou canst and darest." Know that I
fear Thee not. Know that I too have been in the wilderness,
I too have lived on roots and locusts, I too prized the freedom
with which Thou hast blessed men, and I too was striving to
stand among Thy elect, among the strong and powerful,
thirsting "to make up the number." But I awakened and
would not serve madness. I turned back and joined the ranks
of those *who have corrected Thy work.* I left the proud and
went back to the humble, for the happiness of the humble.
What I say to Thee will come to pass, and our dominion will
be built up. I repeat, to-morrow Thou shalt see that obedient

flock who at a sign from me will hasten to heap up the hot cinders about the pile on which I shall burn Thee for coming to hinder us. For if any one has ever deserved our fires, it is Thou. To-morrow I shall burn Thee. Dixi.'"